Reading Bi

C000112329

Wilfred R. Bion is considered a ground-breaking psychoanalyst. 1 113 .... ~
is rooted in Freud and Klein from where it takes an original flight. *Reading Bion*
shows the evolution of his seminal insights in psychic functioning and puts
them in a wider context.

Rudi Vermote integrates a chronological close reading and discussion of
Bion's texts, with a comprehensive approach of his major concepts. The book
is divided into two main parts:

1. Transformation in Knowledge: Bion's odyssey to understand psychic
   processing or the mind
2. Transformation in O: in which Bion reinterprets his former concepts
   from the dimension of the unknown and unknowable.

The running text is put against a background of biographical data and scientific,
artistic and philosophical influences on his work, which are highlighted in boxes
and separate chapters. Bion's concepts are important for anyone dealing with the
mind. His ideas have an ongoing deep impact on psychoanalysis, psychotherapy
and psychopathology. His concepts help us understand psychic change, creativity,
individual psychodynamics and small and large-group phenomena. The discovery
of their value for studies on art, literature, sociology, religion and economics has
just begun.

Reading Bion starts from the very beginning so that it is instructive for people
who are new to his work, but the close reading and background information make
it a meaningful companion for experienced psychoanalysts and psychotherapists
studying his work.

Rudi Vermote, M.D., Ph.D., is a training analyst, past president of the
Belgian Society of Psychoanalysis and Professor at the University of Leuven.
He has published and lectured on Bion's work and is a member of the editorial
board of the *International Journal of Psychoanalysis* and Honorary Member of the
Psychoanalytic Center of California.

THE NEW LIBRARY OF PSYCHOANALYSIS
TEACHING SERIES
General Editor   Dana Birksted-Breen

The New Library of Psychoanalysis was launched in 1987 in association with the Institute of Psychoanalysis, London. It took over from the International Psychoanalytical Library which published many of the early translations of the works of Freud and the writings of most of the leading British and Continental psychoanalysts. The purpose of the New Library of Psychoanalysis is to facilitate a greater and more widespread appreciation of psychoanalysis and to provide a forum for increasing mutual understanding between psychoanalysts and those working in other disciplines such as the social sciences, medicine, philosophy, history, linguistics, literature and the arts. It aims to represent different trends both in British psychoanalysis and in psychoanalysis generally. The New Library of Psychoanalysis is well placed to make available to the English-speaking world psychoanalytic writings from other European countries and to increase the interchange of ideas between British and American psychoanalysts.

Reading Bion was commissioned for the series when Dana Birksted-Breen, predecessor to Alessandra Lemma, was series editor; due to her ongoing support and advice to the author in bringing this project together over time, she is listed as series editor for this book.

Current members of the Advisory Board include Giovanna Di Ceglie, Liz Allison, Anne Patterson, Josh Cohen and Daniel Pick.

Through the *Teaching* subseries, the New Library of Psychoanalysis publishes books that provide comprehensive yet accessible overviews of selected subject areas aimed at those studying psychoanalysis and related fields such as the social sciences, philosophy, literature and the arts.

For a full list of all the titles in the New Library of Psychoanalysis main series and the New Library of Psychoanalysis 'Beyond the Couch' subseries, please visit the Routledge website.

TITLES IN THE NEW LIBRARY OF
PSYCHOANALYSIS TEACHING SERIES

Initiating Psychoanalysis: Perspectives Bernard Reith, Sven Lagerlöf, Penelope Crick, Mette Møller and Elisabeth Skale

Infant Observation Frances Salo

Reading Anna Freud Nick Midgley

Reading Italian Psychoanalysis Edited by Franco Borgogno, Alberto Luchetti and Luisa Marino Coe

Reading Klein Margaret Rustin and Michael Rustin

Beginning Analysis: On the Processes of Initiating Psychoanalysis Bernard Reith, Mette Møller, John Boots, Penelope Crick, Alain Gibeault, Ronny Jaffe, Sven Lagerlöf, and Rudi Vermote

Reading Bion Rudi Vermote

THE NEW LIBRARY OF PSYCHOANALYSIS:
TEACHING SERIES

Series Editor: Dana Birksted–Breen

Reading Bion

Rudi Vermote

LONDON AND NEW YORK

First published 2019
by Routledge
2 Park Square, Milton Park, Abingdon, Oxon OX14 4RN

and by Routledge
711 Third Avenue, New York, NY 10017

Routledge is an imprint of the Taylor & Francis Group, an informa business

Translated from the author's original Dutch by Anneleen
Masschelein and Elisabeth Allison

British Library Cataloguing in Publication Data
A catalogue record for this book is available from the British Library

Library of Congress Cataloging in Publication Data
A catalog record for this book has been requested

ISBN: 978-0-415-41332-9 (hbk)
ISBN: 978-0-415-41333-6 (pbk)
ISBN: 978-0-429-49198-6 (ebk)

Typeset in Bembo
by Swales & Willis Ltd, Exeter, Devon, UK

MIX
Paper from
responsible sources
FSC® C013056
www.fsc.org

Printed and bound in Great Britain by
TJ International Ltd, Padstow, Cornwall

CONTENTS

List of boxes   vii
Acknowledgements   ix

Introduction   1

Part I
Before the caesura: transformations in knowledge   37

1 Biography, 1897–1966   38

2 *Experiences in Groups and Other Papers* (1961)   48

3 Papers on psychosis (1953–1960)   64

4 *Learning from Experience* (1962)   80

5 *Elements of Psychoanalysis* (1963)   95

6 *Transformations* (1965)   114

Part II
After the caesura: transformations in O   131

7 Biography, 1967–1979   135

8 *Attention and Interpretation* (1970)   140

9 Second thoughts: commentary on the *Selected Papers on
   Psychoanalysis* (1967)   169

10 *A Memoir of the Future* (1977)   177

11 Lectures, seminars and some short texts as preparation for
    the lectures (1973–1979)   190

12 Autobiography   213

13 The further development of Bion's ideas   228

    Conclusion   234

Addenda   **237**

    Listening to and reading Bion   238
    James S. Grotstein

    My indebtedness to Bion   244
    Antonino Ferro

    Discovering Bion: a personal memoir   249
    H.B. Levine

    References   253
    Index   266

BOXES

1.1	The Northfield Experiments	40
1.2	Betty Jardine	42
1.3	Bion in the 1940s: three portraits	44
2.1	John Rickman	48
2.2	Wilfred Trotter's influence on Bion's theory	52
2.3	Binocular vision as a cornerstone of Bion's work	53
2.4	The protomental matrix	56
2.5	The matrix: Foulkes–Bion	57
2.6	An experience in a group of Bion	58
2.7	The matrix: other views	62
3.1	Beckett and Bion: an imaginary twin?	66
3.2	Beckett and the psychoanalyst (Anzieu)	68
3.3	Projective identification	72
3.4	The obstructive object versus the containing object	73
3.5	Psychosis: further developments	77
4.1	Functions	80
4.2	The Seven Servants	81
4.3	Dreaming and dream-work-α in Bion's early and late work	82
4.4	Ogden's elaboration of Bion's notion of reverie	87
4.5	The alphabet of psychoanalysis	90
5.1	Elements	95
5.2	Changing attitudes towards the Grid in Bion's work	96
5.3	β-elements and α-elements: two poetic examples	103
5.4	André Green's work of the negative	110
5.5	Antonino Ferro: the transformational mind during the session	112
6.1	Transformations	114
6.2	A rose: essence and representation, noumenon and phenomenon	124
6.3	The noumenon: two examples	128
II.1	Caesura	132
II.2	Continuity before and after the caesura in Bion's work	134

8.1	The language of achievement	141
8.2	Some quotes about O	143
8.3	The experience of O	149
8.4	The state of mind during the sessions: being just above sleep	151
8.5	Bion's different notions of O	154
8.6	The unknown and the attitude of the analyst	157
8.7	Evolution of the psychoanalytic object as a concept in Bion's work	162
8.8	Negative capability: Keats and Bion	164
8.9	James Grotstein: the transcendent position	166
9.1	A poetic anthology for the psychoanalyst	171
9.2	Some philosophical background of the mental attitude to facilitate T(O)	175
11.1	Pilgrimages with Bion	191
11.2	Ignorance	197
11.3	The Alpheus	202
11.4	Transformation in O, example	209

ACKNOWLEDGEMENTS

I would like to express my gratitude to Dana Birksted-Breen, editor of this teaching series, for her confidence in inviting me to work on this book and for the patience and help to get the project accomplished.

Bion's ideas have an experiential impact on psychoanalytic work and understanding. The dialectic between solitary work, and sharing and discussing, is the position from which I transmit something of his work. I would like to express my gratitude to my analysands and trainees and to all the colleagues with whom I could present, discuss, write and share ideas with, in particular James Grotstein, Antonino Ferro and Howard Levine, who helped add text to this book; Chris Mawson and David Taylor for their careful and thought-provoking remarks, and to Avner Bergstein, Monica Horowitz, Joe Aguayo, Larry Brown, Catalina Bronstein, Annie Reiner, Jan Abram and many others. My thanks to the friends and colleagues at the PA societies (the Belgian, Dutch, Swiss, Italian, Swedish, Australian, Taiwanese, Californian, Russian, Portuguese, Austrian, Israeli and Japanese) who invited me to present and discuss the application of Bion's ideas. Also special thanks to David Tuckett at UCL for his invitations and open-minded support of this work, and to Albert and Jennifer Mason for introducing me to the LA of the late Bion.

My thanks go to my Belgian friends working on a similar line, Trui Missine, Jan Cambien, Lut Derijdt, Diana Messina, Willy and Michele Van Lysebetten, Jef Dehing, and Marc Hebbrecht, to name only a few, and to my close co-workers at the University Psychiatric Center KUL.

As I am not a native English speaker, I am grateful for the help first of Anneleen Masschelein and later of Liz Allison, to whom I am deeply indebted. On top of her busy schedule, Liz relentlessly devoted herself to this project. Without her editorial skills and her clarifying feedback as an analyst, this book would not have been possible.

Writing takes time and this was often at the cost of being with close friends and family. Therefore I dedicate the book to my wife Dominique and to my children Lobke, Kasper, Zoe and Samuel for their warm support and understanding.

INTRODUCTION

How to read this book

I have made a great effort to be true to the complexity of Bion's work while writing in a clear and simple style for readers who are starting to get to know his work. I have taken the following steps to achieve this aim:

First. The largest part of the book is a chronological study of Bion's work, to enable the reader to follow the development of his ideas and technique. The text can be read on its own, but is set up as a companion to a close reading of Bion's original texts, either in a group or on one's own.

Second. As will be discussed in the book, we can discern a major break in Bion's work, a 'caesura', to use Bion's term. Literally, a caesura means 'a pause in a line of poetry, especially near the middle of a line'. To reflect this, the book is divided into two parts: before and after the caesura. Before the caesura Bion focused on the psychic elaboration of emotional experiences, described as Transformations in Knowledge. After the caesura Bion focused on transformations at a non-represented level of experience, which he called Transformations in O, which he thought were more powerful in terms of psychic change.

Third. Bion (1967) advised his readers to keep reading until they reached the end of his texts, even if they did not understand completely. He hoped that his ideas would find their own path and integrate with the experience of the reader at the moment of reading, and that with each reading new realizations would happen. Because Bion's texts are multilayered, I offer several perspectives in boxes that may enhance the reader's experiences and interpretations of the text. This format allows them to be read or omitted according to each reader's level and way of reading. This method, which is comparable to the technique used in travel guides to highlight points of interest on a journey, is also used in *Reading Freud* by Jean-Michel Quinodoz (2005). As the boxes stand on their own, it is best to read them as such, otherwise they disrupt the reading of the text which closely follows Bion's writing.

Fourth. Readers who do not wish to follow the chronological development of Bion's ideas but would prefer to go straight to the heart of his theory should start by reading the chapters about Bion's four theoretical books on psychic functioning and psychic change (*Learning from Experience, Elements, Transformations, Attention and Interpretation*). The boxes may help to put the concepts encountered in a broader context.

Fifth. To give some background to the evolution of Bion's ideas, there are sections on Bion as a character, the philosophical influences on his work and the links between his work and that of Freud, Klein, Winnicott, Jung and Lacan. A biographical background is also given, but like Bion's work and this book as a whole, this is divided into two parts, before and after the caesura, also found in his life. The first part is at the beginning of Part I, while the second part is found at the beginning of Part II.

Sixth. In an addendum some short testimonies are offered by distinguished so-called Bion scholars (a term understood by some as a fundamental misunderstanding of the approach necessary if one is to gain a proper view of Bion's method): Grotstein, Ferro and Levine.

I hope that in this way I have succeeded in being true to Bion's spirit, offering a kind of guide to an experience and in-depth reading of Bion's work without simplifying or teaching.

Situating this book in the Bion literature

There exist a number of excellent and noteworthy publications – as well as numerous articles in journals and books, two dictionaries, quite a number of monographs and collections of essays – that are indispensable to those who want to continue their journey into Bion. I will here sketch a very brief overview, indicating the main sources of reference that have implicitly and explicitly nourished my reading and that may serve as guidelines for further reading. Bion's wife, Francesca Bion, collaborated with Bion on his work. After his death, she has continued to devote herself to his legacy by posthumously publishing seven volumes – his autobiographical texts (*The Long Weekend, All My Sins Remembered* and *War Memoirs*), seminars (in Rome, Rio de Janeiro, New York, London and Tavistock), notes (*Cogitations*) and letters to his family (*The Other Side of Genius*). His oldest daughter, Parthenope Bion Talamo, who practised as an analyst in Turin, Italy until her tragic, premature death in 1998, translated Bion's work in Italian and co-edited a number of volumes on her father's work, *WR Bion Between Past and Future* (2000) and *Bion's Legacy to Groups* (1997), but the work she began writing on Bion's oeuvre was unfortunately never finished.

Bion's influence on British colleagues from the 1960s onwards, such as Herbert Rosenfeld, Hanna Segal, Roger Money-Kyrle, Frances Tustin, Donald Meltzer, Elisabeth Menzies-Lyth and Ronald Britton, can be detected in their work. In the 1970s Bion accepted an invitation from the Californian Kleinian group and stayed in Los Angeles for nearly 12 years. An influential

Kleinian and later Bionian group gradually formed, including James Grotstein, Albert Mason and Susan Isaacs in LA. Later, in San Francisco, Thomas Ogden – while starting mainly from the work of Winnicott – developed a far-reaching interest in the work of Bion. In New York, Michael Eigen published on Bion's work from a mystical point of view and Mark Epstein from a Buddhist point of view. There is also a group in Boston whose main representatives are Howard Levine and Lawrence Brown, who organized one of the Bion conferences and published on Bion. However, the most prominent American 'Bionian' author is James Grotstein. His monograph, *A Beam of Intense Darkness* (2007), is the extraordinary result of a lifetime with Bion and his work. An analysand of Bion in the 1970s, Grotstein was one of the first to devote a 'memorial' to Bion. He entitled this *Do I Dare Disturb the Universe?* (1983). It contains several important papers, including 'Who is the dreamer who dreams the dream and who is the dreamer who understands it?'

In *A Beam of Intense Darkness* Grotstein offers 'his own personal diary of reading Bion' (Grotstein 2007: 7). It is very close to Bion but it is more a creative digestion of Bion's work and a presentation of Grotstein's own psychoanalytic theory. Grotstein takes a number of radical options. He discusses Bion's major texts, except for *A Memoir of the Future*, and he quotes Bion extensively, but his writing is synthetic, conceptual and personal, rather than chronological and systematic. The weight of his reading falls on the later 'mystic' Bion from the 1970s. Moreover, while he relies on his own analysis with Bion and on his personal memories of him, he refrains from using biographical material. This lacuna can be supplemented with Gérard Bléandonu's (1994) *Wilfred Bion: His Life and Works 1897–1979*. Bléandonu's insightful biographical account of Bion is based on Bion's autobiographical writings and on interviews, and seems to focus more on the early period in Bion's work. Bléandonu also includes a discussion of *A Memoir of the Future*. His reading is indebted to his own work with groups on the one hand and to the French tradition of psychoanalysis on the other (including thinkers like Didier Anzieu and André Green, who provide a bridge between Freud, Lacan and Bion), and therefore he offers a somewhat different perspective.

When in his 70s, Bion began to give lectures and seminars outside of California, mainly in Great Britain and the United States, but also Italy and Brazil. This has led to a diverse reception in different national traditions. An early introduction, originating from his first visit to Brazil (Grinberg, Sor and Tabak de Bianchedi, 1975), was substantially revised and updated as the *New Introduction to the Work of Bion* in 1993. This book offers concise, intelligent summaries and discussions of the main theoretical works and is a good starting point for studying Bion. The society of Sao Paolo is particularly indebted to Bion. Paulo Cesar Sandler is the most prolific contemporary writer of this group. His monumental, comprehensive and profound *The Language of Bion: A Dictionary of Concepts* (2005b) is essential reading for every student of Bion.

Bion's work evoked a considerable response in Italy. Parthenope Bion worked as an analyst in Turin and together with Silvio Merciai she organized the first international conference in 1997 in Turin. Antonino Ferro integrated Bion's work with the field theory of the Barangers (1983, 2008a,b) in a highly creative, imaginative and vivid way. Besides many seminars and papers, he has published several books on his clinical application of Bion's theory (Ferro 1999, 2002, 2005, 2006, 2008). Other important Italian writers from a Bionian perspective are Claudio Neri, Franco Borgogno, Marco Conci and Giuseppe Civitarese, amongst others. *Lire Bion* (2006) is the French translation of a collection of predominantly Italian authors (Correale, Fadda, Neri). Although the book shares the title of this book and also aims to present a faithful reading, it takes a different approach from ours. It mainly collects the views of different authors on Bion's theoretical work on the one hand, and on his theory of groups on the other.

Actualité de la pensée de Bion (2007) presents a number of contemporary perspectives on Bion in the Francophone and Latin analytic world. Because of the dominance of Lacan, the work of the British school in general – Klein, Segal, Winnicott – was less influential in the 1960s and 1970s. Bion's work was introduced in France by André Green, especially *La psychose blanche* (Donnet and Green 1973), which draws inspiration from Bion's ideas. André Green was a friend of Bion and has played a crucial role in bridging the gap between the French psychoanalytic school and the developments in the Anglo-Saxon world. Although Green starts explicitly from Freud, his book on *The Work of the Negative* (1993), amongst others, is in line with many of Bion's ideas. Likewise, Didier Anzieu was very important for the legacy of Bion in France. He published a great deal on Bion's work on groups (Anzieu 1984) and his book *The Skin Ego* (*Le Moi peau*) is an elaboration of Bion's container-contained theory (Anzieu 1989). Since the 1970s, the French school of psychosomatics (Marty and De M'Uzan 1963; Marty 1991; Luquet 2002) has developed their own theory of psychosomatic illnesses, using Bion's work on thinking and feeling, based on a lack of symbolization: in Bion's and Green's terms, a lack of 'thinking' of affects, which is conceptualized in the Paris Psychoanalytic School as 'operative thinking'. The Botellas (2001) used Bion's ideas about the existence of a hallucinatory layer of thinking. More recently, Monica Horowitz writes and organizes conferences about Bion's work.

Other books which – because of a lack of space – I will only mention focus on particular aspects of Bion. For instance, Joan and Neville Symington (1996) consider Bion's clinical thinking, Malcolm Pines (1985) and Lipgar and Pines (2003) concentrate on Bion's work on groups. Didier Anzieu's (1992) *Beckett et le psychoanalyste* offers an imaginary account of Bion's encounter with Samuel Beckett early in his life. Finally, the two dictionaries of Bion's work, by P.C. Sandler (2005a) and by Rafael E. López-Corvo (2003), are complementary. López-Corvo's (Toronto) *Dictionary of the Work of WR Bion* is a good, concise reference book that situates concepts within Bion's work and provides useful information on the philosophical background of some of Bion's borrowed notions. The same author's *Wild Thoughts Searching for a Thinker* (2006) is much freer and tries to situate Bion clinically within the psychoanalytic tradition. Sandler's already mentioned hefty volume, on the other hand, focuses on Bion's concept of transformations by working with quotes from Bion's work. The work is encyclopaedic in its scope (Sandler 2005a). Sandler had access to Bion's library and to the annotations in his books. Parthenope Bion began writing a book on the books that influenced Bion, but as indicated above this unfortunately remained unfinished at the time of her premature death. Harry Karnac (2008), the founder of Karnac books, has produced an extensive bibliography of primary and secondary sources of Bion's work. *Bion Today*, edited by Chris Mawson (2010) for the New Library of Psychoanalysis, explores contemporary uses of Bion's ideas in different fields (conceptual, clinical, aesthetic, groups) with contributions from colleagues who are distinguished teachers of Bion's work. Some of the contributors worked closely with Bion. C. Mawson has also edited the *Complete Works of Bion* for Karnac, which were recently published (Bion 2014) in 15 volumes. *Bion and Being* was published by Annie Reiner (2012) which represents the experience of the late Bion in a personal, clinical and beautiful poetic way. The scholarly 'Bion's Sources', edited by Nino Torres and Robert Hinshelwood (2013), gives a detailed and thoughtful background. New texts of Bion saw the light thanks to Jo Aguayo and Bernard Malin (2013), who edited the tapes of the *Los Angeles Seminars and Supervision*. Ian Miller and Kay Souter (2013), each from their side, shed additional light on the early Bion in their *Beckett and Bion*. The *W.R. Bion Tradition*, edited by Howard Levine and Guiseppe Civitarese (2016), is a collection of papers by contemporary British and North- and Latin-American European analysts that gives scope to the use and expansion of Bion's ideas.

Some impressions of Bion as a person

Dr Albert Mason recalled that once, when he greeted Bion on the street with a friendly 'How are you?', Bion replied with, 'At 75, I think that I am beginning to get the hang of it'. This reveals the pervasiveness of Bion's profound awareness of not-knowing, being abysmally ignorant (Bion 1997). It also gives us a glimpse of Bion as the enigmatic, ironic man he was. It is tempting to try to construct a coherent image of a person from data, as Valery did in writing about Da Vinci (Nakagawa 1988), but to do this with Bion would be totally un-Bionian and 'stupid, arrogant' (Bion 1957/1967). Alternatively, one can gradually allow an image of a person to emerge, as Kobayashi did in his biography of Mozart: his starting point was a vivid memory of the notes of the 40th symphony, which came to mind in the midst of a crowd. As readers, we each create our own Bion (O' Shaughnessy 2005) and it is probably better to do this from an 'experiencing Sphinx' point of view, tolerating the mystery and not-knowing and achieving an emotional contact, than as an 'investigating Oedipus'. Bion suggested that the way to do this was to look for invariants during transformations and constant conjunctions. I will proceed in this way. Let us see what emerges.

I never met Bion; he died in 1979, about the time when I started reading his work. At the Bion centennial conference in Turin (July 1997), I interviewed his daughter, Parthenope Bion, for the *Revue Belge de Psychanalyse* (Vermote 1998). The interview took place in a room where Bion's presence was manifest through his paintings (a few of which are reproduced in *All My Sins Remembered* (Bion 1985). During the interview, Bion's second wife Francesca and their son and daughter joined us for a while. This impressed me in an ambiguous way; I felt like an uninvited guest in his world. Once, after I had given a conference presentation about Bion's work (2005), I asked Francesca Bion if she thought that I had presented Bion's ideas correctly. She said that it would not have mattered to Bion whether I had reproduced exactly what he said, but that he would have been glad to see that his ideas had led to some thoughts in other people.

Meltzer and Williams (1985) state that it is probably easier to get to know Bion from his autobiography, in which he radically focused on inner truth, than would ever have been possible through knowing him in real life, as he was intensely private.

Bion was born in the Punjab in 1897, where his father was a civil engineer in irrigation at the height of British imperialism. His father, who was descended from the French Huguenots, was a devout Catholic and colonial; a tiger hunter. In *The Long Weekend*, his unfinished autobiography, Bion described his mother as both close and distant. She was probably Anglo-Indian, but Bion is not clear about this, while he is clear about the warmth of his Indian nanny or ayah. We can imagine that the mystery and warmth, and the smells and colours of his Indian childhood, remained with him as 'memories in feelings' (Klein 1957), as a deep layer in himself. He only planned to visit India again towards the end of his life but did not succeed in doing so before his death.

When searching for the essence of psychoanalysis, Bion identified the unknown and mystery as core elements together with solitude (Bion 1963: 7, 15, 63). Experiences of solitude marked Bion's early life. When he was eight years old, Bion was sent from India to Bishops Stortford, a public school near Cambridge. He was a boarder for months on end, only occasionally spending a weekend with the family of a friend. Bion's traumatic experiences while still an adolescent in the Great War (see Chapter 12), in which one third of his fellow soldiers were lost, probably strengthened this feeling of ultimately being on his own. This is painfully expressed through his statement that he died on 8 August 1918 during the Battle of Amiens (Bion 1982: 265) and could never sing again afterwards. Both his first and his second wife were singers.

Everybody suddenly burst out singing – I did not; not even after the war. Never, never again. I was not unhappy – Indeed I often felt that I was much happier than most. But no more singing: never.

(Bion 1986: 191)

Although his mother stayed in England during World War I, in order to be with him when he was able to leave the front in France for a few days, he felt unable to communicate with her. He even described the terrible war experience as a vacation compared to being with his mother during his days off.

Relations with anyone I respected were intolerable, notably with my mother; I wanted nothing except to get back to the Front just to get away from England. I can only hope she had a similar wish to get rid of me. At last I had said good-bye and was leaning out of the train window. 'Mind the door', I warned her, 'it's filthy'. 'Everything', she said, near to tears, 'is dreadful . . . I mean nothing is really cleaned up nowadays'. And so we parted.

(Bion 1986: 266)

This immense solitude is painfully rendered in his description of the attack in Amiens: he lay on the frozen ground and fantasized about being held in his mother's arms (Bion 1986). This is difficult to reconcile with his wish to get away from her. Parthenope Bion suggested that Bion needed to preserve his mother as an idealized internal figure in order to survive. She writes:

I also feel that it is no coincidence that although the diaries were dedicated to his parents, it is his mother alone who is invoked every now and again as a reader, as though Bion felt that she was a fundamental participant in an internal dialogue. It is perhaps not too fanciful to suppose that the fact that he had not 'written letters' during the war had not only been part of a desire to spare his mother pain, but was also an unconscious attempt to preserve her in his own mind as a container as undamaged as possible by hideous news, and hence as a part of the personality capable of alpha-function.

(P. Bion in Bion, W. 1997: 310)

This goes back to his experiences as a lonely child in the boarding school in England, while his parents were in India.

By the time that we should have been looking forward to Christmas dinner, Heaton and I were feeling ill – very ill. The nature of the malady – disinclination for food, a sense of impending death, a craving for maternal love – was made worse for me by the absence of my mother.

(Bion 1986: 65)

Bion gave the mother function a central place in his theory of thinking, but he named this function containment; a military term.

Painful losses also marked Bion's life. His first wife died three days after she had given birth in London while he was away at the front in Normandy in the World War II. In his autobiographical writings, parts of these traumatic experiences return over the years as undigested material. It is not surprising that Bion saw solitude as one of the essences of psychoanalysis (Bion 1963). He could be detached, alone in the presence of others, and he thought that this was a condition of being able to think, and to analyse. As Rice and Wilson are both reported to have said, 'Bion can sit farther behind his own face than any other man I know' (Rice quoted in Lyth 1980; Wilson quoted in Trist 1987).

Bion saw his shyness as one of his strengths (Bion 1986). As a child, he could encapsulate himself in his own fantasy world where 'Our Father' in the prayer became 'Arf-Arfer', or he understood 'electricity' as 'electric city' (Bion F. 1982). Later, his capacity to tolerate and experience the paranoid-schizoid position was probably a vital source of his intuition in dealing with psychotic patients. He was convinced that a fragmented psychic functioning was inherent in all of us, which he linked to the origin of creativity. Later he called it a hallucinatory layer (Bion 1997), an embryonic infinite layer, the origin of all psychic life. In the same vein, he saw regression as part of the human condition: 'Winnicott says patients *need* to regress. Melanie Klein says they *must not*: I say they *are* regressed' (Bion 1992: 166).

This was not how he appeared: the above was contained in an iron frame. Bion was tall and robust. At school, he excelled in sports; he was a rugby and water-polo player and captain of the team. Later his sporting achievements and career helped him to win acceptance as a candidate at the UCL Department of Medicine. He always continued to train, was a North Sea swimmer and later in his 70s, when living in California, he still swam his lengths every day in a cold swimming pool. He also continued to practise pistol shooting (Trist 1987). While in the army, he seems to have preserved something of the sporting and comradely spirit of the public school for a long time, even during the catastrophes of the war. The military discipline and membership of a group were important to him. He described how thrilled he was as a soldier, when he saw the Prussian guard attack in close formation (Bion F. 1982).

Bion's motto was '*fluctuat nec mergitur*' (be rocked and remain balanced; also the motto of the city of Paris). This was rooted in his public school training and his experiences of the Great War, during which he had to keep his emotions under control in order to avoid arousing panic in his men. The imperturbability of a gentleman who could accept emotions without being overwhelmed by them was his first model of containment (Bion 1967). The self-ironic style of the British gentleman may have softened the edges of this discipline. He cultivated this style for a long time, still wearing a bowler hat as late as the 1960s. At the end of his life he stated that this style felt a bit like a prison (Bion 1991).

Francesca Bion describes how she learned to know him as 'a lover of good food, fine wine and the best cigars' and only later encountered the iron man within (Bion F. 1981): 'I do not recall ever hearing him raise his voice in anger, but angry he certainly could be – the look in his eyes and a cutting remark were signs of stormy weather' (Bion F. 1995). Later, when practising in Los Angeles, he retained his British, somewhat otherworldly demeanour, and a young patient described him as 'a strange Sherlock Holmes' (Mason 1989).

Bion's outer appearance and often somewhat arrogant self-confident attitude hid his inner world, which he only revealed at the end of his life. In his autobiography (*The Long Weekend*) the 80-year-old Bion tells how despite his athletic figure, he was rejected when he applied to the Inns of Court Officer Training Corps during the Great War, because he appeared too much of a schoolboy. He felt humiliated in front of his father, who had to use the influence of his acquaintances to get him into the OTC. He described a similar experience when he was walking in his uniform (Bion 1986); he heard the adoring remarks of two girls walking behind him. When they passed by and saw his baby face they started laughing. With self-lacerating irony he described himself in his autobiography as 'clumsy' and 'a milksop'. Even the war decorations (he might as well have been court-martialled, he ironically said) did not alter his feeling that he was a failure, which goes back to his feelings in early adolescence.

> I was big, dreamy, unbelievably incompetent . . . My voice had become deep and somewhat uncontrolled. I became famous for saying 'Have you any Swizz-milka?' in somewhat stereotyped and mourning tones. 'Swizz-milka' became my team call. I tried to get rid of the 'milka' but could not: by the time I achieved 'condenny' it was too late. My nickname was 'Swizz' till I entered senior school.
>
> (Bion 1986: 76)

This self-disclosure brings us to another of Bion's characteristics, a kind of stubborn truthfulness that made him vulnerable, courageous and reliable. There are many examples of this: not only was he a hero in the Great War (see Part II), he was also a pioneer in changing the psychiatric help available to soldiers in World War II. He had the courage to educate his baby himself as a young widower and later took the risk of leaving his safe position as a renowned psychoanalyst in London and moving to Los Angeles, where he was attacked as a Kleinian analyst and even accused and interrogated by the police for practising illegal medicine. But he remained at his post, as he had in the trenches.

This independence went together with a creativity and originality: he developed methods for the selection of candidates for leading positions in the Army and for rehabilitation in the Northfield experiments (see Box 1.1);

for studying and conducting groups at the Tavistock Clinic, he elaborated a clinically rooted theory of psychic functioning and change; and finally, he rethought his entire theory from the perspective of transformations in O. This book will trace these developments, which took place over many years.

It is difficult to reconcile Bion's introversion and distance with the fact that he was asked to assume several positions of leadership. He ironically stated in *Experiences in Groups* that 'a new leader is in my experience without exception, a thoroughgoing psychiatric case' (Bion 1968: 119) who fits best with the current basic assumption of a group. He was a captain in the rugby team at school, a tank commander, an army psychiatrist responsible for the recruitment of soldiers, a Chairman of the Executive Committee of the Tavistock Clinic, a president of the Medical Section of the British Psychological Society, Director of the London Clinic of Psychoanalysis and president of the British Society of Psychoanalysis. And this brings us to another of Bion's paradoxes: he was an anti-leader. He was unable to identify with the establishment and may even have had some problems with authority. This attitude towards the establishment often made his life more difficult than it needed to be; during the Great War, he missed out on the Victoria Cross because of his reluctance to tell the authorities that he had killed an enemy, and he missed several nominations in World War II out of a kind of stubbornness. As a teacher, he had problems with the school establishment and when practising in LA, he never applied for membership of the LA Psychoanalytic Society, only becoming recognized as a member posthumously.

Bion's studies of the dynamics of leadership are far-reaching. He invented leaderless groups as a method for selection, and perceived how the choices and actions of a leader are determined by unconscious group dynamics. Later, when focusing on O, he discussed leadership and the establishment in relation to the so-called genius function (Bion 1970); the establishment needs to create a set-up that allows new and growth-provoking ideas to originate in the group; at the same it must make them digestible to the group and protect the group from being destroyed by them.

Bion did not write much about sexuality. As a child of his time this was not easy. He felt guilty about the masturbatory activity that as a child he called 'wiggling' and he described the school as a gigantic pressure cooker under the watchful eye of masters.

> I had reduced my sexual life to perfunctory prayers of the 'Oh God, save me from self-abuse' type. I did not care what happened; one also suspected that God must have had other matters to attend to.
>
> In the intervals between bothering about sex, cosy sex, very rare and exciting capital SEX of the 'poison-in-the-food' variety, I played games and did work of the kind that is usually mentioned in the prospectus.
>
> (Bion 1986: 79)

Furtiveness, guilt, frustration, in alternation or all together – such was my experience for many years, the most impressionable years of my life, the matrix from which passionate love supposedly will spring.

(Bion 1986: 74)

As an adolescent he felt disgruntled and sulky (Bion 1982) and in his war writings he reflected on the risk of getting oneself killed through unconscious guilt feelings, like because of masturbation. He wrote not only of his inexperience in these matters with his story of falling in love after the war with a girl who sent him wild roses but dropped him for someone else, but also of his violent fantasies of shooting them when by coincidence he met the couple at the beach.

If I had had my service revolver with me I would have shot him. Then I would have shot her through the knee in such a way that the joint could not be repaired and she would have had a permanently rigid leg to explain to her future lovers.

(Bion 1985: 29–30)

After the Great War, he studied history in Oxford and became a teacher at his former school, Bishop's Stortford College. He was accused by a mother whom he invited for tea of improper behaviour towards her son, which looks like a rendezvous that turned out badly. The accusation was groundless according to Bion and could not be substantiated by an investigation, but he decided to leave the school and stopped being a teacher at the end of his term. These inner conflicts were probably the reason that he went into therapy in the early 1920s (see Chapter 1).

Years later, as an officer in World War II, he fell in love with and married Betty Jardine (see Box 1.2), a comedian and one of the first movie stars. He had seen Betty performing in a comedy about a girl falling in love with an officer. According to the letters of Rickman, who befriended them, they were well matched. Tragically, she died a few days after childbirth while he was with the army in Normandy. After some years as a widower, and suffering the painful feelings connected with his loss, raising his little daughter alone, he fell deeply in love with Francesca, then a young research assistant at the Tavistock Clinic and also a widow. The love letters in *All My Sins Remembered* testify to a devoted love.

Later, in *A Memoir of the Future*, which Francesca edited and which Bion considered his *magnum opus*, an attempt to render psychoanalysis in a living form and not in jargon, love and passion have a major place. Rosemary, the daughter of a prostitute, is a good illustration of Bion's ideas about sex and love, about real love (L) and possession (-L), which he considered opposites although they may resemble each other superficially. Bion compared his much-discussed notion of O with passionate love. As an analyst, the late Bion saw sexual feelings as too sensuous and as a distraction from the non-sensuous world where feelings originate, and thought that they prevent the patient's opening to new psychic experiences in the session. Sex is like sherry, he said, an easy way to cheer oneself up. Bion trained himself to be dispassionate, to prevent his analytic view from being blurred by passion. The only link of a psychoanalyst with a patient should be the K-link (knowledge) and not Love or Hate. Sexuality from the side of the psychoanalyst destroys the psychoanalytic process and is an expression of hatred of psychoanalysis. He considered sexual images and feelings in an analysis in the same way as all other thoughts and feelings – as forms and preconceptions that can contain experiences in their process of transformation.

Bion came from a religious family. During the war he often felt rather ashamed of being part of what he called 'the pious brigade'. He seems to have lost his religious faith in the war. Later he used concepts from mysticism to try to understand the unknown reality behind representations, and returned to terms like Faith as a mental attitude to enable contact with this reality that is not yet put into forms.

Bion studied history and philosophy, went to France to study French, could endlessly quote poems even in the trenches, and was interested in mathematics, physics, anthropology and philosophy of science, as was the vogue in his time of great discoveries. Without ever giving many references, he transformed and integrated many of these theories into his own theory of the mind. At the time of her death, Parthenope Bion was researching the influence of her father's reading on his work (Joseph 1999).

Some great men crossed Bion's path and influenced him, like Trotter, for instance (see Box 2.2), who was the King's surgeon and author of *Instincts of the Herd in Peace and War* (1942), and Rickman (see Box 2.1), whose involvement in psychoanalysis, groups and social psychiatry was similar to Bion's and who was his first analyst, and later brother-in-arms, friend and mentor. As a young psychotherapist Bion had Beckett in treatment (see Box 3.1) and we may speculate about the influence each man had on the other's later evolution. Bion also painted, in a style that was classic in form and frame, but he often chose the wild seas in his beloved Norfolk as his subject matter.

Bion was an attentive observer with an open mind and eschewed judgements in terms of good and bad, which he saw as an omnipotent substitution for thinking.

The caesura

In my opinion (see also Borgogno and Merciai 2000) a major caesura occurred in Bion's work and life, a qualitative sudden change (a catastrophic change (Bion 1965)) after a quantitative progression, so to speak. We do not know what happened to precipitate this change. Bion is reported to have told his colleagues (Grotstein 1983) that he did not want to be loaded with honours and sink like a stone, and his wife Francesca wrote that he finally set himself free from his duties, which had become something of a burden. Personally, I think that the insight he achieved at the end of *Transformations* and when writing *Attention and Interpretation* was the driving force behind the change. While Bion initially focused on the process by means of which something becomes psychic and symbolized or represented, he finally realized that profound psychic change was rooted in pure experience and being (becoming). From then on, he focused on what happens at the basic layers of psychic experience. He accepted the consequences of his discovery and began to seek a living, experiencing form of psychoanalysis from an attitude of radically not-knowing. Rather than teaching, he tried to evoke an experience in other colleagues. He started to write in a form that he hoped would influence the content in a living way. *A Memoir of the Future* and his autobiography are examples of this. The changes he made were an attempt to break free, but many people thought that he had 'lost his marbles'. However, when Donald Meltzer was invited by Albert Mason to give a lecture in LA, he visited Bion and concluded that this was not at all the case. Although Bion suffered a small stroke while being in LA (A. Mason, personal communication), he was in good mental condition. Bion's later style was deliberate. Using Socratic questioning, not-knowing and long pauses led some to assign him a kind of guru status, while others saw it as a rather narcissistic performance, deploring his loss of his former scientific discipline. With the benefit of his new insights he reformulated all his earlier theoretical views. I hope to make this clear in this book.

Bion's shift to a stance of not-knowing is not uncommon in psychoanalytic writers and thinkers. Think of Winnicott who encountered considerable resistance to his later text on *The Use of an Object* (Winnicott 1969), in which he stated that the analyst must adopt an open and unknowing attitude rather than giving bright interpretations, and Lacan who did not want to be a 'sujet supposé savoir' and subsequently dissolved his school, not wishing to be a master.

In sum, the Bion that I encountered in my reading of his works and who evolved into 'my' Bion (O'Shaughnessy 2005) is a disciplined man who developed a timeless theory about essences and psychic change. We see him struggle to write from his experience as a psychoanalyst. With a passion and a sense of urgency, it takes form but then each time he sets it free again with self-irony and humour, with an attitude of openness and ignorance. Reading his work has an opening effect which paradoxically also engenders a feeling of security and comfort. His office in Los Angeles was almost empty, containing only a couch and a chair in the middle of the room – it was the patient and the interaction that mattered. Not only was the unnecessary furniture thrown out, he also trained himself to do the same mentally, keeping only a few theories. Frances Tustin, one of his analysands (Tustin 1981), experienced him as a rock around which the most intense emotions evolved. He assumed his loneliness and observed a thorough, dispassionate state of mind, looking at the non-sensuous origin and the essence of the things the patient said, seeing the transformations at a deeper level. James Grotstein, who was in analysis with Bion (see Box 11.1), compared this experience with deep sea versus scuba diving. It was enabled by his radical openness to the unknown. At the same time there was compassion – compassion of a man who lost so much in his life. But the quintessence is that Bion brought psychoanalysis into contact with something that transcends us, an undifferentiated layer of psychic being that great men are open to – the ungraspable, life-giving quality of which we only see an emanation. His ability to do this touched genius.

This ability was probably due to a mixture of his extreme privateness and the extraordinary life events that he went through: his Indian background full of warm mysteries; the long and nearly orphan-like solitude in childhood; boarding school and the Great War; living as a widower for a long time; the painful experiences and iron discipline in school, sports and army mixed with British irony; the intensity of his encounters with extraordinary people like Beckett, Patton, Rickman and Klein, to name just a few; and his lifelong dedication to being a psychoanalyst. I think that Bion was able to tolerate the lonely, empty, infinite, undifferentiated essence in himself in a dispassionate way and to experience how thoughts and feelings emerge from this large unknown field, and he had the philosophical, poetic and psychoanalytic background to think and write about it and apply it to his psychoanalytic experience.

Bion and Freud, Klein, Jung, Winnicott and Lacan

Freud and Bion

As already stated, we can distinguish two periods in Bion's work. The focus of the first period is transformations in knowledge, or in other words the thinking of emotional experiences. This theory can be seen in large part as an extension of Freud's theory.

In the second period, Bion's concern is transformations in O: in other words, the contact with or the becoming of an undifferentiated life-giving psychic zone. In this period Bion continues to refer to Freud but diverges more from him.

Transformations in knowledge

The theory about transformations in knowledge is largely based on Freud's (1911) 'Formulations on the two principles of psychic functioning'. Among the few references given in Bion's first theoretical book *Learning from Experience*

(1962), this is the most important. In his text Freud described how thinking originates in contact with external reality. This was of major interest to Bion, who was trying to develop a theory about the psychoses, which he saw in the first place as thought disorders.

In Freud's view, the capacity to think developed in order to allow us to perceive, adapt to and change reality. The ability to do so requires modifications to the primitive unconscious thought processes which are based on wish fulfilment, what Freud called the pleasure principle in his 1911 paper on 'Two Principles of Psychic Functioning', a paper much quoted by Bion.[1] In the unconscious primary process thinking, the libido moves freely between 'thing representations' according to the pleasure principle. To be able to adapt to reality and for instance not to hallucinate feeding but to be able to intentionally arrive at having something to eat: a logical and practical thinking[2] was developed for which a more fixed relationship between representations was needed as in language. Freud called this relationship between verbal representations, which is governed by the reality principle, the 'secondary process'. This is in contrast with the free relationships by displacement (Verschiebung) and condensation (Verdichting) between the thing representations in the unconscious, for which he coined the term 'primary process' which is governed by the pleasure principle. These are the two principles of psychic functioning.[3] This implies that instead of relying on wish fulfilment, a frustration tolerance is necessary and that conscious perception, memory and judgement must be present. Bion, following Freud, links the origin of thinking to frustration tolerance. A thought originates by tolerating that something is not present instead of hallucinating it as a kind of wish fulfilment as in some dreams. Freud described fantasy as in daydreaming as being an escape from the reality principle – while awake the mind can linger in a wish fulfilment mode.

In his further development of the reality principle and thinking, Freud suggested notation, attention and inquiry (judgement) before action takes place. Bion takes exactly the same steps and he later consequently put them in the horizontal axis of his Grid that reflects the use of elements of psychoanalysis (Bion 1963).

At this level, there are, however, several major differences with Freud. The first is that in Freud's model, thinking only takes place as a way to change reality. This is the kind of thinking that Bion will call *Reason* as discerned from *Idea*. *Idea* is what he calls 'thinking' and later 'transformation in knowledge'. It is a spontaneous, automatic transformation that he derived from Kleinian Phantasy (see section below on Klein and Bion). This thinking is not so much about an adaptation to reality, but a way of automatic processing emotional experiences or changing beta-elements to alpha-elements (see below) by what he called an internal breast. Second: Bion explicitly reduces Freud's pleasure-pain principle to evasion of painful experiences or modification of them. Third: Bion does not view fantasy as an escape from the reality principle as Freud did; on the contrary, Bion's thinking, which he also calls dream thought, corresponds largely with the Kleinian notion of phantasy, which is a kind of constant stream underlying all psychic-emotional activity (see section below on Klein and Bion). It is the base of the psychic elaboration of emotions and perceptions and the base of what he will call the contact-barrier between Cs and Ucs. This way it can even be seen as an ego-function in Freudian terminology. This is different from Freud's concepts of fantasy, which is more a kind of escape from the reality principle. Fourth: Bion stated that a mental apparatus is needed to think the thoughts that already exist, while for Freud thoughts arise from the contact with reality. Fifth: This mental apparatus is only present in rudimentary form and will need the mother, or more precisely the mother's capacity for reverie, to help with the digestion of emotional experiences and thoughts and to develop further. This necessary intersubjective step is a step that is not explicitly present in Freud. Sixth: Freud saw the unconscious and its representations as something given, present in the psyche from the beginning of mental functioning. This is not the case to Bion, who observes that in psychoses representations are often lacking. Bion therefore elaborated a model in which he studied the origin of the representations. He hypothesized unknowable beta-elements, which are not psychic yet, and alpha-elements that are just psychic. These alpha-elements then form the building blocks of dream thought and representations. With these elements thinking can happen. Not only are alpha-elements the building bricks of thinking, they also make the separation of conscious and unconscious possible. Bion describes how alpha-elements cohere to form the contact-barrier, a kind of living semi-permeable membrane composed of alpha-elements. In his model delusions and hallucinations are evacuated beta elements, forming bizarre objects which are a conglomeration of these evacuated beta-elements with attacked and split-off ego-functions.

Seventh: Dreaming is essential in Bion's theory just as in Freud's. However, according to Bion we do not dream to protect sleep; rather, we sleep in order to dream. These dream thoughts go on day and night and are therefore also present in waking life: the waking dream thoughts (which are only present in a footnote in Freud, and elaborated on by Klein). To Bion the dream thoughts are the foundation of psychic functioning, while for Freud dreams can be understood as expressions of unconscious psychic conflicts, which we can decipher by understanding the primary process. Bion's focus was psychic functioning itself while Freud was concerned with content and intrapsychic conflict.

Eighth: Like Freud and later Klein, Bion relied on the life and death drives. Later he described them as Love and Hate links (L, H) between objects but he added a third link: the epistemophilic instinct or the Knowledge or K-link. He saw the death drive as attacks on these three forms of linking –L, –H and –K.

Ninth: Splitting, which Freud (1940) had introduced at the end of his work, is much more elaborated in Bion's work and became a cornerstone of it. He conceives a non-psychotic and a psychotic part in each personality. The latter functions by means of splitting and evacuation. For psychosis, he extends splitting to fragmentation. In Bion's later work splitting is an essential feature of each personality, like Freud (1940) who suggested that because of splitting, fault lines exist in psychic structures as in a crystal. The so-called late Bion (1970) extended this idea of splitting in seeing psychic functioning as happening on different vertices that may or may not interfere. Furthermore, in his way of listening to patients Bion specifically relied on the integration of a split view, which he compared with the view in a binocular microscope, seeing different layers (see Box 2.3).

Transformations in O

In the second part of his work, Bion focused on the transformations that happen at a level where there are no representations yet. These transformations occur in a formless, undifferentiated, a-sensuous zone which he calls O. In O there are already some constellations but they are not yet experienced in a sensuous form, like a figure that is already present in a block of marble which a sculptor still has to reveal. Changes at this level or T(O) are different from T(K). They are about the contact with and the experiencing (becoming) of this zone. As this zone is a-sensuous and transformations in sensuous forms originate from there, Bion concluded that an approach based on the senses is not apt and may even be a hindrance to facilitating and apprehending T(O). Bion (1970) found most of the Freudian concepts, like repression, unconscious-conscious and thinking, too much linked with the sensorial pleasure principle (Lustprinzip), wishes and desires. O is of a different order and Bion suggested that the vector finite–infinite is more suited when talking about O than Freud's unconscious–conscious distinction. On the infinite–finite vector something gains form out of the infinite layer and becomes more finite.

However, later Bion (see Chapter 11) used a model in which he distinguished an undifferentiated, life-giving, hallucinatory zone which is separated by a caesura (a notion from Freud) from a zone of verbal thought. This is rather similar to Freud's topographical model. A difference with Freud is that in Bion's model, the movement is from the undifferentiated zone to verbal thought (O finds K), rather than the conscious conquering of the unconscious found in Freud. Getting in contact with O (which is the same as becoming O or a Transformation in O) is to Bion (1970) both a conscious and an unconscious process; the conscious process consists of being maximally open to the Unknown. In order to be in touch with this a-sensuous reality that is O, Bion advocates no memory, no desire, no understanding, no coherence. As Wieland (2013) rightly puts it, Bion draws in several places on a letter of Freud (Pfeiffer 1963) to Lou Andreas Salome in this regard: where Freud describes how he needs to artificially blind himself to focus all the light on one dark spot. The conscious is seen as maximally receptive (instead of intentional like in Freud). Bion (1965) compares the conscious with a tropism: like plants who turn to the light spontaneously, the conscious lets a 'contained' be found by a 'container' (see *Transformations*) and not vice-versa, and this on a vector going from infinite to finite.

Klein and Bion

Groups

Bion developed his theory of groups before he became a psychoanalyst. It is only after his analysis with Klein which ended in 1953 that he reformulated his original theory from a Kleinian psychoanalytic point of view in the final chapter of *Experiences in Groups* (Bion 1961). In that chapter, he described group dynamics in terms of Klein's primary stages, namely the paranoid-schizoid and the depressive positions, and formulated an understanding of the dynamics between group members in terms of splitting and projective identification.

Transformations in Knowledge

Bion's theory of thinking emotional experiences (1967) is primarily based on concepts of Freud (see section above on Freud and Bion) but also relies heavily on the Kleinian concept of unconscious phantasy. As Segal puts it, Kleinian psychoanalysts take the view that unconscious phantasy, which was a subject of the controversial discussion during World War II, underlies every mental function. In his elaboration of the notion of 'waking dream thought', Bion fully adopts this point of view.

Bion also uses Klein's concepts of splitting into good and bad, envy and reparation, and paranoid-schizoid versus depressive positions. However, he makes them more abstract and frees them from the psychopathological and moralistic connotations that Klein's original formulations were vulnerable to. Thus Bion uses the formula PS-D to refer to the paranoid-schizoid and depressive positions, and rather than seeing them as genetic positions, he sees them as states of mind that oscillate. This mental movement is necessary in the transformation process of psychic elements. The formula PS-D describes a movement from desaturation and incoherence to unity and coherence, and vice-versa. It is a model of transition between elements of thinking, as represented in Bion's Grid. This transition based on PS-D oscillation is one of the pillars of Bion's theory of thinking and became his model of creativity. While Klein linked creativity to the depressive position, for Bion creativity corresponded to the oscillation between PS and D.

Klein's notion of the good internal breast is another cornerstone of Bion's theory of thinking. In Bion's terms the good internal breast is the containing-detoxifying function that comes to be internalized in the interaction with the primary caregiver. Bion spoke of an internal breast and understood Klein's projective identification not as a defence mechanism but as the way mother and baby communicate, so that unprocessed beta-elements which are put into the mother by projective identification can be digested and detoxified by the internal breast.

Following Klein, Bion gives an important place to the epistemophilic instinct. He sees it as a third link between objects: love, hate, knowledge (L, H, K). Bion also gives the death drive, manifest as envy, an important place in his work. Envy transforms L, H, K into -L, -H, -K. This broadens, for instance, the Kleinian insight in narcissism that relies on the dominance of these negative links, described by Rosenfeld's concept of an internal Mafia gang (1987) or the concept of deadening attacks at an internal life-giver (Symington 1993).

Klein's harsh, primitive super-ego is translated by Bion (1967) into the obstructive object, whose attacks on linking are the basis of psychosis (see Box 2.5).

For Bion as for Klein, splitting is a core concept. For Bion, however, it is not only a primitive defence. Many of his concepts on psychic functioning are based on splits. His idea of a psychotic and a non-psychotic part of the personality is one example. While in the non-psychotic part, emotional experiences are 'thought', in the psychotic part, they are split and evacuated. Later Bion (see Chapter 11) expanded this view and presented the idea that mental functioning is split, even fragmented, and that this is a universal human condition. In *A Memoir of the Future* he represents the inner world as a constant interaction of a group of partial and whole inner objects (e.g. four somites, PA, Bion), which is similar to Klein's world of internal part and whole objects. Many of his concepts, like binocular view and two levels of functioning (psyche/soma, mature/immature) separated by a caesura, are based on the notion of split functioning.

It is my impression that Bion was a Kleinian to the backbone and often used this way of thinking without referring to it explicitly. It is the base from where he started. Clinically, most of his analysands experienced his approach as classically Kleinian (see Box 11.1).

Nevertheless, there are also some fundamental differences. Projective identification no longer occurs at a phantasy level as in Klein. To Bion, projective identification is something that happens in reality between people: something psychic is really put into the other and may be contained there. The interaction with a mother does not occur only at a phantasy level; the mother is necessary to catalyse and enhance psychic functioning.

Klein described unconscious phantasy as functioning in everyone. Bion does not take this phantasying for granted but sees it as an achievement. In schizophrenics, it may fail. In trying to understand severe psychopathology as disorders of thinking, Bion elaborated a clinical model of how phantasy functioning originates and what happens in psychotics when this fails or is attacked. Furthermore, Bion's approach was radical in focusing on psychic functioning rather than the content of phantasies. In developing his theoretical model of thinking, Bion was more philosophical and mathematical than Klein, who started from clinical observation in her play therapy with children.

Bion's concept of an unknown psychoanalytic object (see Box 8.7) that needs at least three grid categories to be apprehended is different from Klein's notion of an internal object. In relation to the unknowable psychoanalytic object Bion always focused on the constant conjunctions between psychic elements. He preferred this approach of seeing patterns to an explaining, understanding and cause–effect approach. In Bion's approach there is less room for judgement and thinking in terms of good–bad, something which is more present in Klein's idea's such as seeing the depressive position as a developmental advance on the paranoid-schizoid position or her ideas on envy and gratitude. Good–bad categorizing was often to Bion a kind of omnipotent approach reflecting a primitive form of thought. Another difference of emphasis is that while Klein laid stress on the depressive position and the better integration of split internal objects, Bion's focus was on psychic processing *per se* – especially on how emotions are dealt with internally and how this can lead to psychic change.

Transformations in O

The late Bion who is discussed in the second part of the book still relies on Klein, but introduces a whole new approach focused on transformations in O at an experiencing level, letting new experiences emerge from a state of fundamental not-knowing and being less inhibited by the senses and reason. This is different from Klein who put great stress on understanding and interpreting content. Klein's picture of the internal world looks denser, a theatre full of interacting whole and part-objects (Meltzer would say 'homunculi'). Bion's is full of empty spaces, the unknown and uncertainty. If one were to compare Freud's model to mechanical physics with drives, dynamics and resistances, then Klein's would be electrical with positive and negative split parts while Bion's resembles that of modern physics with huge empty spaces and the uncertainty principle.

Winnicott and Bion

Winnicott (1896–1971) and Bion (1897–1979) knew each other. Winnicott was twice president of the British Psychoanalytical Society (1956–1959 and 1965–1968) and Bion was president in the period in-between (1962–1965). In the Selected Letters of D.W. Winnicott (Rodman 1987), three are to W. Bion. The letters are short except for the first one from 1955 in which Winnicott states to Bion that he thinks of him as the big man of the future in the British Psychoanalytical Society. He hopes that Bion will become president soon, but finds it a pity that Bion is insulated in the Kleinian group, while he will need to be there for the whole Society. In the same letter Winnicott complains that the Society gets bored with what he calls the plugging of terms by the Kleinians, like envy and projective identification, which Winnicott says have been used several hundred times the last few months and hopes that Bion will be part of the attempt to get beyond these disruptive tendencies.

The two men were not close but both were influential at the British Society of Psychoanalysis. Winnicott was only one year older than Bion. They both had independent but quite different personalities, with Bion seemingly more introjective and Winnicott more anaclitic, to use Blatt's (2008) polar categories. Their backgrounds seem to have several things in common. As a child Winnicott was surrounded by eight women taking care of him but with a depressive mother and a rigid father who seemed to have painfully neglected the feelings of his son (Rodman 2003), probably the reason why Winnicott was so sensitive to intrusions of the core self. Bion from his side was a kind of orphan, on his own in England from the age of eight while his parents remained in India. Both were products of the Edwardian School system, Bion at a boarding school near Oxford, Winnicott in Cambridge, and both studied medicine (respectively London and Cambridge). Both enjoyed sports and volunteered for the Great War; Winnicott in the marines (the blue uniforms that were made in the family firm in Plymouth suited his blue eyes best, he said), Bion at the new tank corps. While Bion had a traumatic war experience as tank commander, this is less documented for Winnicott who had been a probationer surgeon on a Destroyer. Both remarried in 1951 after what looks like lonely difficult periods in their lives; Winnicott after an unhappy marriage that lasted 20 years and Bion as a widower. Both were typically British upper-middle-class gentlemen and shared the same British humour and irony. Winnicott had a lively style and was experienced by some as a bit effeminate partly due to his high-pitched voice, while Bion was tall and had an athletic, austere, even somewhat military outlook. Winnicott was a playful man wearing nice suits (he wrote to his tailor that he hoped to live up to the standard of the suits) and driving an oldtimer two-seat Rolls Royce, while Bion was remote. In studying their work I have the feeling that Winnicott can be seen as an intuitive poet at heart full of paradoxes in his clinical work and research, while Bion was an art and poetry lover but with a more scientific state of mind in clinical work and writings.

Transformations in K

Both Bion and Winnicott were much influenced by Klein. Bion was analysed by Klein and became a Kleinian analyst; Winnicott had Klein's son in treatment and was not analysed by her, but by James Strachey and later by Joan Riviere. Strachey recommended him to seek supervision with Klein towards the end of his analysis (circa 1922). While Bion worked with Klein's concept of the internal phantasy world and her ideas about the way the psyche deals with the inborn death instinct, aggression and envy, Winnicott developed theoretical concepts that were contrapuntal to Klein's notions: the importance of the reality of the environment and the conceptualization of subjective objects versus Klein's internal objects – the intrusiveness of the environment versus inborn aggression. Bion focused on the psychic processing of emotions in the mind, while the emphasis of Winnicott was more on relationships, i.e. the role of the environment on subjective states of mind.

Both gave a primary place to the mother and the baby's intersubjective experience with her in their model of psychic development; Winnicott described this in terms of a holding function, while Bion thought in terms of a mental containing and digesting function. Holding refers to the presence of the mother who can buffer intrusive experiences so that the child can go from illusion to disillusionment in a non-traumatic way. The presence of the mother and her dealing with the environment enables an intermediary space between the baby and the surrounding to exist as a 'me–not me' transitional space, where there is a place for playing and fantasy (Winnicott 1971). In his analytic work, Winnicott privileged holding as a psychic phenomenon related to transitional phenomena and on rare occasions took this to involve a sometimes quite literal holding of the patient physically in his arms and managing the patient's external environment in various ways (Letley 2014). Bion did not agree. He was less focused on realizing an intersubjective protected space but more on an analytic version of the mother detoxifying and processing the baby's negative unmentalized experiences through her reverie, relaxed attention, alpha-function communicated to her by means of projective identification.

Overall, Winnicott as a paediatrician saw thinking as developing from a good enough environment where one can play, as in his famous squiggle game and in his playfulness in life; Bion saw the development of thought as based on the tolerance of frustration, not unlike Freud. Winnicott wrote in clinical paradoxes (for instance, the good-enough mother; the capacity to be alone in the presence of another; the mother who has to be there, to be found; the fear of breakdown is about a breakdown that already happened; the destruction of the object to be able to meet the object), while Bion tried to developed a precise meta-theory.

Both gave creativity a major place in their work: Winnicott (1965) described it in terms of an ability to play and live with an internal world – being alive, while Bion conceptualized it in terms of the PS-D oscillation and the emergence of thoughts and forms.

In the 1955 Winnicott–Bion letter that I quote above, the difference between Winnicott and the so-called early Bion is well illustrated. It is interesting that in this letter, Winnicott comments on the clinical case in the presentation of Bion. The letter was written after Bion's presentation to the British Society of Psychoanalysis of his paper: 'Differentiation of the Psychotic from the Non-Psychotic Personalities', which was published two years later in the *International Journal of Psychoanalysis* (Bion 1957). Bion described during the lecture how the patient turned from one side to another on the couch and said 'I don't suppose I shall do anything today. I ought to have rung up my mother' (Bion 1957: 53). Then he said: 'No; I thought it would be like this' and then after a long pause: 'nothing but filthy things and smells' and then: 'I think I've lost my sight'. Bion writes that he himself was really in the dark. He did not understand the patient's saying that he should have rung up his mother, as if the patient's mother would have known what to do. The mother was presented in the analysis as a simple working-class woman. It is interesting how Bion further focused on the movements of the patient, as a child that is hungry, that wants something. It reminded him of Freud's statement about a baby who can do away with tension by a kind of motor movement. This brings Bion to the idea that the psychotic part is evacuating the tension by motor movements (later he will say beta-elements) instead of thinking the frustration. Winnicott, however, proposes an alternative interpretation in his letter to Bion. To him the patient moving to and fro on the couch and then saying that he ought to have telephoned his mother cries for an interpretation about communication. Winnicott states that he would have said:

A mother properly oriented to her baby would know from your movements what you need. There would be a communication because of this knowledge which belongs to her devotion and she would do something which would show that the communication had taken place. I am not sensitive enough or orientated in that way to be able to act well enough and therefore in this present analytic situation fall in the category of the mother who failed to make communication possible; in the present relationship therefore there is given sample of the original failure form the environment which contributed to your difficulty in communication. Of course you would always cry and so draw attention to need. In the same way you could telephone your mother and get a reply but this represents a failure of the more subtle communication which is the only basis for communication that does not violate the fact of the essential isolation of each individual.
(Winnicott 1955, in Winnicott and Rodman 1999: 91)

We see in this quote how Winnicott would have recognized the need of the patient in the current and past environment while at the same time valorizing what he will later call the 'incommunicado true self '(Winnicott 1963) and showing that he is not this mother (not coinciding with the bundle of projections of the patient), as he will develop much later in his paper *The Use of an Object* (Winnicott 1969).

While looking at it from different dimensions, both analysts surprise by their observational acumen and theoretical creativity in the transferential situation.

'Being' was always at the heart of Winnicott's work (Abram 1996). Bion developed the notion of an infinite, non-verbal, a-sensuous, unknown O. We find something similar but less dark in Winnicott: it is the true self that cannot be defined and verbalized (in contrast with the false self). It is an experience – a place to retreat and relax. To Winnicott this zone of regression is vitalizing and more conflict-free than Bion's notion of more frightening infinite spaces. It is protected by a false self, a kind of social oil. As Eigen (1992) stresses, the unintegrated in Winnicott goes hand in hand with 'wholeness'; it is a relief to be in this regressed state. Winnicott's later technique (Bollas 2013) focused on the regression that takes place during analysis. In Bion's view, by contrast, human beings are already regressed and must learn to deal with it.

Bion saw the aim of analysis as rendering the a-sensuous essence of a patient to the patient; similarly, for Winnicott it was making contact with the feeling true self that mattered, a true self that he saw as incommunicado. Eigen (1992: 285) states: 'One of the wonderful things in Winnicott's cases is the room he provides for experiencing reality, non-being, deadness, so that "aliveness" can say yes and has a chance of emerging'.

Bion advocated an attitude of no memory, no desire, no understanding, no coherence in order to get in contact with the unknown O of a psychic experience and to facilitate a transformation in O. In his much-discussed paper 'The Use of an Object and Relating through Identifications', Winnicott (1969) suggested silence and not giving clever interpretations to allow the patient to discover the yet unknown real object once he had been able to destroy his transference illusions.

Although taking very different forms, freedom and humour were paramount to both authors: a difficult-to-characterize British humour that enables one to put one's own ideas into perspective; Bion's ironic humour probably mainly sprang from what he called a binocular vision that enabled a freedom of thought; Winnicott's was playful, seeking to remain in contact with a youthful part of himself that was full of poetic fantasies.

Jung and Bion

When Beckett ended his therapy with Bion at the Tavistock Clinic, they had dinner together and went on to hear Jung give a lecture at the Clinic in 1953 (see Box 3.1). In the discussion, Jung answered a question about the patient by saying that 'she had not been born entirely'. This statement made a deep impression on Beckett, who recognized his own psychic problems in it.

There are certain points of similarity between Jung's and Bion's theory, not so much at the beginning of Bion's theoretical work, but rather in his late work.

Jung's emphasis on the influence of pre-natal life is one of the watermarks of his theory, and this is something that becomes explicit in Bion's late theory as well, for instance in *A Memoir of the Future*. As Culbert-Koehn (1997) quotes, Jung wrote in *Symbols and Transformations* that 'Therapy must support the regression and continue to do so until the prenatal stage is reached' (Jung 1953: par. 508).

Jung's Self is formless, irrepresentable and can only be present through its manifestations. As Dehing (1994) remarks, this is very close to Bion's concept of O (see Box 8.5). Bion variously defines O as the ultimate reality, the godhead, the infinite and the thing-in-itself, just as Jung (1936: par. 247) states that 'the "self" is a pure borderline concept, similar to Kant's Ding an Sich' (quoted in Dehing 1994).

Jung is famous for his use of myths. Likewise, Bion relies on several myths as organizing preconceptual narratives (Oedipus, Garden of Eden, Tower of Babel). Bion explicitly wonders, 'I don't see why Jung would not call the Oedipus figure an archetype if he wants to, or say that an equivalent of the Oedipus figure exists in every human being' (Bion 1977: 422). However, Bion saw no need to expand Freud's theory with the notion of a collective unconscious (Dehing 1994).

Nevertheless, the Jungian archetypes, understood as psychic structures that are already present in the formless self and that become realized when meeting experiences, are close to Bion's concept of psychoanalytic objects (see Box 8.7) which in the later Bion became a-sensuous forms or essences present in O that can be transformed into more finite and sensuous manifestations.

Lacan and Bion

Jacques Lacan (1901–1989) and Wilfred Bion knew each other. Lacan visited Bion and Rickman shortly after World War II (Lacan 1947) as he was impressed by their work with groups and in social psychiatry and by their war experiences. Bion and Lacan were psychiatrists and psychoanalysts at that time, although their meeting took place before their thought-provoking publications, which appeared from the 1950s on.

The physical contrast between the two men was striking. Lacan had been rejected from active military service because he was too thin. At that time, he was an intellectual involved with the artistic movement of surrealism. During World War II, he served as a doctor in a military hospital. Physically, the silent presence of Bion, the athletic hero from the Great War, was very different (see Lacan's report of his visit in Box 1.3).

In first encountering their work, some similarities are striking. Both authors began to develop their theories from their experience of work with psychotic patients, worked for a period with mathematical formulae and wrote in a difficult, often enigmatic style. Their psychoanalytic work has philosophical roots, although they draw on different traditions. Lacan was influenced by and influenced structuralism, while Bion's ideas are rooted in the empiricist and later in the idealist tradition.

There is a change of focus in Bion's work from symbolization or the thinking of emotional experiences (transformations in Knowledge) to the non-represented and infinite (transformations in O); a similar change seems to happen in Lacan who moves from a theory about the signifier towards a theory that starts from being.

Transformations in K

For Bion the mother plays a major and interactive role in the process of symbolization by containing the experience of the baby, digesting and detoxifying it through her reverie so that it can become mental and find a form. In Lacan's early work, the baby is imprisoned in the world and the desire of the mother. They are linked by an imaginary talk that only the two of them understand. A third is needed to get the baby out of this functioning and inscribe him in a symbolic register so that thinking and communicating with others becomes possible. This symbolic register is a language which is already there and consists of signifiers. The driving force to enter this symbolic order is the father, castration anxiety, the lack of the phallus. Entrance to the symbolic order introduces a lack. This lack opens the closed dual world with the mother. If entry to the symbolic order does not take place, psychosis is the consequence. Once in the register of the symbolic order, the child loses his immediate contact with the mother. This lack is translated into a desire, a moving force between human beings.

Transformation in O

As Verhaeghe (2011) described in his Klein-Lacan seminar, Lacan, like Bion, questioned what was behind the repressed, dynamic unconscious of Freud. In the Bonneval conference (Lacan 1966) concerning the kernel of the unconscious, Lacan did not agree with Leclaire's idea that it consists of phonemes, or with Laplanche's idea that it consists of sensory imagoes. As Verhaeghe puts it, to Lacan this kernel is 'une cause béante', an undifferentiated zone that can be compared with a germ cell, a meaningless carrier of possible further development. Here we are in the domain of the Lacanian Real. This is close to Bion's idea of an infinite, undifferentiated O out of which more finite transformations may emanate, but which may contain a-sensuous patterns, psychoanalytic objects (see Box 8.7). In Lacan's view we do not have contact with this zone, just as Bion conceives of a caesura between functioning in K and in O. Lacan thought that the loss of contact with this undifferentiated zone, what he saw as eternal life (Lacan XI seminar, 1964) and metaphorically referred to as the 'lamelle' (Verhaeghe 2011), brings another lack on top of the lack that results from entering the symbolic order, as described above. Lacan linked this with his notion of the 'object a' and jouissance and the wish to return to an original state, which also means death. On the other hand, Bion did not conceive loss of contact with the undifferentiated life-giving zone O as absolute; he thought that it is possible to regain contact with O, albeit indirectly; it is O that will find sensuous, knowable forms or K in a movement that goes from O to K, not the opposite. To Lacan, the original contact is lost forever but the primary jouissance may be inscribed in the body thanks to the mother. This cannot be represented or symbolized but the body knows it and it is a driving force in the contact between man and woman. The jouissance is in the Real of the body. In conclusion, while Bion is looking for direct contact with O, Lacan thought that we are excluded from this zone of primary jouissance, and therefore fundamentally divided, but the profound lack that results is a driving force. This powerful driving force reinforces the desire that originated from entry to the symbolic order as described above.

Philosophical background of Bion's psychoanalytic epistemology

Bion's psychoanalytic theories about knowing, being and psychic change are based on philosophy, although he was not meticulous about referencing the philosophers whose work he drew on. Bion studied history at Queen's college in Oxford after World War I between 1919 and 1921, then taught and later undertook medical training at University College Hospital, London. As a historian, Bion studied some philosophy and was much influenced by Herbert James Paton, who was a notable Kantian who also had a lot of military intelligence experience. Sandler (2005b: 570–575) gives a detailed scheme of the philosophers mentioned by Bion in his complete work. We might wonder (Cambien 1998) why it is a rather short list and why Spinoza, Kierkegaard, Wittgenstein, Heidegger, Schopenhauer, Husserl and Bergson, for instance, are lacking. All these philosophers can easily be linked with Bion's work, especially the phenomenologists (Thys 2005). Torres (2013) found that Bion had in pencil extensively annotated Bergson's *Matter and Memory*.

The organization of this book follows the clear division between Bion's work on transformations in Knowledge and his work on transformations in O. Bion's use of philosophical ideas also reflects this division. Bion's theories on thinking or *transformation in Knowledge* are linked to the theories of the British empiricists. R.B. Braithwaite influenced Bion in his search for a mathematical notation of the sessions (see the Grid) (Harris and Redway-Harris 2013), just as the Nobel prize-winning French mathematician and philosopher of science, Henri Poincaré, who wrote about the role of intuition mathematics and of the 'selected fact' in dealing with complex problems as in psychoanalysis.

Bion's later work on *transformation in O* is closer to the work of idealist philosophers such as Plato and Kant.

Bion's concepts on 'transformation in Knowledge' and the British empiricist philosophers

For the British empiricists, knowledge and thinking originate in the mind as a result of experience. John Locke's theory was a reaction against Plato's claim that *Ideas* exist outside the mind as transcendent *Forms* of which reality is an imperfect reflection, and that they realize themselves in sensuous forms. For example, a triangle may be seen as a Platonic transcendental Form or Idea that is manifest in different ways in nature but exists as such outside the mind. For Locke and Hume ideas do not have an independent existence, but originate in the mind. Locke took the view that they originate in the mind from experience of external reality. This experience gives rise to a *sensation* (Lowe 1995: 21), which leads to simple *Ideas* that can develop into complex and abstract ideas. It is the link with experience that gives an *Idea* its liveliness.

Later, Hume also took the view that ideas originate in the mind and are then projected onto the external world that we constitute in this way (Norton 1993). He differentiates between *Impressions* and *Ideas*. *Impressions* are more forceful and vivid and are 'all our sensations, passions and emotions as they make their first appearance to the soul' (Norton 1993: 6). *Ideas* enforce themselves less urgently and are faint images of these impressions. They are linked to each other by what Hume calls 'constant conjunctions', a notion that Bion adopted.

Like Locke and Hume, Bion based his theory of thinking on a building block theory of mental elements (Cavell 2003). Bion's β-elements are comparable to Hume's *impressions*; they are also vivid and charged with emotion. If we think of α-elements as β-elements stripped of too much vividness so that they can be taken in by the mind, they are close to Hume's notion of an *Idea*. The following passage from Hume comes very close to the way Bion conceives the formation of a thought, a thought for a no-thing.

> The invariant succession of paired objects or events of particular causes and effects, and, although our experience never includes even a glimpse of a causal connection, it does arouse in us an expectation that a particular event (a 'cause') will be followed by another event (an effect) previously and constantly associated with it. Regularities of experience give rise to these feelings and this determines the mind to transfer its attention from a present impression to the idea of an absent but associated object.
>
> (Hume 1739, quoted in Norton 1993: 10)

Hume thought that ideas are linked by what he calls 'automatic mental associations', or imagination. He states that 'thinking is a custom that operates before we have time for reflection' (Hume 1739/1985: 153). Hume calls this automatic process *reverie* (ibid.: 318). It corresponds to Bion's dream-work α or waking dream thought, which he named reverie just as Hume had.

Bion's concepts on 'transformation in O' and the idealist philosophers

Bion's later model of 'transformation in O' is influenced by the philosophy of Kant and Plato. Kant accepted Hume's argument that the origin of all ideas is mental and that the mind is responsible for the constitution of the world, but he radicalized Hume's point of view. He realized that if everything is mental, it is important to be aware of the limits of our thinking. This is the theme of his *Critique of Pure Reason* (Kant 1929/1781). Because all ideas are mental and the capacities of our mind are limited, we cannot know the world as it objectively exists in itself. Our knowledge is bound by *a priori* concepts like space and time and these *a priori* concepts of our understanding do not apply to the reality-in-itself. Therefore, no matter how sophisticated our perceptions, even when they are enhanced by devices, with regard to objective knowledge our minds are bound to that world of appearances created by the limitations of our minds. This implies that we can hypothesize by Reason that there is a reality that transcends the limits of our knowledge and perceptions. Kant calls the Ideas made by Reason about the unknowable reality 'Things-in-themselves'. 'Things-in-themselves' are to Kant thus not the 'world-as-it-is' but ideas about it that delineate the limit of our knowledge. Kant calls these ideas *noumena* (not belonging to the world of appearances, sensorial phenomena, but of the mind) to distinguish them from a *phenomenon*, which belongs to the world of sensorial appearances. Our knowledge is at the level of these appearances, the phenomenal realm.[4]

Kant not only radicalizes Hume's notion that it is the mind alone that is the base for the constitution of what we know as the objective world; he goes a step further. In contrast to Hume, he posits that the ideas in the mind have a transcendental base. In this respect he is like Plato, but for Plato the transcendental ideas exist outside the mind, while for Kant they exist in the mind. Ideas or noumena are transcendental Forms in the mind that are at the base of our construction of reality. For Kant, there are also ideas (noumena) to which no sensorial appearance or phenomena correspond and of which we can know absolutely nothing. God is such an idea.[5] While Bion's conceptualization of transformation in Knowledge seems to be linked with empiricist epistemology, transformation in O seems embedded in Kant's and Plato's philosophy. Kant saw practical thinking and being guided by the senses at a phenomenal level as a distraction from the noumenal world. In the same way, Bion saw the senses and practical reason (the pleasure-pain principle) as a hindrance to 'seeing' and 'becoming' O. He stated in this sense that 'Reason is a slave of the passions' (Bion 1970) which is derived from Hume's famous statement, in which he saw the aim of practical reason only as a way of achieving a goal set by passion and desires and not to attain higher values. In the same vein, Kant wrote that 'we sold our soul for a wooden pot' (Appelbaum 1995), meaning that practical thinking alienates us from our being. Also Bergson, whose *Matter and Memory* Bion pencilled, stressed the utilitarian character of mental functions (Torres 2013). Bion as well stressed the inadequacy of operative intellectual thinking again and again and mentioned, just as Bergson did, another form of knowledge: intuition (Torres 2013). In the same vein, Bion advocated freeing oneself from thinking based on the pleasure-pain principle: no memory, no desire, no understanding, no coherence. Instead he advocated an attitude of 'Awe' and of 'Faith' towards the Unknown, which resembles Kant's attitude towards the Sublime which is beyond what we can think.

For readers with a philosophical background it is important to acknowledge that Bion is not conceptually clear in his use of Kantian concepts. While for Kant 'Things-in-themselves' are a transcendent idea and not the unknown reality-in-itself, Bion seems to use 'Thing-in-itself' to mean both an idea and the existing unknown reality-in-itself. This is reflected in his definition of O: 'When I use the letter, O, I mean it to indicate noumenon, the thing itself of which nobody can know anything' (Bion 1990: 69). In this sense, he misuses Kant's notion (Schermer 2003), no longer seeing it as an idea but as a reality.

Another major difference is that Kant never suggested the possibility of an intuitive contact with an unknowable reality as Bion did. This approach is based on the possibility of a form of observation without thinking, a 'pure experience' (Nishida 2001) which is closer to the way mystics deal with a reality that is beyond reason.

I have the impression that in Bion's last works (like the *Seminars* and *Clinical Discussions*) he saw a-sensuous conjunctions or patterns not only as something happening in the mind like Kant, but also as existing independently of the mind, not unlike Plato. He proclaimed the necessity of a potential for a state of abysmal ignorance, philosophical doubt and intuition in order to get in contact with these conjunctions. However, he did not elaborate on this last point of view.

Notes

1 Wieland (2013) gives a comprehensive list of all places in Bion's work where he quotes Freud. Of the 100 quotes, 39 are on the Freud (1911) 'Two principles' test.
2 Bion (1990: 99) later called this thinking 'the monkey-like trick', as he saw it as hindrance to be in contact with 'O'.
3 Matte-Blanco (1988) took this up in his ideas on symmetrical and asymmetrical psychic functioning. The unconscious functioning with displacement and condensation where one thing can stand for many is a symmetrical relationship as in mathematical infinity (a part of the infinite is infinite as well). This is in contrast with verbal, logical thinking which is asymmetrical, finite. In dreams there is a mixture of asymmetrical and symmetrical thinking.

4 For Kant, this distinction between appearance and 'Thing-in-itself' also applies to the mind itself.

5 For the sake of completeness it may be important to mention that in Kant's conception, the emotional belongs to 'the aesthetic' and is treated in his *Critique of Aesthetic Judgement* (in relation to the beautiful and the sublime) and in his anthropology, but not in his *Critique of Pure Reason*. This contrasts with the approach of Locke and Hume, where emotions are at the origin of sensations, impressions and ideas.

W.R. Bion bibliography

From H. Karnac's (2008) *Bion's Legacy*, pages 1–8, except the 1967 LA seminars (2013). The 24 works of Bion, referred to as WRB 1–WRB 24:

WRB 1 *Experiences in Groups and Other Papers*. London: Tavistock Publications and New York: Routledge 1961; reprinted Hove: Brunner-Routledge 2001.

WRB 2 *Learning from Experience*. London: William Heinemann Medical Books 1962; reprinted in Seven Servants with WRB3, WRB4 and WRB6, New York: Aronson 1977; reprinted London: Karnac Books 1984.

WRB 3 *Elements of Psychoanalysis*. London: William Heinemann Medical Books 1963; reprinted in Seven Servants with WRB2, WRB4 and WRB6, New York: Aronson 1977; reprinted London: Karnac Books 1984.

WRB 4 *Transformations*. London: William Heinemann Medical Books 1965; reprinted in Seven Servants with WRB2, WRB3 and WRB6, New York: Aronson 1977; reprinted London: Karnac Books 1984.

WRB 5 *Second Thoughts: Selected Papers on Psychoanalysis*. London: William Heinemann Medical Books 1967; reprinted London: Karnac Books 1984.

WRB 6 *Attention and Interpretation*. London: Tavistock Publications 1970; reprinted in Seven Servants with WRB2, WRB3 and WRB4, New York: Aronson 1977; reprinted London: Karnac Books 1984.

WRB 7 *Bion's Brazilian Lectures 1 – São Paulo*. Rio de Janeiro: Imago Editora 1973; reprinted in *Brazilian Lectures* (revised and corrected ed.) with WRB 8 in one volume, London: Karnac Books 1990.

WRB 8 *Bion's Brazilian Lectures 2 – Rio de Janeiro/São Paulo*. Rio de Janeiro: Imago Editora 1974; reprinted in *Brazilian Lectures* (revised and corrected ed.) with WRB 7 in one volume, London: Karnac Books 1990.

WRB 9 *A Memoir of the Future Book 1 – The Dream*. Rio de Janeiro: Imago Editora 1975; reprinted in *A Memoir of the Future* (revised and corrected edition) with WRB 10, WRB 13 and WRB 15 in one volume, London: Karnac Books 1991.

WRB 10 *A Memoir of the Future Book 2 – The Past Presented*. Rio de Janeiro: Imago Editora 1977; reprinted in *A Memoir of the Future* (revised and corrected edition) with WRB 9, WRB 13 and WRB 15 in one volume, London: Karnac Books 1991.

WRB 11 *Two Papers: The Grid and Cæsura*. Rio de Janeiro: Imago Editora 1977; reprinted (revised and corrected edition) London: Karnac Books 1989.

WRB 12 *Four Discussions with W.R. Bion*. Perthshire: Clunie Press 1978; reprinted in *Clinical Seminars and Other Works* with WRB 18 in one volume (edited by Francesca Bion), London: Karnac Books 2000.

WRB 13 *A Memoir of the Future, Book 3: The Dawn of Oblivion*. Rio de Janeiro: Imago Editora 1977; reprinted in *A Memoir of the Future* (revised and corrected edition) with WRB 9, WRB 10 and WRB 15 in one volume, London: Karnac Books 1991.

WRB 14 *Bion in New York and São Paulo*. Perthshire: Clunie Press 1980.

WRB 15 *A Key to A Memoir of the Future*. Rio de Janeiro: Imago Editora 1977; reprinted in *A Memoir of the Future* (revised and corrected edition) with WRB 9, WRB 10 and WRB 13 in one volume, London: Karnac Books 1991.

WRB 16 *The Long Weekend: 1897–1919 (Part of a Life)* (edited by Francesca Bion). Abingdon: Fleetwood Press 1982; reprinted London: Free Association Books 1986; reprinted London: Karnac Books 1991.

WRB 17 *All My Sins Remembered: Another Part of a Life and the Other Side of Genius: Family Letters* (edited by Francesca Bion). Abingdon: Fleetwood Press 1985; reprinted London: Karnac Books 1991.

WRB 18 *Clinical Seminars and Four Papers*. Abingdon: Fleetwood Press 1987; reprinted in *Clinical Seminars and Other Works* with WRB 12 in one volume (edited by Francesca Bion), London: Karnac Books 2000.

WRB 19 *Cogitations* (edited by Francesca Bion). London: Karnac Books 1992; new extended edition London: Karnac Books 1994.

WRB 20 *Taming Wild Thoughts* (edited by Francesca Bion). London: Karnac Books 1997.

WRB 21 *War Memoirs 1917–1919* (edited by Francesca Bion). London: Karnac Books 1997.

WRB 22 *Clinical Seminars and Other Works* (edited by Francesca Bion). London: Karnac Books 2000 [single-volume edition containing *Four Discussions with W.R. Bion* (WRB 12) and *Clinical Seminars and Four Papers* (WRB 18)].

WRB 23 *The Italian Seminars* (edited by Francesca Bion and transl. from the Italian by Philip Slotkin). London: Karnac Books 2005 [earlier edition *Seminari Italiani: Testo Completo dei Seminari tenuti da W.R. Bion a Roma*. Edizioni Borla 1985].

WRB 24 *The Tavistock Seminars* (edited by Francesca Bion). London: Karnac Books 2005.

Part 2 – Chronological list

1940 War of Nerves, The in *The Neuroses in War* ed. Miller and Crichton-Miller (pp. 180–200) London, Macmillan 1940.

1943 Intra-group tensions in therapy (with Rickman, J.) *Lancet* 2: 678/781 – Nov. 27 1943 WRB 1 pp. 11–26.

1946 Northfield Experiment [The] (with Bridger, H. and Main, T.) *Bulletin of the Menninger Clinic* 10: 71–76.

1946b Leaderless Group Project *Bulletin of the Menninger Clinic* 10: 77–81.

1948a Psychiatry in a time of crisis *Br. Jnl. Med. Psy.* XXI: 81–89.

1948b Experiences in Groups I
Human Relations I: 314–320 WRB 1 pp. 29–40.

1948c Experiences in Groups II
Human Relations I: 487–496 WRB 1 pp. 41–58.

1948d Untitled paper read at the Int. Cong. on Mental Health London 1948, pubd. in Vol. III *Proceedings of the International Conference on Medical Psychotherapy* 106–109 London, H.K. Lewis and N.Y., Columbia U.P. 1948.

1949a Experiences in Groups III
Human Relations 2: 13–22 WRB 1 pp. 59–75.

1949b Experiences in Groups IV
Human Relations 2: 295–303 WRB 1 pp. 77–91.

1950a Experiences in Groups V
Human Relations 3: 3–14 WRB 1 pp. 93–114.

1950b Experiences in Groups VI
Human Relations 3: 395–402 WRB 1 pp. 115–126.

1950c Imaginary Twin, The read to *Br.PsA Soc* Nov. 1 1950. WRB 5 pp. 3–22.

1951 Experiences in Groups VII
Human Relations 4: 221–227 WRB 1 pp. 127–137.
1952 Group Dynamics: a review.
IJP 33: 235–247 also in *New Directions in Psychoanalysis* ed. Klein, M. et al pp. 440–477
Tavistock Publ. London 1955 WRB 1 pp. 141–191.
1954 Notes on the Theory of Schizophrenia *IJP* 35: 113–118 WRB 5 pp. 23–35.
1955 Language and the Schizophrenic in *New Directions in Psychoanalysis* ed. Klein, M.
et al pp. 200–239 Tavistock Publ. London 1955.
1956 Development of Schizophrenic Thought, The *IJP* 37: 344–346 WRB 5 pp. 36–42.
1957a Differentiation of the Psychotic from the non-Psychotic personalities, the *IJP* 38:
266–275 WRB 5 pp. 43–64.
1957b On Arrogance *IJP* 39: 144–146 WRB 5 pp. 86–92.
1958 On Hallucination *IJP* 39: 341–349 WRB 5 pp. 65–85.
1959 Attacks on Linking *IJP* 40: 308–315 WRB 5 pp. 93–109.
1961 Melanie Klein – Obituary (with Herbert Rosenfeld and Hanna Segal) *IJP* 42: 4–8.
1962 Psychoanalytic Study of Thinking, the *IJP* 43: 306–310 (pub'd as A Theory of Thinking)
WRB 5 pp. 110–119.
1963 *The Grid* WRB 20 pp. 6–21.
1966(a) Catastrophic Change Bulletin of the *Br. PsA Soc* #5.
1966(b) *Medical Orthodoxy and the Future of Psychoanalysis*, K. Eissler. New York, I.U.P.
1965 (review) *IJP* 47: 575–579.
1966(c) *Sexual Behavior and the Law* ed. R. Slovenko. Springfield, Thomas 1964 (review)
IJP 47: 579–581.
1967 Notes on Memory and Desire *Psychoanalytic Forum* 11/3: 271–280. Reprinted in
Melanie Klein Today Vol. 2 – Mainly Practice: 17–21 ed. E. Bott Spillius London Routledge
1988.
1967 *Los Angeles Seminars and Supervision*. Aguayo, J. and Malin, B. (eds) London: Karnac
2013.
1976a Evidence Bulletin of the *Br.PsA Soc* 1976 WRB 18 pp. 313–320.
1976b Interview with A.G. Banet Jr. Los Angeles, 1976
Group and Organisation Studies vol. 1 No. 3: 268–285 WRB 24 pp. 97–114.
1977a Quotation from Freud (on a) in *Borderline Personality Disorders* ed. P. Hartocollis.
New York I.U.P. 1977 WRB 18 pp. 306–311.
1977b *Emotional Turbulence in Borderline Personality Disorders* ed. P. Hartocollis New York
I.U.P. 1977 WRB 18 pp. 295–305.
1977c *Seven Servants* (with an introduction by W.R. Bion) containing Elements of
Psychoanalysis, Learning from Experience, Transformations, Attention and Interpretation
New York: Aronson.
1978 Seminar held in Paris, 10 July 1978 (unpublished in English), published in *French
Revue Psychotherapie Psychanalytique de Groupe* 1986.
1979 Making the Best of a Bad Job, Bulletin of the *Br.PsA Soc* 1979 WRB 18 pp. 321–331.
In 2014 Karnac published the Complete Works of W.R. Bion in 16 volumes, edited by Chris
Mawson, training analyst of the British Psychoanalytic Society and Francesca Bion, the wife of
Bion. They follow the biographical list of Harry Karnac and are mainly ordered chronologically:

Volume I
The Long Weekend: 1897–1919 (Part of a Life)

Volume II
All My Sins Remembered: Another Part of a Life
The Other Side of Genius: Family Letters

Volume III
War Memoirs 1917–1919

Volume IV
The 'War of Nerves' (1940)
On Groups (1943)
The Leaderless Group Project (1946)
Psychiatry at a Time of Crisis (1948)
Group Methods of Treatment (1948)
Language and the Schizophrenic (1955)
Experiences in Groups and Other Papers (1961)
Learning from Experience (1962)

Volume V
Elements of Psychoanalysis (1963)
Taming Wild Thoughts (I): The Grid (1963)
Transformations: Change from Learning to Growth (1965)

Volume VI
Memory and Desire (1965)
Catastrophic Change (1966)
Second Thoughts: Selected Papers on Psychoanalysis (1967)
Notes on Memory and Desire (1967)
Attention and Interpretation: A Scientific Approach to Insight in Psychoanalysis and Groups (1970)
Book Reviews (1966)

Volume VII
Brazilian Lectures:
1973 Sao Paulo Lectures
1974 Sao Paulo Lectures
1974 Rio de Janeiro Lectures

Volume VIII
Clinical Seminars:
Brasilia 1975
Contributions to Panel Discussions:
Brasilia, a New Experience (1975)
Sao Paulo (1978)
Bion in New York and Sao Paulo: New York (1977)
Sao Paulo (Ten Talks) (1978)

Volume IX
The Tavistock Seminars (June 1976–March 1979)
The Italian Seminars (1977)
A Paris Seminar (July 1978)

Volume X
Two Papers:
The Grid (1971)
Caesura (1975)
Four Discussions (1976)

Four Papers:
Emotional Turbulence (1976)
On a Quotation from Freud (1976)
Evidence (1976)
Making the Best of a Bad Job (1979)
Interview with Anthony Banet Jnr (1976)
Taming Wild Thoughts (II): Untitled (1977)

Volume XI
Cogitations
Review of Cogitations, by Andre Green

Volume XII
A Memoir of the Future: Book 1

Volume XIII
A Memoir of the Future: Book 2

Volume XIV
A Memoir of the Future: Book 3 (with expanded key)

Volume XV
Unpublished papers:
The Conception of Man (1961)
Penetrating Silence (1976)
New and Improved (1977)
Further Cogitations (1968–1969)
Appendix A: The Days of Our Lives (1994), by Francesca Bion
Appendix B: 'Catastrophic Change' and 'Container and Contained Transformed': a comparison,
    by Chris Mawson
Appendix C: Standardized Bibliography of Bion's Works, compiled by Harry Karnac

Part I

BEFORE THE
CAESURA
Transformations in Knowledge

---

1 BIOGRAPHY, 1897–1966

Leaving India at the age of eight and going through the British public school system on his own left its mark on the young Bion. When he was 19 he volunteered to fight in the Great War. His war experiences would have a lasting influence on his attitude and his theory. He wrote a short factual report of the horrors he experienced during and shortly after the war (Bion 1997) and a long biographical account in later life (Bion 1982). The autobiographical writings are typical of Bion's approach in his later work and they will therefore be discussed in chronological order in Part II of this book.

Immediately after the war Bion went to Oxford to study history at Queen's College. In 1922 he accepted a position as a teacher at his former school, Bishop's Stortford College. In spite of his popularity, Bion left the school rather abruptly after an unpleasant incident with a student's mother. After Bion had rather awkwardly invited her for tea, she accused him of making advances to her son (Bion 1982). Bion clearly indicates that the mother's accusations were groundless and although the school investigation failed to substantiate the mother's accusations, Bion decided to leave at the end of the term (Bion 1985: 16–17). Realizing that he was not cut out to be a schoolteacher, and aiming at becoming a psychoanalyst, he went on to do medical training at University College London, where he felt more at home than in Oxford. In London, he was taken under the wing of Sir Jack Drummond, a distinguished biochemist, who was murdered in 1952 in France in a notorious criminal case (Bion 1985: 46). At the hospital, Bion was impressed by the surgical skills of Wilfred Trotter (Bion 1985: 37–39). Trotter's work on the herd instinct may have influenced the young Bion, although he does not acknowledge this in his autobiography and bibliography (see Box 1.3).

At around this time, Bion had his first experience of psychotherapy with Dr J.A. Hadfield. Although he was a war hero, Bion wrote of himself as very insecure and sexually immature at that time, and described how he felt extremely hurt and angry when a beautiful girl who he started to date after she sent him wild roses, and to whom he proposed, left him without explanation for someone else (Bion 1985: 28–33). Bion's trust in his therapist was shaken when Dr Hadfield made clear his expectation that he would receive a fee from Bion for referring patients to him, a frowned-upon practice known as 'fee-splitting'

(Bion 1985: 42–43). Although Bion won a gold medal for surgery (to which he referred with the same ironic ambivalence as his war medals) he nevertheless opted for psychoanalysis, his initial choice. After receiving his medical degree, he began work at the Tavistock Clinic in 1933. The Tavistock Clinic was rapidly growing as a treatment and training centre. It was staffed by part-time doctors who were able to offer low-fee therapy to people with a low income because they were allowed to see patients privately at the same time. His psychotherapist Dr Hadfield was a training director and mentor at the Tavistock. He advocated a kind of reductive analysis, explicitly not working with transference but linking current symptoms through a kind of forced fantasy to specific incidents in the past (Dicks 1970 in Miller 2014). Bion therefore ironically called him 'my "Feel it in the Past" (FiP) analyst' because of his tendency to reduce everything to past trauma, including recent grief or hurtful events (Bion 1985: 34), like an unhappy love affair. Later numerous Hadfieldians including Dicks, Bion and Geoffrey Thompson formed a 'rebel' group who went on to formal training at the Institute of Psychoanalysis (Dicks 1970: in Miller 2014). Towards the end of his apprenticeship at the Tavistock, in 1937, he was the first psychiatrist of the clinic to go into psychoanalysis with John Rickman (see Box 2.1).

Initially, Bion worked for some years with Dr Hadfield (Trist 1985). Bion had a part-time practice in Central London in 'a prestigious but sordid room' on Harley Street, where Rickman, Trotter and most doctors of the Tavistock Clinic had their offices (Bion 1985: 42). Meanwhile, he was also working at the Portman Clinic, then an independent centre which specialized in those with sexual perversions, committing crimes and delinquency. It is now connected with the Tavistock Clinic.

World War II

Bion's analysis with Rickman ended in September 1939 (Bléandonu 1994). Bion rejoined the army in 1940.

In the RBMC (Royal British Medical Corps), psychiatrists had a double task: on the one hand, to find better means for selection of soldiers, on the other hand, to provide therapy for soldiers suffering from war neurosis, shell-shock, trauma, etc and to investigate procedures to rehabilitate soldiers back into the army or into civilian life more efficiently. Bion started working with shell-shocked and traumatized soldiers at Craigmile Bottom Hospital. Soon, he was appointed as 'Command psychiatrist' for the Western Command, i.e. a specialist adviser to other medical officers and a consultant for all patients, at the David Hume Military Hospital in Chester.

In 1941 Bion was suddenly transferred from Western Command to Area Command in York. There, he was assigned to work on psychological selection tests for the army. In this context, he proposed his 'Leaderless Group project' to replace the lengthy individual tests by a two-and-a-half-hour-long group experiment. The project is described at some length by his collaborator and friend at the time, Eric Trist (1985), and by J.D. Sutherland (1985). Putting the recruits together in a leaderless group allowed observing army officials and medical staff to assess the candidates' attempts to organize the group from within and to judge their suitability for army life. The main focus was to ensure that good leaders were selected, because according to Bion's rationale 'the social role and "adaptability to persons" was central to the officer's job' (Harrison 2000: 91).

> I can recall vividly how struck I was by the simplicity of the notion, and yet what a stroke of genius it was to create in this way a living manifest sample of personal relationships in a situation in which the conflict between self-interest and a concern for others was an active reality.
>
> (Sutherland 1985: 50)

With Rickman, Bion wrote a report for the army's psychiatric service in order to improve the situation in the medical hospitals, proposing to treat neurosis through group therapy. This would eventually lead to the Northfield experiments. Although he was respected by army officials because of his heroism in World War I, Bion was not appointed as head of the Research and Training Centre. The lack of recognition may have been due to a growing hostility within the army to psychiatry in general and certainly to Bion's revolutionary experiments, which were considered to be potentially subversive or even communist-inspired (Bléandonu 1994: 59).

After he was fired as Command psychiatrist without any forewarning or explanation (Trist 1985: 11), Bion asked to be transferred to the Northfield Military Hospital in Birmingham, where he joined his friend Rickman (see Box 2.1) and was put in charge of the Military Training Wing. Together they initiated a series of experiments with group therapy designed to treat war neurosis, known as the Northfield experiments. In his autobiography, Bion was rather sarcastic about this (Bion 1985: 50) (see Box 1.1).

Box 1.1   The Northfield Experiments

At Hollymoor Hospital, Northfield, Birmingham, a rehabilitation clinic for soldiers with war neuroses, two experiments were conducted. As Harrison points out, 'Foulkes, Bion, Rickman, Main and Bridger showed how the enemy could be defeated, but failed to convince their superiors' (Harrison 2000: 182). Indeed, these experiments were conducted not only because of the need for mass treatment of war neuroses, but also because these pioneers had psychological insights into how to make army life more human and effective. They are regarded as the basis of group therapy and of the therapeutic communities.

The first Northfield experiment was conducted by Bion and Rickman in 1942–1943. They tried to bring hospital functioning closer to the functioning of a military unit by putting the patients together in small groups. In these groups, they did not try to 'steer the discourse when handling the groups', but rather focused on the actual dynamics of the group (Harrison 2000: 187). Bion's vision was rooted in his leaderless group experiment in selecting officers. Bion took a scientific approach. He wanted to focus on the management of problems in interpersonal relations within a group, in order to allow group members to gain some distance from their situation and to gain understanding of their problems. He reorganized the training wing of about 100–200 patients, imposing strict discipline, with a daily parade to make announcements, and by creating different work groups.

While the initiative initially stirred a lot of discussion in the group, Bion soon observed that only 20% of the residents did all the work while the others shirked their duties. In order to address this problem, he did not rely on an authoritarian or moralistic approach but told the group members to study the organization of the work with scientific seriousness and to come up with their own solutions for the problems. The group, which was like both society and individuals in its unwillingness to deal with psychological distress, had first to be made aware that the nature of the distress was psychological, otherwise they would not have been able to use their energy for self-cure. Bion did not suggest practical solutions until the psychological dynamics had become clear and could be discussed.

Although the situation on the wards improved after a month and the number of patients that were able to return to their duties as soldiers indicated the experiment's dramatic success (Bridger 2005), it was abandoned after six weeks. Different accounts are given of the abandonment of this first experiment. Bion and Rickman failed to convince their rigid commanding officer Pearce, who felt that their method was too Freudian and too slow (Harrison 2000: 191). As a result, the structure was prematurely closed down after an unexpected supervision at night where the military staff discovered that the wing was a mess. The floor of the cinema hall was covered with newspapers and condoms (de Mare 1985).

One of the collaborators at Northfield, Bridger, has a somewhat different analysis. On the one hand, he points out that there were also differences in approach between Bion, Rickman and other staff members such as Foulkes and Bierer (who continued the second experiment in which Bion did not take part). Secondly, Bridger also suggests that Bion's authority problem, also evident in his writings about his experiences as a soldier, may have played a part. According to Bridger, 'he neglected – and was indeed somewhat disparaging of – the more immediate environments of the hospital and traditional reactions of the bureaucratic aspects of the military machine' (Bridger 1985: 97). Moreover, Bion was not prepared to compromise. Thirty-five years later, Bion still considered the experience a betrayal and resented his superiors (Bléandonu 1984: 62–63). Accounts of the experiment by Bion can be found in a paper for the Bulletin of the Menninger Clinic (1946) and in the first paper of

(continued)

(continued)

Experiences in Groups (1961). Analyses of both Northfield experiments (and the differences between them) are found in Pines (1985), which collects first-hand observations by collaborators of Bion at the time and in Harrison (2000), who describes the relationship between psychiatry and the army from a more sociological perspective.

Early in World War II, probably while socializing with other officers, Bion got to know the well-known actress Betty Jardine (see Box 1.2). They married during the war in about 1943. Trist, his friend, described Bion's first wife as a warm, gifted, mature person, who matched him perfectly. Their presence as a couple, the proud, athletic and heroic officer and the beautiful actress, attracted envious looks. Bion does not write a great deal about this marriage in his autobiography, but he and his wife seem to have been fairly happy and active in this period. Bion started writing his paper a small, little-known – in Harrison's (2000: 53) view, not very well written – article on the 'war of nerves' for a summary of military psychiatry (Bion 1940). Betty became pregnant. Bion accepted a new project, the 21st Army Corps, for which Bion seems to have been Montgomery's first choice (Bléandonu 1984: 64). It had been found that it was better to treat emotional disturbances of soldiers close to the unit, and Bion wanted to use his group method for this. Therefore, he was in Normandy when he was informed that Betty had given birth to a baby daughter, Parthenope, on 28 February 1945. Betty died of a pulmonary embolism three days after giving birth. It took the army a week to locate Bion. In his autobiography, he describes his dissociated reaction to the news, showing how traumatized he was by it. ('The long-distance call from Brussels to the War office brought the reply "Can you hear me? The baby is very feeble. Can you hear me?" "Yes, yes get on the blast with it, I'm not deaf". "Betty died last Wednesday". "Thank you very much. No, no, not at all. I can arrange"' (Bion 1985: 27). He describes how when he returned to London, he found himself alone with a baby daughter who he wanted to care for himself, an insecure future and £8,000 left (equivalent to £250,000 today), which he and Betty had saved.

Box 1.2 Betty Jardine

Elisabeth Kittrick Jardine, alias Betty Jardine (born Cheshire, England, 1904, died 28 February 1945), started out as an actress in Manchester in 1926, staying with the same company for seven years. She stayed in London from 1933 till her death. In 1934 she played in *Whatever Happened to George*. In 1936 she played for a season on Broadway. Her major success was *The Corn is Green* in 1938, which Bion saw according to Bléandonu (1994: 54). Bléandonu informs us that Emilyn William was the writer of the play and took the role of the main protagonist. The play was about an internal conflict between taking up scholarship at Oxford and looking after his illegitimate child. Betty Jardine played a cynical, seductive young woman.

Betty Jardine appeared as Lavinia Pepper in *Almost a Honeymoon* (1938), as Daisy Johnson in *Mail Train* (1941), as Mathilda Wrench in *A Girl in the News* (1941), as Edna in *The Ghost Train* (1941), as Doris in *The Remarkable Mr Kipps* (1941), as Miss Bohne in *We'll Meet Again* (1942), as Helen in *Rhythm Serenade* (1943), as Fee Baker in *A Canterbury Tale* (1944), a mystical fairy tale about an American sergeant and a British male and female soldier who cross the country, and as Teresa King in *Two Thousand Women* (1944), a comedy-thriller in which a group of woman hide airmen for the Germans. A film critic said later: 'The script is full of glorious moments and gives most of the actresses a chance to shine. Betty Jardine is worth noting'. This was her last film and she died a few days after childbirth the following year which, on the evidence of her performance here, was a great loss to British cinema.

After World War II Bion returned to the Tavistock Clinic. During the war a Council was voted and a Planning Committee was put together to prepare the Tavistock Centre for the post-war situation. Bion finally became the chair of this committee. He organized a broad social psychiatry programme with several kinds of groups. In 1945 Bion undertook a second training analysis, this time with Melanie Klein, which was often very difficult (as he describes in *All My Sins Remembered*) but he remained close to her until her death. In 1946 the Tavistock had to prepare to enter the National Health Service and had to meet criteria about therapy. Bion became chairman of the executive committee. In 1947 Bion became chairman of the medical section of the British Psychological Society. In those years, he was preoccupied with the role of psychiatry in general, as is evident from his presidential address to the British Psychological Society, 'Psychiatry in a time of distress' (Bion 1948), in which he explicitly takes a stand for reform based on the psychoanalytic method. In 1948 the Tavistock entered the National Health Service and the Council decided to focus on psychoanalytically oriented psychotherapy. Bion had several kinds of groups: patients, students and industrial. He saw groups mainly as study groups. He was a little surprised that his colleagues at the Tavistock thought that groups could be used for healing, but he was prepared to make the experiment. At that time he started writing the papers that would be collected in *Experiences in Groups* (Trist 2000). The transition to the NHS brought a lot of tensions within the Centre; not all colleagues could stay and new colleagues were attracted; there were interviews and requests of training. It testifies a clear insight that Bion decided to offer a group for the

Staff members and therefore decided to step down as chairman. The safety and the patience that he offered helped to clear the problems and when this group was less needed, Bion disappeared gradually from the Tavistock and the field of social psychiatry. During all these years he had been in the firing line and developed far-reaching new ideas like the basic assumptions and the protomental matrix. Now he started to focus solely on psychoanalysis in his private practice. The end of these ten years of intensive working with groups in the 1940s coincided with the start of a new life. After being a widower with a small child for seven years, he founded a new family.

Box 1.3   Bion in the 1940s: three portraits

In accounts of Bion's works with groups, his natural leadership and sense of power are stressed by all who worked with him at the time. Portraits are sketched by Sutherland, by de Maré and by Lacan:

'Bion had the great advantage of an imposing military presence. He was a large man wearing the ribbons of his distinguished record as a soldier in World War I – the British Distinguished Service Order and the French Legion of Honour. Apart from this visible record which, in the senior member of the technical team, was of enormous value in facilitating our acceptance in face of the widespread suspicion and underlying anxiety with which psychiatrists were generally received, he quickly made an impression on everyone of "power" in the best sense. He was quietly spoken, unfailingly courteous and attentive to others, and always sensitive and thoughtful about their views. His remarks were usually brief and penetrating and he had the most delightful sense of humour expressed in dry pithy phrases along with occasional amusing personal anecdotes to make a point'

(Sutherland 1985: 48).

'Bion . . . was a massive man, balding with a thick black moustache, high-coloured cheeks, thick-lensed gold-rimmed spectacles, smoking a large Sherlock Holmes pipe. He looked very much the officer of the "old school" and indeed came from an upper-class Edwardian background with British Raj connections. He was an extremely shy man, which was belied by his imposing presence. He rarely spoke, and when he did so it would always be in the form of cryptic comments. In the seminars which he conducted separately from Rickman, he would sit in the circle in profound silence, smoking his pipe and occasionally, after someone had vouchsafed a comment, would emit a loud prolonged sniff which was somewhat disconcerting, since it was ambiguous. What could it all mean? Indeed he would only rarely reveal his thoughts, seated ostensibly as an unobserved observer, but always the centre of unvoiced attention. I remember one comment was that "the working class is always in a state of war", and on another occasion that a Tank

Officer in the previous war had been seen to be wearing a bullet-proof waist-coat under his uniform, which comment was followed by a contemptuous sniff with the inference that the offender was regarded by fellow-officers as a "poor type", clearly not a "good man", terms which were rife at that time. In contrast to this approach much talk centred on the Gestalt quasi-Marxist approach of Kurt Lewin and Brown'

(de Maré 1985: 111–112).

'Thus, I am going to represent these two men for you *au naturel*, men of whom it can be said that the flame of creation burns in them. In the first, this theme is as if frozen in a motionless and lunar mask accentuated by the commas of a thin moustache which no less than the high stature and swim-mer's thorax which support him, give the lie to Kretchmerian formulations, since everything about him alerts us to the fact that we are in the presence of those beings who remain solitary even in the utmost commitment, as is confirmed in his case by his exploit in Flanders where he followed his assaulting tank with whip in hand and thus paradoxically forced the weft of destiny. In the other, this flame scintillates behind a lorgnette to the rhythm of a verb burning to return to action, in the man who, with a smile which makes his fawn brush bristle, likes to recall how he completed his experi-ence as analyst with the management of men, tested in the fire at Petrograd, in October 1917. The former, Bion, and the latter, Rickman, have published together in the issue of the 27th November 1943, of the *Lancet,* which is the equivalent both in its audience and its format to our *Presse médicale,* an article which, through amounting to only six newspaper columns, will mark a historic date in psychiatry'

(Lacan 1947: 293–312).

In March 1951, Bion met Francesca, a research assistant at the Tavistock. She was also a widow and trained as a singer. They got engaged in April and married on 9 June 1951. The Bions bought a beautiful large house, Redcourt in Croydon, Surrey, which is pictured in *All My Sins Remembered.* It is described as an elegant grade II listed Edwardian house with spacious lounges and a Ming cottage-style dining room overlooking several acres of landscaped gardens.

A letter from Bion to Francesca reveals his gratitude to her for enabling him to be a responsive father to Parthenope (Bion 1985: 85).In his marriage with Francesca, Bion seems to have found the happiness and stability that he craved. They had two children together, born 1952 and 1955. Bion worked very hard. According to Bléandonu (1994), it was seven years before the Bions spent a holiday together. Bion became director of the London Clinic of Psychoanalysis (from 1956–1962). In 1959 he fainted in the Underground and had to be hos-pitalized for some weeks for a check-up. This recalls Rickman, his beloved friend who also undertook several public duties and died at 60 from a heart attack (Conci 2010). Bion profited from his hospital stay to write 'Attacks on Linking' (Bion 1959). Already in the 1950s Bion was considered a kind of genius amongst his peers, although he did not consider himself as such, and thought that Hanna Segal was the most brilliant (Bion 1985).

In 1961, Bion presented his legendary paper, 'A theory of thinking', at the 22nd International Congress in Edinburgh. It was the start of his major theoretical corpus. He wrote it when he was over 60 and like most analysts, during weekends and holidays (Bion, F. 2000: 13). His theoretical corpus comprises four theoretical books that are difficult to read, but take us on a journey into the mysteries of the origin of the psychic processing of emotions – what Bion calls thinking. Some people think that Bion deliberately wrote in a cryptic way while others argue that he struggled to put his original ideas into words and that we are fortunate to witness this process (e.g., Bion 1985: 103, 131).

> It was also a time of institutional involvement and leadership. He was President of the British Psychoanalytical Society from 1962–65; Chairman of the Publications Committee and the Melanie Klein Trust; and member of the Training Committee from 1966–68. He never asked for these positions. As an administrator he was an outstanding influence; he could pinpoint the crux of a problem and keep discussion 'on track' in committee. With his acute mental vision and unerring instinct he never allowed the trees to obscure his sight of the wood.
>
> (Bion, F. 1995)

During the week he was absent from home, being at the British Psychoanalytical Society for two or three evenings a week and this after long working days. Francesca Bion states that

> He was skilful in pacing himself – he regarded this as highly important in any job – he could carry a heavy load of work without any apparent falling off in quality. He was also able, like Winston Churchill, to fall asleep for a few minutes and wake refreshed.
>
> (Bion, F. 1995)

Bion enjoyed family life at Redcourt and the Bions bought the 'Little Cottage' at Norfolk, where they spent holidays and where Bion wrote, swam in the North Sea and painted. Together with some of his other paintings, there is a painting of the 'Little Cottage' by Bion in *All My Sins Remembered* (Bion 1985). His paintings were exhibited at the Bion centennial in Turin in 1997, at Meltzer's suggestion (1997). They are not as wild as we would expect from the analyst who was so open to unexpected feelings and wild thoughts. They depict his beloved landscapes. It is possible to argue that Bion's inner freedom only fully surfaced later, after a catastrophic change that we will discuss in Part II. It might be interesting to compare his paintings with the works of Milner, an Independent analyst of the same period and author of *On Not Being Able to Paint* (Milner 1957) who, like Bion, relied on the unconscious ongoing phantasy process and the negative capability of Keats (1817), although in a different way.

The 1960s seem to have been years of happiness:

> Looking back, it surprises me that in the midst of so much work and so many commitments, we had any time for a private life. However, weekends were sacrosanct times for relaxing with the family, conversation, listening to music (our tastes were catholic but favourites were Bach, Mozart, Haydn, Britten and Stravinsky), reading, contemplating and writing. He once said, 'I want to be a psychoanalyst. But I do not want that experience to make it impossible for me to have a life worth living where I could never go to the theatre or a picture gallery or paint or swim.' The children looked forward to his reading to them at bedtime; he was their friend, talked to them as equals, was gentle and even-tempered. I do not recall ever hearing him raise his voice in anger, but angry he certainly could be – the look in his eyes and a cutting remark were signs of stormy weather. He derived intense pleasure from the children's successes, but never made them feel diminished by their failures which he regarded philosophically as a normal part of life. He restrained his natural anxieties to allow them to go their own ways, although he was always ready to offer advice, based on his own experience, which was usually given in a light-hearted, amusing way.
>
> (Bion, F. 1995)

Bion's psychoanalytic epistemological odyssey during this period resulted in a paradigm shift for psychoanalysis. The four theoretical books that develop his meta-theory are *Learning from Experience* (1962), *Elements of Psychoanalysis* (1963), *Transformations* (1965) and *Attention and Interpretation* (1970). This is a remarkable rate of production, given that Bion was over 60, had a full private practice and was holding society positions at the time when he was writing his theoretical works. The last book was published while he was in the US but written while he was still in London. He called the four books his Seven Servants, in an allusion to a verse of Kipling's poem in the 'Just so stories'. During these years he also presented the three papers entitled 'Memory and desire', 'Negative capability' and 'Catastrophic changes' to the British Society (Lyth 1980).

2 EXPERIENCES IN GROUPS AND OTHER PAPERS (1961)

Introduction

Experiences in Groups is a collection of Bion's essays on groups, written during and after World War II. He wrote the first essay in collaboration with John Rickman, his former analyst (see Box 2.1). As Parthenope Bion pointed out (Vermote 1998a), elements of Bion's later ideas are already present in these first texts, such as the resistance against learning from experience, the hatred of thinking and the existence of an undifferentiated protomental matrix. Bion's descriptions of his experiences in groups are pre-analytic writings. It is only at the end of his book that he re-interprets his findings from a psychoanalytic point of view.

In my experience, it is possible to apply some of these findings to individual psychology and psychotherapy. As in a Bionian sense the individual may also be seen as a group, basic assumptions can be seen at work within an individual.

Box 2.1 John Rickman

John Rickman (1891–1951) came from a Quaker background and trained as a psychiatrist. He was among the pioneering British psychoanalysts who had analysis with Freud in Vienna in the 1920s. Freud encouraged him to work with psychotic patients (Rickman 2003: 13). He had further analysis with Ferenczi and later a longer period with Klein until he joined the army. He was considered part of Klein's circle (Harrison 2000: 41), but because of the impartiality of his mediations between the warring parties in the Controversial Discussions, he was seen as more of the Middle Group. Like Bion, Rickman was tall and powerfully built and had a discreet, courteous, traditional English style. He could be a non-dogmatic communicator and facilitator of ideas – building bridges between disciplines and groups. He had an international role at UNESCO during the war. From 1935–1948, Rickman was editor of the *British Journal of Medical Psychology* and of the

---

International Journal of Psychoanalysis and president of the British Psycho-Analytical Society. Rickman also played a role in diminishing the tension between the Tavistock, which offered applied psychoanalysis and training, and the British Psychoanalytic Institute. 'There seemed to be a guru quality about Rickman, a prodding inspiration rather than an administrator or an academic writer' (Harrison 2000: 8). As well, he had a good reputation as an administrator when President of the International Journal of Psychoanalysis because he was responsible for signing a long lease on its Mansfield House, New Cavendish Street. Rickman wrote numerous papers on Freudian psychoanalysis, on the Quakers, but also on the air raids and military psychiatric rehabilitation (an article on the Northfield experiment is co-authored by Bion and Rickman). Rickman was the first to apply Klein's ideas to group psychology. He supported and recognized Bion's originality in public in a paper he gave in 1949 to the Royal Anthropological Society. Conci (2010) quotes:

> The study of group-tension deals with the moment-to-moment oscillations between group-cohesive and group-disruptive forces . . . The pioneer in this field of research, in my view, is Dr. W.R. Bion, whose first exposition on group tensions was published in *The Lancet* in 1943, and whose later contributions were published in *Human Relations* (1948). No one should even begin to undertake this kind of work who desires above all things to conduct a peaceful life. In the group interview of the kind I have in mind, it is often found that one of the first things the group does is roundly to attack the person they have called in to help them.
>
> (King 2003: 155)

Harrison rather convincingly demonstrates how much Rickman's ideas on social psychology (along with Trotter earlier) influenced Bion's ideas in this period (Harrison 2000: 44–53). In their work on groups they shared the ideas of field theory as developed by the communist intellectual Kurt Lewin, who emigrated to the US. Field theory is at the foundation of Bion's basic assumptions theory. Bion respected Rickman and regretted that his analysis with him was prematurely ended in 1939 by the outbreak of World War II, although it may also be that the ending was caused by was some sparks flying between them, rather than by the turbulence of the times:

> there was some kind of emotional turbulence, with its high and low pressure areas, which extinguished the analysis as far as Rickman and I were concerned. It stopped; though not before it had also extinguished any spark of respect that might have been entertained for me by my pre-psycho-analytic colleagues, and before I had penetrated far enough to be independent.
>
> (Bion 1985: 46)

(continued)

(continued)

The short analysis with Rickman was of tremendous importance for Bion. His strong feeling of being a failure dissipated and his courtship of Betty Jardine may be seen as one of its results. His former therapy with a psychotherapist whom he described as 'Dr. Feel in the Past' (Dr Hadfield, one of the founders of the Tavistock Clinic) did not seem to have resulted in a lasting psychic change.

During the war, both Bion and Rickman were drafted by the army as majors. They became close friends, although they were different in age and demeanour. Even after the failed Northfield experiment (1942–1943), Bion and Rickman remained in touch. When in 1948, Bion tried to stir up a psychoanalytic revolution within psychiatry, Rickman was beside him (Trist 1985: 27). Rickman also participated in one of Bion's study groups with business people, which Bion initiated at the Tavistock Clinic. Conci (2011) studied their correspondence from 29 January 1939 to 17 June 1951, the year of Rickman's untimely death. The letters reveal a warm picture of Bion and also show how far the so-called early Bion identified with Rickman (Vermote 2011).

One of the unexplored influences of Rickman on Bion might be the indirect effect that he may have had as a Quaker – a religion that was in a way neo-Platonic, based on one, hidden truth and mystery as we find in Plotinus, Bohme and the Upanishads. We may see many facets of this hidden truth, revealed in the late Bion (Velleman, personal communication). Moreover, Bion's family were the offspring of the exiled French Huguenots, many of whom became Quakers.

Bion's attitude in conducting groups: the group as study group

Already from these first texts on, Bion showed his non-dogmatic point of view. Bion thought that working with groups differs fundamentally from a classic psychoanalytic approach. He saw psychoanalysis as based on a two-person situation and therefore mainly focusing on 'pairing': sexual relationships and Oedipal dynamics. Bion makes the surprising suggestion that in contrast, a group's main concern is reality. This is why within the Oedipus myth, Bion sees the figure of the questioning sphinx as the most important figure for a group. In retrospect, Bion writes in his introduction:

> I am impressed, as a practising psychoanalyst, by the fact that the psycho-analytic approach, through the individual, and the observations these papers describe, through the group, are dealing with different facets of the same

phenomena. The two methods provide the practitioner with a rudimentary binocular vision. The observations tend to fall into two categories, whose affinity is shown by phenomena, which, when examined by one method, centre on the Oedipal situation, related to the pairing group, and, when examined by the other, centre on the sphinx, related to problems of knowledge and scientific method.

(Bion 1961: 8)

The sphinx is also an image for the position of the analyst in a group, who is 'invested with feelings that would be quite appropriate to the enigmatic, brooding, and questioning sphinx from which disaster emanates' (Bion 1961: 162; Vermote 1994).

Consequently, in his work with groups, Bion always placed the link with reality and knowledge in the foreground. He saw all his groups as study groups and maintained the stance of a researcher, explicitly refraining from assuming a position of leadership (see Box 2.2). From the position of an ordinary group member, he adopted an observing, thinking rather than a psychoanalytic or therapeutic attitude as Main, Foulkes and Pines did (see Box 2.5). Bion's theory of groups is based on his findings from this observing position. Partly in reaction to his attitude, the groups inevitably regressed. Bion noticed that there were few critical judgements in his groups but rather an emotionally charged atmosphere that affected all group members. One of his main observations was that the level of talk in the group was more superficial than in normal interaction and that the group clearly sought a leader in him (Bion 1961: 38). As a technique, he decided to intervene only when the attention of a group was directed towards an individual, including himself: 'the interpretations would seem to be concerned with matters of no importance to anyone but myself' (Bion 1961: 40). When he did intervene, he did so in a deliberately free-floating manner: 'it must seem to be a contribution as impertinent as it was likely to be accurate' (Bion 1961: 41). He further observed that the process that took place around him had not so much to do with him, but was a group phenomenon that would later be displaced to someone else. Moreover, certain themes were ignored when they did not fit in with the group's common concern. When an individual tried to introduce such a topic, it was invariably not heard. From these observations, Bion postulated the existence of a *group mentality* (the expression of the will of the group to which individual members contribute anonymously and unconsciously) that determines the group's emotional orientation and mental life. An individual needs this group mental life in order to feel fulfilled and will try to satisfy this need by being a member of a group. In the group there is a tension between fulfilment of individual needs and the group mentality, and this gives rise to a specific group culture.

Box 2.2   Wilfred Trotter's influence on Bion's theory

This note is based on a research paper on this subject by Torres (2003). Wilfred Trotter (1872–1939) was a professor of surgery at University College Hospital (UCH) and the honorary surgeon of King George V as well as Freud. He was also a sociologist, and coined the concept of the herd instinct (Trotter 1916). Trotter is the person who introduced Ernest Jones (he was Jones' brother-in-law) to Freud's writings. He attended the First International Conference of Psychoanalysis in 1908. When Bion studied medicine at UCL, he won the gold medal in surgery as Trotter's attendant dresser. Torres convincingly demonstrates the influence of Trotter's ideas on Bion. In Trotter's view, humanity's main problem was how to reconcile a weak rational mind with gregariousness, operating by suggestion (Bion's group culture, basic assumptions and valency). Trotter's basic instincts (self-preservation, sex, nutrition) are very close to Bion's basic assumptions (fight-flight, pairing, dependence). Trotter insisted on resistance against new ideas and mental pain and anxiety as the price of learning, just as Bion did later in his theory on thinking. The main focus of both was mental functioning. Like Bion, Trotter stressed truth as the nourishment of the mind and lies as poisonous. With Trotter, Bion shared the ideas of a psychosomatic unity, which can be the cause of group diseases (see Bion's protomental system). Moreover, both used metaphors of digestion and muscle activities to describe mental functioning. Trotter saw the improvement of the group morale as a curative factor and the suspension of leadership as a sign of a developed group. Bion later experimented with a Leaderless Group Project and refrained from taking the role of a leader in his study groups.

In 2013, Torres published an update of his original research paper in his book on Bion's sources co-edited by R.D. Hinshelwood. This stresses even more how Bion identified and introjected Trotter to such an extent that he even forgot to refer to him when using Trotter's ideas, for example in commenting on 'The Imaginary Twin 'in Second Thoughts:

> he (the patient) must have been the first patient to make me wonder whether the idea of cure was not introducing an irrelevant criterion in psychoanalysis.
> (Bion 1967: 135; quoted in Torres and Hinshelwood 2013: 8)

This is an idea that Trotter had mentioned in his 1916 book on the herd instinct and in Bion's fundamental conviction about the dubious role of reason in psychic growth:

> Man cannot support the suspension of judgment which science so often has to enjoin. He is too anxious to feel certain to have time to know . . . reason intrudes as an alien and hostile power, disturbing the perfection of life and causing an unending series of conflicts.
> (Trotter 1916: 35 quoted in Torres and Hinshelwood 2013: 11)

To reveal this group mentality Bion experimented with a technique that he would continue to use throughout his life, the so-called 'binocular vision' (see Box 2.3).

> I am reminded of looking through a microscope at an overthick section; with one focus I see, not very clearly perhaps, but with distinctness, one picture. If I alter the focus very slightly I see another. Using this analogy for what I am doing mentally, I shall now have another look at this group, and will then describe the pattern that I see with the altered focus.
>
> (Bion 1961: 48)

Thus, for instance, Bion focused on two people who had been absent for a few sessions. These absentees spoiled his feeling that the group was doing well. However, when the focus on this situation was slightly displaced, the hardworking group who was present suddenly appeared hostile and resistant towards the work they had to do. From this perspective, the absent members became in fact the true leaders of the group who expressed their contempt for the group by not coming; the other group members were followers. Subsequently, the passive attitude of the group could be regarded as very active in its resistance, affording 'splendid opportunity for evasion and denial' and 'equally splendid opportunities for observation of the way in which these evasions and denials are effected' (Bion 1961: 49–50).

These evasions and denials were not verbal but were manifest in gestures and facial expressions and remained on a general and anonymous level.

> Mr M played an interesting part; I found it necessary to devote careful attention to it. Before I could give an interpretation that would be comprehensible by the group I had to observe the expression on his face, and the order in which he called upon the members of the group to participate. It was as if one were watching a silent film of a man conducting an orchestra: what sort of music did he wish to evoke? Mr M's function was to keep hostility alive so that no one could fail to notice my impotence to effect any change whatever in the situation.
>
> (Bion 1961: 70)

Box 2.3   Binocular vision as a cornerstone of Bion's work

Bion uses the term binocular vision in different places in his work. He uses it for the first time in *Experiences in Groups* (Bion 1961), where he describes its origin: it is like looking through a binocular microscope at different levels. It

(continued)

(continued)

allowed him to see how a group that appeared to work well together revealed a completely different picture on a different level. He uses the notion explicitly in *Second Thoughts* (Bion 1984/1967: 54, 86, 104).

Apart from these literal quotes, Bion's work is characterized by an approach in which different points of view that at first sight are incompatible are allowed to co-occur and reveal something that cannot be perceived from just one dimension. Bion's work is full of examples of looking from coexisting perspectives: the basic assumptions, PS and D, transformations in K and transformations in O. His Grid is an exercise in seeing phenomena from various perspectives, and the psychoanalytic object which is the focus of Bion's observations and interpretations can only be seen from a co-occurrence of three Grid categories.

Transformations also takes as its starting point the co-existence of various layers: sleeping and waking, conscious and unconscious, pre-natal and post-natal, pre- and post-catastrophe, sensorial and ineffable, imaginative speculation with wild and stray thoughts and a disciplinary, very strict frame. This approach of looking from multiple coexisting points of view in order to reveal an underlying pattern will be formulated explicitly with the introduction of the notion of vertices in *Attention and Interpretation*. The adoption of different perspectives is also explicitly present as a method in *A Memoir of the Future*, where Bion explains in the introduction how much he relied on reversed perspective to write the book.

In the same vein, Bion had no problem combining diverging perspectives and sometimes contradictory ideas of mathematicians, poets, religion and philosophers like Hume and Kant. Grotstein (2007) expresses this characteristic of Bion's thinking in terms of a convergence of the functions of the left and the right half of the brain. Mason (2000), from his personal experience of Bion as a friend, gives some striking examples of the ever-present binocular vision in Bion's attitude and wry humour. Kernberg and Ahumada (2000) and Sandler (2005b) point out that the notion of binocular vision also occurs in Locke's notion of common sense and in the work of Hume, as a constant conjunction between two images brought about by the two eyes.

Basic assumptions

A peculiar phenomenon that Bion noticed was that when in a group two people seemed to get together, the group acknowledged this without trying to interfere. This was strange, given the fact that normally group members were quite intolerant of one person receiving more attention than the rest:

> Whenever two people begin to have this kind of relationship in the group – whether these two are man and woman, man and man, or woman and woman – it seems to be a basic assumption, held both by the group and the pair concerned, that the relationship is a sexual one. It seems as if there could be no possible reason for two people's coming together except sex.
>
> (Bion 1961: 62)

Bion explained the tolerance of the group towards the exchanges of a couple (e.g., smiling etc.), which were allowed to continue endlessly, even if a conflict with the group mentality could arise, by positing that there is a shared *basic assumption* (*ba*) that groups meet for the purpose of sex or reproduction; in other words, that groups mainly get together in order to maintain the group. This basic assumption will be called 'pairing' and abbreviated as *baP*.

A second basic assumption, *baF* (*fight-flight*), also serves to save or preserve the group. 'The group can only fight-flight, find an enemy – if you do not find or create one, then find a leader to whom the presence of an enemy is obvious' (Bion 1961: 68–69). A third basic assumption, *baD* (*dependency*), is that the group has gathered in order to obtain security from one individual on whom they depend and whom they will in turn revere. The three basic assumptions satisfy different needs: a sense of protection by and reverence of the leader in the case of *baD*; of effective action and strength in the case of *baF*; and the hopeful expectancy of an unborn, future saviour (a Messiah) in *baP*. Bearing in mind that the two other basic assumptions are always dormant presences in the protomental system, one can easily see how shifts within a group can occur: the structure of group and leader remains the same but the patterns and the associated needs and goals change.

The three basic assumptions serve to preserve the group on an unconscious level and in order to do this they go against the interests and welfare of individuals. This is why, according to Bion, groups can hardly be therapeutic for an individual.

The protomental system and the basic assumptions

Group mentality can now be defined as 'a machinery of intercommunication that is designed to ensure that group life is in accordance with basic assumptions' (Bion 1961: 65). Each basic assumption has its proper feelings and emotional states which are linked to each other as in chemical reactions and are antagonistic. For instance, safety and dependency in the *baD* go together with feelings of inadequacy and frustration in comparison with the omnipotence attributed to the leader. All groups function in one of these three basic assumptions. There is no conflict between the basic assumptions; whenever one is predominant, the other two are dormant in the background. The background presence of non-expressed basic assumptions is called a '*protomental system*' (Bion 1961: 101). Psychological and physical symptoms or emotional states can often be understood as coming from this protomental system. In the protomental system, where there is no differentiation between the psychological and the physical, prototypes of basic assumptions are nonetheless present but they are not yet perceivable. The undifferentiated psychosomatic protomental system also provides the matrix of diseases (Bion 1961: 102). At this point, Bion sees diseases as being related to the large and small groups to which an individual belongs, on the one hand by the individuals' relation to the basic assumption group, and on the other by the protomental stages of the other two assumptions (that are not manifest).[1]

The dynamics of a group result from the transitions of one basic assumption into another. For instance, a fight–flight group can turn into a pairing group. During these moments of transition, there is room to discuss individual needs. A good leader manages to mobilize emotions associated with basic assumptions without endangering the individual's freedom.

Box 2.4 The protomental matrix

Bion was influenced by Trotter's idea that the gregariousness of mankind is a result of basic instincts that assure the survival of the species. The weak rational mind and the maintenance of individuality are of no concern to these instinctual forces. Bion's war experiences fortified this view. Lewin's notion of a field (Lewin 1935) allowed him to frame his vision psychoanalytically. This concept of the field was imported by Eric Trist, Bion's friend and colleague at the Tavistock, after his stay in the United States, where Lewin was working after his emigration from Nazi Germany. Lewin saw a group as a Gestalt, not just externally but also internally, and he formulated his 'field theory' for group dynamics as $B = f (P \times E)$ – B being behaviour, f function, P personality and E environment (Ancona 2000).

The unconscious primitive influence of the group was further explored by Bion using Kleinian concepts of psychic functioning such as projective identification of part-objects in a group (Bion 1961). In any case, it was clear for Bion that the unconscious cannot be disconnected from a group dynamic field; even when one is alone, the unconscious is determined by a group. To Bion this field, which he also called 'the protomental matrix', is a zone where soma and psyche are not yet differentiated, but where there are constellations of undifferentiated thoughts and feelings that coexist and shift. This point of view is unique. These constellations are always present, even before a form contains them. Only one is expressed at the time. The others are latent, in the background. Bion discerns three such primitive constellations or organizations of fields: dependency, fight-flight and pairing, which are emotional states of mind: 'soft, warm, sustained' versus 'danger, threat, defence, thinking, action' and 'seductiveness, play, creativity, couple'. They can be powerful and Bion thought that disease emerged from these non-expressed fields. According to Bion, the task of the group leader/psychoanalyst is to use binocular vision to see the unexpressed basic assumptions at work and evoke them. Making an unexpressed basic assumption manifest may result in shifts. One could say that health comes from a dynamic expression and interaction of all three fields in an individual, a couple, a group or a society. It is surprising that Bion did not extend this approach to understanding groups in terms of basic assumptions to illuminate what happens in the psychic constellation of an individual. Torres (2013) discusses the protomental matrix from a philosophical point of view. He stresses that the term protomental has been used to describe Bergson's and Whitehead's ideas on matter. However, this was later than when Bion first used the term in 1950. Anyway, as Torres remarks, Bion first studied history and therefore had a philosophical and historical background. He was less influenced by the dualistic background of medicine, where in the early 1950s psychosomatics were seen as the mind influencing the perfect functioning body machine. Bion's idea of an undifferentiated matrix with energy and where bodily sensations and mental phenomena are one is an original point of view in psychoanalysis. His idea of alpha-elements is close to this point of view.

Bion (1971) returned to the notion of a matrix much later, now thinking in terms of an undifferentiated unconscious layer from which thoughts arise. He envisioned a hallucinatory undifferentiated matrix in each person with transitions to differentiated, finite thoughts and feelings. This became central in his later model.

Box 2.5   The matrix: Foulkes-Bion

Bion's vision of the matrix in a group is often opposed to Foulkes' view (Brown 1985, 2003). Foulkes greatly influenced group therapy and came from a similar background to Bion: both experienced World War I (although Foulkes was not a front-line soldier) and Foulkes arrived at Northfield three weeks after Bion left. Together with Tom Main, he worked in the Northfield Experiment II. This experiment may be seen as providing the basis for the later Therapeutic Communities and institutional psychoanalytic psychotherapy as practised in the Cassel hospital, where Main started a therapeutic community. The major difference between Bion and Foulkes is that Foulkes was already a psychoanalyst and did not – like Bion – adopt a military attitude. In his view, traumatic neuroses could not be cured by creating group morale as Bion had tried to do in the Northfield Experiment I, but by means of treatment of individuals in a group. Foulkes saw the matrix as a Gestalt, the whole of what individuals share in a group on a latent and on a manifest level. In this sense it is closer to Winnicott's transitional zone than to Bion's notion of a protomental matrix. Foulkes' conception of the matrix is not based on a primitive and negative power like Bion's; it is a therapeutic force that helps individualization and that is a surplus for the treatment of an individual in a group. While Foulkes treated individuals in a group, Bion always addressed the group and in his groups at the Tavistock, he let the group regress until the basic assumptions were revealed. In Foulkes' groups these regressions were not as intensive, and basic assumptions seldom became clear. In the opinion of Pines (1987) Foulkes' groups were more therapeutic in effect,

(continued)

(continued)

while Bion's contributions made the unconscious dynamics in groups and large groups, especially non-therapeutic groups, more understandable. Bion always saw groups as study groups. It is, however, difficult to support Pines' conjecture: while it is clear that Bion's non-therapeutic focus evoked resistance, it is unproven that his method had less therapeutic effect than groups run narrowly on Foulkes' lines.

The work group

Leaders are chosen because they accord with the basic assumption of the group. Often, the leader may turn out to be a pathological individual, for instance a paranoiac will spontaneously be chosen as leader of a fight–flight group. According to Bion, the characteristic of a leader that accords with the basic assumptions is that he should possess 'magical' qualities, which inspire awe, rather than proposing scientific solutions. In a basic assumption group 'hatred of learning by experience' (Bion 1961: 86) prevails. Bion's approach to groups, however, is opposed to that of a leader with magic or religious capacities. His intention is to introduce a 'binocular view' to the group, hoping to produce shifts in the internal dynamics.

Bion concluded that there are two levels of group functioning: a *'basic group'* level, formed by shared basic assumptions and feelings (which takes place at the level of the protomental system and which he also calls *valency*), and a *'sophisticated or work group'* level, dealing with reality. The work group is rewarded for doing a task and is formed through cooperation. Because the sophisticated group interferes with the basic assumption of the basic group, there will be the appearance and effect of a conflict (Bion 1961: 97).

Box 2.6   An experience in a group of Bion

Some 25 years ago, I was a member of what I think was the last 'study group' taken by Bion in this country, as part of a group relations course spread over three months or so, and directed by Ken Rice at the Tavistock Institute in London.

Looking back, I cannot recall much of the detail of what happened and was said at those meetings. I do retain a strong visual impression of the room we met in in Devonshire Street, with its high windows and polished floors, and of my fellow members. They included a prison governor, a prison psychologist, a couple of businessmen, a journalist, a young social worker and an equally young myself. (At the time I was a Project Officer at the Tavistock, working on action research projects, mainly in industrial settings.)

They were somewhat torrid days at the Tavi. The Institute had recently split into two factions, headed by Eric Trist and Ken Rice. I belonged to Eric Trist's faction and was only allowed to attend the course at all because Bion was going to take a group. Of Bion himself I remember mostly the persona: his way of walking into the room and sitting down, the evenness of his speech, his air of intense, dispassionate curiosity. It had something of the quality of being faced with what might be called a 'pure culture of enquiry'. It was extraordinarily unsettling, and in retrospect extraordinarily moving.

I want to comment on two other, partly related, memories. The first, which I was very keenly aware of at the time as were some other group members, is that Bion never gave the slightest impression of being the author of *Experiences in Groups*. Some of us had read this beforehand with varying degrees of understanding and frustration. We were primed to spot 'basic assumptions' at work and to be offered the evidence from our experience of their reality. We were to be sadly disappointed and then intrigued. Nothing Bion said seemed to connect to this bit of conceptual apparatus; whereas in the inter-group events run by Ken Rice, Isabel Menzies, Bob Gosling, Pearl King and, I think, Pierre Turquet over two weekends, dependence, pairing and fight-flight were everywhere, and I think genuinely to be found.

Bion's preoccupation was elsewhere. But where? In the early sessions he often spoke about 'naming' and the use of names: the way naming has an illusory quality, as if it were felt to be the answer to a question rather than the question for which an answer needs to be sought.

'I'm David Armstrong' seeks to identify a boundary around an entity that is myself: to use the language of Bion's later writing, to bind a constant conjunction with a name, which Bion refers to as a definitory hypothesis. But this binding can also be used to restrict enquiry. A boundary for exploration (who is David Armstrong?; what is he?; where is he here and now?) becomes a barrier for defending – this is 'me', that is 'not me'. A limit is set; the unknown is robbed of its power to disturb. The revenge of the unknown is that one can be left feeling curiously empty, unable to make contact with the group, or even with oneself in any way that has the ring of something authentic.

In later sessions, a recurring theme was knowledge and the fear of knowledge expressed in rules, morals and judgements. The meetings of the group took place at the time of the notorious Profumo affair. I recall Bion's bafflement (maybe that's too strong a word) at the moral energy this released in the group, as if we could not entertain the thought that this affair, like the affairs that sometimes surface in group relations conferences, could be understood, to adapt a phrase of Clausewitz or Bismarck about war and diplomacy, simply as the pursuit of politics by other means. Morality was the lie invented to conceal a thought, there for the finding.

(continued)

(continued)

Naming, knowing, inventing lies, finding thoughts: these are recurring themes throughout Bion's later writing. I wish to suggest that they are as fertile a ground for exploration in the field of the group as they are in that of the individual. More than that, I also believe that these two fields provide, in Bion's phrase, a 'binocular vision' for exploring and understanding the ground of human knowing and un-knowing, becoming and be-ing, without which we are prisoners of our fears and terrors, in our private and our public life.

(Armstrong 1992: 262–264)

A psychoanalytic theory of groups and its ensuing technique

In the 'Re-View' at the end of *Experiences in Groups*, Bion interpreted his theory of groups from a psychoanalytic point of view for the first time. He was in analysis with Klein at the time of writing the Re-View and reformulated his findings from a Freudian and Kleinian point of view, although Klein herself was not so keen on his work with groups (Lipgar and Pines 2003). From a Kleinian perspective, Bion can be seen to have foregrounded the importance of psychotic mechanisms in basic assumptions. Although Bion, like Freud, and in contrast to Trotter, repeatedly rejected the existence of a herd instinct, he did believe that man is fundamentally a group animal and needs a group to fulfil this aspect of his being. What happens in a group is fundamentally different from the pair of analyst/analysand in the psychoanalytic situation. Therefore, the model of transference and countertransference cannot be used to explain group dynamics. A group that is bound by the valency of a basic assumption, however, has a number of characteristics that are reminiscent of the Freudian unconscious: it does not know time, the level of complex verbal exchange is low, it resists development or learning from experience. Although Bion started to use the term 'therapeutic group' for his groups with patients, this is confusing because his experiments with groups did not aim at therapy; the main goal was to study group dynamics. Bion was convinced that group therapy was not an economical approach to the treatment of individual patients (Bion 1961: 79), because the basic assumption preserves the group at the expense of the individual's needs (Bion 1961: 182–183).

Along these lines, Bion sees the therapeutic group as a group in which the basic assumption of dependence is dominant, and therefore in a massive state of regression. This entails that the psychiatrist/leader is expected to cure all individual disorders in a magical way, rather than cure being effected through cooperation of group members. To Bion's mind, giving in to the impulse to give interpretations is a symptom of distress rather than an illumination of external reality. Instead, the therapist should aim to produce shifts in the basic assumptions by keeping a binocular view and offering interpretations at more than one level, in order to reveal the group's underlying structure. In doing this, the therapist will try to mobilize the group's work function, which is forced to grasp the new situation by thinking. A work group can be compared to Freud's ego-functions. It maintains contact with reality and proceeds to solve problems in a scientific manner.

Bion tested his model against other theories of groups, ranging from philosophers like Plato, St Augustine and Nietzsche to early anthropologists like Le Bon and McDougall as well as analysts like Freud and Klein.

In society, the three basic assumptions can be found in three institutions that have been traditionally studied by philosophers and psychoanalysts, whose theories are not so much wrong as partial. The Church is a typical example of a dependent group, the Army is a fight-flight group, while Aristocracy is the group centrally concerned with pairing or sexual relations and breeding. Each of these institutions are in fact work groups that have devised successful ways of dealing with the specific fears and dangers of the basic assumptions underlying them.

Bion in the end appealed to Melanie Klein's views on the pre-Oedipal stages of development to explain the basic organizations to survive as a group. Whereas the work group, functioning through cooperation and identification, can be compared to the Freudian ego (an apparatus for reality testing and perception-consciousness) and has an Oedipal structure (and is therefore prone to neurotic disturbances), the mechanisms of the basic assumption group must be described in terms of the primary stages described by Klein, i.e. the paranoid-schizoid and the depressive positions. When this is transposed to the therapeutic group, it means that the members of the group will try to 'cure' themselves by splitting and projective identification. The analyst should be aware of when he is being 'used' in such a group dynamic.

> It is my belief that these reactions are dependent on the fact that the analyst in the group is at the receiving end of what Melanie Klein (1946) has called projective identification, and that this mechanism plays a very important role in groups. Now the experience of countertransference appears to me to have quite a distinct quality that should enable the analyst to differentiate the occasion when he is the object of a projective identification from the occasion when he is not. The analyst feels he is being manipulated so as to be playing a part, no matter how difficult to recognize, in someone else's phantasy – or he would do if it were not for what in recollection I can only call a temporary loss of insight, a sense of experiencing strong feelings and at the same time a belief that their existence is quite adequately justified by the objective situation without recourse to recondite explanation of their causation.
>
> (Bion 1961: 149)

The members of a group will try to expel the 'badness' of the group by locating it in an individual member who is subsequently ignored or rejected. On the other hand, the group members will seek cure by splitting off good parts of their personality and placing them in the analyst. In this way the feeling of 'being treated' that these individuals receive from the group is the achievement of a state of mind akin to the 'loss of individual distinctiveness', spoken of by Freud, on the one hand, and the depersonalization that we meet with the psychotic on the other hand (Bion 1961: 184).

Conclusion

Bion's ideas about groups are highly original and were formulated before he started to work as a psychoanalyst; he only formulated them in psychoanalytic terms retrospectively.

It is peculiar that Bion sees the task of a group as dealing with reality. This is the level of a work group. However, approaching groups as study groups and taking an observing attitude enabled Bion to reveal an underlying layer that he compared to psychotic functioning, which should always be revealed in working with groups. This layer is the protomental matrix that consists of three basic assumptions, of which one is expressed while the other two are dormant in the background. These unconscious mechanisms, whose only aim is the preservation of the group at all costs, mean that individual needs have no place and a group cannot be used for therapeutic purposes. However, a group leader can make these dynamics manifest by taking a binocular view and thus stimulating shifts; in the moments when this happens individual needs can be approached.

The notions of an undifferentiated layer in psychic functioning, primitive communication by projective identification and a binocular view to reveal these psychic phenomena will be paramount in Bion's further theories.

Box 2.7 The matrix: other views

The idea of a non-differentiated layer of psychic functioning is found in the work of several psychoanalytic authors, whether they are influenced by Bion or not. It is the basis of Balint's notion of the 'Basic Fault' (Balint 1968). Patients who react from this layer tend to interpret behaviour, feelings and thoughts in a general, undifferentiated way. They listen more to the music than to the content of words. This listening at different wavelengths may result in misunderstandings, as often happens with borderline patients, for instance.

Integrating Freud's understanding of unconscious functioning and Bion's mathematical notions of infinite-finite, Matte-Blanco (1988) described psychic functioning as a range from fully undifferentiated functioning to fully differentiated, with countless possibilities of degrees of mixtures of undifferentiated-differentiated in between. Grotstein (Vermote 1999) compared this model of psychic functioning with the simultaneous playing of a thousand CDs, a thousand programs of psychic functioning, each with their own specific mixture of differentiated-undifferentiated functioning. The deepest layer of the unconscious is a functioning at a pure infinite level. Matte-Blanco further links Freud's unconscious primary processes of displacement and condensation with the characteristics of infinity. In both, a part can stand for the whole and vice versa. The conscious, with the secondary process, is on the side of the differentiated way of functioning and the finite. In dreams, according to Matte-Blanco, we have a typical mixture of the differentiated and undifferentiated functioning

The interpersonal field as such was later explored by the Barangers (1983, 2008a,b) and following them, Ferro (1999) introduced the notion of the bipersonal field in relation to the analytic setting. Lichtenberg-Ettinger (1997) explores the notion of the matrix (the mother's womb) from a Lacanian perspective. Bion (1971) will later call this zone the hallucinatory matrix, with which one can make contact through deep regression, a point which is also elaborated by French analysts like de M'Uzan (1989) and the Botellas (2001). Ogden (1989) apprehended this zone in his description of the 'autistic-contiguous continuum'. This rudimentary zone (Bion speaks as well of the 'ruddy matrix') has a great impact in psychotherapy and change at this level proves to be a major therapeutic factor (Vermote 2005, 2009).

An intrapsychic zone which is unknowable, undifferentiated, infinite and which is our primum movens is also the basis of most mystic philosophers like Plotinus, St Augustine, Meister Eckhart, Jacob Böhme, Jan van Ruusbroeck and St John of the Cross; this idea had an influence on Bion's development of transformations in O.

Note

1 Indeed the most prominent diseases are sociocultural related (e.g. cardiovascular) at a psychosomatic level (e.g. the influence of stress on the immune system). Even in very concise causes like an infection or the effect of a bullet, the proneness to it depends in part on the unconscious dynamics in the field. This is poignantly described by Bion in his war writings (see Chapter 12).

3 PAPERS ON PSYCHOSIS (1953–1960)

Introduction

Bion's clinical psychoanalytic papers on psychosis were written in the 1950s. He reproduced them unaltered and collected them in *Second Thoughts* (Bion 1967) together with an accompanying 'Commentary'. The Commentary will be discussed in Part II as I discuss the texts in chronological order. It is also easier to understand the perspective that Bion takes in the 'Commentary' if the evolution in his thinking in the 1960s is kept in mind.

The series of papers on psychosis (1953–1959) start with his membership paper ('The Imaginary Twin') and paved the way for his classic 1960 meta-psychological paper on thinking. This latter paper laid the foundation of the four theoretical books that would follow and is one of the cornerstones of contemporary psychoanalysis. These papers of the 1950s give more of a sense of Bion's clinical observation and his intuitive approach at work than we can gain from his later four theoretical books where he refrained from giving extended clinical examples.

In these texts of the 1950s Bion develops his well-known views about splitting, the psychotic and the non-psychotic part of the personality, verbal thought, psychotic functioning and hallucination, bizarre objects, attacks on linking, and the obstructive object. All these are crucial in his understanding of psychosis and finally led to his theory of thinking. In this chapter I give an overview of all the texts included in *Second Thoughts*. I would suggest that readers who are already familiar with Bion's ideas on psychosis turn to the section concerning *On Arrogance* (pp. 71), which is a highly original paper, and of course the section on Bion's classic text: *A Theory of Thinking*.

In contact with the psychotic mind

Bion's writings on schizophrenics are extremely dense. His own thinking was often seen as condensed and allegoric, perhaps even sharing some of the features of schizophrenic thinking. Francesca Bion describes how deeply he tried to understand and identify with his patients' difficulties in dealing with mental experiences:

He often talked to me about his feelings of being totally in the dark, unable to make any headway towards fathoming a patient's behaviour. There were infrequent occasions when he felt he had a glimpse of understanding, only to fall back almost immediately into doubts about the possibility of any effective treatment. He would say, 'I'm in the wrong job', or, 'It's beyond me', or, 'I can't make head or tail of it'. He would sometimes emerge from his study, where he had been deep in thought, struggling with these seemingly intractable problems, looking pale and what I can only describe as 'absented'. It was alarming until I realised that he had been digging so deep into the nature of the psychotic mind that he had become 'at-one' with the patient's experience. Very rarely, he was elated by a sudden flash of understanding; I remember him exclaiming, 'I must be a bloody genius'. But he would soon after decide that it had been a 'blinding flash of the obvious'.

(Bion, F. 1995)

Much later, Bion fully explored these capacities of tolerating fragmentation and reversing perspectives and considered how these capacities could be used in psychoanalytic technique (see Chapter 11).

The Imaginary Twin

In 'The Imaginary Twin' Bion described how, in the course of analysis with a certain patient, he gradually realized that many conversations mentioned by the patient in the sessions were in fact conversations with imaginary figures, split-off parts of his personality. One character turned out to be a double of the patient. Bion tried to reunite these figures and parts by his interpretations and became aware that the patient did not react to his endeavour. In the rhythm 'association–interpretation–association' Bion felt that actually it was the analyst who was placed in the position of a twin, so that any difference could be denied. A dream made this clear:

He was driving in a car and was about to overtake another. He drew level with it and then instead of passing it kept carefully abreast of it. The rival car slowed down and stopped; he himself conforming to its movements. The two cars were thus parked side by side. Thereupon the other driver, a man much the same build as himself, got out, walked round to his door and leaned heavily against it. He was unable to escape as, by parking his car near to the other, he had blocked egress from the far door, while the figure blocked egress from his door. The figure leered menacingly at him through the window.

(Bion 1984: 8)

Here Bion made a major discovery that would mark the further evolution of his thinking. When Bion interpreted this peculiar psychic functioning itself rather than the content of the dream, a psychic change happened. This switching of the focus from content to psychic functioning that we also see in the work of Klein, Segal, Rosenfeld and Joseph, amongst others, characterizes the Kleinian approach and profoundly changed the technique and theory of psychoanalysis.

Subsequently, in this text the patient is compared with two other cases in which a twin also appeared in the material. In each there was a conjunction between the twin theme and vision, which Bion linked with a new capacity for exploring the environment and the emergence of intellect. The theme of vision also leads to the primal scene and the relationship between the parents and hence the resurgence of Oedipal material.

Box 3.1 Beckett and Bion: an imaginary twin?

According to Anzieu (1983, 1986, 1989, 1992), the imaginary twin may refer to the therapy that Beckett had with Bion. We can only suspect that the meeting between Beckett and Bion created a powerful storm with a deferred effect (Connors 1998):

> When two personalities meet, an emotional storm is created. If they make sufficient contact to be aware of each other, or even sufficient to be unaware of each other, an emotional state is produced by the conjunction of these two individuals, and the resulting disturbance is hardly likely to be regarded as necessarily an improvement on the state of affairs had they never met, and since this emotional storm has occurred, the two parties to this storm may decide to 'make the best of a bad job'.
>
> (Bion 1979: 321)

During Beckett's psychotherapy with Bion, from January 1934 until December 1935, both were still publicly unknown. It was only in 1969 that Beckett received the Nobel Prize for literature and Bion became one of the most influential psychoanalysts. Beckett suffered from fear, a writer's block and numerous psychosomatic complaints (cysts, colds, arrhythmias) when, after his father's death, he was put under extreme pressure by his tyrannical mother to whom he was strongly attached in a love-hate relationship. Three times a week, Beckett visited the Tavistock Clinic to see Bion, who had just finished his studies in medicine and was still in training to become a psychotherapist. It was two years after Bion joined the Tavistock Clinic as an assistant (Knowlson 1997). Bion was then 37 years old and had been in therapy with a psychotherapist, to whom he referred as 'Dr Feel-it-in-the-Past' since this was his answer to all current problems. This was presumably Dr J.A. Hadfield, an eclectic psychotherapist who seemed to have been a very influential figure at the Tavistock at the time (Connors 1998). With Beckett, Bion probably used Hadfield's method of reductive analysis focusing on Beckett's relationship with his mother (Knowlson 1997). Bion's fruitful analysis with John Rickman would only take place later (1939–1940).

During his treatment Beckett wrote several plays: 'A Case in the Thousand' (1934), which is clearly linked to his analytic treatment, and 'Murphy' (1938), which mentions a meeting with a schizophrenic patient in a mental hospital. According to Anzieu (1986), Pim and Pom, two characters in 'As it is', probably refer to Bion, whereas Connors (1998) sees a reference to Bion in the character of Mr Endon in 'Murphy'. But this is all speculative, as Oppenheim (2001) correctly argues. Nevertheless, Beckett and Bion have several themes in common (Stevens 2005), such as the focus on mind over acting, nothingness (with two sorts of nothingness: non-thought and nothing or naught), psychotic versus non-psychotic, the chaos of the mind and the importance of being able to bear this, the Unnameable, a distrust of language and at the same time the painterly use of the word, inner speaking (the Voice) as something that comes from the outside, splitting, and autistic objects. In Beckett's texts, we can see extreme examples of instances of –K and attacks on linking as described by Bion.

Stevens (2005) suggests that Bion was able to bear 'the sane psychotic' in Beckett, which inspired Beckett and which supposedly had a great influence on his creativity. Later, Bion would locate the source of creativity in the paranoid-schizoid position. However, both Beckett and Bion considered the psychotherapy as incomplete when it finished. Bair states in her biography of Beckett (Bair 1978/1990: 208): 'on February 1935 he noted that he was about to complete his one hundred and thirtieth session with Bion, a never-ending "squabble"'. When Beckett decided to stop, Bion and Beckett had dinner together in the Etoile restaurant in Charlotte's street (Knowlson 1997) before attending a lecture together, given by Jung, the third of a series that Jung gave at the Tavistock. Beckett was strongly influenced by Jung's notion of the unborn self or the unborn part of the self, which is closely related to Beckett's fears of the womb. In Bion's texts, the 'unborn self' is an important theme in *A Memoir of the Future* (Bion 1991), which takes the form of a trilogy like Beckett's series (*Malone, Molloy, The Unnameable*). Anzieu (1983, 1986) saw Beckett as Bion's 'imaginary twin'. Stevens (2005), who knew Beckett, suspected that the clinical examples given in both 'Attacks on Linking' (Bion 1959) and 'The Imaginary Twin' (Bion 1950) refer to Beckett's psychotherapy. However, the title leads one to suspect a strong identification, of which Bion distanced himself in his Commentary (1967) (Stevens 2005). Further, there is a striking resemblance between Beckett's *The Unnameable* (1955) and Bion's idea of 'nameless dread' (Bion 1967).

From Beckett's work and Bion's later autobiographical writings it is clear that both recognize the feeling of an inner void and a lack of an inner containing object. Beckett and Bion seem to have shared a lethargy and a strong introjective attitude which enabled them to sink deep into themselves. They use words sparingly and strip their writing of emotions (Bion before his Californian period) which are nevertheless strongly present. Although both writers were somewhat strict, and were known for their silence, distance and scansions in speaking, the way they dealt with their inner world is different. Bion's natural dispassionate

(continued)

(continued)

interest found its way in a psychoanalytic frame of mind and he could grasp his psychic functioning in a psychoanalytic theory. Beckett let his inner world exist, he listened to it and let it come up; he described its nothingness and uselessness in a non-aesthetic, non-narrative and cold manner (like Bion's no memory, no desire, no understanding, no coherence). Both Bion and Beckett are characterized by a self-disciplined style which exerts a great influence and attraction on others and produces a kind of stillness. In 'Disjecta' Beckett (1949) wrote: 'The expression that there is nothing to express, nothing with which to express, nothing from which to express, no power to express, no desire to express, together with the obligation to express' (cited in Katz 1999: 1).

We find these themes especially in Bion's later texts, where they are stripped of their pathological interpretation:

> I find myself in the state of mind with which I am distressingly familiar – the state of mind in which I can only say that I am abysmally, literally and metaphorically, ignorant. That is one reason why it is a matter of some urgency to me to be able to find some sort of network in which I can catch any thoughts that are available.
>
> (Bion 1977: 31)

Bion developed a more free-living and social side than Beckett and became a family man, although he remained strongly ambivalent towards social life: in 1968 when moving to LA he left his social life behind to be more on his own. Beckett also showed a growing sparing simplicity in his later life, although he was Joyce's pupil in the sultry artistic Parisian scene. It is striking that neither Bion nor Beckett wanted to collaborate on the monumental biography that Bair (1978) wrote on Beckett.

Box 3.2 Beckett and the psychoanalyst (Anzieu)

For those interested in the connection between Bion and Beckett, Anzieu's book *Beckett et le Psychanalyste* (1992) is highly recommended. Anzieu wrote his work after a thorough study of Beckett's texts, an undertaking to which Beckett himself responded without much enthusiasm (Anzieu 1983: 1989).

Anzieu was an influential French psychoanalyst (1923–1999) who was in analysis with Lacan until he discovered that Lacan's well-known case 'Aimée' was in fact his mother. Anzieu was much influenced by Bion's work and elaborated on Bick's (1968) 'second skin' in light of Bion's thoughts (Anzieu 1989a, 1989b, 1990) and on Bion's theory about the group unconscious (Anzieu 1984). Since the 1950s, Anzieu was fascinated by Beckett's work, seeing in him a re-actualization of Blaise Pascal's work (Anzieu 1992). One day Anzieu was reading 'Molloy' aloud to his wife in a Parisian park when Beckett and his spouse passed by – Beckett looked up but kept his distance. In 1989 Anzieu started an intimate and fanciful diary in which he describes the significance of Beckett and the meeting between Bion and Beckett with an inner voice through his own perception (Anzieu 1992). Under the influence of Beckett, the father of the Nouveau Roman, Anzieu is trying to find a new style, just as Bion did in *Memoir of the Future*. Anzieu's work is not a conventional biography that attempts mastery of its subject; rather, it evokes Beckett experientially. By listening to his own inner voice and without trying to write a story, Anzieu evoked Beckett from his own inner world. Anzieu thus shows his inner dynamics as a psychoanalyst, just as Bion did in his later texts. Reading Anzieu's (1992) *Beckett and the psychoanalyst* is an experience.

A theory of schizophrenia

The largest part of *Second Thoughts* comprises clinical studies in psychosis published in the *International Journal of Psychoanalysis*, focusing on the use of verbal thought in psychosis. In *Notes on the Theory of Schizophrenia* (presented in 1953) Bion observed that language does not always correspond to verbal thought. It can be a mode of action, as in projective identification and in splitting the object. Bion gives the example of a patient who tries to split the analyst by speaking about something in a drowsy manner, while at the same time the content incites the analyst's interest. Another patient who tried to provoke the analyst into giving two opposite interpretations at the same time expressed his wish to split the analyst in a striking image: 'How does the lift know what to do when I press two buttons at once?' (Bion 1967: 25). Bion also observed that the use of verbal thought can bring more pain because it sharpens the awareness of psychic reality and internal persecutors. It is related to the capacity to integrate and the depressive position. The psychotic patient experiences this evolving capacity for verbal thought as the cause of the pain and anxiety. In a defensive reaction, the psychotic patient will attack his premature capacity for verbal thought by resorting to splitting. Indeed in treating schizophrenic patients, it is often precisely when one gets the impression that the patient is on the point of dropping his delusion that he is most at risk of a new psychotic breakdown. The analyst is faced with a dilemma (Vermote 2002): when the patient begins to be able to use his capacity for verbal thought there is a risk of reviving the internal persecutors and becoming more aware of the pain of the depressive position, and therefore the analyst is tempted to give into the impulse to reassure the patient. Bion, however, is clear that reassuring will undo the analytic work.

In 'The Development of Schizophrenic Thought' published in 1956 in the *International Journal of Psychoanalysis* Bion elaborates the idea that not only schizophrenics but everyone possesses both a psychotic and a non-psychotic personality. This is not unlike Klein's notion of positions but differs from the Lacanian point of view where a psychotic person has no access to the symbolic order and remains in the imaginary order. Bion thought that in the psychotic part of the personality, there are attacks as a result of the innate death drive on the apparatus for the perception of internal and external reality and on verbal thought. These result in a minute fragmentation and subsequent evacuation through projective identification leaving the patient empty. The expelled particles of the apparatus for perception and of the ego continue to 'lead an independent and uncontrolled existence outside the personality' in the external objects that 'encapsulate them', and are called '*bizarre objects*'. This is how Bion explains hallucination.

Bion's oft-quoted illustration is of the patient's perception of a gramophone engulfed by an expelled part of the patient's apparatus for perception – vision or hearing. When the gramophone is playing, the patient feels that he is being watched or listened to by the animated gramophone (Bion 1967: 40). Hanna Segal's equally well-known example given in her 1957 paper 'Notes on Symbol Formation' of a patient who equated playing a violin with masturbating in public has some similarities.

In 'Differentiation of the Psychotic from the Non-Psychotic Personalities' from 1957, Bion further explores how the psychotic part of the personality is characterized by the splitting and projection of the part of the personality concerned with awareness of internal and external reality, creating bizarre objects which can be confused with thoughts, and which may subsequently be taken back inside through a 'reversed projective identification' in an attempt to restore the ego and the capacity to think. These non-thoughts are then agglomerated as opposed to being processed by thinking in the non-psychotic part. The patient may give the impression of using verbal thought when he has merely become skilful in 'this type of agglomerated rather than articulated speech'. It may look like verbal thought but it hides a very different and destructive form of psychic functioning.

In 1958 this study is continued in '*On Hallucination*'. The psychotic undergoes his experiences as if they are coming back to him from the outside:

> if the patient says he sees an object it may mean that an external object has been perceived by him or it may mean that an object is coming back to him through his eyes: if he says he hears something it may mean he is ejecting a sound – this is *not* the same as making a noise.
>
> (Bion 1967: 67, Bion's italics)

In this paper, Bion also expresses his view that the dreams of psychotic patients are actually evacuations and therefore hallucinations. 'To the psychotic a dream is an evacuation of material that has been taken in during waking hours' (Bion 1967: 78), while in the non-psychotic part this material is processed by verbal thought. From this point of view, it is not surprising that psychotics are rarely able to coherently reproduce their dreams.

On Arrogance

On Arrogance (1957) is a wonderful short text that testifies to Bion's originality and clinical acumen. Bion thought that the psychotic part of the personality might be dominant not only in psychotics but also in severe neurotics (whom nowadays we may describe as patients with a borderline personality organization). It is important to uncover this in therapy. The way that Bion does this is typical of his style of working. It is not by logical deduction or perception but by discerning a recurring pattern of co-occurring phenomena (which he will call later 'constant conjunctions'). In a number of his patients, Bion observed the co-occurrence of references to curiosity, stupidity and arrogance. Arrogance differs from pride: 'in the personality where life-instincts prevail, pride becomes self-respect, when death instincts predominate, pride becomes arrogance' (Bion 1967: 86). When references to curiosity, arrogance and stupidity coincide, this indicates a patient in whom the psychotic part of the personality is dominant and who has suffered an earlier psychic catastrophe in which there was a destruction of the ego. Bion's idea is that this is caused by a failure of normal projective identification; as a consequence of this the sexually orientated Oedipus situation is rendered intolerable. This important link with the environment has to be destroyed, resulting in the destruction of the ego.

To illustrate the connection between curiosity, arrogance and stupidity, Bion proposed a reading of the Oedipus myth as a story in which the quest for knowledge (curiosity), arrogance (taunting the gods), stupidity and catastrophe (psychosis) co-occur (Steiner 1985). In Bion's (1967: 86) words:

> the sphinx, who asks a riddle and destroys herself when it is answered, the blind Teiresias, who possesses knowledge and deplores the resolve of the king to search for it, the oracle that provokes the search which the prophet deplores, and again the king who, his search concluded, suffers blindness and exile.

In his work with this type of patient, Bion describes how he manages to tolerate what the patient put into him through projective identification, in other words to provide something that did not happen in the patient's earliest history. Thus, he arrives at a first definition of containment.

> Put into other terms, the implicit aim of psycho-analysis to pursue the truth at no matter what cost is felt to be synonymous with a claim to a capacity for *containing* the discarded, split-off aspects of other personalities while retaining a balanced outlook. This would appear to be the immediate signal for outbreaks of envy and hatred.
>
> (Bion 1967: 88–89, my italics)

Box 3.3   Projective identification

Klein introduced the concept of projective identification in 'Notes on Some Schizoid Mechanisms' (Klein 1946). It was hard to foresee that this concept would become the 'trademark' of Kleinian psychoanalysis. Klein used the term projective identification to describe the omnipotent phantasy that parts of oneself can be put into someone else and can be controlled there. In his work with primitive pathology, Bion made a distinction between normal and pathological projective identification and remarked that the phenomenon implies more than a phantasy; there is a real effect as well (Spillius 1992). Something psychic is really deposited into the other. Joseph (1985) elaborated this in her ideas on the transference as a total situation. According to Grotstein (2005a), Bion subsumed Klein's intrapsychic notion of projective identification and brought it to an interpsychic level. He widened the scope of the concept from a pathological defence mechanism at a phantasy level to a primitive means of communication between mother and baby, between patient and therapist. Current neurobiological research, such as the discovery of mirror motor neurons (Gallese et al. 2007), confirms that there is indeed non-verbal and unconscious communication as well as verbal and conscious communication and that we are pre-wired to receive the feelings of others. (Damasio 2000). Furthermore, Bion links the origin of psychic processing to projective identification: what is put in the mother can be digested there by the mother's reverie. This faculty of psychic processing can be adopted by the infant, introjected as a primary internal breast. In Bion's view projective identification is the basis of the primary relationship between mother and infant and a dimension of all relationships. In this sense Bion distinguished between a normal, realistic and a pathological, excessive projective identification. This insight had fundamental implications for the technique of psychotherapy. The therapist was no longer seen as a blank screen in the transference but as an actively and unconsciously involved person. His/her task is to contain, like the mother, through reverie and relaxed attention, what is put into him/her.

Grinberg (1962) coined the notion of 'counteridentification' to indicate how an analyst can be in the grip of what is put into him by projective identification. Only in a second phase, the analyst becomes conscious and able to actively work through this. In Britain, Joseph's work (Feldman and Bott Spillius 1989) is close to the container/contained model of Bion. Grotstein (2005) further elaborated Bion's use of projective identification with its intra- and interpsychic, conscious and unconscious, verbal and preverbal subliminal characteristics and named it 'projective transidentification'. Britton (1989) described a psychic space through communication in projective identification and the containment of the mother, in which there is also room for triangulation and an observing attitude of the patient towards himself. A useful overview of the post-Bionian evolution of the concept of projective identification can be found in Quinodoz (2007).

Attacks on Linking

This text shows the genius of Bion before he was recognized as such; we see a shift from theories with which he felt at ease to a new theoretical unknown territory (Ferro 2017). Bronstein and O'Shaughnessy (2017) edited a book in which *Attacks on Linking* is revisited nearly 60 years later from a current psychoanalytic perspective (A. Ferro; E. and E. da Rocha Barros) and a Kleinian perspective (R. Blass; R. Britton) and illustrated by clinical cases (M. Horovitz; C. Nemas; E. O'Shaugnessy), also comparing it with his later works (N. Ferro; R. Vermote).

In the paper Bion points out and illustrates that in psychosis, there is not only a catastrophe that happened in the past – but a catastrophe that goes on in the present. Patients not only attack the creative link with the analyst, in analogy with the attack on the breast and the creative couple as described by Klein, but also attack verbal thought itself. This leads to dreamless nights, blank spaces, convulsive attacks and feeling murdered.

Bion emphasizes that splitting the capacity for verbal thought can result in the agglomeration of persecutory objects to form a massive obstructive object (see Box 3.4), functioning as a primitive, cruel super-ego. According to Bion, in the treatment of psychosis it is crucial to understand how this obstructive object is formed and how it functions.

In this context he gives again a definition of containment: 'An understanding mother is able to experience the feeling of dread, that this baby was striving to deal with by projective identification, and yet retain a balanced outlook' (Bion 1967: 104). Bion sees the link between the analyst and the so-called psychotic parts of a patient as based on the mechanism of projective identification. This process can go wrong because of an overly strong envy of the patient that attacks the interpersonal process of processing and digestion by means of (normal) projective identification and/or because of a lack of receptiveness in the environment to the patient's projective identification. The result is excessive projective identification and a deterioration of development. If receptiveness to the projective identification is lacking, a self-attacking obstructive object will be formed by the elements that are not contained and digested. However, a kind of linking can exist, which gives the misleading impression of verbal thought because it is rational or logical, but this is never based on an emotional linking.

Box 3.4 The obstructive object versus the containing object

The obstructive object is a psychoanalytic concept that can help us to understand borderline and psychotic patients, in whom there is a dominance of the psychotic part of the personality and where attacks on linking are found.

(continued)

(continued)

The obstructive object is defined by Bion as an agglomeration of persecu-tory objects, a primitive, cruel super-ego. It is an unconscious phantasy that actively attacks psychic functioning. In psychotic patients it may manifest itself by concrete actions; I think, for instance, of a psychotic patient who castrated himself or another who wanted to pierce his eyes because of masturbation. But we may also see manifestations of the obstructive object in borderline or neu-rotic patients, in whom it may be revealed by attacks on mentalization just as in psychotic patients and by self-destructive actions, for instance in relationships and in professional activities. This internal representation of the obstructive object may be reflected in transference reactions and in relationships.

Eaton (2005: 8) gives a good definition of the obstructive object:

> an internal object that perpetuates an atmosphere of intense mental pain, violence, and self-attack . . . Chronic self-attack, including attacks on link-ing, blocks the growth of a sense of personal agency that would ordinarily allow a person to receive help and to cooperate in his or her own analytic transformation.

The core characteristic of the obstructive object is that it is a projective identification-rejecting object. Bion states that

> Denial of the use of this mechanism, either by the refusal of the mother to serve as a repository for the infant's feelings, or by the hatred and envy of the patient who cannot allow the mother to exercise this function, leads to a destruction of the link between infant and breast and consequently to a severe disorder of the impulse to be curious on which all learning depends. The way is therefore prepared for a severe arrest of develop-ment . . . Feelings of hatred are thereupon directed against all emotions including hate itself, and against external reality which stimulates them. It is a short step from hatred of the emotions to hatred of life itself.
>
> (Bion 1993: 106–107)

Eaton continues that the task of the analyst is

> to learn to describe (and in doing so, contain and bring awareness to) the shifting levels of pain and anxiety that the patient experiences, moment to moment and session to session. Over time, the mindfulness and reverie that we demonstrate for our patient is internalized and becomes part of the patient's own projective identification-welcoming object world.
>
> (Eaton 2008: 22)

By this openness to projective identification, the opposite of the obstructive object is created: a containing object, which is a kind of a good internal breast. This idea of a containing object is described in detail by Mitrani (2001).

'A Theory of Thinking'

The papers as brought together in *Second Thoughts* culminate in 'A Theory of Thinking', an original theory about the thinking of emotional experiences. This paper is the base of all Bion's subsequent theoretical thinking, and all Bion's later work can be seen as an elaboration of his 'Theory of Thinking'. From here Bion started his own original theoretical odyssey. In his paper, Bion appealed on the one hand to Freud's (1911) text on the origins of thinking ('Formulations on the Two Principles of Mental Functioning'), and on the other to the Kleinian notion of the always present phantasying (Isaacs 1948) or 'waking dream thought' (Bion 1962). He also used philosophical and mathematical notions, but without referring to them in an explicit way. His aim was to offer a kind of 'applied philosophy' that would be useful for the analyst confronted with disturbances of thinking.

Bion's starting point was that thoughts are not the result of thinking; rather, 'the apparatus that I shall provisionally call thinking . . . has to be called into existence to deal with thoughts' (Bion 1967: 111). This means that for Bion, thoughts precede thinking. Thoughts can be classified in different categories according to their development. Pre-conceptions are akin to Kantian 'empty thoughts' (e.g., the innate or a priori predisposition of an infant to expect a breast); they turn into conceptions when they meet with a realization (e.g., the infant meeting a breast). However, these conceptions are not yet proper thoughts. Drawing on Freud, who related thinking to frustration (the pleasure principle), Bion hypothesizes that a thought only arises when a pre-conception does *not* meet with a realization but with frustration:

> The model I propose is that of an infant whose expectation of a breast is mated with a realisation of no breast available for satisfaction, an absent breast.
>
> (Bion 1967: 111)

Only when the capacity to tolerate this frustration is sufficiently developed can the 'no-breast' become a thought and an apparatus for thinking develop to process these thoughts, which in turn will further enhance the capacity to tolerate frustration. This is what happens in the non-psychotic part of the personality.

In psychosis or the psychotic part of the personality, where the capacity to tolerate frustration is not sufficient, the absent breast will not develop into a thought but will instead become a bad object that has to be evacuated by projective identification. This results in a hypertrophy of the apparatus for projective identification in order to clear the psyche of the accumulation of bad objects. No thoughts arise; there is only permanent, repeated evacuation. Time stands still in the psychotic part, as in the 'Mad Hatter's tea party' in *Alice in Wonderland*, where it is always four o'clock (Bion 1967: 113).

At an intermediary stage, when frustration tolerance is just sufficient that the patient need not resort to evacuation, but not yet enough to allow thinking to develop, people may resort to a omniscient categorizing in terms of good and bad. This kind moralizing is often used but may be seen as a primitive form of thinking.

Bion further integrates the ideas of his former texts on psychosis. He conceives of the development of thinking as an interactive process in which the infant communicates with a caregiver by a normal use of projective identification. The mother's capacity for reverie is the receptor organ for the infant's sense-data of the self, communicated by projective identification.

In this paper Bion gives a more elaborated definition of containment than in the former texts:

> If the infant feels it is dying it can arouse fears that it is dying in the mother. A well-balanced mother can accept these and respond therapeutically: that is to say in a manner that makes the infant feel it is receiving its frightened personality back again but in a form that it can tolerate – the fears are manageable by the infant's personality.
>
> (Bion 1967: 114–115)

When the mother cannot tolerate these projections, the infant reintrojects nameless dread. Projective identification and reverse projective identification will continue. This process is experienced as a parasitic internal object inside the infant, 'a greedy vagina-like "breast" that strips of its goodness all that the infant receives or gives leaving only degenerate objects' (Bion 1967: 115).

When the mother is able to tolerate the infant's projections, the infant can use the mother as an instrument for psychic processing of sense-data, as it does not yet possess this ability. In this way the projections may become psychic and the personality develops consciousness. At this point, Bion introduces the concept of alpha-function (short for 'dream-work α') that 'converts sense-data into alpha-elements and thus provides the psyche with the material for dream thoughts and hence the capacity to wake up or to go to sleep, to be conscious or unconscious' (Bion 1967: 115).

After defining the alpha-function, Bion now refers to the material that has become psychic through the processing of the α-function, as the α-elements. They are the basic blocks of further dreaming and thinking. Emotional experiences and sense-data that are not psychic yet are named β-elements.

Patterns of relatedness are further established by language – which is another important step (Bion 1967: 118–119). This leads to what Bion calls 'correlation'. In other words, through verbalization and thoughts, different sets of sensory perceptions and emotions can be linked to each other, creating a sense of truth. A counterpart of this 'common sense' is the 'common emotional view', which entails that a 'sense of truth' is experienced if the view of the object which is hated can be conjoined to a view of the same object when it is loved and the conjunction confirms that the object experienced by different emotions is the same object.[1]

Conclusion

Bion understood psychosis primarily as a thought disorder, in the sense of a failure to make emotional experiences mental and process (think) them further. He developed an 'applied' theory of psychosis for the practising psychoanalyst by integrating Klein's theories (of phantasy, projective identification, the internal object, the paranoid–schizoid and the depressive position) with the Freudian conception of the mental apparatus (conscious – unconscious) and the pleasure-reality principle, and subtly adding useful insights from philosophy (concepts of Hume and Kant like pre-existing thoughts, reverie, consciousness) (see Introduction) and his own insights about the role of communication in the origin of thoughts (alpha-function, containment, beta and alpha-elements).

Box 3.5   Psychosis: further developments

Bion lived in the heyday of the treatment of psychosis and was treating several psychotic patients in the 1950s. Melanie Klein's theory (Klein 1946) and the further evolution of the concept of projective identification made it possible to conceive of contact with the psychotic. As is well known, Freud believed that no transference occurred in psychoses, hence his distinction between transference neuroses and narcissistic neuroses or psychoses. The Kleinian approach that presupposes a zone of psychotic functioning in everyone with transference by projective identification greatly expanded the indications for psychotherapy of psychosis.

In the essays discussed so far, we see how Bion relied on Freudian and Kleinian notions like the death drive and splitting, and developed an original theory of schizophrenia with splitting to a degree of fragmentation, the psychotic and non-psychotic parts of the personality, attacks on thinking and perception, the formation of bizarre objects and a projective identification-refusing internal object: the obstructive object.

Bion's contribution to the understanding of psychosis is unique because although he attended to object relations and the content of the clinical material, his primary focus was on verbal thought itself. In his view, the capacity for verbal thought and unconscious functioning (Freud) or phantasy (Klein) cannot be taken for granted in psychosis. This is indicated by the fact that psychotics are unable to dream and to form dream thoughts. Also, there is no adequate

(continued)

(continued)

contact-barrier between primary and secondary processes. In his study of the foundations of verbal thought, Bion defined alpha-elements as experiences that are just psychic but not further elaborated, the building bricks of thinking. In contrast to these alpha-elements, he proposed the notion of elements that are not yet psychic (beta-elements) and also underlined the necessity to think already existing, given thoughts (thoughts are there before thinking). In his view, the capacity to think can only be developed intersubjectively, with someone else's assistance. More precisely, a person with a maternal role functions as a container into which unthought elements can be evacuated through projective identification and transformed into a psychic form. Bion connects the automatic process of thinking emotions (or dream thoughts) and the depressive position. Thinking can only occur when frustration tolerance is sufficient, because it entails pain and grief. When the capacity to think does not develop, there will only be continuous splitting and evacuation so that experiences do not become psychic and cannot be elaborated psychically by the alpha-function, and already existing thoughts are broken up again (like a house of lego-bricks being scattered) by an alpha-function in reverse. These split-off parts conglomerate with split-off parts of the ego to form bizarre objects that are experienced as existing outside the mind. Because of these split-off parts of the ego, seeing, hearing and smelling are experienced as coming from outside: this is how Bion explains hallucinatory phenomena. Once it has started, the splitting goes on, leading to destructive psychic fragmentation; the psychotic enters a 'maelstrom', to use Freud's term. This malign splitting is enhanced by a primitive, persecutory internal object which Bion sees as the core of a psychotic process (see Box N). Good summaries of Bion's theory of psychosis can be found in Grinberg et al. (1993) and de Masi (2000). Grotstein's model is comprehensive in that it incorporates neurobiological findings (1999).

Bion's revolutionary ideas are based on his clinical practice. In Anglo-Saxon psychoanalysis, it is rare to find texts on psychosis and schizophrenia that do not refer to Bion. The theoretical corpus of another innovative psychoanalyst, Jacques Lacan, also began from the relation between psychosis, philosophy, language and mathematics. While Lacan's approach is predominant in Francophone psychoanalysis and Bion's in the Anglo-Saxon world, both models are found in the South American community and other non-Anglo-Saxon countries. In the 1970s and 80s numerous other centres and authors treated psychotic patients analytically. To name but a few: the famous Chestnut Lodge in the US (Searles, Feinsilver, Pao); Meltzer, Murray and Williams in the UK; the clinic of La Borde in France, following a more Lacanian line (Oury, Guattari). Bion's model was introduced in France by André Green's book on *La psychose blanche* (Donnet and Green 1973). Other centres on the continent can be found in Switzerland (Benedetti and Ciompi), Italy (Lombardi), Scandinavia (Rosenbaum, Culberg and Larssen) and Belgium (Van Bouwel, Thys, Vermote, Dehert, Pieters, Peuskens).

Many of these treatments were institution-based. Under the pressures of the biological model, de-instutionalization, evidence-based approaches to psychotherapy and managed care, many of these institutions have disappeared in recent years. However, the fact remains that a model of the mind has been formulated that is rooted in the treatment of psychosis and that strongly influenced psychoanalysis, including the treatment of non-psychotic problems. Currently, the clinical applications of Bion's model of thinking are primarily found in the treatment of personality disorders.

Note

1 This corresponds to the Kleinian notion of the depressive position.

4 LEARNING FROM EXPERIENCE (1962)

Box 4.1   Functions

In *Learning from Experience*, Bion adapts the mathematical concept of functions. This concept was introduced by Galileo. A function consists of variables or factors that operate in consort. It is a precise statement of a relationship between variables. The algebraic expression of such a functional relationship is called a formula (Kline 1967). It is typical of the mathematical theory of functions in that it not only allows working with known, but also unknown factors. If a function is constant, one can study how unknown variables change in relation to each other.

Introduction

In this book, Bion further elaborates his theory of thinking by applying the mathematical theory of functions (see Box 4.1) to it, together with some epistemological ideas.[1] In *Learning from Experience*, experience has a philosophical meaning in the British empiricist tradition: in other words, it is about what happens when something impresses itself on the mind. It concerns the unknowable forerunners of thoughts (see Introduction). Bion supposed that it is at this level that something goes wrong in psychotics, where thought disorders are the major problem. His aim was to develop an applied theory of thinking as a clinical, practical aid for the psychoanalyst dealing with psychosis.

However, Bion warned his readers that although he used concepts from philosophy and mathematics, he did not feel bound to their disciplinary rules and conventions. He was aware that he might be criticized for 'mis-using' words and concepts with an established meaning, but he wanted to maintain this ambiguity because the ability to apply already existing concepts in new and unexpected contexts is a capacity of the human mind that is essential for psychic growth and therefore vital in psychoanalysis. In the same vein, Bion advised the reader that 'the book is designed to be read straight through at once without checking at parts that might be obscure at first' (Bion 1962: Introduction). The book has lost none of its freshness 50 years later.

Box 4.2   The Seven Servants

Bion developed his theory of thinking further over the course of four books: *Learning from Experience* (1962), *Elements of Psycho-Analysis* (1963), *Transformations* (1965) and *Attention and Interpretation* (1970).

Later when these four books were re-published in a single volume he chose the title Seven Servants according to the verse of Rudyard Kipling (1936) in 'Just so stories', where the seven pillars of wisdom are six servants: What, Why, When, How, Where and Who; the seventh is not named. Grotstein (2007) sees it as the consciousness for psychic qualities and the quest for truth. The four books are indeed about external reality, perception, experience and how it gets transformed and transcended psychically.

As suggested by Bléandonu (1994), amongst others, the four books are a kind of psychoanalytic epistemological odyssey.

In reading the four books or the corresponding four chapters of this book*, you will notice that there is a progression in Bion's thinking that at a certain moment leads to a shift from transformations in knowledge to transformations in O. After this point he changed his style, his life and reformulated his findings. The shift occurs at the end of *Transformations*. We have used this caesura in the work of Bion as the dividing line between Part I and Part II of this book.

Therefore *Transformations* is discussed in Part I and *Attention and Interpretation* in Part II. This last book was published while he was in the US but written while he was in London.

*As I mentioned in the Introduction, I would suggest reading the chapters on the four theoretical books first as a whole, without many interruptions, and without reading the Boxes except the ones about the mathematical concepts at the beginning of each chapter. In this way, you may see the path that Bion followed. On a second reading you can use the text and the boxes as a companion for a close reading of the four books – which will be easier once you have a broad view.

The fundamental question: how do we learn from emotional experiences?

As in his 'Theory of Thinking' paper (Bion 1962), Bion returns to Freud's (1911) text on the 'Two Principles of Mental Functioning' but now with the concept of functions in mind (see Box 5.1). In this paper, Freud focused on thinking in relation to the sense-impressions of external reality and the pleasure and reality principles. Bion adapts this in viewing sense-impressions from the 'outer world' and emotional experiences from the 'inner world' as existing at the same level. He further reduces the Freudian pleasure principle to an evasion of frustration and the reality principle to a modification of frustration (see Introduction). He links this evasion and modification with the alimentary metaphor: spitting out versus taking in and digesting.

Evasion is what happens in the psychotic part of the personality, while in the non-psychotic part something analogous to a digestion takes place, which Bion will study as an unknown function: the alpha-function that he already mentioned in his 'Theory of thinking'. In so far as the alpha-function is successful, alpha-elements are produced. Both alpha-function and alpha-elements are unknowable and Bion will keep these terms 'deliberately devoid of meaning' (Bion 1961: 3).

Alpha-elements are suited to storage (the Freudian notation and memory) and are the building blocks of dream thought. When the processing of the sense impressions, emotions and thoughts that press on the mind into alpha-elements is inoperative, they remain unchanged and are referred to as beta-elements.

Dream thought

For Freud, fantasy allowed a retreat from the reality principle to a mental space still governed by the pleasure principle. Daydreaming is a specific example of this. Klein's conception of fantasy was different. In her view, drives are always caught up in fantasy. As Segal (1991) put it, phantasy in the Kleinian sense is the vast continent under the sea rather than an island on the sea as it is in the Freudian model. It was to differentiate their conception from the Freudian view of fantasy that the spelling 'phantasy' was adopted.

In developing his concepts of 'dream thought' or 'dream-work alpha' (the latter is the term he used in his *Cogitations* in 1959 (Bion 1992: 62)), Bion relies on this notion of phantasy (see Introduction). As a Kleinian, he sees phantasy as the basis of psychic functioning and he understands 'thinking' as a continuous mental processing of feelings, perceptions and thoughts. 'Waking dream thought' is this ongoing unconscious process, which he indicates as *I* or Idea and which is different from Reason or *R*.

Box 4.3 Dreaming and dream-work-α in Bion's early and late work

In *Cogitations* Bion (1992) also refers to dream-work-α as 'waking dream thought'. It is 'a continuous process belonging to the waking life and in action all through the waking hours, but not usually observable then except with the psychotic patient' (Bion 1992: 38). He therefore compares it later (Bion 1979: 257) with the Alpheus, the mystic subterranean flow that only surfaces now and then. Dream-work-α produces the unconscious, according to Bion (1992: 71). It allows conscious elements to become unconscious and vice-versa and allows for the possibility of conscious and unconscious levels of functioning that remain separate yet in touch. When the process fails, a kind of hallucinosis will be the consequence: 'these elements remain detectable because the patient cannot make them unconscious and therefore available to him' (Bion 1992: 71). This point of view is different than Freud's for whom the unconscious is already there. It is also worth mentioning that to Freud, what one observes in psychosis are not overt, unrepressed unconscious contents but rather the results of a 'Heilungsversuch' (an attempt to recover, Freud (1914)) an attempt of the psychotic to recathect objects that partly fails and remains at the level of word presentations rather than thing presentations. The result is a bizarre secondary process where words are linked in a way that normally happens in the primary process.

In *Cogitations* Bion points out that alongside its Freudian meaning, resistance also consists of a 'felt need to convert the conscious rational experience into dream, rather than a felt need to convert the dream into conscious rational experience. The "felt need" is *very* important' (Bion 1992: 184). In dealing with dreams it is important to be aware of the patient's need to process experiences, which can be 'obscured by the analyst's insistence on the interpretation of a dream' (ibid.).

Dream-work-α is to Bion an essential part of ego-functioning: 'α is concerned with, and is identical with, unconscious waking thinking designed, as a part of the reality principle, to aid in the task of real, as opposed to pathological, modification of frustration' (Bion 1992: 54). In this sense Bion further states that 'in my idea above, the dream symbolization and dream-work is what makes memory possible' (Bion 1992: 47).

For Bion we sleep in order to dream, but dreams are not dream-work-α; they are but a reflection of what happens at this unconscious level during sleep. At one point, Bion suggests that a dream indicates a kind of spillage of the alpha-dream-work, or in alimentary metaphors:

I suggest that what is ordinarily reported as a dream should be regarded by us as a sign of indigestion, but not simply physical indigestion. Rather it should be taken as a symptom of mental indigestion . . . That there has been a failure of dream-work-α.

(Bion 1992: 68)

In this hypothesis, which Bion does not develop further, there are no dreams when dream-work alpha is sufficient. In this interesting but unusual point of view found in his notebooks, he does not see dreams as the result of alpha-function but as a kind of garbage produced when alpha-function is insufficient.

(continued)

(continued)

Bion also claims that in order to allow for dream-work-α, containment by someone else or by an internalized aspect of them, an interiorized breast, is necessary. Beta-elements, mixed alpha and beta-elements and Ideas present themselves to this 'breast function' to be transformed. Only after this digestion has taken place do they become available to be appropriated by the psyche. This means that psychic elements, even dreams, can remain in a state of not being appropriated by the psyche. This may explain the common clinical fact that there are patients who are characterized in waking life by a lack of psychic processing and who resort to evacuative mechanisms like acting out, and yet may sometimes nevertheless show a separated rich dream life. It is as if their dream life is not available to them and they cannot gain from it without the help of the waking dream function of the therapist. Following this reasoning, this would mean that beta-elements (non-psychic) can include thoughts and dreams as well and that they also need a dream-work-α to become available to the psyche of the patient. Little is known about this work of the analyst at the gate, at the caesura of the unconscious-conscious world, between what Bion will later call the pre-natal and the post-natal mind (Bion 1989). From this perspective, dreaming can be seen as happening in another place, having a life of its own and not only being a transformation of experiences. In other words, instead of one psychic place where experiences are transformed by the alpha-function into psychic elements, the late Bion thought in terms of a separated dream world, with only few gateways to the conscious world. This is what Bion seems to have in mind when he wonders about a patient: 'Where were you last night?' (Bion 1997: 36) He compared this world with the Alpheus emerging now and then to the surface and called it the emmatures, the hallucinatory layer of psychic functioning.

Alpha-function as a factor of the contact-barrier

Bion sees the ongoing dream thought or alpha–function as a *contact* with the unconscious and at the same time as establishing a *barrier* and a distinction between conscious and unconscious functioning. The contact barrier[2] is a dynamic mechanism that depends on the supply of alpha–elements[3] that may be clustered or ordered narratively, logically or geometrically.

I shall now transfer all that I have said about the establishment of conscious and unconscious and a barrier between them to a supposed entity, that I designate a 'contact-barrier'; Freud used this term to describe the neuropsychological entity subsequently known as a synapse. In conformity with this my statement that a man has to 'dream' a current emotional experience whether it occurs in sleep or in waking life is reformulated thus: The man's alpha-function whether in sleeping or waking transforms the sense-impressions related to an emotional experience, into alpha-elements, which cohere as they proliferate to form the contact-barrier. This contact-barrier, thus continuously in process of formation, marks the point of contact and separation between conscious and unconscious elements and originates the distinction between them. The nature of the contact-barrier will depend on the nature of the supply of alpha-elements and on the manner of their relationship to each other.

(Bion 1962: 17)

Applying the mathematical function theory, one can see the unknown alpha-function as a factor of the contact-barrier, which is an unknown function in itself. Although both are unknown, 'function theory' allows Bion now to presuppose that an improvement of the alpha-function will lead to improvement of the contact-barrier, resulting in better contact with emotional experience and in learning from it. This corresponds to what he observed clinically: the capacity to learn from emotional experiences improved when he intervened at the level of psychic functioning, instead of intervening at the level of meaning. Today we are used to this shift in technique, but Bion's move from a focus on meaning to a focus on psychic functioning was revolutionary at the time. From now this theme will run through his whole work.

The failing of the contact-barrier in the psychotic part of the personality

To understand psychopathology with his model of alpha-function, Bion further relies on Kleinian ideas about envy and splitting. If alpha-function is attacked and destroyed by envy, only beta-elements remain. As a result, the contact-barrier fails and the distinction between conscious and unconscious thinking dissolves. This leads to a kind of rational thought in psychotics which is characterized by a particular lack of 'resonance' (Bion 1961: 15). The psychotic will live like an automaton in a world of beta-elements. He can speak in a clear and articulate way but his speech is one-dimensional; it has no overtones and undertones of meaning. No thoughts can emerge from it.

In the psychotic personality existing alpha-elements are further stripped of their psychic characteristics (an alpha-function in reverse) to become beta-elements which can form a *beta-screen* by compression rather than a living contact-barrier. This replacement of the contact-barrier by a sterile beta-screen is a dynamic process, intended to evade frustration. A delusion is an example of such a beta-screen: a delusion is logically coherent, but does not change; the same rational explanation is offered for all emotional experiences as if time stands still. One can compare a delusion to a piece of plastic that protects the individual from emotional experiences, while the contact-barrier, which consists of alpha-elements, is more like a living psychic skin. This is illustrated by a case of mine:

John is a psychotic patient who developed a delusion in which his frustration as an adolescent was explained by external factors related to reactions to his superior qualities. His paranoid delusion was based on a few false premises (for example, that he was a threat at the university because of his superior intelligence and therefore was blocked in his progress by a conspiracy of the academic staff) but in itself was logically tightly coherent. For some months John repeated the same delusion over and over; all new material acquired a place in the delusion. Time stood still. Instead of a psychic elaboration of new experiences, they were warded off by the delusion, which was like a hard impermeable skin. Often he literally expelled emotions when he felt confronted by questions, by making loud noises and movements without answering the question. When something painful happened in his life (he was rejected when he applied for a job), he repeated the same delusional story as ever, but in a more agitated style. I had the impression that something had happened, which he denied and split away. It was as if he was covered by a blanket and all I could see was that there was some movement under the blanket, but he could not tell me or be in touch with what had happened and what it meant to him.

Bion (1961: 25) re-defines the bizarre objects which he discussed in his texts on psychosis as the origin of hallucinations (see *Second Thoughts*) as beta-elements, with split-off parts of ego and super-ego sticking to them. When the analyst receives these bizarre objects through projective identification, s/he will be prodded into an attitude of praise or disapproval by their ego and super-ego characteristics, without realizing why. When this happens s/he is at risk of reverting to a primitive attitude of non-thinking rather than adopting an open, dream-like alpha-function.

Delineating some factors of the alpha-function

Although the alpha-function is unknown, Bion developed some models to account for its origin. He noted that the earliest emotions experienced in the relationship with the mother, like love, must be transmitted in some way or other with the mother's milk. It is at an oral level that a baby first comes into contact with emotional experiences and that he must learn to handle them. To Bion this implies that the alpha-function is related to the alimentary canal of the baby, or at least to the psychosomatic expression of it. It is on this basic level that a 'wanted' breast will at a certain moment be 'felt' as an 'idea of a breast missing' and when this frustration is tolerated it can give rise to a thought. The alimentary canal is thus burdened with proto-thoughts, although it is not suited for this. Bion emphasizes again and again how difficult the origin of thinking is: proto-thoughts like the wanted breast are in fact negative, greedy objects that are hard to tolerate.

This is what happens on the side of the baby. The question remains how a mother passes on love at this alimentary level, in other words: through her milk? The answer is somewhat surprising: through 'reverie' or 'the capacity of relaxed attention'. Bion uses Hume's notion of reverie (without further explanation or reference) as a factor in the mother's alpha-function. The mother's reverie can bear the proto-thoughts like the wanted breast and makes them suitable for the alpha-function of the baby, which will be fortified by this process.[4]

Bion thought that communication between baby and mother initially takes place by means of projective identification. Here his view is in contrast to that of Klein (1946) who saw projective identification as an omnipotent phantasy in which mostly unwanted parts of the self are put in the other. Bion does not view projective identification as taking place only on a phantasy level. He saw it as something that is actually happening: in projective identification one really is putting something in the other's mind. Thus, projective identification is a form of basic communication and the origin of a primitive form of thought. As such it is one of the factors of alpha-function (see Box 3.3).

In his theory about the origin of thinking, Freud (1911) opposed the pleasure and reality principles. In Bion's model, the projection of unwanted emotional experiences into the mother suits both the pleasure and the reality principle. Indeed, provided that the mother's capacity for reverie is sufficient, projective identification diminishes pain and is at the same time in the service of the reality principle, since putting parts into her through projective identification makes it possible for thoughts to arise.

Bion emphasizes that in evolutionary terms the capacity to deal psychically with emotional experiences is probably a fairly recent requirement for which the human organism is not really equipped. We need others to bear the frustration and develop the capacity to 'think' emotional experiences (*Idea or I*). This is fundamentally different from the world of thoughts based on logical thinking (*Reason or R*).

Box 4.4 Ogden's elaboration of Bion's notion of reverie

Ogden focuses on the intersubjective experience of the analytic couple. In his papers of the 1990s, he conceived this along Winnicottian lines as an intermediary zone – a third area of experience, an analytic third (Ogden 1994). This third is something new, a creation. Reveries are seen as metaphors created to give shape to the analyst's and patient's experiences in this area (Ogden 1997) and to form an envelope for this mental space. This is based on Winnicott's conception of 'the place where we live' and where we are creative and alive.

(continued)

(continued)

In 2004a Ogden integrates Bion's unconscious waking dream thought into his model and he states that the psychoanalytic function of the personality is the experience of dreaming and that 'containing is the enhancement of the capacity for dreaming one's experience' (Ogden 2004c: 1356). Ogden sees from then on the task of the analyst as helping the patient to contain these parts that are not mentalized yet; in other words, 'to participate in dreaming the patient's undreamt dream' (Ogden 2004c: 1360). In this sense, he distinguishes (Ogden 2004b) between night terrors (undreamt split-off parts – beta-elements) that have to be dreamt and nightmares which are actual dreams. The intersubjective analytic third is now seen as an unconscious emotional field where the patient can come to life by 'becoming increasingly able to dream one's experience, which is to dream oneself into existence' (Ogden 2004b: 862). For people who do not have this capacity yet, he developed a technique: 'talking as dreaming' (Ogden 2007), in which what looks like talking about books, films etc is actually 'an improvisation in the form of loosely structured conversation (concerning virtually any subject) in which the analyst participates in the patient's dreaming previously undreamt dreams' (Ogden 2007: 577).

K: the processing of emotional experiences in psychoanalysis

In the functions theory (see Box 5.1), a function relates unknown factors – a relation which can be expressed in a formula. In looking for a formula to express the alpha-function, Bion starts with the principal factor of this function: emotions. Emotions can be seen as expressing a link between subjects. To keep it simple, Bion proposes to determine the dominant link for a psychoanalytic session; in other words, the dominant link of the transference. The simplification of a relationship to a dominant link does not prevent it from being complex, but with the dominant link kept as a constant factor, it is easier to study other unknown factors of the alpha-function. Bion discerns three basic emotional links: L(ove), H(ate) and K(nowledge). The last term refers to the Kleinian epistemophilic instinct and it is important to note that Bion also sees the K-link as emotional: Knowledge must involve feeling, it is not logical thinking. In the relation between analyst and analysand, the analysand's relation to the analyst may be described in terms of any one of the three links, but the analyst's relation should always be a K-link and no other. This cannot be taken for granted. In contrast with a group where the K-link is dominant (see *Experiences in Groups*), in a couple the L-link is facilitated by the basic assumption of pairing and therefore many analysts work from the L-link (e.g. holding, mothering, reliving Oedipal fantasies in the transference-countertransference).

We must stress again that Bion defines K as the thinking of an emotional experience, which is different from rational thought. Moreover, K is a getting-to-know, and not a possession of knowledge. Already in this first book, Bion states that a fully open, unsaturated, ignorant attitude is necessary to allow for the K-link. It is a pitfall to understand Bion's K as an attempt to understand or look for causality. Even if it were possible to know an emotional experience, this attitude would destroy the K-link. Indeed Bion will call this possessive attitude towards knowledge −K (minus K), the opposite of K.

As K is the opposite of evasion (which Bion linked to the pleasure principle), he sees it as always painful and he warns that this must never be forgotten in an analysis. −K is then a premature closure in order not to feel this pain.[5,6]

Model, abstraction and theory

In exploring the question of how an analyst can think an emotional experience (K) without pinning it down in knowledge (−K), Bion further relied on what is known as the model-abstractions approach. A model is concrete and precisely fits the experience, like an image. It has sensorial and often narrative qualities. An abstraction is more loosely related to a concrete experience, further removed from it and less saturated. It is more concerned with patterns of connections between objects. Abstractions are not narrative and cannot be logically derived; they are 'seen' in a spontaneous process. Therefore, they are more appropriate to contain experiences still to come and in this way can be seen as pre-concepts. Bion supposes a movement between these two meta-levels: model and abstraction.

Abstractions can be related to each other to form a theory. A theory is characterized by the fact that the elements of which it is composed are coherently connected and in this way, a theory may help to reveal connections in the clinical material. However, the elements of a theory can also be disconnected so that they can be used as a concrete model to fit with specific emotional experiences.

According to Bion, around six theories should suffice to derive models and abstractions for psychoanalysis. The Oedipus myth is a good example, although the fixed narrative connection of the elements of the myth may be a problem for the use of separate elements (for example, in using the Oedipus myth in psychoanalysis, it is usually from the perspective of Oedipus, and seldom from the perspective of the Sphinx or Tiresisas).

An abstraction is about seeing links, connections and patterns, or in other words: functions. This corresponds to Bion's definition of K. Through reverie and through dream-like presence in a state of relaxed attention an analyst can allow a pattern (a realization) to emerge and be seen. To give a concrete form to this realization, a model is needed. One could compare the abstraction with seeing a constellation in the thousands of stars that are visible; a model like the Big Dipper is then necessary to fix and name this realization.

Learning from Experience *(1962)* 89

Logical thinking differs from K in that it is not based on such a spontaneous realization of a pattern (abstraction) and the illumination of this pattern by a model. When in psychoanalysis a pattern does not emerge spontaneously from emotional experience but is deduced logically, it is something sterile that will result in psychoanalytic jargon. Concerning the use of models to name these patterns, Bion stresses that because a model is more concrete and sensorial than an abstraction, its sensuous qualities may affect our thinking.[7] For example: Bion is using an alimentary model for psychic processing with digesting, spitting and milk, and this brings its own sensuous connotations.

Box 4.5   The alphabet of psychoanalysis

Bion was looking for a system that could be used as a model and an abstraction. A model is concrete and maps on to a particular emotional experience. In other words: a realization that illuminates a part of reality, like a beam in the dark. An abstraction is further removed from concrete experiences and may fit different experiences. While a model is so concrete that it has sensorial qualities (e.g., an image), an abstraction can be a concept (e.g., projective identification). An ideal system to approach what happens in the thinking process of patient and analyst would therefore be both concrete and abstract, and therefore flexible, like the letters of the alphabet. They are abstract, yet they allow us to form specific words.

This is the reason why Bion turned to the geometrical theory of elements. Elements can be lifted out of an abstract system and reconnected to a concrete experience, thus producing a realization, while maintaining the characteristics of the abstract system.

Selected fact

To describe what happens in the realization of an abstraction (in other words a pattern or a constant conjunction), Bion refers to the intuitive geometry of Poincaré. In a row of elements in which no coherence is seen, suddenly a connection can light up that gives coherence to the whole. In intuitive geometry, this phenomenon is called a 'selected fact'.[8]

He relates this to what Klein described as the paranoid-schizoid and the depressive position: the capacity to tolerate a non-coherent paranoid-schizoid position (PS) until coherence suddenly brings about a depressive (D) position. Bion uses an abstract notation (PS) which does not carry the connotations of fear and persecution as in the original Kleinian definition. 'PS–D' and 'selected fact' are thus factors of the α-function.

To facilitate the emergence of a selected fact, Bion advises relaxed attention and reverie, which he had already described as the right attitude to facilitate alpha-function.

One of the elements of the constant conjunction can be used as a name[9] for the conjunction. Thus, we have on the one hand the selected fact or seeing of a conjunction (abstraction), and on the other the name or the representation to which this conjunction is related (model).

The psychoanalytic object

According to Bion, psychoanalysing involves allowing selected facts to emerge; in other words, the realization of constant conjunctions, and hypotheses that some elements are constantly conjoined (Hume 1735–1985). Such a K attitude of the analyst towards an emotional experience stimulates the growth of the patient's personality. At this point, Bion can state that these constant conjunctions are the objects of psychoanalysis[10] (see Box 8.7). They do not exist at random because they have a counterpart in the unknown essence of the personality (which may be compared to the Kantian thing-in-itself).

So psychoanalytic objects (functions of the personality in the form of constant conjunctions) have Kant's primary (the ineffable essence or noumenon) and secondary (phenomena, what is perceived.) features (see introductory text to this chapter on philosophy). We cannot enter directly into contact with the primary features.[11]

The notion of the psychoanalytic object put in a formula

In his endeavour to make an applied theory for the practising analyst about thinking and therefore relying on the mathematical theory of functions (see Box 5.1), Bion put the psychoanalytic object, which is a function in a formula. A formula describes the constant relation between unknown factors. The formula of the psychoanalytic object is $(+/-Y)\ (\&)\psi(\xi)$. It consists of an unknown constant ψ (for instance an inborn preconception) and an unsaturated element (ξ) (for instance the emotional experience) that gives value to ψ. So $\psi(\xi)$ could be the inborn conception of a breast that is filled in by the concrete emotional experience of meeting a breast. In psychoanalysis, both the preconcepts and the concrete emotional experiences are related to the personality $(\&)$. Moreover the psychoanalytic object can be used to disclose, or to ward off; this is why the factor 'growth of the personality' is included in the formula $(+/-Y)$. The formula of the psychoanalytic object thus becomes: $(+/-Y)\ (\&)\psi(\xi)$.

For example, a patient feels that she wants to help a friend with a relational problem (ξ), and realizes that this often occurs: when people are sad, this triggers in her a reaction of wanting to help (ψ). This seems related to her personality and history $(\&)$. She may explore this realization or close it off. In other words it may change her personality in a positive or negative way $(+/-Y)$.

Container and contained and proto-organizations

In *Learning from Experience* Bion abstracts his former notion of container-contained to ♀ (container) ♂ (contained.) and explores it from the point of view of functions. The mother receives the contained by projective identification, the contained is detoxified[12] and the infant can gradually take over the alpha–activity represented as ♀♂. In other words, K or thinking as a function can be represented by ♀♂.

Bion further plays with the ♀♂ abstraction. Following Elliot Jacques, he uses a reticulum, which is a small network of cells or fibres in the body, as a model with which to compare ♀♂. ♀ can be seen as the slots of the reticulum and the emotions as the threads. We have therefore a ♀+ ♀+ ♀+ ♀ growth in which '+' represents the emotions. The content c' can be contained in the slots ♀, but note that in Bion's model it is always ♀ that is searching for c'. To make ♀♂ possible, ♀ must remain integrated without becoming rigid so that ♂ can fit and be integrated, connected by the reticulum.

A second metaphor is that of ♂ content, seen as something that protrudes from a base that is unknown. A two-dimensional image is provided by the parabola (Bion 1961: 92). In order to let c' grow, insecurity or doubt – the state of mind of the PS position – must be tolerated. This is represented as ♂. ♂. ♂. ♂ in which '.' is a constant representing doubt.

It is important to know what emotions (+ and.) in ♀+ ♀+ ♀+ ♀ and ♂. ♂. ♂. ♂ are compatible with K. When + is for instance envy, a commensal relation between ♀+♂ will be impossible and we get –K instead of ♀♂. Instead of growth, a denudation of meaning, stripping of goodness and deterioration take place.

Conclusion

In this book Bion attempts to elaborate the theory of thinking which he developed for clinical use by the analyst, especially in the treatment of patients with thought disorders. His question is akin to that of the empiricist philosophers: how does the human mind process what impresses itself on it (perceptions, theories, emotions)? Bion focuses on the unknowable forerunners of thinking, unknowable proto-thoughts before verbal thought. In a baby this must happen at an alimentary level or the psychosomatic equivalent of it. At this point these impressions can be spit out or digested. For his study, he resorts to the mathematical functions theory, which makes it possible to make hypotheses about unknowable factors like the ones he is dealing with, by looking at how they are related. He asks, 'What are the factors of the alpha-function and how are they related?' Important factors are emotions and the relationship between mother and baby. He brings in several theories from psychoanalysis, philosophy, philosophy of science and mathematics in trying to apprehend these factors of thinking. His idea of the communication between mother and baby is a development of the Kleinian concept of projective identification. Thinking or the further psychic processing of the emotions is an unconscious spontaneous process, different from Reason. This idea of thinking is in line with a number of philosophers that Bion studied like Hume, Whitehead and Bergson. In his hypothesis about how the mother handles the emotional experiences that are put into her by projective identification, Bion is at the same time referring to Hume's automatic reverie. He equates this analytically with the Kleinian notion of unconscious phantasy, a constant flow that links emotions.

Bion further studies how these ideas of thinking or alpha-function can be of use in psychoanalytic sessions, and concludes that this is about spontaneously seeing patterns of connections which are the essence of a personality. Seeing these a-sensuous essences is what psychoanalysis is about, according to Bion, and he therefore calls them psychoanalytic objects. In applying the functions theory to 'thinking', he produces a formula for them that expresses the constant relation between unknown variables. He hopes to reveal psychic reality in this way.[13] What is paramount in his idea of spontaneous thinking is the sudden realization of a constant conjunction between elements (a psychoanalytic object). He compares this with the realization of a selected fact as described by the intuitionist mathematician Poincaré. In psychoanalytic terms, he links this process with the Kleinian concept of the two positions after having made them abstract as an oscillation between PS and D. Bion's formula of thinking or psychoanalysing can be seen as a meta-theory: the factors of the formula can be filled out from many different theoretical approaches. Letting this thinking process happen in a session, in other words seeing these patterns or conjunctions, establishes a K-link with the patient and has more clinical effect in severe patients than focusing on the meaning of what a patient brings. Bion describes the frame of mind that is necessary to create the conditions in which this can happen: relaxed attention or reverie, just like what happens between a mother and her baby. Bion will further elaborate this process in his next two books.

Notes

1 His footnotes refer to Semple and Kneeborn, Frege, Popper, Braithwaite, Poincaré and Kant.
2 The idea of a contact-barrier derives from Freud's Project and is related to neuronal synapses. Freud postulated three systems of neurones for perception, memory and consciousness that are impermeable at their contact-barriers but become permeable when psychic quantity (Qn) passes (Sulloway 1979).
3 This model of the necessity of α-functioning implies that primary process and unconscious thinking are not self-evident, as was implicit in Freud's model of the unconscious and in phantasy functioning in Klein's model.

4 Note that thinking and feeling, internal objects and physical sensations are related in this model. Bion was very aware of the psychosomatic nature of the mother's feeding, nursing and general care of her baby (as vehicles for her reverie).

5 This will later be developed as the second column in his Grid.

6 This is a much-debated statement. It is different, for instance, from Winnicott, for whom psychic development does not depend on the tolerance of frustration and can develop through playing. However, both authors stress the need for the caregiver's protection. In Bion the frustration needs to be contained by the mother and in Winnicott the caregiver needs to protect the child from too much intrusion of reality so that a psychic space and growth can develop.

7 The way in which the senses may inhibit the spontaneous perception of a-sensuous pattern of relations will be discussed in depth in Bion's *Attention and Interpretation*.

8 In photography Roland Barthes (1981) calls such an organizing moment a *punctum*, something that attracts the viewer's attention among all the detail and gives the picture a (personal) meaning.

9 This is the definitory hypothesis in the first column of the Grid that he will develop in *Elements*.

10 This is in analogy with mathematical objects: the objects of which mathematics consist.

11 This theme and its clinical implications will later be worked out in *Attention and Interpretation* (Bion 1970).

12 The notion of detoxification in relation to containment is widely used in the literature, but not by Bion himself who used metaphors of digestion.

13 Braithwaite, a philosopher of science to whom Bion refers, thinks along the same line. See Harris and Redway-Harris (2013).

5 ELEMENTS OF PSYCHOANALYSIS (1963)

Introduction

The two chapters that follow, on *Elements of Psychoanalysis* and *Transformations*, are the most complicated of this book. In *Elements* Bion tries to categorize the elements of thought scientifically and continues this attempt in a nearly mathematical way in *Transformations*. I try to systematize and to give background and explanations, but oversimplifying would not do justice to the process that Bion went through.

Bion's Grid presents his work in the form of a simple and useful tool, which the analyst can develop further in his own way and introject so that it becomes part of his intuition (Vermote 1998b, 2000a). The major themes of Bion's approach are inherent in the Grid and its use: the attitude of not-knowing and openness, the absence of moralistic judgement, the focus on psychic functioning, a binocular view and the development of reverie and imagination, the need to use it 'without irritable searching after certainty' and analysing without taking a cause-effect approach but rather looking at the co-occurrence and the relatedness of phenomena, at how invariants are expressed at very different levels. Bion constructed the Grid as a tool to develop the intuitive capacity to see the constant conjunctions between elements. According to him, this is what psychoanalysis is about.

> In the practice of psychoanalysis I am convinced that the emotional experience can be discerned as a constantly changing pattern of emotional experience. If the psychoanalyst develops his capacity to intuit these experiences he can become aware that there are certain experiences that are constantly conjoined and that these constant conjunctions are themselves experienced as repeated conjunctions. These constant conjunctions become manifest to the analyst after a period of time (provided he resists an irritable searching after certainty) as a kaleidoscopic change: the sensuous change will bear a resemblance to elements of the C categories that are found amongst his models.
>
> (Bion 1989: 11)

It is also important that the Grid can be used to apply both the former part of Bion's theory (transformations in knowledge) and the later part (transformations in O) (see Box 5.2). As with all his achievements, Bion was ironical about this major one (see Box 5.2), but he continued to refer to the Grid to the end of his life and even started to make a Grid version of his *Memoir of the Future*.

On 2 October 1963 Bion presented a paper on his Grid to the British Psychoanalytical Society,[1] which may be seen as a forerunner to his publication of the Grid in *Elements*. He never published this text, but Francesca Bion edited it in 1997 (Bion 1997). Bion's *Cogitations* (Bion 1992), also published posthumously by Francesca Bion, contain some preliminary thoughts on the elements as well. Years later, Bion published a paper on the Grid based on a lecture that he gave in Rio de Janeiro in 1971 (Bion 1977). Francesca Bion further published some tape-recorded musings that he made in preparing a lecture given in Rome in 1977, and in which he refers widely to the elements and the Grid (Bion 1997), but as the main text of this book offers a chronological reading of Bion's work, I will add a note on these texts from the 1970s in Box 5.2, in order not to disrupt the chronological structure of this book.

Box 5.2 Changing attitudes towards the Grid in Bion's work

Bion was working on the idea of a Grid while writing *Learning from Experience*, and he presented a paper to the British Society of Psychoanalysis about the Grid on 2 October 1963, shortly after the publication of the book. Bion never published this paper himself but in 1994 Dr Rosa Beatrix Pontes Miranda de Ferreira sent literal notes of it to Francesca Bion, who published it in 1997 (Bion 1997).

It is a remarkable paper about how the Grid helps in seeing and dealing with constant conjunctions, the core of Bion's approach to psychoanalysis. In this paper he already mentioned transformations and O. This shows the seminal role played by the approach of delineating elements in the further evolution of his thinking.

The Grid proved to be an important tool in maintaining openness and fostering T(K). It sharpens observation and intuition. It allows for the possibility of speculative imagination and creates a psychic attitude in which new thoughts and the seeing of constant conjunctions can arise. When Bion later shifted his focus from T(K) to T(O), the Grid remained useful. For T(O) the Grid can be used as what he called 'a reality scale', indicating the distance from a thought or feeling to O. In other words the Grid shows movement on the vertex undifferentiated-differentiated, and in this way it may be used to indicate when transformations happen in O.

There are many different interpretations of the Grid, such as those by Bleandonu (1994), Grinberg et al. (1975, 1993), Grotstein (2007), Lopez-Corvo (2003), Symington (1996) and Vermote (1997, 1998, 2000, 2005), but Bion himself had different attitudes towards the Grid. He insisted that the Grid is always a meta-system, only working at the level of representations, never at the level of the Thing that is represented. In Brazil he made a humorous comparison of the Grid to a ruler that can be used to slap the fingers (Brazilian Lectures 1974: 98). He toyed with the idea of making a 3D Grid, and he imagined that the distances between the lines of the grid would become so thin that it would become a grating (Bion in New York and São Paulo 1980: 92). On the same occasion, he also said: 'As soon as I got the Grid out of my system, I could see how inadequate it is . . . only a waste of time because it doesn't really correspond with the facts I am likely to meet' (Bion in New York and São Paulo 1980: 56). Francesca Bion gives a review of Bion's comments about the grid in her introduction to her publication of Bion's 1963 paper (Bion 1997).

Bion continued to use his Grid until the end of his life and even contemplated making a grid version of *A Memoir of the Future*. In his tape-recorded musings of 28 May 1977 (Bion 1997), preparing one of his seminars in Rome, he associates about β, α and C-elements while making long detours. He stresses again that β-elements are not psychic, and therefore darkness. He wonders to what element of the Grid the phenomenon corresponds of a mother not being able to breastfeed her baby because of an erection of her nipples responding to a genital erection of the baby. To what elements correspond the archaic remnants in our minds which are comparable to the branchial clefts in our body that refer to a fish stage in human evolution and are no longer of any use? Can these archaic mental remnants proliferate as the remnant branchial clefts may develop to branchial tumours (Bion 1987)? Or what happens to memories that remain particularly intense during life for unknown reasons, such as Bion's memories of the rubbing of an animal against the metal bars of his cage in the zoo that he saw as a child and the bagpipe music that moved him during an attack in the Great War? What kind of elements, conjunctions and transformations are they?

Bion saw the Grid as a cage to contain his wild thoughts, a system of transformation like a DNA-helix, an approach to the Unknown.

The essence of the book Elements

So far, in his exploration of 'thinking emotional experiences', Bion had developed concepts such as the contact-barrier, the alpha-function, L, H, K, ♀♂, PS-D, the selected fact and psychoanalytic objects. In a further attempt to discriminate his basic concepts and their relation, he now used the theory of elements (see Box 5.1).

In a first attempt to delineate the essential elements of psychoanalysis, Bion took some of the notions mentioned above plus some features that he found essential in his psychoanalytic practice: loneliness, pain and growth. However, he was not satisfied with this approach. For example, it is not logical to retain ♀♂ as an element, as the notion ♀♂ or container-contained must be filled in by other elements to be meaningful. Therefore it cannot be considered as a basic element.

In a second attempt, he defined the elements of psychoanalysis now as the different forms of thought described in *Learning from Experience*, going from concrete to more abstract (β-elements, α-elements, dream thoughts, preconception or model, conception, concept or abstraction, theory) and he put them on a vertical axis. This vertical or 'genetic' axis can therefore be seen as describing the genesis of thoughts. On the horizontal axis he indicated the different ways that these different forms of thought can be used by the patient and by the analyst. In this way he constructed a Grid with two axes and at least 42 categories – at least, because he leaves the Grid open. These categories were finally considered as the elements of psychoanalysis, as everything that happens in a session can be categorized as one of these elements. Any thought, act, statement or feeling of analysand and analyst during a session finds its place in the Grid.

It is most important that Bion will further manage to formulate the relation and transition between these elements using the notions of ♀♂, PS-D and selected fact that he described in *Learning from Experience* (see below, 'Reconsidering the theory of thinking as the transition between elements'). This bringing together of '♀♂, PS-D and selected fact' in relation to the elements of psychoanalysis constitutes a formula and a new definition of thinking. We now have a clear and distinct description of what may be happening in psychoanalysing: a meta-theory that may serve as a compass in each session and over a longer term of a psychoanalysis. The aim of this meta-level is to help a psychoanalyst to see exactly what is happening and to communicate with other colleagues about it. Defining the categories of his Grid as the elements of psychoanalysis will also lead to a new definition of the object that psychoanalysis is concerned with: an unknown object that is reflected in constant conjunctions that need at least three Grid categories to be described (see Box 8.7).

Bion's Grid of elements

The vertical axis of the Grid

Rows A–H of the vertical axis represent the stages of thinking an emotional experience.

A. β-elements: unprocessed raw sensorial and emotional impressions are placed at this level. They are not psychic yet and therefore they are inanimate and saturated and do not have possibilities of growth. Until β-elements are transformed into α-elements they are not suitable for thinking. Existing thoughts that have not yet been appropriated by the psyche and therefore have the status of a thing may also be considered as β-elements. Bion gave the example of certain psychotic patients who 'regard "thoughts" as "things" [and] show every sign of regarding what I am used psycho-analytically to believe are phantasies as "facts"'(Bion 1963: 97).

   Untransformed β-elements can only be evacuated by projective identification or acting. This is expressed in the row on action in the horizontal axis: A6. For instance, an unpremeditated blow can be seen as a β-element (Bion 1963/1997) or alcohol abuse or self-mutilation as evacuation of psychic pain by acting instead of thinking it.

   β-elements cannot be used as unsaturated elements; in other words, as containers or preconceptions that are open to allow an experience to be noted and contained. Therefore they are not present in the open rows on the horizontal axis of the Grid: A3, A4, A5 do not exist or have the same characteristics as A1.

B. α-elements: a passage through the internal good breast or α-function transforms the β-elements into α-elements, the building blocks of dream thought. They can be seen as primordial thoughts and feelings (Bion 1997: 23).

C. Dream thoughts, dreams, myths: in contrast to α-elements and β-elements, which are hypothetical constructs, there is direct evidence that dream thoughts, dreams and myths exist. These C-elements are the result of a further elaboration of the α-elements by waking dream thought (see Box 5.2), which is the base of Bion's theory of thinking.

   There are, however, many thoughts and myths that already exist in culture and it depends on the openness of the analysand and analyst whether they can use these in a growth-provoking way.

THE GRID

	Definitory Hypo-theses 1	ψ 2	Notation 3	Attention 4	Inquiry 5	Action 6	$\cdots$ n
A β-elements	A1	A2				A6	
B α-elements	B1	B2	B3	B4	B5	B6	... Bn
C Dream Thoughts Dreams, Myths	C1	C2	C3	C4	C5	C6	... Cn
D Pre-conception	D1	D2	D3	D4	D5	D6	... Dn
E Conception	E1	E2	E3	E4	E5	E6	... En
F Concept	F1	F2	F3	F4	F5	F6	... Fn
G Scientific Deductive System		G2					
H Algebraic Calculus							

D. Pre-conception: an element which expresses an expectation but in relation to a narrow range of phenomena which it fits well. It is close to the notion of model that Bion elaborated in *Learning from Experience*, where a model was defined as an empty thought and therefore unsaturated. For instance, it might be an image that fits a specific experience. It can be inborn like the pre-conception of a breast or given by language or culture.

It reminds me of an anecdote, when I was walking in the fields with my youngest son, being a toddler then. He was learning his first words. We had one of these small cardboard books with simple iconic images of a horse, a cat and so on. At once we crossed a real horse on the road. He had never seen a real horse which actually did not look at all like the small iconic image in bright yellow in the book. It was huge, smelled, and was brown, impressive in its movement and noise. He pointed at it and pronounced the word horse, as he was used to do when we were turning the pages of the booklet. He had a pre-conception ready for the experience of meeting a real horse in reality although this experience was more impressive and very different than the small image in the book.

E. Conception: when a pre-conception or an empty thought meets what is expected, a realization occurs (like the pre-conception of a breast meeting the real experience of a breast) and the pre-conception is saturated, becoming a conception. This conception can be used again in an unsaturated way so that in its turn, it is then open for a larger range of phenomena as a preconcept.

F. Concept: a concept is farther removed from concrete sensorial reality and therefore open to more phenomena, like the notion of a chair as a seat with four legs, that fits to very diverse seats. Or the notion of depression, for instance, which is far more abstract and corresponds to a group of symptoms, than the seeing and feeling of a particular person who is sad, which is at the pre-conception, conception level. A concept is close to the notion of abstraction.

K. Scientific deductive system: concepts and hypotheses that are logically related.

L. Calculus: a scientific deductive system represented by algebraic calculus. It is unsaturated. If psychoanalytic objects could be put into algebraic formulae, psychoanalysts would be able to predict phenomena. In physics or geometry, this happened: algebraic geometry, for instance, was no longer tied to the senses because of the transition from a visual to a mathematical notation, and in physics, we do not rely on our perceptions of electricity to work with it and calculate it. Bion hoped to make such a system for psychoanalysis; the Grid is part of it and the mathematical notations in *Transformations*.

The horizontal axis of the Grid

The horizontal axis (Columns 1–6) is concerned with different uses of the levels of thought delineated in the vertical axis. The degree of openness to self-knowledge is an important factor in understanding the distinctions that Bion makes between the different ways of using these levels of thought. In this way, the first (definition) but especially the second column (denial) can be considered as closing, while columns 3, 4, 5 are opening.

1.   Definitory hypothesis: when a constant conjunction is seen, this can be named by a definitory hypothesis. Distinguishing it from what it is not, is in this sense always limiting. For instance, 'what you are experiencing now is what most people would call a depression'.
2.   ψ: this column is concerned with using an element not to experience. This closing, denying or lying can take place at all levels of the vertical axis, from concrete to abstract elements. When, for instance, defining somebody as depressed, and using this as a filler that gets in the way of allowing new experiences and thoughts to happen in the contact with the patient, then it is no longer using a concept as definition (C1), but as a barrier (C2).
        As there are many ways to close oneself from an emotional experience, a whole negative Grid could be derived instead of one ψ column (Bion 1963: 101; Meltzer 1978). To Bion, psychoanalysis as a scientific system does not exist yet. It is at the level of description and not a combination of theories and notation that may help us to predict and fundamentally change mental phenomena, as physics and chemistry succeed in doing in their domain, by formulating in an abstract way connections between elements that are not manifest. Bion therefore places the scientific system of psychoanalysis in the second row in which also lying is put (G2).
3.   Notation: this refers to note-taking and memory. Bion took Notation and the next category 'Attention' from Freud's (1911) description of the functions of the ego in his 'Two Principles of Mental Functioning'. In general, notation in a session means 'a representation of a present and a past realization, a kind of brief summary' (Bion 1963: 18). Bion found myths the most compatible notation system because in a myth elements have been linked for centuries. In this way, by using myths for notation, unnoticed links between various elements in the clinical material can become clear.
4.   Attention: although Bion names this category in analogy with Freud's (1911) notion of attention in the 'Two Principles of Psychic Functioning', for Bion it is not as active a state. Rather it is a state of mind of passive receptiveness,[2] free-floating or relaxed attention in expectance of a selected fact, of a coherence to be seen. In this respect there is an affiliation with the notion of pre-conception. C3 combines

attention (column 3) and pre-conception (row C), a non-saturated element par excellence. According to Bion it is therefore the element in terms of which the love of the analyst for his patient, which is expressed by a K-link, that can be described.

5. Inquiry: an investigation to illuminate something or to release further material. Earlier, Bion called this column Oedipus (Pontes Miranda de Ferreira 1997) because curiosity and stubbornness are connected with a wanting to know. This can be related to hubris, which is punished by the Gods. Bion was keen on this idea and we see it reflected in the myths he often uses: the Garden of Eden, the Tower of Babel and Oedipus (Bion 1963a: 46).

6. Action: this can be acting out at the level of β-elements (for instance, evacuating pain by self-harm without it becoming psychic); it can also be an action like an interpretation – transition from thought into verbal formulation. Bion describes how lonely an analyst is in this action but also how important it is never to lose this sense of loneliness.

Box 5.3 β-elements and α-elements: two poetic examples

Bion (1990: 41) gives the example of a β-element, not yet transformed but available to the mind, in a verse of John Donne that he quotes at length in (1979: 257):

> Her pure and eloquent blood
> Spoke in her cheeks, and so distinctly wrought,
> That one might almost say, the body thought
> It has a deep freshness and a bodily vividness.
>
> (Donne, *The Second Anniversary*)

Anzieu et al. (1993) and Parthenope Bion (1997) both give 'les madeleines de Proust' as an example of an α-element. It is an Idea as sensation (see Introduction) which is still vivid and sensorial but already appropriated by the psyche. As Anzieu (Anzieu et al. 1993) remarks, the philosophical notion of sensation is Anglo-Saxon and already involves something psychic; this is different from its meaning in French, for instance, where it corresponds more closely to a sensorial experience.

The use of the Grid

The Grid may be used like Mendeleev's periodic table. For instance, it may be used to clarify which elements are *not* seen in the material during a session and therefore go uninterpreted. By way of exercise, Bion suggested that the analyst try to place what happens, what is said and what is thought in a session in the different categories of the Grid. This can help to clarify on what level of abstraction (the vertical axis) thinking is situated and how it is being used (horizontal axis) by analysand and analyst. If the analyst places the session's happenings, utterances and thoughts in various Grid categories, the Grid can help him or her to see how something could have been interpreted in other ways, i.e., which elements were not present in the analytic session. Moreover, it can facilitate an assessment of whether analyst and analysand are on the same wavelength of communication (Lucas 1993). The same communication may have very different meanings when uttered by a psychotic patient at the level of the first row to evacuate a feeling, or by an analyst in order to put an experience into words and solicit a further exploration.

Bion insisted that the Grid should always be used outside the sessions, but its use nevertheless leads to a particular way of handling clinical material. As a result of using the Grid, the analyst will start to think in a particular way about clinical experience which will have an implicit influence on his/her practice. It provides practice, analogous to the musician's scales and exercises.[3] When interiorized by frequent use, it will develop and sharpen the analyst's intuition. The object of such extra-sessional work is to substitute creative thinking for laborious and frequently meaningless note-taking. It helps the analyst to develop an ability to arrive instantaneously at conclusions that would otherwise be the hard-won fruits of laborious intellectualization (Bion 1963: 72).

One of the games Bion proposed for the analyst was to play with the Oedipus myth and to replace all columns and rows by a different component of the myth: column 2 then becomes Tiresias; column 5 (inquiry) Oedipus. A similar game to enliven the Grid involved putting in each category the proper name of someone who was a good example of that category, so that the Grid was like a chess game that involved living persons rather than wooden pieces.

The Oedipus myth as a whole can also be put in a category, for instance in C or G etc. As C4, for instance, it is a pre-conception-premonition; as F2 it is a theory that is used to close the analyst off from experience.

The major aim of the Grid is to help the analyst to see patterns and transitions between elements. It is not constructed to detect causal links. Everyone can make their own Grid with the elements that are important from their own experience and theoretical background. In Bion's view, it is more beneficial for an analyst to know a limited number of theories in depth through intensive use than to know a lot of theories in a superficial and rational way.

Reconsidering the theory of thinking as the transition between elements

Bion's delineation of the elements enabled him to deepen his understanding of thinking. He elaborated his theory of thinking by studying the transition between elements. To go from column to column on the horizontal or use-axis, a desaturation, a decoupling of the experience and the representing element, is always necessary (PS). This must be tolerated until a sudden spontaneous perception of a new coherence (D) arises, as Bion elaborated in *Learning from Experience*. Bion compares the emergence of this new coherence in the analyst with the notion of a 'selected fact', as described by Poincaré in intuitive mathematics.

> Melanie Klein's discoveries of the paranoid-schizoid and depressive positions required a theory that in certain situations, apparently unrelated elements, associated with feelings of persecution, come together as an integrated whole associated with feelings of depression. I shall employ this theory together with the term 'selected fact', borrowed from H. Poincaré. Each use classified under the categories 1–6 of the schematic axis depends on the operation of this mechanism on the elements A–G.
>
> The process of change from one category represented in the grid to another may be described as disintegration and reintegration, Ps ↔ D.
>
> (Bion 1963: 34–35)

A coherence can be put in a definitory hypothesis of the first column. It can be noted or named (third column – notation) or it can be used in an open way to allow further coherences to emerge (fourth column – attention). This can be further studied (fifth column – inquiry) and eventually be used to do something, for instance providing an interpretation (sixth column – action). In this way, there is a transition from column to column, always starting from desaturation.

Opposed to these open transitions, there is a closing way of using thoughts. When a connection is seen (column 1), it can be used to block further exploration of the unknown. This defensive attitude to prevent further thinking-feeling is expressed in column 2, ψ. As already mentioned, the closing use is so diverse and extensive that column 2 could be made into a separate Grid in itself.

While a transition between elements on the horizontal (use) axis happens by a PS-D movement, in a transition between the rows on the vertical axis (the genesis of thoughts) it is the relation container (♀) – contained (♂) which is primordial. The container is seen as a pre-conception that finds something that fits into it, which is a realization that leads to a conception. Each conception can in turn be desaturated again and used as preconception.[4]

The distinction between changes on the horizontal axis (PS-D) and the vertical axis (♂♀) is rather complicated and artificial and Bion finally integrates the two movements:

It is tempting to suppose that the transformation of β-elements to α-elements depends on ♀♂ and the operation of Ps ↔ D depends on the prior operation of ♀♂. Unfortunately this relatively simple solution does not adequately explain events in the consulting room; before ♀♂ can operate, ♀ has to be found and the discovery of ♀ depends on the operation of Ps ↔ D. It is obvious that to consider which of the two ♀♂ or Ps ↔ D is prior distracts from the main problem.

(Bion 1963: 39)

From now on, thinking is seen as a transition between categories based on a convergence between '♀♂ and PS-D and selected fact'. This became Bion's formula for thinking. 'On the PS ↔ D operation depends the delineation of the whole object (seeing the conjunction); on the successful operation of ♀♂ depends the meaning of the whole object' (Bion 1963: 90).

Bion also described a minus state: instead of PS-D moving through saturation-desaturation towards a greater integration, there is also a − (PS ↔ D, ♀♂), where instead of giving meaning, a stripping of meaning occurs, 'which leads to disintegration, total loss and depressive stupor, or, intense impaction and degenerate stuporose violence' (Bion 1963: 52).

The relation between the elements and the psychoanalytic object

The psychoanalytic object was defined in *Learning from Experience* in terms of the functions theory with the formula $(+/-Y) (\alpha)\psi(\xi)$. The use of elements now allows Bion to define it in a different and simpler way.

[T]he elements of psycho-analysis are ideas and feelings as represented by their setting in a single grid-category; psycho-analytic objects are associations and interpretations with extensions in the domain of sense, myth and passion . . . requiring three grid categories for their representation.

(Bion 1963: 103)

A psychoanalytic object belongs to subjective psychic reality (*myth*, what scientists call fiction compared to facts), mobilizes strong emotions but not destructive aggression (*passion*) and can manifest itself in phenomena that can be perceived (*senses*). Bion proposes this definition in Chapter 3 of *Learning from Experience* on p. 11. However, on p. 101 he states that the psychoanalytic object has three dimensions: sensa, mythology and analytic theory, and relates these dimensions to rows B (alpha-elements), C (personal myth) and G (theory) of the Grid. It is unclear to me why he replaced passion here with theory. On p. 103 he returns to the first definition without any explanation and he sees the psychoanalytic object again as 'associations and interpretations with extensions in the domain of sense, myth and passion, requiring three grid categories for their representation'. These Grid categories may come from all classes, A–F. If ideas and feelings are represented in a single Grid category, they are considered as elements.

Myths as fact-finding tools

In psychoanalysis, myths are often used to provide content and meaning. In his focus on revealing conjunctions or functions, Bion rather uses myths as 'fact-finding tools' or ♀. Myths find new elements, show the relation between elements and can indicate that elements are lacking in a session. In this way they are a kind of primitive scientific system. Bion takes the example of our relation to knowledge, the guiding thread in his work. There are three myths about our relation to knowledge that reveal specific facets of this relationship: the Tree of Knowledge, the Tower of Babel and Oedipus and the Sphinx. All three myths demonstrate the difficulty human beings have with acquiring knowledge and describe how the gods punish man for it. For example, in the Oedipus myth, the oracle of Delphi is pronounced by a monster and it is followed by a series of disasters: the plague in Thebes, the death of the King, the suicides of Jocasta and of the Sphinx and Oedipus' blinding. In this sense the Oedipus myth sheds light on the relation with knowledge and not only on L and H relationships.

In analysis where thinking itself (in the sense of *Idea*, the spontaneous, automatic dream-like processing of emotional experiences, which is different from *Reason* or logical thought) is the problem, this dealing with knowledge is our paramount experience. Bion gives a clinical example to illustrate this:

> The analyst is and thinks he is in a consulting room conducting an analysis. The patient regards the same fact, his attendance in analysis as an experience affording him the raw material to give substance to a day dream. The day dream thus invested with reality is that he the patient being extremely intuitive, is able without any analysis, to see just where his difficulties lie and to astonish and delight the analyst by his brilliance and friendliness. The patient reports and the analyst believes that he, the patient, has had a dream. The patient reports, but does NOT believe that he has had a dream. The dream, an experience of great emotional intensity, is felt by the patient to be a straightforward recital of the facts of a horrifying experience. He expects that the analyst in treating it as a dream requiring interpretation will give substance to his day dream that it was only a dream . . .

> The 'dream' . . . is something that would emerge in the session as a hallucination when the capacity for day dream weakened.

(Bion 1963: 49–50)

Bion called this phenomenon reversible perspective. An illusion of agreement is created, but the patient uses the interventions of the analyst in a totally different way than the analyst intended them. The agreement is obvious but not the disagreement.

Bion compares the foregoing example to the classic image of the Rubin vase that depending on the perspective may look like a face or a vase. Although it appears from the outside that both analyst and patient are talking about the same thing and agree, they have completely different ways of seeing it. One must bear in mind that the type of deformation in the clinical example is always a sign of great pain and that it is hard to discover because of the apparent accord between analyst and analysand. It demonstrates the usefulness of the Grid as a tool when the problem is thinking of emotional experiences itself. With the Grid it became possible to be aware that the patient was at another level of psychic functioning than the analyst. The patient wanted to ward off psychic pain, while the analyst intended to explore. If we use the Oedipus myth as a fact-finding tool, by looking at the conjunctions of what happens in the session in the light of the conjunctions present in the myth, we can say that the problem was not at the level of content, a conflict between father and son (Laius versus Oedipus), but at the level of thinking itself (the Seer Tiresias who knows the truth versus Oedipus 'who turns a blind eye' (Steiner 1985) to it.

What the patient says may be thematically evocative of Oedipal content, but when placed in the Grid it may appear to be scattered debris after ego-destruction. In a situation like this, the patient does not have a good apparatus to think the Oedipal and attention must focus more on the thinking apparatus than on the interpretation of Oedipal content.

Myths and the relation between pain, growth and knowledge

Bion's practice taught him that mental pain is an essential element of psycho-analysis. His theory of thinking is based on the capacity to tolerate frustration. Increasing the 'capacity to suffer pain' is a necessary part of analysis and psychic growth, although both patient and analyst obviously hope that the pain itself will decrease. This is why the analyst must prepare himself to see the pain that is present for his analysand. A focus on pain does not entail that the analysand must suffer unnecessary pain during his analysis. The analyst can be in touch with the underlying pain and how the analysand deals with it by his intuition before it becomes manifest to the patient. The example above of reversible perspective shows how the Grid may improve this intuition.

> Pain cannot be absent from the personality. An analysis must be painful, not because there is necessarily any value in pain, but because an analysis in which pain is not observed and discussed cannot be regarded as dealing with one of the central reasons for the patient's presence. There is a need . . . more obvious in some cases than in others, for the analytic experience to increase the

patient's capacity for suffering even though patient and analyst may hope to decrease pain itself. The analogy with physical medicine is exact; to destroy a capacity for physical pain would be a disaster in any situation other than one in which an even greater disaster – death itself – is certain.

(Bion 1963: 61)

The relation between growth, pain and knowledge is described in the myths of Oedipus, the Tree of Knowledge, the Tower of Babel and the Sphinx. We may expect that they will also appear in analysands' material and in this way the myths are fact-finding tools. In his musings in 1977 on the Grid (Bion 1989), Bion adds The *Royal Cemetery at Ur*, in which he actually sees two myths. The first is the procession of the notables in 3500 BC, probably under the influence of hashish, into the pit where the King will be buried together with them in all their splendour. The pit was located in the city's refuse heap, maybe implying that the human remains are rubbish. Bion links it with magic, religion and death. The second is that around 3000 bc the cemetery was visited by plunderers driven by the power of gain and surpassing magic and religion – Bion calls them the forerunners of science. He further adds the death of Palinurus (Virgil, *Aeneid* Book V) where Neptune requires the life of Palinurus who was steering the ship by the stars (knowledge), as a sacrifice to allow the Trojans to reach Italy safely. Bion drew on these myths because he felt that they offered images of omnipotence-helplessness for practising analysts to make use of. With these five myths, the analyst has a set of tools to facilitate the perception of constant conjunctions.

Feelings and the Grid

Hitherto Bion's approach has focused on knowledge. However, 'I know that you hate me' is not so far removed from 'I feel that you hate me'. Thoughts are preconceptions for something else, and the same can be said for feelings. A feeling is then a premonition in the literal sense of the word, preserving the connotations of fear and warning. Sexual feelings, for instance, are then not merely seen as an expression of sexuality but as a precursor of something else. Bion prefers to interpret on this 'precursory level', namely to interpret 'what is obvious to the analyst but unobserved by the patient' (Bion 1963: 74). Bion often refers to the need for the analyst to be sensitive to the analysand's feelings that are hinted at but not yet fully emerged. He felt there was little reason to state what is already obvious.

As premonitions, feelings can be used to open or to close. Feelings can be placed in the Grid like thoughts. They can also have degrees of sophistication (vertical column) and differences in use (horizontal axis). Feelings and thoughts cannot be separated. A feeling can be a forerunner of an Idea or can even represent an Idea; sometimes it can also serve to close an Idea. The link between feelings and thoughts can become clear with the Grid.

Negative growth

What is growth? Do PS-D and ♀♂ automatically entail growth? The PS-D, ♀♂ dynamics in the Grid can lead both to more abstract and to more sophisticated thoughts (descending in the Grid) and to more concrete thoughts that are closer to experience and more vital (ascending in the Grid). Rising to the more concrete is called negative growth; descending in the Grid is called positive growth. The notions of 'positive' and 'negative' must be understood in a mathematical sense; they indicate a direction and do not entail value judgements. Both movements are important. This must be related to Bion's starting point in this book: the dilemma between model and abstraction.

A negative growth moving from a more abstract form to concrete experience must be clearly distinguished from 'attacks on linking', which can also be read as an ascending movement in the Grid, but which entail a denudation of meaning rather than a development of the personality. These attacks on linking are the – (PS ↔ D, ♀♂, selected fact) that were discussed above.

Box 5.4   André Green's work of the negative

Bion's work is based on a great tolerance of fragmentation and regression. In *Attention and Interpretation* (1971) Bion states that we are all regressed, a statement that could be supplemented by 'we are all fragmented'. Throughout his work Bion asserts his tolerance of having no mental grip, of being in a state of abysmal ignorance. This is not a mental state of tranquility, but rather of anxiety and functioning under impending disaster. The importance of tolerating a lack of control is also seen in his ideas of being able to allow the non-present breast, a thought for a no-thing, leaving the elements of the Grid open, desaturation of ♀, allowing PS, the infinite, being in the Unknown (O) and finally no memory, no desire, no coherence, no understanding. Finally, this tolerance is manifest in Keats' concept of Negative Capability. Bion's approach is always concerned with the dialectic movement from fragmentation to coherence, but the creative process he is aiming at requires both.

When there is no movement, there is destruction instead of a creative force, usually as a reaction to psychic pain. Then there will be –♀♂ and –K, –L, –H. 'Greedy points' arise, attacks on linking, denudation of meaning and psychosis.

In *The Work of the Negative* (1999) André Green, who befriended Bion, works out the idea of the negative based on Freud. During the 1997 Bion Centennial in Turin, Green gave a key lecture where he linked his notion of the work of the negative to Bion's work. Green explains the negative as follows:

> I have proposed gathering together all these related mechanisms: repression, splitting or disavowal, foreclosure or rejection and negation, in the concept of 'the work of the negative'. This gathering is justified by the fact

that all these mechanisms are elaborations of the prototype of repression. All of them imply a judgment of acceptance or refusal: a question whose answer has to be given in terms of yes and no. This question is posed, as we have seen, in many ways, grounded in different contexts, dealing with various materials (instinctual impulses, affects, representations, perceptions, words, etc.) in Freud's conception. Among the various defence mechanisms described by Freud, Anna Freud and Klein (whose contribution includes denial) etc., this group is different from the others because its constituents directly imply this basic choice of acceptance or refusal in consciousness of derivatives that are rooted in the unconscious or the id.

So it is easy to show that Bion's ideas opposing the 'no thing' to the 'nothing' are deeply justified and can be related to Freud's elaborations even if one may stress the influence of Melanie Klein between them.

In this discussion of Bion's ideas, what is important is to make the distinction between the absence of the breast and the annihilation of the breast. In the first instance – the absence – which is found in normal and neurotic conditions, this situation leads to representations or, in other words, to fantasies. Freud's framework is applicable here. The other case – annihilation – would be more linked to the psychotic part of the personality and deals with a situation predominantly marked with destruction, a more precise form than abolition. This destruction, which can be understood either along Freud's line of foreclosure and rejection or according to Melanie Klein's annihilating anxieties, results not so much in archaic fantasies of destruction but even more, as Winnicott and I have shown, in a destruction of the psychic activity of representation which creates 'holes' in the mind, or feelings of void, emptiness etc. When Freud describes Schreber's delusions, he interprets them as processes of restitution after the withdrawal from reality. In other words, patchworks hiding scars or spaces that show some kind of loss of substance. Bion describes similar occurrences but for him the destruction takes the form of the consequence of excessive projective identification that evacuates the unassimilable contents of the mind: the ß-elements.

(Green 1998: 660–661)

PS-D, selected fact links versus narrative links

Finally, it is characteristic of Bion's approach that he is more interested in links between elements than in content. Narrative connections hinder the investigation of conjunctions between elements because causal or logical or narrative connections are predominantly produced by *Reason* rather than by a spontaneously emerging *Idea*. Logical Reason connections are closing and therefore usually situated in column 2.

Bion focuses radically on the spontaneously occurring creative links that result from a PS-D movement, instead of making deductions by reasoning.

Conclusion

The theory of elements and the construction of the Grid enabled Bion to develop his theory of thinking further. With the Grid as a tool, he could now describe in a fine-grained way how transitions between levels of thought and feelings happen and how these can go in the direction of psychic growth or not. Dealing with omnipotence and the capacity to suffer pain is crucial in this. Moreover, he could put thinking or the transition between elements in an abstract formula, which he hoped would facilitate communication between analysts and improve the intuition of the a-sensuous psychic reality that psychoanalysis requires. His Grid even enabled him to show the relation between the elements or categories of his Grid (representations, phenomena) and this a-sensuous, unknowable psychic reality, for which he coined the term psychoanalytic objects, and which may be compared with noumena. It takes at least three categories of the Grid to get a glimpse of such a psychoanalytic object.

Box 5.5 Antonino Ferro: the transformational mind during the session

Antonino Ferro has written several books about his imaginative and lively use of Bion's ideas in a private clinical psychoanalytic practice with both children and adults (Ferro 1996, 1999, 2002, 2005, 2006, 2008). Ferro's starting point is that of the Barangers (2008), Latin-American Kleinian psychoanalysts who saw the analytic situation as an unconscious couple phantasy, a bipersonal field. Ferro views this bipersonal field as an emotional field full of unmetabolized mental elements. Patient and analyst take elements from this field and transform them.

To conceive of this transformation Ferro relies on Bion's theories of thinking and transformation. The mind is the place where the unmetabolized sensorial β-elements of the bipersonal field are transformed by patient and analyst into α-elements, the bricks of symbolization. Ferro calls this 'alphabetization'. It is an original word for the 'waking dream thought' in the patient and analyst that Bion described. At some point Ferro compares the situation in the session with two mills transforming the elements of the emotional bipersonal field.

Ferro suggests that there is an β-α-gradient and the analyst must take care lest this gradient be reversed. This may happen when the mind of the patient or analyst overflows with or is flooded by unmentalized elements. Instead of α-elements being formed from β-elements, the existing α-elements are then evacuated from the psyche. Ferro describes the α-elements in a more concrete way than Bion did. In his view they can be occasionally experienced as oneiric, dream-like visual flashes that can occur during the session. The α elements can be linked and expressed in more elaborated metaphors, stories, which are often visual: the so-called C-elements of Bion. The analyst can use these C-elements to help the patient's 'mental apparatus for thinking thoughts' (the container-contained and PS-D oscillation) to transform the elements of the bipersonal field during a session. Ferro gives numerous clinical examples of this process.

Ferro adds a new dimension to this understanding of the transformational process of the bipersonal field: that of narratology (Umberto Eco). The metabolized elements of the emotional field or the α-elements can be seen as elements, with which a story can be created (a narration). Ferro calls them 'narrative derivatives'. They are inanimate or animate characters that can be told in different ways. Each session offers a virtually infinite number of possible stories. In order to allow one possible story to be told, many others are suppressed (what he calls 'narcotization'). To allow these stories to unfold, the analyst must maintain a very open and permeable state of mind of the analyst (Keats' negative capability).

An opposite attitude is a theoretization of what happens. This colonizes the emotional bipersonal field, hinders the free movement of the characters and blocks the unfolding of stories. In Ferro's view the analyst's role is not to decipher the meaning of the stories that occur in the transformation of the emotional bipersonal field but rather to co-narrate this field, helping to create the story or film. The creation of the bipersonal field is a continuous process and the link of existing stories and images with the emotional field is seen as unsaturated, as the story-making is a continuous process. Transformations that took place outside the session (for instance, night dreams) can be used in the session, like the rewinding of a recorded TV programme.

Ferro's focus is always the transformational process of the emotional field during the session and psychoanalysis is radically seen as the enhancing of this transformational capacity of the patient. From this point of view Ferro redefines the criteria of the analysability of a patient, the analytic frame, sexuality and aggression.

Notes

1 It was handwritten by Dr Hans Thorner and given in 1971 to Dr Rosa Beatrix, who gave it in 1994 to Francesca Bion, who published it in 1997.
2 Bion puts a lot of emphasis on the spontaneous perception of constant conjunctions when one is in the right relaxed state of mind or reverie. Therefore he calls Cs (conscious) a tropism; it turns effortlessly to the selected fact.
3 Bion saw his Grid as a mental climbing frame with which to train oneself outside the sessions.
4 Preconception is used in a broader sense here than a category in row D. In order to distinguish the two (Bion 1963: 73) Bion will use 'preconception' when he is concerned with the use of a thought (column 3 and 4) and 'pre–conception' when discussing a stage in the development of thinking (row D).

6 *TRANSFORMATIONS* (1965)

A transformation is a one-to-one mapping of a set of points. When this is done in the same plane, all the lengths remain the same. This is the case for translations, rotations, reflections and glide reflections. These transformations are called isometries or rigid motion transformations. It was the arts and the problem of perspective that brought the problems of projection and section. Projective geometry was taken a step further by Pascal, whose theorem states that the property of a geometrical figure is that it is invariant under section and projection.

This property of invariance under transformation will help Bion to delineate the psychoanalytic object further (see Box 8.7); he is now able to define it as a constant conjunction – an invariant connexion of elements.

When Descartes was confronted with new problems, mainly concerned with movements like curves in the trajectory of projectiles, the properties of light and heliocentric theory, he started from scratch, applying the algebraic method to geometry. Once he had freed himself from the limitations of visual representation on which Euclidean geometry was based, it became possible to study the curves of projectiles. The evolution in geometry showed that Euclid's definitions of basic concepts like point and line were no longer satisfactory for more complex problems like the projection of a circle on a sphere. Algebraic geometry could calculate four-dimensional geometry, a concept used in the theory of relativity which included a space-time dimension that we cannot perceive. In this way, our intellects are no longer limited to place and space.

Bion was familiar with theorems like those of Riemann and Poincaré, who studied the implications of changing the number of dimensions. Riemann extended algebraic geometry to n-dimensions. It is impossible to visualize or to grasp this from our basic sensuous three-dimensional knowledge of the world. The implication of non-Euclidean geometry of more than three dimensions is that the human mind reaches beyond common sense, experience, the data of the senses and intuition (Kline 1967). Mathematics are no longer seen as a body of truths, as they had been for more than 2,000 years, but rather as a body of unknowing and uncertainty.

Introduction to Transformations: *the essence of the book*

Bion had hoped that it would be possible to read *Transformations* without knowledge of his previous work, but he thought that he had failed in this aim (Bion 1965: Introduction). Indeed *Transformations* is a difficult and complex book. The experience of reading it creates the PS-D situation that Bion probably experienced himself, while writing it. Towards the end of the book and in the next book, *Attention and Interpretation*, a shift occurs and an illumination sets in.

To summarize: in *Learning from Experience* and in *Elements*, Bion had defined thinking as the transitions between the elements of psychoanalysis by means of 'PS-D, ♂♀, selected fact'. In *Transformations* he will study these transitions in more detail, making use of the geometrical theory of transformations (see Box 6.1). Drawing an analogy with algebraic geometry, Bion hoped that by using algebraic formulae, psychoanalysis could be freed from its descriptive limitations. He even asked for the assistance of a mathematician. The result is a difficult, strange and often confusing amalgam of mathematical and philosophical terminology. As Meltzer (1978) stated, Bion's mathematics became 'Dodgsonian' (after Charles Dodgson, the author of *Alice in Wonderland* whose *nom de plume* was Lewis Carroll).

By the end of *Transformations* he will reach the insight that one can not know the origin of what is transformed, which he calls O, and that knowledge remains at the level of representations. This insight will provide the basis for a major shift: Bion will change his focus from the representations of experiences to the unknowable reality itself behind these representations (O) and to the transformations that happen at this level (transformations in O). He will realize that mathematics and geometry fall short of apprehending this unknown reality of O and therefore he will look for new metaphors. Along with the algebraic notion of infinity, he will rely on Platonic Forms and the Kantian thing-in-itself and finally borrow expressions from the mystics who throughout the ages had also been confronted with the task of apprehending and conveying an unknowable, ineffable experience. After a long and difficult theoretical ascent, Bion will arrive at a clear and strong vision of 'transformations in O', which he will develop in his book *Attention and Interpretation*. Bion's insight about what he calls 'transformations in O' marks a caesura, a qualitative jump in the progression of his ideas. As a consequence, he will reformulate all the concepts that he had previously developed in reference to O. As I explained in the Introduction, I have used this caesura in Bion's work as a structuring principle in writing this book.

Visual metaphors of Transformations

In order to give an idea of the difficulty of apprehending what lies behind the representations in psychoanalysis, Bion uses the analogy of the relation of a field of poppies with the painter's representation of it on canvas. The painting is a transformation in which a number of things have remained invariant, allowing the field of poppies to be recognized as such. The position of the analyst in a session can be compared to the position of a person who is looking at the painting, while attempting to grasp what is happening in the field of poppies in reality. Bion evokes the analyst's position by still another image. The analyst is like one who perceives the reflection of a tree in water agitated by the wind. Emotions may be compared with the wind that distorts the reflection further. The analyst deals with a transformation in which certain aspects remain unaltered; these are called invariants. These invariants reflect the original reality. In the same vein, when psychic catastrophe occurs it is important to look at what is invariant in the pre-and postcatastrophic stage.

In a 1963 paper on the Grid that was first published in 1997 by F. Bion, Bion used the same example of the field of poppies and the transformation by painting. In this paper he proposes to represent the original reality of the poppies by O, and states that for psychoanalysis this O must always be an emotional experience.

Focusing on transformation

O is the ever unknown emotional stimulation, and Bion refers from the beginning to the notion of 'Das Ding an sich' from Kant. O gets transformed to something that can be perceived in the session, be it an act or a feeling or an image or an idea; in short, the categories or the elements of the Grid. If O is a shared experience in the session, it is easier for the analyst to have an idea of the transformations of O in the patient and to see the difference with the transformations in the analyst. Bion starts from clinical vignettes. He describes an imaginary patient referring to three different patients. The transformations of the patient can of course be in all the elements of the Grid. For the transformations of the analyst, the analyst has his psychoanalytic pre-conceptions as a tool, theories with their own invariants and transformations.[1] Bion refers to theoretical concepts of transference, the Oedipal situation and projective identification. Unlike the late Bion of 'no memory, no desire, no understanding, no coherence' (see Part II), Bion at this point sees the task of the analyst to see the transformations of the patient from the original authentic experience, by a transformation in his psychoanalytic pre-conceptions, and to give it back to the patient in as precise English as possible. This can be blurred by strong emotions. The analyst can also be blinded by looking from a cause-effect focus instead of looking at the constant conjunctions of invariants throughout the transformations. The imaginary patient suffers from hypochondriac pains in his knee and goes through a psychoanalytic controlled breakdown with a violent psychotic change after the breakdown. Bion looks at the pre- and postcatastrophic invariants.

In example A, Bion describes a psychotic breakdown and the invariants in the pre- and postcatastrophic phase in the patient and how this constant conjunction can be reflected in the theory of projective identification that the analyst uses. Example B is about a patient who uses splitting and projective evacuation of fragments as Bion described in his text *On Hallucination*, these theoretical pre-conceptions help Bion in his analytic transformation. Example C illustrates what Bion calls parasitism of the patient or 'chronic murder' by the patient: interventions by the analyst from his psychoanalytic pre-conceptions are all plausible but have no effect. The focus is on the transformations instead of on the content and meaning and this shows that there is an attack, destruction of the analytic activity by the transformations of the patient. The patient angrily reports during the session that the milkman has called, and here Bion makes the difference between a rigid motion and a projective transformation. If the expression about the milkman is transferential and says something about his relation with the analyst, this would be rigid motion transformation (his feelings to the analyst are repeated to the milkman), but here the patient is angry that the analyst seems not to notice that the milkman called – meaning for the patient that the milkman part of the analyst has visited his house and the analyst does not seem to know that. This is not a repetition but a huge deformation.

Applying geometrical concepts to transformations

As already mentioned, the notions of transformations and invariants are borrowed from geometry (see Box 6.1). We may argue that Bion applied three different geometrical transformations to psychoanalysis. First: *Rigid Motion Transformations* are transformations within a two-dimensional plane like in Euclidean geometry; the important characteristic for Bion is that they do not entail much deformation. For example, a square remains a square whether it is glided or rotated. To Bion this is a metaphor for what happens in the classical transference of whole objects in psychoanalysis. The repetition of Oedipal rivalry in transference would be an instance of such a classical situation. In a rigid motion transformation, the relationship between the invariants remains easy to perceive during the transformation.

Second: Compared with a rigid motion transformation in the same plane, a transformation from three dimensions to two dimensions, a *projective transformation*, geometrically causes gross deformations of the original object. For instance, when a sphere is projected onto a plane, it becomes a circle. This kind of transformation may be a metaphor for projective identification in the transference, where what is transmitted is deformed. The characteristic of deformation is what is important to Bion. The relation between the invariants remains stable but is much more difficult to recognize than in a simple projection. Bion gives the example of a patient who adds all kinds of material that has nothing to do with the experience that he is talking about, so that the invariants of the original experience become almost unrecognizable in the session.

Third: In geometry, *transformation in infinity* occurs when there is a projection within a space with infinite dimensions. This kind of geometrical transformation may be a metaphor for what happens in sessions with psychotic patients. Bion compares the position of the analyst in these cases with the position of the nuclear physicist where there are also no boundaries. He gives the example of a patient talking about ice cream, a word which comes back many sessions later without any link and may now be heard as 'I scream'. The use of the words 'Ice cream – I scream' are like widely separated points in space. In this kind of transformation it is very difficult to recognize the invariants and their conjunctions, which reflect the original object. Bion also refers to this transformation as a 'transformation in hallucinosis'. Links are attacked and disappear; points are scattered in infinity. There are no longer any thoughts to hold on to in infinity; it is experienced as an enormous frightening space without thoughts that can be seen as lines that give a frame. What remains for psychotics is as Pascal puts it: 'Ces espaces infinies, m'effrayent' (Bion 1965: 171).[2] Instead of thoughts giving rise to a three-dimensional containing space, there is continuous destruction of thoughts by the obstructive object in psychosis, which can be seen as a greedy, destructive, all-absorbing point.

Bion indicates that in transformation in hallucinosis it is less important to observe the content than the patient's relation to the material: a severe splitting and evacuation and a 'frail but stubborn warding off '. These phenomena are invariants that indicate the presence of a transformation in hallucinosis. Such patients appear to be in control, but actually they cannot tolerate anything that does not fit in with the way they see the world. The invariant relationship is characterized by an envy that attacks any new idea: the patient already knows everything. Frustration is not tolerated. No verbal thoughts exist; actions speak louder than words. The mind functions as an evacuating muscle. Any new thought is fragmented and evacuated. Bion compares this visually with a hyperbole; what we see is something that exceeds, that is no longer contained. There is no openness but an attitude of predetermination. The patient gratifies all his needs by means of his own creations; he is independent and above all rivalry, greed and meanness.

A new concept: the origin of transformations or O

In transposing the concept of transformations to a psychoanalytic session, Bion hypothesized that there is an unknowable emotional experience (O), which leaves an impression in both analysand and analyst. What is important in psychoanalysis is that part of O that is shared between analyst and analysand. When a container ($\female$) finds the experience, it can be 'realized' or transformed into a representation or thought. In this way each party will develop a different transformation of the emotional experience. A psychoanalysis can be regarded as a collection of such transformations.

Invariants in transformations and the psychoanalytic object

In geometry, the projected object can be derived by looking at the relation of the invariants: the position of some points remains the same throughout the transformations. For example, when a sphere is projected on a plane, this will result in a circle whose points maintain the same relation as in the sphere. As we have discussed, this relation between invariants is easy to discern in rigid motion transformations, difficult in projective transformations and nearly impossible in transformations in hallucinosis.

The ineffable psychoanalytic object can be apprehended from the constant conjunction between invariants during the transformation. These constant conjunctions cannot be logically derived, but they can be perceived and experienced in the ever-changing and transforming representations that reflect the psychoanalytic object, as the shadows reflect reality in Plato's allegory of the cave. As outlined in *Learning from Experience* and *Elements*, the perception of the conjunction between invariants (the psychoanalytic object), which remains the same in a flux of transformations, may happen as a selected fact (Poincaré). In order to allow this realization to happen, an open attitude of relaxed attention or reverie (corresponding to the C3, C4, D3 and D4 categories of the Grid) is required. In other words, one cannot know the psychoanalytic object, but one can experience or 'become' it. Bion here adopts Kant's terminology and posits O and the psychoanalytic object as a hypothetical 'Ding an sich' (thing-in-itself) which can manifest itself through secondary characteristics (phenomena) or transformations but remains in itself unknowable (a noumenon) (see Introduction).

Transformations in K

Looking for conjunctions in the material is different from looking for meaning and logical connections. Hume saw our understanding of the relations between phenomena as based on our perception of co-occurrences rather than on accurate perceptions of what he called necessary connexions (i.e. causal relationships). Looking for causality hinders our receptiveness to noticing conjunctions (and therefore it is put in the second column of the Grid). Although this way of thinking may be questionable for physical reality (for instance, when we put a nail in the wall, we can observe a clear link between cause and effect), Bion found the model of spontaneously detecting conjunctions a helpful way to think about the experience of the analyst dealing with emotional reality.

The fact that the analyst is not looking for cause-effect or narrative relationships does not mean that the patient will not do so. The patient's narrative explanations will depend on the emotional links (L, H, K and also –L, –H, –K), but Bion advises that the analyst should not pay too much attention to these narratives; it is better to be as open as possible and to allow ♀ to find and contain unknowable experiences and conjunctions between elements in the patient. These ♀ are not only verbal and visual but may be olfactory, sexual or auditive. Actually Bion is always giving the same message, advocating the need for relaxed attention, tolerance of frustration, adopting the PS position, not claiming to understand and letting ♀ find a ♂ (contained) spontaneously. The more his understanding of the thinking process deepens, the stronger this message becomes.

Attitudes that close down the transformational process

For Bion, the formation of a thought depends on the capacity to tolerate frustration when a sense-object is not present in reality. When this psychic experience of non-presence is found by a ♀, a thought happens: a thought for a no-thing. As in *Learning from Experience*, Bion continues to stress the link between K and frustration tolerance. This means that suffering and solitude constitute essential parts of psychoanalysis and the analyst must respect this. He repeats that when a patient closes himself to an emotional experience (column 2 of the Grid), this is a sign of suffering, indicating that frustration is too great.

The place of the analyst is in K and therefore it is not his aim to provide emotional gratification. Bion states that the analyst's openness to a constant conjunction (the analyst's K-link) may be hindered by a desire (unconscious) or a memory (unconscious), which leads arrow to a closing (column 2 of the Grid). Desire (arrow pointing to the right above desire) points to the future and memory (pointing to the left above memory) to the past, and both interfere with the analyst's openness in the present.

This closing psychic functioning can be destructive when the links are destroyed, as in psychosis. Bion discussed this as denudation of meaning, –K or –(♀♂, Ps ↔ D), the formula of thinking that he discussed in *Elements*. As we discussed under transformation in psychosis, this results in greedy, envious, hallucinatory no-objects that can be linked with what Bion had already called an internal obstructive object (see Box 3.4), which can be seen at work in severe personality disorders and psychosis. Bion experiments with space, time, notations by Greek mathematicians, envy and greed in psychosis and then combines this with his Grid. A point (.) can represent the no-thing (the not present thing), that can be thought. This thinking can be represented by movements in the Grid: ← ↑ and thus becomes ←.↑; when the dot is not present, we have a hallucinatory no-object ← ↑.

> The problem posed by ← ↑[3] can be stated by analogy with *existing* objects. ← ↑ is violent, greedy and envious, ruthless, murderous and predatory, without respect for the truth, persons or things. It is, as it were, what Pirandello might have called a Character in Search of an Author. In so far as it has found a 'character' it appears to be a completely immoral conscience. This force is dominated by an envious determination to possess everything that objects that exist possess including existence itself.
>
> (Bion 1965: 102)

> −K 'space' may be described as the place where space used to be. It is filled with no-objects which are violently and enviously greedy of any and every quality, thing, or object, for its 'possession' (so to speak) of existence.
>
> (Bion 1965: 115)

This means that annihilating something – for instance, a creative capacity or the love for someone because of envy or jealousy or hate or pain – becomes a kind of black hole that is not just a hole but a psychic place that exerts a negative destructive influence, not unlike what Freud described as the 'Maelstrom around the hole created in psychosis'.

Perception and naming of conjunctions

One of the elements of the constant conjunction can be used to name or define the constant conjunction, for instance 'Daddy' or 'Cat'. This is column 1. It differs from notation in column 3 in that the latter situates the constant conjunction within a larger whole by relating it to other constant conjunctions, for instance by relating it to the other elements in the Oedipus myth. This is why column 3 intrinsically involves more narrative and cause-effect characteristics. Deliberately looking for connections must never take over the Ps-D approach in which the perception of connections occurs spontaneously. When this deliberate searching does occur, the result is a closing and judgemental attitude, a moral outlook and therefore a primitive reaction. The perception of a connection can be related to Freud's conscious (Cs), which is determined by Bion as a tropism. A tropism is a spontaneous involuntary movement like that of a plant towards the light. Bion considers a ♀ spontaneously seeking and finding a ♂ in the same way. The direction of this Cs can again be marked by the movement on the Grid, ←↑ which reflects ♀ in search of ♂, what Bion calls 'in search of existence'. This tropism can also be negative: a greedy destructive internal object stripping off meaning; then it is represented as − ←↑.

The state I have represented by − ←↑ is one I can also represent in terms classifiable as C3, thus: − ←↑ may be personified by a non-existent 'person' whose hatred and envy is such that 'it' is determined to remove and destroy every scrap of 'existence' from any object which might be considered to 'have' any existence to remove. Such a non-existent object can be so terrifying that its 'existence' is denied, leaving only the 'place where it was'. This does not solve the problem because the place where it was, the nothing, is even more terrifying because it has, as it were, been further denied existence instead of being allowed to glut itself with any existence it has been able enviously to find. Denial of the existence of the 'place' where it was, only makes matters worse because now the 'point', marking the position of the no-thing, cannot be located.

(Bion 1965: 111–112)

Infinite and finite modes of psychic functioning

Bion remarks that when using the Grid, one must not forget that one is working at the level of representations or signs, rather than on the level of the emotional experience itself, with which there can be no direct contact. In this sense, we must also remember that O is nothing but a sign of the unknowable emotional experience in the session. This is a crucial insight and from now on, Bion will focus on O. The advantage of working with signs is that invariants and especially the connections between them can more easily be seen/experienced. In other words, signs facilitate a ♀ finding a ♂.

However, this also entails a problem. The representations and the connections between the representations take place in a finite world, whereas the links in O happen in an infinite world. Therefore, our models and the links we establish in three dimensions are inaccurate.[4] Bion felt that it was vitally important always to bear the distinction between a finite and an infinite mode of psychic functioning in mind, a distinction which he will finally consider to be more important than the distinction between conscious and unconscious psychic functioning: 'the differentiating factor that I wish to introduce is not between conscious and unconscious but between finite and infinite' (Bion 1965: 46).

A turning point in Bion's work: looking for direct contact with transformations in O

At this point in Bion's work, we witness a major transition, a turning point in his approach. Until this point he had studied the origin of thinking emotional experiences, in other words how they become mental representations and are further transformed. He hypothesized an unknowable reality behind the representations, which he named O. Now, after his long search about how experiences and perceptions are transformed in representations, he shifts his focus from the representations to O itself. He illustrates with an example how difficult it is to be in contact with O through representations.

> Imagine that the original transformed (O) is a number of marbles of a different color and diameter. A first transformation consists of putting in a second tray as many 1-inch diameter marbles as there are green marbles in tray one. This is the O for the following transformation, in which it is asked that as many marbles are put in tray 3 as there are blue marbles in tray 2. When we do not know the rules of the transformation, it will be quasi-impossible to deduct from tray 3 the original tray 1(O).
>
> (Bion 1965: 127)

In the same way, the Grid was used to elaborate signs in an attempt to see connections and transitions. The Grid is not bound to one theory but offers a meta-theoretical tool for describing how feelings and thoughts are transformed, which helps the user to adopt a non-closing attitude. By using the Grid one avoids making causal links to the past, to memories or to psychoanalytic theories. However, the contact with what the sign O represents is not established by using the Grid because the Grid and T(K) remain at the level of the representations.

This is a major realization which marks a turning point, a caesura in Bion's work. It can be situated in the transition from chapter 10 to 11; more precisely on page 138 of the Karnac 1984 reprint of *Transformations* (Bion 1965). Bion will now direct his attention to the possibility of making direct contact with what is behind the representations. This direct contact is called a 'transformation in O or T(O)'. This is distinct from a transformation in K, which was represented by the ♀♂ and PS-D movement between the elements of the Grid. According to Bion, a T(O) brings about a major change; it makes psychoanalysis terminable (Bion 1970). Bion compares the contact with O to what happens in a state of passion. To use Lyotard's (2000: 19) phrase, 'It takes you from behind'; you cannot want it.

Defining O

It is impossible to *know* O but one may experience or become O. This becoming O involves a change called a 'transformation in O'. We have a resistance towards this experience of O, a tendency to close ourselves off from it. Actually all logical thinking about clinical material and pinning it down with intellectual understanding are forms of resistance to the contact with O. Real thoughts stemming from O do not need a thinker.

While he now began to concentrate on O itself, Bion did not abandon his former approach, but he formulated a new model that could serve as a pre-concept, an unsaturated ♀ for this Unknown. This new model is based on Plato, Kant and religious mysticism. These three sources have in common a concern with the inaccessibility of reality behind a curtain of illusions.

Plato supposes Forms which are unknowable. According to Plato, meaning is nothing but a reference to these Forms. Kant makes a similar distinction between the ineffable noumenon and the reflection of it in phenomena (see Introduction). According to the mystics, finally, there is a spiritual essence that is unknowable but that can be incarnated and experienced. Paraphrasing Meister Eckhart, this is godhead, of which god is but the representation.

Because O is by definition unknowable, and the sign O is but an attempt to represent something ineffable, Bion gives a negative definition of O.

To qualify O for inclusion amongst the column I categories by defining its definitory qualities I list the following negatives: Its existence as indwelling has no significance whether it is supposed to dwell in an individual person or in God or Devil; it is not good or evil; it cannot be known, loved or hated. It can be represented by terms such as ultimate reality or truth. The most, and the least that the individual person can do is to be it. Being identified with it is a measure of distance from it. The beauty of a rose is a phenomenon betraying the ugliness of O just as ugliness betrays or reveals the existence of O. L, H, K are links and by virtue of that fact are substitutes for the ultimate relationship with O which is not a relationship or an identification or an atonement or a reunion. The qualities attributed to O, the links with O, are all transformations of O and *being* O. The rose *is* itself whatever it may be *said* to be. The human person *is* himself and by 'is' I mean in both instances a positive act of being for which L, H, K are only substitutes and approximations.

(Bion 1965: 139–140)

Box 6.2   A rose: essence and representation, noumenon and phenomenon

There is a rose as idea, form and essence that takes form in a real rose. The beauty of the rose, its colour and perfection, originates in our mind. Borges (1972: 161), blind himself at that time, wrote a poem about the beautiful, invisible rose that the blind Milton held before his face and could not see but glows forever in poetry. The same year, however, he (Borges 1972: 271) writes about the illumination that the words may allude to but that do not express the eternal rose; they are not a mirror of it but 'a thing added to the world'. This is quite close to the late Bion (see Box II.1) who sees images and words not as a step in the psychic processing of an experience, sensation or feeling but as dimensions (vector) on their own with an own evolution that may touch or not at the experience to whom they refer.

The same idea that a word only alludes to a thing is expressed in Gertrude Stein's (1922) famous 'A rose is a rose is a rose' or in Shakespeare's (1600, *Romeo and Juliet*) 'a rose by any other name would smell as sweet'. Bion (1991: 203) writes: 'Even a "beautiful woman" is a shade of a shade of a shade'.

The realization that there is another unknowable world of which we are part but which is not human-centred is close to Bion's conception of O and is often referred to by the mystics.

The rose is without why; it blooms because it blooms;
It cares not for itself, asks not if it's seen.
(Angelus Silesius (1986 (1737): 285)

The change that results in Bion's approach is great. From K, he saw all feelings and thoughts as preconceptions for possible realizations. But O itself, or Reality, cannot be known or approached through K. Until this point, Bion had focused on seeing constant conjunctions in thoughts and feelings (letting a ♀ find ♂ in a state of relaxed attention). In other words, for T(K) he facilitated a realization of connections between different thoughts and feelings (what he called functions of the personality). For T(O) he focuses on the relation of thoughts and feelings with O.

Growth, truth and openness to O

The concept of O allows Bion to give a new definition of psychic truth. He now defines truth in relation to O, as being open to what O represents, rather than closing it off. Truth is thus not a moralizing judgement in terms of 'right or wrong'. In *Learning from Experience* Bion had already shown how in relation to K or thinking, a moralizing judgement was a way to preclude K. In *Transformations* he repeats this in the light of O: this kind of moralistic judgement is the opposite of openness to O.

The same is true for attempts to use a theory of causation and narration: true or false. Such a theory is based on reason, and closes both the spontaneous PS–D oscillation in T(K) and the openness to O in T(O). It is clear to Bion that 'Evidence of the employment of a theory of causation is evidence of the operation of a theory that is not adequate' (Bion 1965: 63).

The theory of causation is only valid in the domain of morality and only morality can *cause* anything. Meaning has no influence outside the psyche and causes nothing.

(Bion 1965: 59, footnote)

Without truth or an openness to O, thinking is poison for the mind, and can lead to a deterioration of the personality. From this perspective the second column ψ of the Grid can now be defined as a closing off of the emergence of O.

Reconsidering former concepts in the light of Transformations in O

The relation with O casts a new light on former concepts, including transformations in K, the Grid, the psychoanalytic object and psychopathology. I will discuss these dimensions one by one.

Transformations in K: although Bion's focus is now on O and trying to experience-become O, he does not discard his former approach using T(K). However, K is now seen in the light of O. K is the becoming conscious of O. K is the only way to apprehend and represent a T(O) experience, but it is never the experience itself. The movement is always from O to K: it is O that finds K spontaneously, never K that finds O.

The Grid: any element in the Grid can be reconsidered according to its position on what Bion calls the Reality scale, meaning the distance from O. In this way, β-elements are closest to O; theories are far removed from it. On the Reality scale, 'that is Form and reminder, deity and incarnation, hyperbole[5] and evacuation' (Bion 1965: 152–153), O is represented by Form, deity and hyperbole, while reminder, incarnation and evacuation are the points where O can be apprehended by K.

The psychoanalytic object (see Box 8.7): in Bion's new vision, the psychoanalytic object is now redefined as the essence of a personality, the O of a person, the irreducible self that an analyst and analysand can intuitively come into contact with in experience. At this point the aim of psychoanalysis shifts from knowing about O to becoming O: 'The interpretation should be such that the transition from *knowing about* reality to *becoming real* is furthered' (Bion 1965: 153).

Psychopathology: In defining psychopathology in reference to O, we may say that psychotics cannot stand the contact with O; they are not protected. They are 'orphans of O' (Grotstein 2001); they cannot tolerate the infinite as discussed in transformation in hallucinosis because they do not have a capacity for thinking to hold on to. To Bion geometry, for instance, did not originate because geometrical forms reflect reality; it originated to provide a means of getting a hold or creating a space so that infinity becomes bearable. In borderline individuals a contact with O is possible but it is mostly overwhelming. Borderlines have some capacity for mentalization but it is fragile; a way of looking at it is that their psychic skin has holes in it and does not protect them enough from exposure to O. Neurotics, finally, are too closed off from O. They rely mostly on the first and closed columns of the Grid; a defence, a rational harness shields them from O, and hence vitality is missing.[6]

O and mysticism/language of achievement

Bion asserts that we can never grasp O through philosophy, because it is what lies outside our (categorizing) mind. Mysticism adopts a different approach than philosophy by saying that one cannot know O but one has to become it. For the mystic, the direct contact with an Ultimate Reality is a life-changing experience, for which there are no words; it is an experience that can only be addressed indirectly. This experience is described as an illumination or satori in Zen. Bion does not advocate such a mystic experience, but he focuses on the getting to know, the experience of the unknowable emotional essence of a psychoanalytic session. In this sense, he finds that the terminology, metaphors and method of the mystics are more suited to apprehend the unknowable emotional reality of the session than the mathematical descriptions he had used before. Bion uses the language of the mystics to find containers to communicate about a transformation in O, without actually being a mystic. Like Augustine, he suggests suppressing[7] memory, desire, the understanding and the senses in order to facilitate experiencing the O of the emotional experience in a session. From this experience, a 'Language of Achievement' can arise (see Box 8.8). It is no coincidence that Bion turns to poetry to find a language that emerges spontaneously from an experience of becoming. In poetry, language is not defining something (see column 1 of the Grid), but doing something. It creates a new experience, liberating the reader from former ways of seeing, defining and naming.

Conclusion

In studying the transformation of elements, Bion discerned several types of transformations (rigid motion, projective and transformations in hallucinosis). At a certain point, he realized that by thinking in this way he remained at the level of representations. These are transformations in Knowledge, and although Knowledge in Bion's view is different from Reason, logical thought and narration, a more fundamental transformation can take place. Bion suggested that real change happens at a level behind the representations. Because it is unrepresented, this layer is infinite and unknowable. In working from this layer he moves from a philosophical empiricist background to draw on philosophical idealism (Plato, Kant) (see Introduction). The attempt to be in touch with and experience O brings about a new kind of psychoanalysis, now focused on T(O) rather than on T(K). However, the one does not preclude the other, and Bion reformulated the concepts that had taken form in his studies of transformations in K from the perspective of transformations in O.[8]

Box 6.3   The noumenon: two examples

Grotstein (Bion Centennial Meeting Turin, 1997) and Meltzer (Bion Centennial Meeting London, 1997) both gave telling examples of the clinical use of the noumenon, in Kantian terms or psychoanalytic object, in Bion's words: that is, an a-sensuous constellation that is not yet differentiated but that can take many forms or phenomena on the vertex from infinity to the finite.

I recall an analytic session when I remembered an episode from my medical internship. An ex-girl-friend suddenly contacted me unexpectedly and told me that she was flying to San Francisco but would be making a brief stopover at Chicago airport (I was interning in Chicago at the time). We saw each other briefly. I recall being very unemotional about the encounter. Later, when I saw her plane take off towards the west, I experienced a series of uncanny visualizations. First, the image of the aeroplane seemed to darken into a shadowy form. Then it was transformed into the image of a huge raven, and I even imagined that I saw the wings flapping. Next, it became even more eerie, perhaps mechanical, but unlike an aeroplane. Every time I subsequently read Kant or authors who cited Kant, the memory of that uncanny episode returned to me. Finally, when I introduced this into analysis with Bion, he helped me to understand it as a return of the memory of a very early significant loss that had occurred in the first few months of my life, but he employed such terms as 'thing-in-itself', 'beta-element', and 'noumenon' in his analysis of my experience. Thus, if I err in my Kantian scholarship, I feel that I am in very good company indeed.

(Grotstein 1999: 143)

That is the position of the child in relation to these internal parents: as far as really seeing them and seeing them with anything other than this nebulousness, it just doesn't happen. The clearest view we ever get of the internal parents is in our dreams. My patient's dream of the dome of the Duomo is the clearest sight she will ever have of the internal mother's breast – and its beauty, and its meaning to her. It is on this 'Siena – Firenze' axis, which of course is keeping the father's penis at least a few hundred kilometres away from the mother's breast, which is about the state she is in at present – that she can tolerate the idea of the mother's breast, and its meaning to her.

(Meltzer 1997: 65)

Notes

1 Bion states that the analyst is ideally in C3, C4, D3, D4 and has his psychoanalytic theoretical pre-conceptions (so not the category D 'preconceptions' of the genetic vertical axis of his Grid, but 'pre-conceptions' concerning use and therefore the last four columns, and as these psychoanalytic pre-conceptions are theoretical here, the E and the F rows).

2 Later, in *Attention and Interpretation*, both these transformations in infinity and the hallucinatory layer will have a less pathological connotation than they have here and this kind of transformation will become the core of psychic change.

3 A movement in the Grid which represents attacks on linking and stripping of meaning, for instance C or D elements that get denuded to beta-elements. This is different from what Bion formulated as 'negative growth', which is also a movement in the Grid that goes from more abstract elements to more concrete ones that goes with an increased liveliness.

4 In order to represent only a part of the physical world, physics requires at least 30 dimensions, and colours and time only exist because our brain makes them.

5 A manifestation of O may be seen as a hyperbole that is arising from O.

6 In Chapter 13 this idea is elaborated in making a distinction in looking at psychopathology from K and from O, which leads to another point of view of pathology from the O-vertex.

7 In *A Memoir of the Future* (Bion 1991: 232) he suggests that 'opacity' of memory and desire is a better term than repression of it.

8 This may seem abstract and theroretical, but it is actually rooted in clinical practice and has a lot of clinical implications. Indeed insight by verbal thought is a small zone, interaction happens mostly at an unrepresented non-verbal level and real change happens predominantly through new experiences.

Part II

AFTER THE CAESURA

Transformations
in O

Introduction

At the end of *Transformations*, Bion described transformations in O. This was a far-reaching insight that changed his life. While transformations in K are transformations at the level of thinking, which involve giving a mental representation to experiences, transformations in O happen at the level of an experience which is not yet represented. They are new living experiences. I have the impression that this revelation of transformations in O amounted to a 'catastrophic' change for Bion.[1] He revised his theories, began to write in a different style, relocated and began to live in another way. This required of him a radical faith in another zone, a zone that cannot be entered with categorizing reason: another world of psychic functioning which now and then surfaces by taking a form, as in dreams. In order to be in contact with this zone, an attitude which can actually be seen as letting go is needed – a radical psychoanalytic attitude such as thorough free-floating attention. Once one switches to rational, controlling thought the contact is lost. One cannot want it. Bion was already approaching this attitude through his development of reverie and relaxed attention to enable transformation in K. But now it became something different. Metaphorically speaking, a quantitative progression led to a qualitative change. Seen from O, all Bion's concepts and the attitude he advocated acquired another sense. He elaborated and deepened this insight in his last theoretical book, *Attention and Interpretation*, which was also the last book that he wrote in London. After he had completed this book, he felt that his mind had been unfettered and he wanted to reconsider everything he had written from the dimension of O, the Unknown or Ultimate Infinite Reality. This is the only thing that matters to a psychoanalyst, according to him. We now see a remarkable change in his style and way of writing, teaching, talking and living.

Box II.1 Caesura

The world is unknown and mysterious and not what we perceive and think. From the beginning of his work, Bion focused on an unknowable a-sensuous truth that governs the phenomena in a sensuous world. It is in disruptive experiences, cracks in our thinking and perception that it is revealed that there are other ways of looking and thinking about the unknown world. These breaks are embedded in Bion's (1989) notion of caesurae, which are a point where worlds meet. At these points we have the feeling of something else that yet remains the same. It is another transformation of constant conjunctions. Throughout his whole work Bion focuses on 'seeing constant conjunctions' rather than looking for causal and narrative links and reasoning that are limited to one dimension of psychic functioning. Bion mentions many coexisting worlds like conscious-unconscious; psyche-soma; waking-sleeping; past-future; pre-natals-post-natals; dreaming and waking life; differentiated-undifferentiated.

With his paper *Caesura* Bion (1989) envisages a new step, where these worlds move along different vectors that may meet or not. In the same view elements like beta and alpha-elements and container and contained can be seen as different vectors that can meet or not. Conjunctions are then, for instance, the meeting of the vector on which a beta-element moves and the vector on which an alpha-element moves.

From this perspective, chance and the unknown come to play a much greater role. As there are an infinite number of vectors, the probability of observing conjunctions of vectors is small. It is typical that in *Caesura*, Bion sees change as unpredictable and compares it to the game of snakes and ladders. Likewise, Bion sees a personality as an invisible and unknowable essence expressed in and consisting of different layers, like the skins of an onion. These may meet and then constant conjunctions may be revealed in the transformation, a constant conjunction pointing at the unknowable essence.

This way of looking at psychic reality as an infinite number of vectors that may meet or not is a de-constructive approach that breaks our regular thinking and understanding that lives a life on its own. It opens us to an unknown world. There is a resistance to being open to these meetings of vectors, in other words to experiences that have not happened yet. Hence Bion's saying that one rather loves old friends in hell than new friends in heaven (Bion 1989).

Bion (1997) compared the caesura in this sense with a glass painting from Picasso (in *Untitled* and in *A Memoir of the Future*); you may look at the same thing but from different sides, different vectors.

> It seems to me that we need to develop the capacity to use a screen, a resistance, a caesura, as Picasso could use a plate of glass. Look on *this* side and you see a delineation of a psycho-somatic disorder; look on *this* side and you see a soma-psychosis.
>
> (Bion 1991: 487)

> Investigate the caesura; not the analyst; not the analysand; not the unconscious; not the conscious; not sanity; not insanity. But the caesura, the link, the synapse, the (counter-)transference, the transitive-intransitive mood.
>
> (Bion 1989: 56)

The caesurae can be seen as gates where it is possible to be in contact with both sides or vectors and therefore one is able to speak a language of achievement that can penetrate in both worlds.

It is also possible to understand Bion's way of answering questions in the light of the concept of the caesura (see Chapter 11), making long associative detours to subjects that have seemingly nothing to do with the question, letting a meeting happen between these subjects.

Box II.2 Continuity before and after the caesura in Bion's work

After the caesura in Bion's work, there is a radical shift to a focus on transformations in O rather than in K. However, as Bion remarks himself in *Transformations* and in *Caesura*, when a catastrophic change occurs in a patient, there is nevertheless a great deal of continuity of functioning before and after the caesura. Also in Bion's work, even with the dramatically changed focus from K to O, there are invariants in his approach. Bion advocates a non-rational attitude to facilitate transformations in both K and in O and stresses that both types of transformations require a state of mind in which the automatic, creative PS-D oscillation can do its work (see *Learning from Experience* for T(K) and *Attention and Interpretation* for T(O)). Moreover, he sees the essence of psychoanalysis, the psychoanalytic object, as a-sensuous in both T(K) and in T(O). In T(K) he sees it as an a-sensuous essence that needs at least three Grid categories to be revealed (*Elements*), while in T(O) it is a kind of basic a-sensuous Form or constant conjunction existing already in O that finds forms in K to be expressed (*Attention and Interpretation*).

Note

1 A catastrophe is the fourth act in classical Greek tragedy, the climax of tension which is the beginning of the denouement. Bion (1965, 1966, 1970) uses the notion of catastrophic change at several places in his work. It is a disruptive change with an emotional upheaval while there are invariants before and after the catastrophe (see also Box II.2).

7 BIOGRAPHY, 1967–1979

Given his age, Bion needed space and time to express his insights at the time he was formulating his new ideas in *Attention and Interpretation* in the 1960s. He often quoted the lines of Ecclesiasticus (xxxviii, 24), 'wisdom cometh to the learned man by opportunity for leisure'.

He focused more and more on changes in the a-sensuous Unknown of the psyche, as Meltzer expressed well at Bion's memorial by repeating the verse that Bion (1979: 257) quoted from his beloved Milton:

So much the rather Celestial light
Shine inward, and the mind through all her powers
Irradiate, there plant eyes, all mist from thence
Purge and disperse, that I may see and tell
Of things invisible to mortal sight.

(Milton 1674, *Paradise Lost*: 101)

We can observe a shift from Bion's use of mathematical forms or metaphors and an empirical philosophical approach to apprehending psychic transformations to the use of religious mystical metaphors and reliance on transcendental philosophical concepts to apprehend psychoanalytical reality.

The change that took place while Bion was still in London had major consequences, among which was Bion's move from London to the US. Grotstein, Bail and Brandschaft invited several London analysts to Los Angeles. Amongst them were Rosenfeld, Segal, Thorner, Joseph, Guntrip and Winnicott. In 1967, Bion and Mason were also invited to Los Angeles. Following this visit, the Bions decided quite unexpectedly to leave England in 1968 and to go and live in California. The Masons also moved to LA, while Bion's colleague and friend, F. Philips, went to live in Sao Paolo. Later, Philips invited Bion to Brazil several times to give lectures.

Moving from London to LA at 71 years of age was not an obvious course for Bion. He would see his children less and had to leave his friends, patients and students and his house and cottage. His children were still teenagers at this moment, and given his own painful story of separation from his parents as a child, leaving them in boarding school must have been difficult. Moreover, he was obliged to practise without his medical degree and without insurance in a city where psychoanalysis, and certainly Kleinian analysis, was not as well known as London and in fact was regarded with suspicion and even hostility.

Bion gave few explanations concerning his move. Mason (1989) recalls that Bion told him that California reminded him of the warm India to which he had never returned. To Grotstein, Bion said that he did not want 'to be loaded with honours and sink without a trace', but Meltzer (1985) writes that Bion's semi-retirement left his students and colleagues in a state of incomprehension. Mason (personal communication) recalls that at the farewell party for Mason and Bion, Meltzer tried to dissuade him by saying, 'they will chew you up and spit you out like a pip'; Hanna Segal advised them to try it for five years; Money-Kyrle whispered that he wished he could accompany them. Meltzer states that Bion's departure made his London colleagues feel accused of being 'the container that squeezed the life out of the mystic and his ideas' (Meltzer 1985: 520). Pines (1987) suggests that Bion did not want to be Klein's successor. However, Francesca Bion contradicts the speculations of Bion's London colleagues about the reasons for his departure: 'he did not leave in order to retire from the practice of psychoanalysis, nor as a money-making exercise, nor to spend a sybaritic existence in the Californian sunshine' (Bion, F. 2000: 14).

In Los Angeles, the Bions moved into a house in Brentwood near Beverly Hills and Hollywood with a large swimming pool (a former water-polo player, Bion swam 50–100 lengths each morning in an unheated swimming pool). Initially his analytic practice was based at home, in his garage which he converted into a consulting room (as was usual among many colleagues in LA) until the neighbours complained that this was not a business area. Then for a short while he had an office with Mason in Beverly Hills and then took an office for himself, furnished with only a couch and a chair placed in the middle of the room: only the essence of the psychoanalytic meeting mattered. It is difficult to imagine Bion in Beverly Hills, and indeed he remained utterly British. One of his adolescent patients even brought his friend along to the session to see this strange 'Sherlock Holmes' (Mason 1989).

Working in the US was not easy. Many of the colleagues who had invited the Kleinians to come over felt threatened when they began to attract patients and candidates.

Although several Institutes had shown interest in working with Bion, there were no real offers. Bion did not apply to become a member of the LA Psychoanalytic Society. When Mason became the scientific secretary of this society, he organized a lecture about the work of Bion. Bion chose to talk about cures. At the conference Bion described an opera singer who came for analysis and made a loud shriek for some minutes, and then Bion interpreted that perhaps she was putting her anxiety about being thrown out of the building into him. Then he asked: is this a cure? Nobody reacted; the lecture lasted ten minutes. Mason asked two questions, feeling panicked as he had organized the conference. There was further silence and after 20 embarrassing minutes, two thirds of the hall was empty (Mason, personal communication). Bion was also invited to the Psychoanalytic Western (Psychoanalytic Societies of the West Coast) for a conference on the theme: New and Old, where he suggested that participants should come up with new things that were actually old things but improved, but this did not work. Then there was the Menninger lecture, where he shocked his public (see Chapter 11). Grotstein also organized local seminars (Bion 2013).

In 1970 *Attention and Interpretation* was published. This work, which Bion had written in England, was regarded as very controversial in the US. The Los Angeles Psychoanalytic Society and Institute were convinced that psychoanalytic training had to be traditional and not Kleinian. The Institute was split concerning these matters, with Greenson as a well-known opponent of the Kleinians. Ralph R. Greenson was professor at UCLA and an influential analyst who was well integrated in the Californian psychoanalytic, academic and movie scene. Marilyn Monroe and several other film stars were in treatment with him. Once, when asked about the similarity between India and California, Bion answered: 'well, there can always be a tiger at the bottom of the garden'; according to Albert Mason, he was implying Greenson (personal communication, Mason 2014). The police were informed by an unknown analyst that Mason, Isaacs and Bion were practising without a medical license, as many practitioners from Europe did. Thanks to the work of Peter Loewenberg, they were fortunately able to obtain a research psychoanalytic license, which was a new category. During this very difficult period, Susanna Isaacs from London joined Bion and Mason in Los Angeles. She applied to be admitted to the LA Psychoanalytic Institute and was refused, which is strange as she had an American MD and was a respected psychoanalyst in London who had succeeded Winnicott in his practice at Paddington Green (personal communication by Mason, who added that it was maybe due to their second thoughts after having admitted him). *Cogitations* includes the following comment on this stressful period:

> The relationship between myself and my colleagues in Los Angeles could be accurately described as almost entirely unsuccessful. They are puzzled by, and cannot understand me – but have some respect for what they cannot understand. There is, if I am not mistaken, more fear than understanding or sympathy for my thoughts, personality or ideas. There is no question of the situation – the emotional situation – being any better anywhere else.
> (Bion 1992: 334)

When quoting these lines, Francesca Bion adds that she and her husband nevertheless experienced many long-lasting friendships and deeply enjoyed art and music in LA (Bion, F. 1995).

While he was living in California, Bion worked on three projects at the same time. First there was the trilogy *The Dream* (1975), *The Past Presented* (1977, published in Rio de Janeiro) and *The Dawn of Oblivion* (1979, first published by Clunie Press). In 1991, Francesca succeeded in getting these books published in one work: *A Memoir of the Future*. The books are mainly written as a dialogue, and consist of parts and layers that interact and communicate, like visions and developments on different vectors as a reflection of the personality or the mind itself. Bion was perhaps attempting to let the reader experience his insights.

Second, and around the same time as the former books, Bion wrote his autobiography *The Long Weekend*. It was later complemented by Francesca Bion with unpublished letters and texts – *All My Sins Remembered: Another Part of a Life* and *The Other Side of Genius: Family Letters* – and with Bion's theoretical diary and notebook *Cogitations*.

Third, Bion gave several seminars and supervisions in this period. In only a short period of time, he visited Brazil, New York, Rome and London. Francesca Bion edited and published most of these talks posthumously.

It is very enlightening to read these open, truthful works from this period side by side and get in touch with Bion from three different vertices. Meltzer (1985) has written that being able to read these works together offers an opportunity to get to know Bion better than was possible in real life as he was very private.

The last 'Californian' Bion is often presented as the mystical, transcendental Bion, but we can doubt this. The mystical metaphors, which first appeared in *Transformations*, reached their peak of intensity in *Attention and Interpretation*, the last book that he wrote in England. He continued to focus on the Unknown but seemingly more in a Socratic philosophical way while living in the US. In *Elements* Bion represented the process of thinking emotional reality as PS-D, $\female\male$. Unexpectedly he ended *Attention and Interpretation* with the conclusion that for T(O) the same mental stance of PS-D, $\female\male$ and selected fact seems to be optimal, now translated into the oscillation patience-security. The formula thus came to be a container for psychoanalysis itself. With this realization Bion ended his theoretical writings. From this point no more purely theoretical work would follow. Bion's ideas were no longer overtly mystical; we now rather see a Socratic Bion, practising a not-knowing and questioning attitude with an insistence on experiencing.

The work that Bion produced in this last period is marked not only by a change in content, but also in style and tone. His writing is more affective, open and free. He is focusing on truth, less condensed, more tolerant of fragmentation and certainly more provocative. He is looking for a new style of writing that is able to interact with and contain his way of thinking, while preserving a mental freshness and liveliness. We see this change in writing explicitly in the three books of *A Memoir of the Future*. The demarcation of this new period is also manifest in his theoretical diary *Cogitations*, as described by Borgogno and Merciai (2000). Bion's war writings from the 1970s also differ in style from those of the 60s.

Not everyone welcomed this change. Many missed his dry and rational approach from the 60s – based on Knowledge (K). O'Shaughnessy (2005), for instance, labelled Bion's works from the last period as 'less disciplined, less coherent'. As already stated in the Introduction, Bion was still becoming, even at the age of 80, and we may see this profound change as a transformation in O.

At last Bion decided to return to the UK and also to visit India for the first time since his departure so many years ago, and Meltzer started to arrange things in Oxford for him. Francesca Bion describes these last moments:

By 1978 we were seeing less and less of our family owing to their work commitments; after lengthy discussions during that year and early 1979 we decided to return to England but were unwilling to sever ties with California entirely. We sold our house and bought an apartment, hoping to divide our time between the Western world and Europe. Arriving in London on September 1st, Bion set to work (as usual) while I once more went house-hunting in the Oxford area. There were a few analysts in Oxford at that time, including Oliver Lyth, Isabel Menzies, Donald Meltzer and Matti Harris. Bion's arrival added a stimulus to the hope that the nucleus of a psychoanalytic group could be formed where none existed.

Having found a suitable house, we moved in at the beginning of October, the container arrived from the docks, and unpacking began. I recall the hours we spent emptying cartons of books, a tedious job but one mixed with the pleasure of meeting 'old friends' again.

It has been suspected and believed that Bion wanted to return to England because he knew that he faced imminent death, but although it would have been natural for him to accept that at the age of eighty-two his days were numbered, taking steps to keep a foothold in California and agreeing to work with a group in Bombay in January 1980, were not the actions of a dying man – unless he is given to gross denial. Bion was, above all else, scrupulously honest with himself and others.

He became ill in the third week of October: myeloid leukaemia, diagnosed on November 1st, developed with extraordinary rapidity and, mercifully, quickly led to his death on November 8th.

(Bion, F. 1995)

Bion's laconic comment on his diagnosis was: 'life is full of surprises, most of them unpleasant' (Mason, personal communication, 2014).

8 ATTENTION AND INTERPRETATION (1970)

Introduction

In studying the thinking of emotional experiences or transformation in K, Bion developed a theory including concepts such as α-function, β-elements, constant conjunction, PS-D, selected fact and container-contained. He linked together and deepened these concepts by applying first the mathematical theory of functions (in *Learning from Experience*), the theory of elements (in *Elements*) and finally the geometrical theory of transformations (in *Transformations*). The latter produced an insight that led to a catastrophic change in his ideas about psychic change. He realized that with his theory of thinking or transformations in K, he remained at the level of representations, while fundamental psychic changes (transformations in O) happen at a not yet represented, or undifferentiated psychic level. In *Attention and Interpretation* Bion develops the theme of transformations in O further. Focusing on T(O) entails a different kind of psychoanalysis and requires a different frame of mind of the analyst than working with T(K). Bion now redefined the concepts he had developed in his theory of thinking in relation to T(O), as he had already begun doing in *Transformations*.

Language and O

Words have a sensuous background and are therefore closing of T(O). This is problematic as psychoanalysis relies on the use of words. Poetry has the potential to offer a way out of this problem as in poetry words can transcend the concrete sensuous situation and become a 'Language of Achievement' (see Box 8.1), a language that is in contact with the origin of psychic reality, with the a- sensuous, undifferentiated, unrepresentable O. It is a language that is both a substitute for action (as in transformation in knowledge) and an action, something new that happens (transformation in O). Bion even intended to produce a poetic anthology for the analyst (Bion, P. 1997; Bion, F. 1985). He stated that poetic language would be a 'language that has a counterpart of durability and extension in a domain where there is no more space and time' (Bion 1970: 2). However, according to Bion, there is also a danger in using poetry. The beauty of a poetic (and religious) approach may become a substitute for the Truth (as Plato had already warned) rather than an apprehension of it. Moreover, although psychoanalysts are expected to speak a so-called 'language of achievement' (see Box 8.1), a language that is in contact with O and evokes psychic change, we cannot expect psychoanalysts to be artists.

If we cannot rely on poetry and art, how can we overcome this sensuous level of language? As we have seen in *Transformations*, Bion tried a mathematical abstract approach but could not attain the level of a predictive mathematical theory that would relieve psychoanalysis of its reliance on sensorial descriptive language. In the case of T(K), he proposed that the sensuous level could be overcome by focusing on the patterns of invariants throughout transformations rather than trying to understand and looking for causal and narrative relations and meaning. For T(O) he maintained and radicalized this attitude, adopting a stance which eschews understanding, and does not look for coherence, but rather attempts to be in touch with an undifferentiated zone from where thoughts arise.

Box 8.1 The language of achievement

The language of achievement is to talk from O, from where verbal thought originates. It is the language of the Man of Achievement (Keats; see Box 8.8). It is a language that is not a substitute for action, but a prelude to action (Bion 1970). Bion writes of his wish 'to try to pierce through to this "thing" behind (A real poet is able to use language that is penetrating and durable. I would like to be able to use language that did the same)' (Bion 1980: 60). In her unpublished paper 'On the difference between possession and floating the pleasure principle' presented at the Bion Conference in Boston 2009, Nicola Abel-Hirsch quotes 'In the beginning', a poem by Dylan Thomas (2002: 22) talking about the 'ribbed original of love'. Not only this poem, but 30–40 of the 90 poems in Thomas' collected works were written before he was 20. Abel-Hirsch quotes from a text of Moran (2005) referring to Stephen Spender, who bemoaned the shapelessness and meaninglessness of Dylan Thomas' work: 'The truth is that Thomas's poetry is turned on like a tap; it is just poetic stuff with no beginning nor end, shape or intelligent or intelligible control', although Thomas himself did not agree with this. She further points to the fact that Thomas' biographer Ferris (1985) wonders whether what he calls the strangeness of Thomas' early poems owes something to the words and images that rose up in his hallucinatory states of mind between sleep and waking. This is close to what Bion describes as the hallucinatory infinite zone and in this sense, the language that springs from it may be seen as what Bion calls a 'language of achievement', which would be the ideal language of the analyst during sessions to facilitate a transformation in O. Indeed, as Thomas (1985/1934) remarks himself in a letter written to Glyn Jones in March 1934: 'The chief use of meaning in a poem may be to satisfy one habit of the reader, to keep his mind diverted and quiet, while the poem does its work on him'.

Psychic truth

The search for truth, which is different from a moralizing attitude, was central to Bion's view of psychoanalysis. He quoted Doctor Johnson in this respect:

> The physician considers recognition of the pain subordinate to its cure; the psycho-analyst's view is expressed by Doctor Johnson's letter to Bennet Langton: 'Whether to see life as it is, will give us much consolation, I know not; but the consolation which is drawn from truth, if any there be, is solid and durable; that which may be derived from error must be, like its original, fallacious and fugitive'.
>
> (Bion 1970: 7)

Psychoanalysis is different from medicine. It cannot rely on the senses as medicine can, and a problem must not only be realized by the doctor but also by the patient. Moreover, emotional-psychic reality is observed by intuition and is not bound to space, time and causation. This approach to psychic truth is valuable for T(K) and for T(O). In *Transformations* Bion defined truth not in moral terms but as the contact with O, and consequently determined by the distance to O. Real truth finds itself from O, without verbal and categorizing thoughts, where one may see intuitively what is. This truth is revealed effortlessly.

The hallucinatory layer

O can be seen as belonging to an infinite space. It is the base from where everything gets transformed. Verbal thought or transformation in K is such a transformation. T(K) can fall short because experience is too limited to allow a constant conjunction to be discerned, just as certain planetary movements could not be imagined before differential calculus had been invented.

Psychotics lack the capacity for T(K); while at first sight they may appear to be talking about a given experience in a similar way to us, the similarity is superficial.

> What may then appear to the observer as thoughts, visual images and verbalizations must be regarded by him as debris, remnants or scraps of imitated speech and histrionic synthetic emotion, floating in a space so vast that its confines, temporal as well as spatial, are without definition.
>
> (Bion 1970: 12–13)

Bion returns to the example of the psychotic patient talking about ice cream (see *Transformations*). It was an 'I scream' spread out over many years, a moment stretched out into an extremely thin membrane. What is important here is that Bion arrived at the realization of the 'I scream' not through reason but because he was in contact with the layer from which the transformation in the patient occurred, the basic hallucinatory layer.[1] He could see how the transformation evolved. This contact with the undifferentiated, unthought, non-sensuous reality from whence mental phenomena arise is the major difference between the analyst and the theorist or philosopher who relies on thinking, memory and sensuous reality.

O and the preverbal matrix: the layer of hallucinosis

O is the layer from where thoughts emerge and it cannot be defined. Definition relies on another more finite kind of psychic functioning. The notion of a preverbal matrix, which had already been discussed in *Experiences in Groups* (see Box 2.7), is quite similar to the notion of a non-sensuous infinite mental domain. Bion will now also refer to this domain or matrix as the layer of hallucinosis, loosening the connections that the term 'hallucinosis' had with psychosis in his previous work. Being in the O-vertex in psychoanalysis is being in contact with a layer in which thoughts have yet to arise. O is something that has not happened yet; it is the non-sensuous, the not-yet-thought. Beta-elements acquire a new meaning in the light of T(O). For T(K) they are unprocessed, unthought experiences and perceptions – this means that from the perspective of T(O), they are the elements that are closest to O. They are an expression of O, but have not yet been appropriated by the psyche with its categories of time and space.

Box 8.2 Some quotes about O

Freud, Bion, Klein, Winnicott, Einstein, Shakespeare, Bach or whoever it be, was or shall be, were able to formulate verbally, mathematically, or musically, that which has a counterpart in reality. We can no more than suddenly, eternal as long as it lasts, have a transient, fleeting glimpse of 'it' in an intuitive way. The great authors in science and art made formulations that fleetingly apprehended some emanations of reality. In this resides the possibility of a 'real' analysis, a term coined by Bion.

(Sandler 2005b: 15)

My reconciliation between my views and those I believe to be Bion's and Kant's with regard to 'transcendent' as something passing beyond all experience is that O is not experienced per se – that is as an object of experience. O, like the God of Moses in Exodus ('I am that I am') is the subject, something with which one can only subjectively resonate – that is 'become'. Put another way, one does not really experience O; one experiences being O.

(Grotstein 2007: 133)

(continued)

> I do not see why an infinitely small biological particle being that whirls around the galactic centre on a speck of dirt – called by us the Earth – should, in the course of an ephemeral life that does not last even a thousand revolutions around the sun, imagine that the Universe of Galaxies conforms to its limitations.
>
> (Bion 1991: 229)

> I shall use the sign O to denote that which is the ultimate reality represented by terms such as ultimate reality, absolute truth, the godhead, the infinite, the thing-in-itself.
>
> (Bion 1970: 26)

> O describes both the unnameable unrepresentable external reality Grotstein describes as 'the world as it is, the universe without representations' (2011, private conversation) and the individual's primal internal preconception of that natural world.
>
> (Reiner 2012: 6)

The origin and necessity of a finite space for T(K)

From the infinite mental space of O, it became clear to Bion that a finite space is necessary to think, to have transformations in K. Representations or T(K) happen in a restricted, sensuous space – while mental space itself is not restricted. This leads Bion to an original claim: he suggests that we created a representation of three-dimensional space in order to make the thinking of emotional experiences possible, although mental space remains unknowable. Thus, in Bion's view the representation of a three-dimensional mental space did not originate from a realization of the geometric space in material reality; rather, the need to contain emotional experiences lies at the origin of Euclidean geometry.

In psychotics, this finite containing space is lacking. The distance to which fragments are scattered and dissipated seems to relate to the degree of mental disturbance. In psychotics, for instance, they are spread over sessions, even over years.

The representation of a three-dimensional mental world allows for the phantasy that something can be projected and contained. Without spatial representation, the projection enters into a mental space that is so 'large' that it incites a reaction of psychotic fear. Bion compared this to a surgical shock, when all the blood vessels dilate at once and the blood enters into a space that is too large, resulting in a sudden drop in blood pressure. He quotes Pascal: 'Ces espaces infinies m'effrayent' (These infinite spaces scare me) to describe what happens in the psychotic. S/he evacuates an emotion and the containing space, which become non-existent. This non-existence quickly turns into a greedy object that eats anything and might be compared to a black hole. Bion wrote of patients who lack the representation of a three-dimensional world: 'people exist who are so intolerant of pain or frustration (or in whom pain and frustration is so intolerable) that they feel the pain but will not suffer it and so cannot be said to discover it' (Bion 1970: 8). They are able to feel, but cannot think or differentiate. Anything that may bind the emotion, no matter how weak, even a scream, reduces the risk of getting lost in the infinite spaces that terrify the psychotic.

Vertices

Transformations in O happen in an infinite mental space, an undifferentiated layer of psychic functioning, and can be contained in a finite, sensuous three-dimensional space. To further conceptualize this, Bion uses the notion of vertices. In the analyst and analysand transformations occur on different vertices.

For instance, to a psychotic patient an interpretation can be felt as being excluded from a sexual relation and therefore he transforms the insight in a psychotic way to a 'frightful noise' (Bion 1970: 20) while the transformations of the analyst are happening at another vertex. This is a new and more open way of understanding psychotic symptoms, different from Bion's earlier work on T(K) where he would have interpreted the patient's reaction to his intervention as an 'attack on linking'. Now he understands it as a transformation of the patient on a different vertex than the one of the analyst.

Bion uses his Grid as an instrument to help distinguish these different transformations and vertices, and thereby gives it a new meaning in the light of T(O). On one vertex the transformations can be closing for instance by remaining within column 1 and making logical deductions. On another vertex the transformations may happen in an open way: using elements as preconceptions ('fact-finding tools' or 'containers in search for a contained') with transitions happening from column 1 to columns 3 and 4 (Bion 1965). In psychosis the transformations may remain within row 1 at the level of beta-elements, as in the example of the psychotic patient above.

Apprehending psychoanalytic objects

The ability to 'see' a psychoanalytic object depends on the realization that there is an invariant constant conjunction between elements during a transformation. A binocular vision, or the use of several vertices or points of view, is helpful. For instance, stuttering and psychosis may both be transformations of the same psychoanalytic object but on two different vertices. If we are looking only from one vertex, it is much harder to see this psychic, non-sensuous psychic object. In *Elements*, dealing with transformations in K, Bion stated that the psychoanalytic object needs at least three Grid categories to be revealed. In other words, it needs to be seen from at least three vertices.

When considering transformations in O, Bion will again focus on the invariant relation between elements during the transformation and not on what is perceptible or has meaning. The content of a patient's statement is less important. The analyst can see the transformation while he is observing it from the O-vertex and not relying on verbal thought but on intuition, while the patient cannot be conscious of the transformation, as he is not observing from the O-vertex.

Analysing from the O-vertex

The therapeutic impact of interpretations will be greater if they lead to a transformation in O, which is a kind of primary change, a change in experience in being. Therefore the analyst must be in contact with O and must not allow himself to be blinded by reasoning and the sensuous appearance of the patient. The success of an analysis depends on the analyst's capacity to maintain the O-vertex. He must be able to distinguish which events are evolutions of O and to assess what is hindering or helping the process of experiencing or becoming O.

In order to be able to do this, it is essential for the analyst to have experienced a T(O). This is why a training analysis is a necessity. In Bion's view, however, there are some side-effects to a training analysis that may have an opposite effect, like the tendency to identify with the methods of one's training analyst as well as the influence by psychoanalytic habits and theories. These are hindrances that can divert the future analyst from what is really at stake – the experience of being in contact with O.

From the O-vertex an interpretation should focus on an evolution of O, when it has evolved to a point where it becomes manifest in K and is therefore knowable. An intervention from O evokes a new experience.

> I shall use the sign O to denote that which is the ultimate reality represented by terms such as ultimate reality, absolute truth, the godhead, the infinite, the thing-in-itself. O does not fall in the domain of knowledge or learning save incidentally; it can be 'become', but it cannot be 'known'. It is darkness and formlessness but it enters the domain K when it has evolved to a point where it can be known, through knowledge gained by experience, and formulated in terms derived from sensuous experience; its existence is conjectured phenomenologically.
>
> (Bion 1970: 25)

The analyst must wait for a T(O) to take place; he cannot want it. As in the case of T(K), the sequence of frustration tolerance, waiting for coherence or selected fact to happen, is also important for T(O). This corresponds to the PS-D oscillation that Bion described for T(K), but for T(O) he describes it as an oscillation between patience and security.

Observation from and contact with O

How can we perceive or be in contact with O during a session? Freud attributed perception to consciousness and he described perception as consisting of attention, notation and memory. Bion largely shared Freud's view[2] in his elaboration of T(K) and suggested that a mental attitude of relaxed attention and reverie was required to let the process of perception and becoming aware of something happen. However, for T(O) he could not maintain this view, since psychic reality at the level of O cannot be perceived by the senses.

> The absence of memory and desire should free the analyst of those peculiarities that make him a creature of his circumstances and leave him with those functions that are invariant, the functions that make up the irreducible ultimate man. In fact this cannot be. Yet upon his ability to approximate to this will depend his ability to achieve the 'blindness' that is a prerequisite for 'seeing' the evolved elements of O. Reciprocally, his freedom from being 'blinded' by the qualities (or his perception of them) that belong to the domain of the senses should enable the analyst to 'see' those evolved aspects of O that are invariant in the analysand.
>
> (Bion 1970: 59)

Bion is quite radical here: an approach from a sensuous vertex hinders perception of or contact with the a-sensuous, undifferentiated O.[3] Such a perception of O is, for instance, perceiving anxiety before it is felt and perceived as anxiety. Realizations from the sensuous pain-pleasure world (memory and desire) will destroy the analyst's capacity for observation from O. Freud's hypothesis that the perception of reality occurs via consciousness does not fit for T(O). The Freudian memory is too much like a container, a mouth ingesting something. The Freudian concepts of preconscious and unconscious suffer the same limitation: they too are conceptualized as containers to put something in. The idea of 'repression in the unconscious' is based on the avoidance of painful memories. In sum, these concepts are based on the senses and governed by the pleasure-pain principle, and are of no use when it comes to apprehending T(O).

> Memory and desire are 'illuminations' that destroy the value of the analyst's capacity for observation as a leakage of light into a camera might destroy the value of the film being exposed.
>
> (Bion 1970: 69)

Bion therefore proposes that the analyst should actively seek to refrain from memory, desire and reason.

Rather than memory, Bion now proposes a dream-like memory that enables opening to the O of the psychic experience and the human personality.

[T]he experience of remembering a dream . . . must be contrasted with dreams that float into the mind unbidden and unsought and float away again as mysteriously. The emotional tone of this experience is not peculiar to the dream: thoughts also come unbidden, sharply, distinctly, with what appears to be unforgettable clarity, and then disappear leaving no trace by which they can be recaptured.

(Bion 1970: 70)

In his experience, when memory and desire are eschewed, and one artificially blinds oneself to sensuous experiences, the capacity for this dream-like memory increases. This memory is spontaneous, automatic and is a kind of afterglow of conjunctions at an a-sensuous level. It reflects the point where O meets K.

I wish to reserve the term 'memory' for experience related to conscious attempts to recall. These are expressions of a fear that some element, 'uncertainties, mysteries, doubts', will obtrude. Dream-like memory is the memory of psychic reality and is the stuff of analysis. That which is related to a background of sensuous experience is not suitable to the phenomena of mental life which are shapeless, untouchable, invisible, odourless, tasteless.
    . . . It may appear that this contradicts the psycho-analytic theory of dreams unless it is remembered that the dream is the *evolution* of O where O has evolved sufficiently to be represented by a sensuous experience. The sensuous elements of a psychotic dream do not represent anything. They *are* a sensuous experience.

(Bion 1970: 70)

The attitude of the analyst in analysing from O

Bion trained himself to adopt this attitude of eschewing both memory and desire both in and beyond sessions, resisting them when they began to arise. He warns us that as we learn to set aside memory and desire our sensitivity is heightened to what remains in us from the herd animal: pairing, dependency, warfare, birth – the basic emotional situations.[4] Practising the discipline that Bion proposed means that feelings of love and hate become almost unbearable. The need for analysis of the analyst may therefore increase again.
    Maintaining the attitude of being in O during a session is more uncomfortable than the attitude of benevolent abstinence recommended by Freud. Bion suggests that rather than being in a neutral state, the analyst who analyses from an attitude of relinquishing desires is in a fearful position. When O manifests itself this may be accompanied by an uncomfortable persecutory feeling. Bion will therefore link the Kleinian idea of the PS position to openness to O, just as he had previously linked the relation between the PS-D oscillation with T(K). At-one- ment with O is frightening, because

the analyst must give up the support of an understanding, categorizing, sensible attitude based on sensuous perceptions.[5]

> The first point is for the analyst to impose on himself a positive discipline of eschewing memory and desire. I do not mean that 'forgetting' is enough: what is required is a positive act of refraining from memory and desire. It may be wondered what state of mind is welcome if desires and memories are not. A term that would express approximately what I need to express is 'faith' – faith that there is an ultimate reality and truth – the unknown, unknowable, 'formless infinite'.
>
> (Bion 1970: 30)

Box 8.3 The experience of O

O cannot be defined or represented and Bion therefore links his notion of O in an allegorical way with concepts from different disciplines such as the Kantian Thing-in-Itself or noumenon, the Platonic Forms, the mathematical infinite and the mystical godhead that can be incarnated. O evokes something transcendental, something 'beyond' the senses that can take form in a sensorial reality. It is not something 'higher'; Grotstein (2007) quotes Kant to say that it is bathos, the deep from where everything starts, the foundation of experience. O is the mute other that lies 'just beyond, within and around' where we are. One does not really experience O; one experiences experiencing O. Bion wanted to express a clinical reality with his use of the concept of O. The difficulty of finding a concept that is able to encompass what is experienced is part of the clinical, psychoanalytic truth that he wished to convey.

O is the base of psychic phenomena, which is in itself a-sensuous and unknowable. If we try to grasp O by perception or understanding, we lose contact with it, like a camera which becomes useless when light leaks in. We can only experience it or become it. It takes you from behind, you cannot capture it; it grasps you. Bion compares it with passionate love. Psychoanalytic objects, which are the focus of Bion's observation and interpretations, are rooted in this senseless base. Bion (1970) uses Eckhart's metaphor in suggesting that psychoanalytic objects relate to O, as the Holy Trinity relates to God. Psychoanalytic objects are the closest our minds can get to O. They form the irreducible essence of personality. They are related to dim constellations that are already present in O, but have no form yet – as the statue is already present in the rock but it needs the sculptor to get it out.

To be in touch with the senseless base (O) and to see the psychoanalytic objects emerge from there, Bion advocates a state of not trying to understand, not trying to remember, not trying to grasp through sensorial perception. It is better to wait in a state of relaxed attention until something finite emerges from this infinite layer. Bion suggests several techniques to help the analyst to let go of categorizing thinking. Speculative imagination and wild thoughts

(continued)

(continued)

may help, says Bion (1980, 2005a, 2005b). It is interesting that another Neo-Platonic thinker, Bishop Nicolas De Cusa, a 15th-century philosopher who was much influenced by Eckhart, proposed the same technique. His 'learned ignorance' is a vision without understanding, which he propagates in his *De Docta Ignorantia*. De Cusa states that man needs speculation, a mixture of science and imagination to apprehend the unknowable God and infinity, just as Bion tried to apprehend O by means of what he calls speculative imagination.

Another of Bion's techniques, focusing not on the content but on the relationships between phenomena (constant conjunctions), can also help us to get a glimpse of these psychoanalytic objects. An attitude of faith is the right mental stance. Interpretation must relate to the point where these psychoanalytic objects arise from the hallucinatory layer. In such a contact the analyst is able to give interpretations about the psychoanalytic object before it is fully transformed into sensuous reality. This requires him to sit back with a clear mind as close to undifferentiated infinite psychic functioning as possible and allow the senseless constant conjunctions that point to a psychoanalytic object to light up in the dark (Bion gives the analogy of 'illumination by a beam of darkness').

It can be argued that in this sense practising psychoanalysis has a meditative aspect. Indeed, it requires the analyst to tolerate the dark and not-knowing, and to maintain the paranoid-schizoid position for a long time until something finite arises from the infinite layer. This empty state of mind is the condition for contact with this basic layer. Being in contact with the hallucinatory layer may result in strong, visual images and feelings as essences take form. The contact with O results in a transformation T(O) which is very different from a transformation that stems from understanding something. In T(O), something that was present but non-differentiated finds its way to become differentiated and finite, in many different forms or vertices.

This result is not a mystical experience but a transformation in O, an experience of change that occurs at an undifferentiated level. Bion found the language and metaphors of the mystics the least inadequate to describe this experience and even method. Augustine talks about transcending memory, transcending the mind, transcending time and speaking a language that is renewing with sentences that have no beginning and no end (Saint Augustine 1998: 195, 221; Lyotard 2000: 45) which is close to Bion's 'language of achievement' (see Box 8.1). To Bion adopting this stance is not a mystical experience in itself; he is not looking for a state of bliss. Bion's aim is not mystical enlightenment but a psychic change within the well-defined psychoanalytic frame, which is different from a religious experience.

The pitfall with a notion like O is that it is not something that can be imagined or thought with verbal thought. It is 'what is', and verbal thought and senses preclude any access to it. It is a-sensuous and unrepresentable. A void or emptiness is maybe close to it, but it is not void or emptiness. The core, the essence of self is nothing and yet all. Psychoanalysis may be the art of dealing with this 'hole' that is the essence of our being and with which the mind-wandering/daydreaming ego is in contact.

Box 8.4 The state of mind during the sessions: being just above sleep

Bion insisted on getting rid of memory and desire and actively resisting the temptation to rely on theories and understanding during the sessions. There is another aspect to this, which he describes in the Los Angeles seminars in 1967 (Bion 2013: 56) as being in a state 'just above sleep'. We find it already in his 'Cogitations' from 1959 when he is developing his theory on the alpha-function:

> Drowsiness is coming to me: it is part of the relaxation I have to achieve if my ideas are to be accessible. I must *dream* along, but then I risk going fast asleep. I have had to shut my eyes because they sting. Then I nearly went to sleep: 'Watch the wall my darling, while the Gentlemen go by.' (Rudyard Kipling. 'A Smuggler's Song'.). A smuggling process I must not know anything about. A wrapping up and packing of the goods I wish to move from the environment. Does that mean that α is to *hide* things from the conscious? If so, it is nearer to Freud's view of dream-work. The conscious is the servant of the unconscious. It is the conscious whose job it is to lie and deceive and protect the unconscious in its activities.
>
> (Bion 1992: 82)

> He drew attention to the state of mind that the analyst has to be in during the analytic session; the margin between being consciously awake, able to verbalise impressions, and being asleep, is extremely small. He found that 'being on the right wavelength is comparatively rare and has to be experienced to be recognised'. He told me that he also sensed this when alone in deep thought; he would 'wake up' to find light had been shed on a previously 'dark spot'. (Freud's words in a letter to Lou Andreas Salomé.)
>
> (Bion, F. 1995)

> If we are to translate our thoughts and feelings into physical or corporeal fact, there has to be a certain focusing of our mental apparatus as a prelude to action. That very act seems to me – putting my thoughts into 'verbo-visual' terms – to involve putting other elements out of focus. It is difficult to practice to de-focus-peripheralize the irrelevant without falling into the opposite error of permanent insensibility; blindness, deafness, repression. That is why I talk of the 'opacity' of memory, desire, understanding.
>
> (Bion 1991: 232)

Faith as mental attitude for an analysis from O, and an Act of Faith as result (instead of a thought)[6]

The analyst must be O: this is a way of life. He must achieve a frame of mind that allows him to be receptive to O. This attitude corresponds to what Bion calls *Faith* (F), surrendering to what has not yet happened, to what cannot yet be known.

Whereas in the K-vertex, the analyst waits in Ps to let unsaturated pre-concepts find elements resulting in a thought, in F the analyst waits from the O-vertex, for the occurrence of an 'Act of Faith' which is O finding a form.

> An act of Faith is peculiar to scientific procedure and must be distinguished from the religious meaning with which it is invested in conversational usage; it becomes apprehensible when it can be represented in and by thought. It must 'evolve' before it can be apprehended and it is apprehended when it is a thought just as the artist's O is apprehended when it has been transformed into a work of art . . . It is only when it has evolved to the point where it can be represented by a grid element that it can be apprehended.
>
> (Bion 1970: 34–35)

Awe, faith and mystery

In relation to an 'Act of Faith', Bion foregrounds not-knowing and the unknowable. We must be able to tolerate ignorance in order to adopt the vantage point from where we must look. O is the symbol or representation of this not-knowing and unknowable. The requisite attitude towards it is awe and faith.[7] When the sense of mystery, awe and faith disappear in an analysis, we are at risk of entering a dangerous, closed world. An attitude of awe towards the unknown is a good basic attitude for the analyst, expressing surrender to and faith in O.

> It is as well to be reminded by the poet Herman Melville that there are many ways of reading books, but very few of reading them properly – that is with awe. How much the more is it true of reading people.
>
> The unconscious – for want of a better word – seems to me to show the way 'down to descend', its realms have an awe-inspiring quality.
>
> (F. Bion, quoting Bion 1981: 4)

> However thorough an analysis is, the person undergoing it will be only partially revealed; at any point in the analysis the proportion of what is known to what is unknown is small. Therefore the dominant feature of a session is the unknown personality and not what the analysand or analyst thinks he knows.
>
> (Bion 1970: 87)

The origin of thoughts on the K and the O-vertex

> A thought has as its realization a no-thing. An 'act of faith' has as its background something that is unconscious and unknown because it has not happened.
>
> (Bion 1970: 34)

To put this more precisely: the way in which Bion considers the origin of the thought from the O-vertex is different from the way in which he conceived it from the K-vertex, in *Elements of Psychoanalysis* and *Learning from Experience*. There, a thought came into being when the individual was able to tolerate the absence of a thing, for which a thought (K) was produced: a thought for a nothing. From the O-vertex, thought is where the non-sensuous, not-yet-thought world meets the finite world, it is not the representation of an experience that has already taken place, but something new that happens.

The 'act of faith' on the O-vertex is the contact with the layer of hallucinosis from where thoughts arise. Bion stated that this basic layer is always present and influencing us, but that we tend to close it off and to be defensive towards it:

> [A state of hallucinosis is] always present but overlaid by other phenomena which screen it. If these other elements can be moderated or suspended hallucinosis becomes demonstrable; its full depth and richness is only accessible to acts of faith.
>
> (Bion 1970: 36)

Great artists seem to be in contact with this zone, like Dylan Thomas (see Box 8.1).

O and the unconscious

O as the not yet happened and the not yet captured is ineffable. It is a kind of transcendent reality behind a curtain of illusions. Or better, it is the internal and external reality that we are in contact with through illusionary shadows, like projections on a screen. This reality is both inside and outside the personality, and conscious as well as unconscious. Therefore the unconscious cannot be equated with O. To Bion the unconscious as a concept is too much of a container, and is related to the pleasure principle as something that secures us, which Bion interprets as evasion of pain. The focus of analysing from the O-vertex is the unknown, without compromise, and this implies the unconscious as well as the conscious. This constitutes a shift from classical psychoanalysis which takes the unconscious as its main focus. The resolution of unconscious conflicts does not guarantee that the patient will come to be more in contact with O.

Box 8.5 Bion's different notions of O

Bion mentions O for the first time in *Untitled*, where a 1963 version of his Grid is presented. It was written when he was finishing *Learning from Experience*. In *Untitled* it is the O of origin, the original and unknown reality that comes to us in a transformed way, as far as psychoanalytic work is concerned, and he sees it as an emotional reality. When he takes up O again in *Transformations*, it has the same meaning: the unknowable origin, the point from where a transformation starts, but it is no longer restricted to the field of emotions.

In *Attention and Interpretation*, Bion explores O using different models: philosophical (the Unknown, the Kantian 'Ding an Sich' which we cannot think); mathematical (infinity); religious (the godhead which is not yet represented as God or the Trinity (Eckhart)). Through these explorations O acquires a more transcendental meaning.

Bion explicitly states that O is not the unconscious and that it is a notion that touches both on unconscious and conscious functioning. Even if all unconscious conflicts were resolved, this would not guarantee contact with O (Bion 1970). Such contact requires a special attitude of no memory, no desire, no understanding and no coherence.

Later, with the notion of the caesura and also in *A Memoir of the Future*, I have the impression that O is seen as a kind of deeper layer of the unconscious, an expansion of the Freudian unconscious. It differs from the repressed and dynamic unconscious and is a zone that we only now and then have any contact with (see Box 11.3). It is a zone of specific mental functioning that Bion gave different names to (emmatures; pre-natals; hallucinatory layer; a kind of sane psychotic functioning).

In my understanding, in his later supervisions and clinical seminars that are characterized by a Socratic questioning from a position of radical not-knowing, Bion used O in a somewhat different way again, as a symbol for the radically unknown a-sensuous psychic reality which we can 'become' by intuition.

O and the pleasure principle

Seen from the O-vertex, Bion conceives pain and the pleasure–pain principle in a different way. Pain now expresses resistance to growth and maturation, in other words resistance to the contact with O, which entails growth. Desire, memory and understanding are based on avoiding pain and keeping faith at bay and in this way they prevent a transformation in O from occurring. The idea that memory and understanding are forms of resistance to T(O) is different from Freud's (1911) 'Two principles of mental functioning' and Bion's (1962) own 'Theory of thinking', which is rooted in the pleasure–pain principle since the emergence of a thought is linked with the capacity to tolerate frustration.

'Faith' (T(O)) versus containment (T(K))

Eigen (1981) emphasizes that for Bion 'faith in O' is a primary methodological principle. P. Bion (2000: 138) stresses that the no memory, no desire attitude should go with awe and mystery – as it opens the analyst more to the projections of the analysand and to the analyst's own psychoanalytic objects that resonate with it. The problem with containment can be that it comes from the wish to help the patient, to understand, to get the patient some relief – this is all from the sensuous domain and may hinder the evolution and the becoming of O.

Bion places the 'desire to understand' in column 2, because it closes. This is an important but radical point of view which many psychoanalysts do not share. To Bion it is, for example, not important to know whether a patient is really married or not; the analyst is at risk of saturating their observation with this knowledge and losing contact with the unknown reality of the patient, with what really is. In the same vein, pre-conceptions belong to the K-vertex and are containers that can be filled. Memory and desire are of the same nature; they are also containers, one for the past, the other for the future. They are all sensuous objects that fill the space.

This psychic reality is found when O evolves to a point where it can be discerned through sense-impressions. This point of meeting between infinite and finite can be captured in words although words cannot do justice to it because they are so charged with sensuous associations. Words allow a contact at the intersection K–O, but what matters are acts of faith: to go beyond and to come into contact with O itself, so that a transformation in O may occur and O can find K.

> The psycho-analyst is concerned with O, which is incommunicable save through K activity. O may appear to be attainable by K through phenomena, but in fact that is not so. K depends on the evolution of O→K.
>
> (Bion 1970: 29)

This contact with O is what Bion had in mind when he suggested that an analyst must place himself on a point in infinity (the multi-dimensional, non-differentiated, hallucinatory matrix); to Bion the movement is always from O to K, not from K to O.

Faith should not be associated with religious faith here, which is saturation. It is a condition beyond understanding in which there is contact with the non-differentiated zone, where one can 'see' (like a seer) how the mental object takes shape out of this zone and is transformed.

> For me 'faith' is a scientific state of mind and should be recognized as such. But it must be 'faith' unstained by any element of memory or desire.
>
> (Bion 1970: 32) (also quoted in
> Eigen 1981 and Grotstein 2007)

Psychosis

From the K-vertex (in *Learning from Experience, Elements, Transformations*), Bion assumed that for both the analyst and the psychotic the core problem is the openness to a psychic experience and the transformation of it in thoughts; in other words the process of mentalizing an emotional experience.

From the O-vertex, Bion saw a major difference between what takes place in the analyst and in the psychotic. Although the analyst and the psychotic both try to keep the sensuous away, for the analyst this means that he should not allow himself to be hindered by the pleasure-pain principle so that he can be in the O-vertex. For the psychotic it is the opposite; he also keeps the sensuous away but his efforts are driven by the pleasure-pain principle, and he tries to evade the pain by saturating everything with meaning and by blocking transformations in K and in O. From the O-vertex, Bion saw psychosis as a way to avoid experiencing O.

In the course of many years of clinical experience, I personally have found that psychoanalysing from the layer of hallucinosis is helpful when dealing with patients with a neurotic structure and sufficient cognitive control. It has seemed to me too risky to rely on T(O) in psychotics and severe borderline patients and I have felt that in treating them, it is better to rely on Bion's first model of T(K), and focus on containment and enhancing the α function in these patients. Bion advises the opposite, and suggests that especially in working with the psychotic part of the personality, the analyst must become at one with the layer from where his patients' hallucinations arise and effect transformations in O→K.

In the preverbal zone (matrix) of the psychotic, the domain of hallucinosis, a transformation in sense-impressions (β-elements) takes place. It is a transformation that has no meaning but that provides pleasure or pain and endures: the less satisfaction the individual experiences, the more greedy they feel, and the more hallucination occurs. This is the reverse of what should happen in T(O) in the analyst: acts of faith in the hallucinatory matrix that can evolve on the O-vertex and that can be met by a thought. Bion already mentioned the example that it was an act of faith that allowed him to see in one of his patients that one moment of time was as stretched out over chronological time as a thin membrane (this is the example of 'I scream'; see above). For the analyst this was illuminating in the vertex of O, but not for the patient who from his vertex further resorted to a transformation in hallucinosis.

Precluding T(O)

In a psychotic T(O) does not take place, because everything happens on a sensuous level. Sexualization of psychoanalysis is a less overt form of hatred of psychoanalysis. It excludes the possibility of seeing how something is the expression of O and is transformed in O. It saturates a perception in O. Likewise, the L, H and K links of the analyst may close off his contact with O. The desire to heal, to be a good mother (L) and to understand (K) prevent contact with O and T(O). 'Development itself cannot be desired. The painful nature of the dilemma is essential' (Bion 1970: 79). In other words, the analyst will be blind to O if he tries to heal, love and understand his patient. This has far-reaching implications for the handling of the transference and counter-transference. It differs from a classical approach in which a psychic processing of the L, H, K field of the transference–countertransference is central.

Box 8.6 The unknown and the attitude of the analyst

Bion stresses that we should always focus on the unknown in psychoanalysis. Although we cannot know what lies outside our knowledge, we do have a sense of infinity and of the smallness of our knowledge. According to Bion this is expressed by 'a sense of Mystery' and the notion of 'Awe'. Augustine, who is considered the first philosopher to write about what happens in the mind, also drew attention to the infinity of our minds in his *Confessions* (Saint Augustine 1998). Now, neuroscience shows that the number of possible neuronal connections is of the same order as figures used in defining the unknown infinite astronomical world. To use one of Plato's ideas, we are like 'a sponge in infinity'. However, we have a conscious mind that adapts itself to a changing environment and tries to make it predictable. This capacity for practical thinking and adapting to ever-changing situations by developing maps and patterns developed for survival (Edelman 1992). It is close to what Freud (1911) described in his 'Two principles of mental functioning'. Our mind defends itself against the Medusan, petrifying qualities of our not-knowing and not-being-able to know. It is difficult to imagine that we originate from and are surrounded by nothingness.

While this practical way of thinking might be life-saving in dealing with physical reality, it limits our ability to deal with emotional realities in psychoanalysis. It is like Kant's statement: 'Little does the mind make note of its prison when the profit is mastery over the physical world'. We tend to close off our intuition of what is behind the 'veil of illusions' that we create to feel secure. A transformation in O can occur when something transcends the capacity of our understanding. For a brief moment, the veil of illusions is ruptured and one may surpass the categories of thinking. First there is horror but what follows is a feeling of delight, when the power of the mind offers a form for what was beyond our thinking. Kant calls this the experience of the Sublime. He gives examples of this happening, for example when we are confronted with overwhelming, awe-inspiring natural phenomena, like seeing a star-spangled sky.

(continued)

(continued)

This is why Bion suggested that we must see each patient each time as if we see him for the first time. Being open to uncertainty, destabilizing our natural habit of trying to grasp, to understand is important to get a glimpse of O and achieve a creative, transforming change.

I would like to quote Mason (2000: 987) here:

Bion once told me that he thought swimming was not really exercise as it was effortless. This I think is a good description of how he worked. Effort is memory or desire – the work we feel we have to do against resistance; but Bion's reverie was a description of him swimming – letting his unconscious do the work while he floated into becoming 'O'. I would hasten to add that Bion's 'effortless' swimming was possible only because of the long years of training he had undergone to acquire this skill.

The relation between ♀ and ♂, reconsidered from O

From the O-vertex, Bion doubts whether the mental domain can be contained in psychoanalysis. A container in search of a contained (the ♀♂ movement) does not seem an accurate metaphor for what happens at the O-vertex. From this perspective, talking about a probe into the Unknown feels more apt than thinking in terms of a container. The idea of a container is restrictive. As an example, Bion raises some thought-provoking questions: can a personality be contained within the person of Mr X? Is acting out a manifestation of something that cannot be contained' within psychoanalysis? Can the clinical reality of psychoanalysis be contained within its theories; are these not too limiting?

As president of the British Psychoanalytic Society, Bion sought to understand the dynamics of institutions from the O-vertex. But how? In order to investigate this, he posed the question of the relation of a genius (the contact with O experienced by a mystic) to an institution (Establishment). As in Nietzsche's *Thus Spoke Zarathustra*, Bion suggested that one function of a group was to create a genius without destroying the group. This balance can be maintained by establishing rules so that everyone can profit from the genius or mystic. The mystic and the group cannot be indifferent to each other. The relationship of mystic ♂ and group ♀ may take one of three patterns of relations: commensal, symbiotic or parasitic.[8] In a commensal relationship both will develop; in a parasitic relationship the one will destroy the other; and in a symbiotic relationship, they cannot do without each other.

Lies

In relation to O, a lie is characterized by the fact that it is related to a thought that requires a thinker. 'Descartes tacit assumption that thoughts presuppose a thinker is valid only for the lie' (Bion 1970: 103). In O or truth, thoughts emerge and are not constructed by a thinker. Bion distinguishes different kinds of lies, according to their relation with the thinker. Here again he will rely on the ♀♂ metaphor: a lie and a thinker. In a commensal lie both will develop; in a parasitic lie, the lie will destroy the thinker; and in a symbiotic lie, the lie and the thinker cannot without each other.

In this new version, lies are not restricted to column 2 of the Grid but can be found in various categories of the Grid. In order to detect lies, it is better to look at invariants, patterns that occur spontaneously, than to ask whether a narrative is logically sound, which will only reveal the liar through the weakness of the causal link.

The fact that only lies need a thinker has important implications. When an intervention is too dependent on the analyst's thinking, it is not really an expression of O. Thus from the O–vertex, Bion turns against narrative because it depends on illusory causal relations that need a thinker from a pleasure-pain background and is in his view always an expression of a thinker.

♀♂ transformed from the O-vertex

As discussed in *Elements of Psychoanalysis*, from the K–vertex, the fitting of a ♀ and a ♂ leading to a realization is the most important. In the K–vertex, it is a ♀ that finds a ♂, a constant conjunction, and one of its elements can then be taken as the name of the constant conjunction. From the O–vertex, however, the ♀♂ relationship is different: liberating O is the most important thing. A meaning and finding a word can now be compared to a sculptor's carving something from a block, liberating the O that is in it. It is O that moves towards K, towards a ♀ or a ♂. In Bion's new vision ♀ and ♂ develop on different lines. Will they meet? If they meet, ♂ can empty ♀ or destroy it and ♀ can suck ♂ dry. It is not the mystic who finds O, but O finds the mystic and he can be destroyed by it. Similarly, society can contain the mystic, destroy him or be destroyed.

New metaphors

When he sought a good model to express his approach from the O-vertex, Bion was unable to find an algebraic analogy and decided to borrow expressions from the mystics like Meister Eckhart and St John of the Cross. His use of these writers does not mean that he conceived psychoanalysis as a form of mysticism.

There is a 'thing-in-itself', which can never be known; by contrast, the religious mystic claims direct access to the deity with whom he aspires to be at one. Since this experience is often expressed in terms that I find it useful to borrow, I shall do so, but with a difference that brings them closer to my purpose.

(Bion 1970: 87)

In the same vein, he borrows models from Plato and Christianity:

The Platonic theory of Forms and the Christian dogma of the Incarnation imply absolute essence which I wish to postulate as a universal quality of phenomena such as 'panic', 'anxiety', 'fear', 'love'. In brief, I use O to represent this central feature of every situation that the psycho-analyst has to meet. With this he must be at one; with the *evolution* of this he must identify so that he can formulate it in an interpretation.

(Bion 1970: 87)

In anybody, in everything, there is a relation of phenomena to ultimate reality. To indicate the point where O meets K, Bion uses an analogy drawn from Meister Eckhart, which expresses this movement on the O-vertex from O to K: the relation of ultimate reality to these qualities is like that of the godhead to the trinity. Trinity is the point where the godhead, which is in itself formless and infinite, becomes apprehensible (Bion 1970: 88). The godhead cannot be named or conceived. Ultimate reality is not grounded in sense experience. This is why psychoanalytic science should also not be grounded in sense experience, as opposed to a scientific approach, music, aesthetics, politics etc. which all have a sensuous base. Fear, panic, love and anxiety have no sensuous background. They are already present at an a-sensuous level before they are expressed; in other words, they have an absolute essence. Through intuitive contact with this essence, it is possible to see a transformation before it is expressed in sensuous reality (T(O)).

Technique

The essence of Bion's technique remains 'to detect a pattern that remains unaltered in apparently widely differing contexts' (Bion 1970: 92). In these different contexts or vertices, one can see an evolution of O towards a point where it becomes apprehensible. The vertex of the dreamer is not the vertex of the person awake; the vertex of the undifferentiated layer is not the vertex of the thinking, understanding analyst. The vertex of the unconscious is not the vertex of the conscious. However, despite these differences, the vertices must be close enough to allow the analyst to see something binocularly (see Box 8.6).

When a pattern remains unaltered, it can again be used in a non-saturated way to see new things or in other words to widen the area illuminated. For instance, Bion links Oedipus, Babel, Eden and messianic expectation because they show a common pattern in their representations of the relation to knowledge. Each version emphasizes a different aspect, but together they suggest a common configuration of knowledge as a danger.

Thinking and acting from the O-vertex

When one begins to think in terms of vertices, even beta–elements can be seen as a separate vertex which can relate in different ways to the development of α. The same holds true for acting and thinking. In Bion's new vision, seen from O, thinking and acting can be seen as two different vertices; they are not necessarily coupled (see also Box II.1). At this point, Bion diverges from the Freudian account of the dynamic between acting and thinking as described in the 'Two Principles' and from his own 'Theory of thinking'. Acting and thinking are two different vertices that can have different relations and for instance may dominate or be commensal with each other. When looking from O, what is most important is that everything can be seen as containing O. The primal question for the analyst is to see – intuit the evolution of O in his patient – and this can be done on different vertices.

The psychoanalytic object revisited

> Freud said that he had to 'blind [him]self artificially to focus all the light on one dark spot'. This provides a useful formulation for describing the area I wish to cover by F. By rendering oneself 'artificially blind' through the exclusion of memory and desire, one achieves F; the piercing shaft of darkness can be directed on the dark features of the analytic situation. Through F one can 'see', 'hear', and 'feel' the mental phenomena of whose reality no practising psycho-analyst has any doubt though he cannot with any accuracy represent them by existing formulations.
>
> (Bion 1970: 57–58)

With a beam of darkness, in blindness the analyst waits to 'see' the evolved elements of O (Bion 1970: 58). In this way, the irreducible, the ultimate, the essence of someone can come to the fore. His freedom from being 'blinded' by the qualities (or his perception of them) that belong to the domain of the senses should enable the analyst to 'see' those evolved aspects of O. These are the non-sensuous invariants in the transformations of the analysand. The further the analysis progresses, the more the psychoanalyst and the analysand achieve a state in which both contemplate the irreducible minimum that is the patient. The aim of the analysis is to give this essence back to the patient. This irreducible minimum is incurable because what is seen is that without which the patient would not be the patient.

Box 8.7 Evolution of the psychoanalytic object as a concept in Bion's work

According to Euclid's open definition, mathematics is about mathematical objects. Likewise, Bion says that psychoanalysis is about psychoanalytic objects. A psychoanalytic object is not known and can appear in a hundred different forms in a flux of dreams, transference, attitudes and postures etc.

In *Learning from Experience*, the psychoanalytic object was defined as a function, which – depending on the way the variables are filled in – can result in a myriad of appearances. In other words, the psychoanalytic objects that we are looking for in sessions are functions that consist of constant conjunctions between elements. The manifestations of a psychoanalytic object can be very different according to the elements which are linked by a given constant conjunction, but the conjunction, the constellation remains the same. This stable conjunction that underlies the changing appearances is ineffable. It creates unity to what we perceive. Conjunctions and psychoanalytic objects cannot be derived by logical deduction. They become apparent by letting go and allowing coherence to occur spontaneously in the mind, in an attitude of relaxed attention. Bion will describe this mental event as the PS-D oscillation and the occurrence of a selected fact. The conjunction between elements is not perceptible by the senses, as the conjunction itself is a-sensuous. Each individual analysis has its specific psychoanalytic objects.

An example of such a psychoanalytic object is presented by a patient who told different stories about sailing and one about crossing a large boat with his tiny boat, which was quite dangerous. At other times, he seemed very interested in the Second World War, etc. Each of these stories expressed a fascination with danger and the presence of a catastrophe. The stories were the changing appearances of an underlying constant conjunction. The meaning of the story and hypotheses about the origin of the story and links with the past of the patient were less important than the fact that this underlying coherence manifested itself and again and again emerged as a selected fact. This psychoanalytic object is of a psychic order, it is not a material given, although it always manifests itself as a sensorial phenomenon.

In *Elements*, Bion attributed the following characteristics to the psychoanalytic object. It is always about something intensely emotional, lively (hence he spoke about passion, except for denuding hate and aggression). It is sensorial in its manifestation, but of the order of the psychic. It is not a material fact, but of the order of myth (or fiction). None of these qualities alone are sufficient to deduce the psychoanalytic object; they must co-occur. The categories of the Grid can reflect the psychoanalytic object as phenomena but are not the psychoanalytic object. The psychoanalytic object is beyond the elements or categories of the Grid. This is why Bion saw the psychoanalytic object as determined by at least three Grid categories.

In *Transformations* Bion approached the constant conjunctions that constitute the psychoanalytic object by looking at the invariant relation between elements before and after a transformation.

In *Attention and Interpretation*, Bion emphasized the psychic, ineffable character of the psychoanalytic object and now came to see it as a Form that comes to be realized (not unlike Plato). The ineffable mental object is described as a Character-Idea, an irreducible part of the personality that realizes itself in a flux of transformations but of which we catch only an afterglow. Bion's sense of the inadequacy of our knowledge in apprehending the psychoanalytic object and the importance he attached to the experience of allowing oneself to be struck by this ineffable object as it emerges led him to turn to the language of the mystics. He wanted to emphasize the experiential side of T(O). Experiencing the psychoanalytic object and letting oneself be affected by it rather than knowing and being defended against it were central in the late Bion's approach. This is the PS-D oscillation that he had already described for T(K) in *Learning from Experience* and now repeated for T(O). For Bion, this is the alpha and omega of the psychoanalytic method.

In order to experience a psychoanalytic object emerging from the undifferentiated or infinite zone, Bion tried to be in a state of 'no memory, no desire, no understanding, no coherence'. The experience of a psychoanalytic object takes the form of the realization of constant conjunctions, selected facts that are intuited in a mental state which is characterized by the movement from patience to security. J. Gooch, a former analysand of Bion, saw Bion's technique as being so receptive that through projective identification there could be resonance between the psychoanalytic objects of the patient and of the analyst. Interpretations can then be made from this emergence (Gooch 2002).

The 'PS-D, $♀♂$' formula for T(K) and T(O)

Finally, Bion presents PS-D and $♀♂$ as the essence of T(O), as he did in *Elements of Psychoanalysis* for T(K). In this way this formula becomes the α and Ω of his work:

It may, therefore, seem surprising if, at this stage and in relatively few sentences, I describe what is perhaps the most important mechanism employed by the practising psycho-analyst . . . In every session the psycho-analyst should be able, if he has followed what I have said in this book, particularly with regard to memory and desire, to be aware of the aspects of the material that, however familiar they may seem to be, relate to what is unknown both to him and to the analysand. Any attempt to cling to what he knows must be resisted for the sake of achieving a state of mind analogous to the paranoid-schizoid position. For this state I have coined the term 'patience' to distinguish it from 'paranoid-schizoid position', which should be left to describe the pathological state for which Melanie Klein used it. I mean the term to retain its association with suffering and tolerance of frustration. 'Patience' should be retained without 'irritable reaching after fact and reason' until a pattern 'evolves'. This state is the analogue to what Melanie Klein has called the depressive position. For this state I use the term 'security'. This I mean to leave with its association of safety and diminished anxiety. I consider that no analyst is entitled to believe that he has done the work required to give an interpretation unless he has passed through both phases – 'patience' and 'security'. The passage from the one to the other may be very short, as in the terminal stages of analysis, or it may be long. Few, if any, psychoanalysts should believe that they are likely to escape the feelings of persecution and depression commonly associated with the pathological states known as the paranoid-schizoid and depressive positions. In short, a sense of achievement of a correct interpretation will be commonly found to be followed almost immediately by a sense of depression. I consider the experience of oscillation between 'patience' and 'security' to be an indication that valuable work is being achieved.

(Bion 1970: 123–124)

'Prelude to or substitute for achievement'

In the development of Bion's work, the idea of fragmentation became more and more important. In his view we are all fragmented, and it is important to be able to tolerate this state of mind. We need to be able to free ourselves from a knowing, categorizing and gripping attitude and to be able to tolerate the so-called psychotic mode where from the hallucinatory layer O finds K. Putting PS to the foreground becomes a cornerstone of his late work. In this regard, Bion (1970: 125) quotes the letter in which John Keats described the 'Negative Capability' of the 'Man of Achievement':

I had not a dispute but a disquisition with Dilke on various subjects; several things dove-tailed in my mind, and at once it struck me what quality went to form a Man of Achievement, especially in Literature, and which Shakespeare possessed so enormously – I mean Negative Capability, that is, when a man is capable of being in uncertainties, mysteries, doubts, without any irritable reaching after fact and reason.

(Keats 1817)

Box 8.8 Negative capability: Keats and Bion

There is an extraordinary degree of overlap between the late Bion's view of the psychoanalyst and Keats' view of the poet, as expressed in his letters.

Keats reacted against Wordsworth and Coleridge, who were Romantic poets like him. He felt that they were seeking a unitary truth by means of intellectual speculations, an attitude which he experienced as full of closing preconceptions and mannerisms that block the inner poetic genius (Bate 1963). This is close to what Bion wrote about the psychoanalytic genius (Bion 1970).

Keats was influenced by Hazlitt's idea on 'gusto', a lecture he had attended shortly before writing the letter to his brothers. Gusto is a kind of passion, liveliness. Keats compared it for instance with the paintings of Titian where 'not only do his heads seem to think – his bodies seem to feel' (Bate 1963: 244). The idea of gusto is linked with Hazlitt's view of the mind as not only automatically self-centred, but directed spontaneously to whatever is around. Keats embraced this view in what is called empathic identification (Bate 1963: 378), which is illustrated in another letter: 'if a sparrow come before my window I take part in its existence and pick about the gravel' (21 November 1817). To be able to attain this state of the moment, both Hazlitt and Keats thought it was necessary to be humble and disinterested. Keats thereby followed Hazlitt's ideas on the natural disinterestedness of the human mind (Bate 1963: 258), a capacity that Keats found maximally present in Jesus and Socrates. In a similar way, Bion talked about the necessity of self-abandonment in the attitude of a psychoanalyst. We must place Keats' famous statement that to have negative capability it is necessary to abstain from 'any irritable searching after fact and reason' in this context. The ability to tolerate the Unknown is of primary importance to Keats. This state of mind typifies the man of achievement, the ideal of a poet without a character of his own – a capability that Keats sees represented at the maximum by Shakespeare. It is a maximum receptiveness, as Keats described: 'it seems to me that we should rather be the flower than the bee'. This is why Keats famously suggested that 'if Poetry comes not as naturally as the leaves to a tree it had better not come at all' (Keats 1817, letter to John Taylor, 27 February).

From his new perspective which emphasized fragmentation and the need to tolerate it, and evolution on different vertices, Bion regarded envy for instance as something that is separate from the personality. It is something outside the personality, split into tiny parts. It is not the person but envy which is split into fragments that each grow separately and result in cancerous growth of envy. 'A single malignant cell that lies waiting to become malignant'. The separate operation of systems led Bion to the idea that the human animal is persecuted by his mind and the thoughts associated with it. Hence the tendency to take refuge in mindlessness, stupor, sexualization or acting out.

In sum, Bion's credo was tolerance of fragmentation and not-knowing while observing from the O-vertex. This observation is of paramount importance: 'The fault [for an interminable analysis] lies in the failure to observe and is intensified by the inability to appreciate the significance of observation' (Bion 1970: 125). But this observation must be from the O-vertex, which is actually the same as being in contact with O. Hatred of psychoanalysis and its reciprocal sexualization of psychoanalysis can occur because the O–vertex is not maintained and the senses, passion, pleasure and pain are allowed to take over.

Bion distinguished between language that is a substitute for action and language that is a prelude to action, and describes the Language of Achievement as both. This resulted in the final lines of *Attention and Interpretation*:

> What is to be sought is an activity that is both the restoration of god (the Mother) and the evolution of god (the formless, infinite, ineffable, non-existent), which can be found only in the state in which there is NO memory, desire, understanding.
>
> (Bion 1970: 129)

The restoration of the Mother may be interpreted as the restoration of the internal thinking breast or T(K), while the evolution of god may be seen as T(O).

Conclusion

Attention and Interpretation is the culmination of Bion's psychoanalytic odyssey. The focus on T(O) brought a radical new way of understanding psychic change, observing, interpreting. He reformulated all the concepts that he used in apprehending T(K) for T(O): like $\alpha\beta$, $\female\male$, PS-D, truth, psychoanalytic object, psychotic part, hallucinatory layer. He succeeded in integrating T(K) and T(O) as a dual track of psychic functioning and change (Vermote 2011). The book reflects a catastrophic change in his theoretical and clinical understanding. After this insight, Bion did not develop any more new concepts; rather, he directed his efforts towards elaborating the insight that he had formulated in *Attention and Interpretation* and experimenting with style, form and clinical practice.

Box 8.9 James Grotstein: the transcendent position

James Grotstein (1925–2015) was one of the Los Angeles analysts who invited Bion to move to California. He was in analysis with him a long time and later became a colleague and friend of Bion at the time that the APA wanted to expel the Californian Kleinian analysts. He was a Kleinian analyst who made the bridge with psychiatry, and who later became famous in interpreting Bion's work. Grotstein knew the emotional experience that Bion writes so indirectly and allegorically about, at first-hand. As an academic, Grotstein studied and provided scholarly interpretations of Bion's concepts.

Moreover, he developed his own way of using, thinking and becoming them. We may perhaps characterize his writing as a hyperbole of O, applying the words that he wrote about Bion to himself: a 'peak in Darien' (Grotstein 2007: 114). Grotstein's Bion is a 'Prometheus Unbound'; he describes the training analyst's task as helping 'his analysand-in-training' to become a competent mystic (Grotstein 2007: 3).

Inspired by Kant, Grotstein sees

> the human being as existentially trapped between the two arms of O . . . that is that it is implicit to the sensory stimuli of emotional experience (from within and without) on the one hand, and to the unconscious inherent pre-conceptions in the unexpressed unconscious on the other.
>
> (Grotstein 2007: 87)

To Grotstein, O is the Ultimate Truth, godhead. β-elements are O's proto-emotional descendants, the ghosts of O (Grotstein 2007: 59), the shadow or imprints of O (Grotstein 2007: 60); α-elements 'indicate that the subject has attributed personalness to the impersonal experience of the β-elements, has claimed them' (Grotstein 2007: 61). Thoughts without a thinker are 'inborn pre-conceptions' and

> O's offspring, they are the 'unborns', the 'intimations of immortality' that we seemingly experience as located within our inner cosmos, but they are placeless, unlocated: they cannot be found because they can never be the object- they are always already the ever-emerging subject.
>
> (Grotstein 2007: 125)

Internal objects and the self are the 'radioactive imprints of O' and this can be revealed with the help of another. This is the goal of psychoanalysis: 'the capacity to experience O is the privilege of the ineffable subject of psycho-analysis . . . the "Man of Achievement"' (Grotstein 2007: 127). To experience becoming O is a drive, a Truth drive. It is a stage that we can reach beyond the depressive position which he names the 'transcendent position'. He puts it in what he calls a Bionic koan: 'We spend and too often waste a lifetime walking in the shadow of our ultimate unclaimed self'.

Grotstein (1983) edited an influential book in memoriam of Bion, shortly after his death, that marked the state of the art of Bionian approaches at this time: *Do I Dare Disturb the Universe?* (Grotstein 1983). He further elabo-rated his own thinking in relation with Bion's ideas in *Who is the Dreamer Who Dreams the Dream?* (Grotstein 2001) and radically interpreted Bion and psychoanalytic practice from what he called 'Bion as a mystic' in *A Beam of Intense Darkness* (Grotstein 2007).

Similar approaches of Bionian ideas from a mystical side include, amongst others, Epstein (1995) and the numerous papers of Eigen (1998, 2001, 2012).

Notes

1 The concept of the hallucinatory layer will be more and more freed from psychopathological connotations in Bion's later work (Bion 1971) and will finally be equated with the infinite basic layer from where thoughts arise.

2 In his Grid, the horizontal row even represented the same steps that Freud (1911) had delineated in his *Two Principles of Mental Functioning*: notation, attention, inquiry, action.

3 This is different from his 1963 point of view in a paper on the Grid (Bion 1997), where he saw O in psychoanalysis as an emotional experience.

4 This is similar to the basic assumptions that he introduced in *Experiences in Groups*: dependency, pairing and fight-flight.

5 While Bion relies on the mystics in trying to find words and images to transmit the experience, the experience of O in a psychoanalysis has another quality for Bion than what we find in mystics like Eckhart and Buddhism, for instance, where perceiving without the senses and the accompanying temporary dissolution of the self is described as a kind of joyful liberation, enlightenment.

6 Although Kierkegaard considered the attitude of faith predominantly from a religious point of view, much of his detailed exegesis of it anticipates and (probably in terms of the dissemination of ideas) inspires Bion's recommendation of faith as part of a scientific stance.

7 This is close to the 'Achtung' that Kant invokes to designate the relation that thinking has with the 'Thing-in-itself' in the experience of the sublime (Lyotard 1991: 76). Kant described how in the experience of the sublime when the mind is in contact with something it cannot grasp (as in scenes of rugged nature), thinking is transcended and a feeling of horror accompanies it.

8 One can imagine that this model can also be applied to the individual psyche as a relation of a genius-part to an establishment-part of the psyche.

9 SECOND THOUGHTS
Commentary on the *Selected Papers on Psychoanalysis* (1967)

Ten years after the publication of his papers on psychosis, Bion collected them and added an introduction and commentary in a book titled *Second Thoughts*. This additional material deserves a separate chapter as it shows Bion in dialogue with himself, using the ideas that he had discussed in his four theoretical works and applying his Grid to his early papers. This allows us to see how Bion departed from his early work. It is difficult to follow this unique document without knowledge of Bion's later work. I have therefore opted to discuss his second thoughts or commentary in chronological order, in Part II, after the caesura.

Notation and presentation of clinical material in psychoanalytic papers

In Bion's papers on psychosis, clinical material was rendered in a way that is usual in psychoanalytic articles. By the time of the *Commentary* Bion had become convinced that this mode of presentation is usually deployed in a closing manner: mostly to confirm an already existing thought. In other words, it belongs to the first, or even worse, to the second column of the Grid. Moreover, he found it absurd to pretend that a so-called factual representation of clinical material would not be distorted. This is inevitable when experiences are given a narrative form and when representation relies on memory (no matter how recent) and on sensuous experience. Psychoanalysis, by contrast, concerns an extra-sensuous reality, an emotional experience that is in itself odourless and colourless. The emotional experience as such can never be rendered. Furthermore, a few changes do not suffice to make the patient unrecognizable. Bion found that this turns the presentation into a fiction of the worst type. If fiction is used it should be in order to bring us closer to psychic reality, but Bion found that this was not the case in his articles from the 1950s. For example, he judged his representation of the patient in the *Imaginary Twin* to be closing, feeling that it read as an attempt to prepare the reader for the triumph of psychoanalysis.

At best the *Imaginary Twin* article can be read as a description of a realization (a form fitting a non-sensuous datum) that occurred at that particular moment. Years later, when the passion has cooled, another realization with equal validity may occur. For example, the monosyllabic listlessness that Bion described in his original representation of the patient can now be seen as an attempt to capture the ineffable experience of his relationship with the patient and describe the patient's depression, which 'cannot be sensuously grasped'.

Since, in Bion's view, the experience of the relationship that the analyst has with his patient is ineffable, the further removed the interpretation is from a state that can be described in sensuous terms, the greater the chance that it will be accurate. According to Bion, the ineffable plays a far greater role than verbal meaning, certainly in the case of psychotics. In the sessions one can be in touch with it, but it is hard to communicate it from writer to reader, even when writer and reader are the same person, as in the case of Bion reviewing his early papers.

The most accurate notation of a session is the representation of a subjective experience of a session, not in the form of what has been (C3) but as a formulation of an image evocative of the future (C4), a non-saturated form that remains open to what can come rather than trying to create an accurate record of the past.[1] It can be an intuitive sense in which direction a patient can evolve given the essence of this person instead of pinning the patient down to how he/she functions at this moment. In any case, each representation in sensuous space and time fails to capture the ineffable experience that is at stake. The models that we use to represent something are saturated too soon and hence they blind us. In 1967 Bion considered this to be the main problem of his papers from the 50s. An analyst must remain open to all possible developments – as wide a spectrum of thought and feeling as possible, pleasant or unpleasant. Bion's point was that one should analyse the possibilities as they occur without memory or desire.

An interpretation can be 'correct', and yet if it is nothing but a manipulation of theories, without regard for the uniqueness of the realization it attempts to capture, nothing can evolve from it. Similarly, the aim of an article is to produce an evolution in its readers. If a paper merely offers a logical application of theories, this will not happen. Moreover, most of the papers describe part of a session and then interpret it. This is insignificant in Bion's opinion, because there are a thousand possible interpretations and associations and one cannot enter into contact with the non-sensuous psychic reality through the senses (hearing, seeing, smelling, touching), but through intuition. It is hard to communicate this non-sensuous reality to the readers of a text; at best one can try to convey the realization of this non-sensuous reality and the ensuing interpretation. Moreover, the words in which the experience of the ineffable is expressed can be too narrow or too broad to contain it. The concept 'model' expresses this well. A model expresses a transformation of something that is not sensuous into another medium. A patient and an analyst may use different models but as they are both in contact with the same non-sensuous reality, this is not so bad. In writing a paper, the use of models becomes more difficult as the reader and the author do not share the same experience. Moreover, which of the many possible interpretations should one convey? In order to see patterns, there must be selection. According to Bion this selection must occur spontaneously through a precipitation of coherence; in other words, via a selected fact. If the selection is based on an attempt to demonstrate something, as is the case in most papers, it is worthless.

Not only language and the senses but also space and time pose difficulties for any attempt to apprehend psychic reality. The difficulties are particularly acute in the case of psychotics like those described in the papers collected in *Second Thoughts*, because their sense of space and time is disturbed and they deny time and distance because they entail too much frustration. Moreover, the obtrusions of the analyst's memory and desire may be understood as comparable attempts to avoid frustration in contact with psychic reality. The analyst needs to be able to grow with the patient without a denial of the psychic reality, otherwise what is happening is not psychoanalysis.

Box 9.1 A poetic anthology for the psychoanalyst

Here is Francesca Bion on Bion's project to write a poetic anthology for the psychoanalyst, from her text at Bion's memorial:

> It is not surprising then, that he had hoped to compile an anthology of poetry; and since psychoanalysis was fundamental to his thinking, the collection was to be for psychoanalysts. Not, he said, for anyone who is merely *called* a psychoanalyst, not the label of certification, but the 'real thing'. The pieces were to be selected, not for the practice of psychoanalytic virtuosity in giving so-called 'psychoanalytic' interpretations, but because a psychoanalytically expanded capacity would fit the reader to have a new experience, however familiar he might think he was with previous experience of the words.

Unfortunately the anthology will have to join the long list of his projected but unwritten works, but I would like to read to you part of what he wrote as an introduction.

> It is easy in this age of the plague – not of poverty and hunger, but of plenty, surfeit and gluttony – to lose our capacity for awe. It is as well to be reminded by the poet Herman Melville that there are many ways of reading books, but very few of reading them properly – that is, with awe. How much the more is it true of reading people.

(continued)

(continued)

Someone asked, 'Why climb mountains?' 'Because they are there' was the reply. I would add that there are some who would prefer to postpone the exercise till their rugosities, heights, depths and declivities have been worn to a uniform flatness. The Grand Canyon will be tamed; Everest, Kanchenjunga neon-lit; the pass of Glencoe deserted by its ghosts; Nanda Devi no longer the home of the Seven Rishis; the Master of Stair a phantom without bones. William Blake, in Gnomic Verses said, 'Great things are done when men and mountains meet; This is not done by jostling in the street'.

I resort to the poets because they seem to me to say something in a way which is beyond my powers and yet to be in a way which I myself would choose if I had the capacity. The unconscious – for want of a better word – seems to me to show the way 'down to descend', its realms have an awe-inspiring quality.

(Bion, F. 1981: 4)

Annie Reiner sketches an anecdote that brings Bion's interest in poetry to life.

The now famously posh Rodeo Drive, two blocks east of Bion's old building, at that time had a hardware store, a bookstore, and other homely businesses on a street now graced only by the likes of Prada and Tiffany's. There were also at least three bookstores within the small radius that is Beverly Hills, which now has a shocking and shameful *none*. One of these was a psychoanalytic bookshop, a small dusty store at the front of which an equally dusty looking old man sat reading at an old wooden desk. He rarely spoke, and when he did his voice coloured by a Hungarian accent was quiet and weak, as if emanating from a distant place . . .

As I wrote a check for my purchases, this usually curmudgeonly man commented on my interest in Bion's work. Obviously impressed by Bion, he added, 'he comes in here all the time, mostly to buy poetry'.

(Reiner 2012: XVII–XVIII)

Psychosis and the relation with infinity

To be able to allow the relation with infinity, to grow is of primary importance. For instance, if there is an idealized father, it is not the distortion of the father image that must be interpreted. Instead this idealization makes it difficult for the patient to have a relation with infinity. It is better to point at how the patient closes his experience to the Unknown in having a fixed image of his father. Only when 'at-one-ment' with O becomes possible, in other words when the patient dares to experience the vast Unknown and thoughts may be born out of this infinity (which is also nothingness), only then does a harmonious growth become possible (Bion 1984: 145). It is only then that real reverence and awe become possible instead of the simulacra of these feelings that result from immature idealization. In contrast with the papers on psychosis of the 1950s in which Bion developed a coherent theory of thinking, he now sees the origin of thoughts as 'won from the dark and formless infinite'. This infinite is unknowable and cannot be put into words. Bion compares this with the dictum of Eckhart, who mentioned that the idea of the Holy Trinity is the closest one can get to the experience of an unknowable, infinite God. In other words, 'Three binds a constant conjunction won from the dark and formless infinite' (Bion 1984: 148).

A totally new outlook on Bion's theory of thinking could now be formulated: infinity is there before finity; thoughts are there before they are thought. When something is thought, it is won from infinity, but at the same time one must realize that there are many other thoughts that have not yet found a thinker. The analyst must be open enough to let those thoughts evolve, to look at the evolution and then to make an economic selection based on selected fact. It is the analyst's task to give the patient back to himself.

The psychotic part can now be formulated as something that is not won from the formless infinite. A psychotic can try to deal with his overwhelming unconscious world in a sane way, meaning that he can develop a religious awe for this infinite. Then we have a change from an insane psychosis to a psychotic sanity. However, if his overwhelming unconscious world is approached from a logical, realistic or scientific point of view, then we have insane psychosis. In insane psychoses, for instance, everything has the same depth and is treated in the same way. The infinity is there but there is nothing finite to get a hold on, in order not to be entirely lost. There is no difference and no finite binding. This is not the case when there is an awe for the infinite, and an openness to allow thoughts to evolve from there. The analyst must be able to see this. Bion gives the example of how the patient's attacks give the analyst the feeling that there is a skin floating between the patient and the analyst, an infinite monomolecular plane. The analyst must be able to intuit, to 'see' how the attacks evolved into this experience. He can only achieve this through a focus on the infinite Unknown. This may sound counterintuitive in dealing with psychotics, where one would expect reliance on thinking and coherence, as Bion proposed in his theory of thinking and in dealing with psychotic patients in the 50s. In his 'Second Thoughts' about these papers Bion advises the opposite: the analyst should be as close to the infinite as possible and should try to see from there. These phenomena in a psychoanalysis can hardly be shared with a third. Psychoanalysis is still in such a state that one needs the presence of the patient to share the experience. Unlike a discipline such as mathematics, there is no abstract method yet to allow one to deal with objects in their absence.

A radical focus on the non-sensuous reality

The importance of contact with the non-sensuous dimension or the O of a session raises questions about conceptions of the psychoanalytic cure based on sensuous experience and on the pleasure principle. Bion stressed that the idea of a cure is a defensive idea that erases the unfamiliarity of the psychoanalytic experience and of the psychoanalytic object. It offers security but stops the work. The patient's improvement that impressed Bion at the time when he was writing his papers on psychosis was not a part of the analytical work, he finds now many years later. The preconceptions were not to mate with a conception but with a memory. Bion's statements are radical: there is moreover no room for desire in psychoanalysis. It is the unknown non-sensuous reality that counts. The analyst must maintain an attitude of philosophical doubt, which the psychotic will try to attack in order to bring the analyst back to memory and desire. As already mentioned above, this is somewhat counterintuitive, since spontaneously, one tends to reserve this attitude for more neurotic patients and to respect the defences of psychotic patients in order not to disturb their fragile relation with reality. Like Klein, Bion is convinced that everyone has a psychotic part and that a psychoanalysis can only be meaningful when this part is uncovered.

In his discussion of 'On Arrogance', Bion stated that it is easier to see the evolving pattern of co-occurrence of curiosity, arrogance and stupidity in a mental state without memory and desire where it evolves from infinity, than at the time of his writing of the paper when he deduced this pattern. At the time of the *Commentary*, Bion would rather interpret the evolution which he sees at a non-sensuous level. Intuition is the sense-organ of the non-sensuous, the mental counterpart of the senses. Every interpretation that comes from the sensuous will be wrong.

Bion (1984: 158) admitted that he used to attach great importance to a diagnosis at the time of his papers on psychosis, in order not to be alone in his vision and thereby find some reassurance. This reassurance is lost when working without memory and desire. The analyst will often find himself on his own, because the patient also seeks some certainty to hold on to. Bion advocates the same attitude towards reading. Reading as a clinical experience – reading and forgetting – can stimulate evolution, but it can also result in a defensive attitude when the text is strong. In the same vein Bion indicated explicitly that it is best to read his work, to forget it and to read it again. He advocates the same approach for dealing with clinical material.

Conclusion

The 'Commentary' is a small text but of particular importance as it helps us see how Bion reinterpreted his former concepts and clinical experience in the light of his new insights about the need to be open to a dimension that he called O.

Box 9.2 Some philosophical background of the mental attitude to facilitate T(O)

We find many of the characteristics that Bion attributes to O and the mental attitude that he proposes in order to experience O in what Meister Eckhart, the medieval Neo-Platonic mystic and bishop, described as an unknowable, undivided divine essence within ourselves. As discriminative verbal thought precludes the experience of this essence, attempts to approach it often involve trying to put off the ego-functions, so that we are not caught in judgements and thoughts that we need for daily reality, hence the Via Negativa of the mystics (i.e. God does not exist) and the paradoxes of the Zen Buddhists (i.e. burn the Buddha). In the same vein, O does not exist – it is just a concept to point at something else. Bion's O is about being, pure experience; Bion's K is about a contact with the unknowable reality by unconscious thinking.

I paraphrase from Eckhart's *Sermons*: the divine essence is at rest, unmoved but moves us. It is not of the order of time and space; there are no words for it and you cannot talk about it. It is as fire in the fire. It only exists in potence, not in something that is, therefore you can get in contact where it gets form and not when it is form already; it is an unborn getting born, a becoming. The only way to experience it is with a poor mind, and an empty spirit (Ledic Gemut) or self-abandonment; it comes of its own accord; you cannot want it. The spontaneous experience of the essence is facilitated by self-abandonment and detachment, in what Eckhart calls 'Gelassenheit' (releasement, letting be) – a maximum receptiveness, forgetting and not-knowing.

Eckhart had a great effect on philosophers like Heidegger and was his primary source in his writing of *Being and Time*. Heidegger sees the same 'Gelassenheit' as a basic state of mind (Visser 2008). Heidegger contrasts mathematical logical thinking (not unlike Bion's Reason) with 'das andenkende Denken' which he sees as the real thinking. It is an accepting, being in astonishment and respect without wanting to grasp; in short it is 'Gelassenheit' (Ijsseling 2015). Heidegger made a 'Kehre' (Turn), not unlike Bion's caesura, in which he leaves the metaphysical position for this state of mind as the best approach to Sein or Being. The language appropriate to this state of mind is an 'Urdichtung', not unlike Bion's use of Keats' language of achievement.

The Chinese Wu-Wei expresses the same state of mind. White (2011) links both Eckhart's Gelassenheit and the Chinese Wu-Wei with Bion. It is similar to Keats' 'negative capability' (see Box 8.8) and we can trace many similarities with Zen Buddhism or with Hebraic mysticism like the Kabbalah. In Bion this basic state of mind for the analyst is found in his 'patience – security' and his 'no memory, no desire, no understanding, no coherence' attitude. Najeeb (2014) makes a link with the Indian Vedic Buddhism.

A position of dispassionate waiting seems at the heart of Bion's psychoanalytic attitude. T.S. Eliot expresses this well in his poem 'East Coker' (1940)

(continued)

(continued)

from the *Four Quartets* where he describes waiting without love and hope and thought but with faith that is in the waiting.

The self-abandonment or *Gelassenheit* of Eckhart was well expressed and practiced by Angelus Silesius.

> The self must make an unconditional surrender of its selfhood. It must lose all sense of self-identity, of particularity, of otherness. Above all, it must be quit of all desires, whether for rewards, for happiness, for a future life, or even for God himself; for the persistence of any desire attests the fact that the desiring self still lives on. It must die. It must cease to be. The categorical imperative of Angelus Silesius is *Sei nicht* – Be not.
>
> (Angelus Silesius 1737/1986: 88)

We find in Bion's approach the same notions of Essence, rendering a person unto themselves, getting in contact with the undifferentiated, infinite core of our psyche by eschewing memory, desire, understanding and coherence.

Note

1 'Now the particular case that I think we ought to be talking about is the patient that each one of you is going to see tomorrow, always – not the one that you saw today, or yesterday, but *tomorrow*' (Bion 1967, first seminar LA in Aguayo and Malin 2014: 2).

10 *A MEMOIR OF THE FUTURE* (1977)

After the evolution of his thoughts on psychic functioning and psychic change in his four major theoretical works (the *Seven Servants*), Bion adopted a more artistic mode of expression as he continued his psychoanalytic odyssey. In keeping with his account of transformations in O, he wanted to allow his readers to experience what he was trying to communicate. He hoped that the unusual style of *A Memoir of the Future* would enable form and content to influence one another; in other words, that it would save the content from being imprisoned in the style; his hope was that the style would facilitate the unknown spontaneous process. In this sense *A Memoir of the Future* has a great deal in common with Bion's autobiographical book, *The Long Weekend*, which was written in the same spirit and in which the 75-year-old Bion did not make any concessions to the reader.

Francesca Bion (1995) stated that 'she saw the change in him and the relief he felt in throwing off some life-long restraints'. She quotes from the epilogue of *A Memoir of the Future*:

> All my life I have been imprisoned, frustrated, dogged by commonsense, reason, memories, desires and – greatest bug-bear of all – understanding and being understood. This is an attempt to express my rebellion, to say 'Good-bye' to all that. It is my wish, I now realize doomed to failure, to write a book unspoiled by any tincture of common-sense, reason, etc., (see above). So although I would write, 'Abandon Hope all ye who expect to find any facts, scientific, aesthetic or religious in this book', I cannot claim to have succeeded. All of these will, I fear, be seen to have left their traces, vestiges, ghosts hidden within these words; even sanity, like 'cheerfulness', will creep in.
>
> (Bion, F. 1995)

Reception of the Trilogy

Although Bion considered the trilogy to be his magnum opus, his readers' reactions to *A Memoir of the Future* were distinctly mixed: Wisdom (1987: 545) states, for instance: 'I failed to understand a word from his *Memoir of the Future*'. Actually, the first two books, which were published in Brazil, were not immediately successful when released. Although Bion spoke highly of the three books, they were ignored for years and only came to be published in the UK after painstaking effort (Sandler 2005a) and at Bion's own expense (Bléandonu 1994). Donald Meltzer, an American analyst who lived and practised as a Kleinian in Oxford, visited Bion when he was invited to lecture in Los Angeles, as he was worried about him.

> As the ensuing years brought news of conflicts within the psychoanalytic community in Los Angeles and the slim volumes of the Memoir began to appear in their shoddy and error-ridden Brazilian edition (1975, 1977), along with the equally unattractive and inaccurate so-called 'lectures' (1973–1974) in Brazil, it seemed that perhaps Dr Bion had not left us but rather had been kidnapped and was being tortured or degraded or perhaps was just becoming senile.
>
> (Meltzer and Williams (1985) in
> Hahn 1994: 521)

> The general reaction to them was one of shocked rejection. 'He was a great man', but he had no experience of writing fiction, a well known literary critic must have said declining to review his books. He was very old, he was not well: he was disappointed by his experience in California: his isolation denied him the modulating influence of his former colleagues – all these remarks have been heard uttered as an excuse for not reading, or not reading carefully, and certainly not rereading the *Memoir*.
>
> (Meltzer 1994: 546)

Meltzer and his wife, the psychoanalyst Martha Harris, therefore decided to publish the third book separately with their own Clunie Press. During their visit they were impressed by Bion's liveliness and the seriousness of his work. The Meltzers gave a series of lectures on the three books in Oxford in 1982 (Meltzer 1985). Meg Harris Williams, the daughter of Martha Harris, wrote three beautiful additional texts on the Trilogy (Harris Williams, 1983, 1985, 2010), now collected in a book. They are dense, poetic and the best so far on the Trilogy. She sees the underlying pattern of the trilogy as different parts of Bion's self in interaction. In the first book this interaction takes the form of a chaotic dream. Over the three books the different parts achieve coherence, integrating the life of Bion in the present, and come to be able to face the approaching catastrophe of death.

The real success of *A Memoir of the Future* came only much later, after the three books had been collected and edited under the care of Francesca Bion, and published with an explanatory key under the title *A Memoir of the Future* (MOF) by Karnac in 1991. I agree with James Grotstein (2005b) that the title probably refers to the Platonic idea that Forms or preconceptions are inherent from before birth; some can develop interactively and others in an independent way, just as we see happen in the different characters of the book.

The style

The art form that Bion used to reflect his psychoanalysis of thinking is comparable to the style of Joyce (the Joyce of *Ulysses* and *Finnegans Wake* rather than of *Portrait of the Artist*) and Beckett. Beckett, who had been in therapy with Bion, also wrote a Trilogy, which also articulated multiple identifications and used a language full of attacks on linking, with words that may have shifting meanings. Bion had already articulated the problem of using verbal language when discussing a language of achievement. Bion and Beckett did not trust words and found that language spoils the contact with what is expressed. Beckett famously said that he wrote because there is nothing to say. *A Memoir of the Future* also shows the influence of Milton's style. As Harris Williams (1983) pointed out, Milton wrote two memoirs in completely different styles. Bion did the same with *A Memoir of the Future* and *The Long Weekend*.

The fictitious characters

Since Bion wanted to bring about a change in the reader without making any concessions to a narrative and logical approach, it is not surprising that reading his Trilogy arouses a strong resistance in most readers (Sandler 2005a). Bion suggests reading in a state of reverie, close to the infinite, which he compared once with a state just above sleep (Bion 1967, third seminar in Aguayo and Malin 2014). *A Memoir of the Future* can indeed easily be read as a dream. The characters represent different parts of Bion's personality and thoughts on different vertices. They form a group. To Bion, the fictitious dream characters are more real than real people. 'Real people have to be treated roughly if the universe is to be made safe for imaginary people' (1991: 92), therefore 'he must be cruel, only to be kind' (Hamlet, III, iv, 179).

Bion offered an explanatory key to *A Memoir of the Future* in which the fictitious characters are elaborated. 'Alice' is a well-educated lady, who suffers the most from the burden of her education, whereas 'Rosemary', the maid and daughter of a prostitute, represents sexuality and authenticity. In the end, their roles are reversed: Alice changes from mistress to lover and to maid of her own maid Rosemary. 'Roland' and 'Robin, his neighbour', on the other hand, are mixed, ambivalent characters, sometimes thoughtful, but often in action. 'Tom' is a powerful servant, 'Man' represents the powers that are occupying England – in this way he represents a certain military masculinity, 'Arf-arfer' – referring to the prayer 'Our Father' – is the primitive super-ego, and 'Priest' represents the minus form of the religious dimension, namely the institutionalized church that risks killing the religious genius, the revolutionary change in point of view and experience offered for instance by Jesus or the Buddha. The unborn self plays a role, just as in Beckett's work (it was a topic in the lecture of Jung that both Bion and Beckett attended). Meg Harris Williams (2011) notes that some of the characters are from Milton's *Paradise Lost* and sees in the figure of Roland a reflection of her father, the poet Roland Harris, who was an analysand of Bion.

Sandler (2005a) views the book as an epistemological work from which he quotes large conceptual excerpts in his dictionary of Bion's range of ideas. He discusses Bion's explanatory key to *A Memoir of the Future* and remarks that Bion-Myself-PA represent three aspects of the same character. The characters Sherlock Holmes, Mycroft Holmes, and Watson also form a gradient: whereas Watson represents acting and Mycroft pure thought, Sherlock combines both characteristics. Meltzer (1994) points out that the characters are functioning under the dread of the catastrophe of occupation by the alien forces. Bion often felt that he was living in dread of an imminent disaster. In Bion's way of thinking, a certain dread seems important for the functioning of Mind and for psychic change.

Since *A Memoir of the Future* consists of three separate books – *The Dream*, *The Past Presented* and *The Dawn of Oblivion* – I will discuss each book separately. The multilayered book has a different effect on most readers and evokes many different ideas and associations. My modest approach to the Trilogy will make no sense to those who have not read the books. I limit myself to giving some hints that may help in reading them.

First book: The Dream

The first book is the most difficult to read, since it attempts to unfetter Bion's writing from the constraints of logical thought. It tries to create conditions in which thoughts may arise of themselves. Like Bion in his recurrent dream of the Steinbeck, struggling in the mud of the trenches, thoughts struggle to find a form and a thinker. Trying to 'imagine' this, Bion chooses a dream form for the first book of the Trilogy. The dream format is an attempt to let form and thought originate spontaneously and find each other to the benefit of both. This dynamic interaction is a reflection of the PS-D oscillation on which the thinking of emotions is based. The hallucinatory basis of thinking, the infinite hallucinatory layer, resists being transformed into a secondary, coherent, narrative form. The reader must be able to let go of the desire to get a grip on the writing by organizing it into a narrative and read without attempting to understand, in order to experience the spontaneous PS-D oscillation for himself. As De Bianchedi (2005: 1533) states: 'One has to read (preferably aloud, in a group context) without memory . . . Taking up Bion's use of Keats's definition of "language of achievement" and "negative capability"'. One has to let something finite emerge out of the infinity of the hallucinatory basis of thinking. The purpose of Bion's text is to expand the reader's thinking. In this text, Bion uses the technique of reversed perspective, first described as a psychotic mechanism in T(K) (Bion 1967), but now seen as a good technique for fostering T(O). Close to this method of reversal of perspective is his use of binocular vision, which helps to foster thinking from different vertices. For example: an analyst may listen to the breath of a patient and focus on the gas vertex and so observe a spectrum of flatus to poisonous gas. Bion likes this approach and seems to enjoy questions based on such a reversal of perspective with a shifting from foreground to background, as in Rubin's vase. Hence questions like: who is the most famous: Nelson or his blind eye? Or Newton or his apple? Using the same binocular perspective, PS and D are now compared to waves and particles in the wave theory. By looking from different vertices, using binocular vision and reversed perspective, Bion exercises in the book a faculty that he calls speculative imagination (Bion 1997). He hopes to touch the infra- and ultrasensorial to which we have no access, and to unleash its powers. Bion thinks that psychoanalysis in its current form remains at a superficial, descriptive level. It is merely 'a stripe on the coat of the tiger' (p. 112). What will happen when we meet the tiger itself?

Bion seeks to break through the crust of secondary thinking in order to regain contact with what is real. He therefore resorts even to shocking images like meeting in the arse of a dinosaur. He seems to find Rosemary (the street-wise daughter of a prostitute) more authentic than Alice (who represents education). In the explanatory key to *Memoir of the Future*, Bion describes the vigorous Rosemary with one sentence: 'she does not like psychoanalysis', the sterile jargon-ridden psychoanalysis that Bion attacks. Bion, much like Beckett, was convinced of the limitations of language that probably only art could overcome. To preserve the vitality in his words, Bion at times uses potentially offensive and blasphemous language, a 'cuntish language', for example when he says that 'Psychoanalysts are gasbags'. Blasphemy is used as an antidote against dead, sterile psychoanalytic jargon.

Second book: The Past Presented

I see the second book or *The Past Presented* as a living Grid, like a chess game with living pieces. The different players are like thoughts in various stages, belonging to different grid categories. Du for example is a very primitive thought that lies close to the Central Nervous System (α-element), Roland verbalizes thoughts that resemble abstraction (G), Tom represents the primitive and the acting out (A6), Edmund is very abstract and represents the astronomic point of view (G), Alice is stuck in her own system, therefore column 2, Moriarty represents a closed cynicism (column 2), Watson is rather column 1 (he secures something but does not think further), and

Holmes is Inquiry or column 3. These categories can also be seen as vertices (the psychoanalyst, the priest, the servant, etc.). The character called P.A. keeps these vertices together.

As in *The Dream*, Bion's unsaturated approach provides no narrative cohesion in this book. He frustrates the reader in his search for a meaning. The effect is that the book is difficult to read and as the reader's attention is not held by a kind of narrative tension, it can be annoying. But to Bion this challenge to the capacity for frustration tolerance is an essential step in catalysing thinking.

Rather than a story, Bion offers a kind of basic hallucinatory layer with its chimera. As a reader in a PS state of mind, one can be in touch with emerging thoughts from the non-differentiated basic layer that Bion evokes.

The best strategy is to try to read with a penetrating darkness, not-knowing and being sensible to connections that may emerge as a feeble light. Bion quotes the poet G.M. Hopkins: 'Be shellèd, eyes, with double dark / And find the uncreated light' (p. 271). One needs an inner eye, apart from the senses.

Bion masterfully describes the birth of thoughts from the basic layer or matrix. The character Du is an embryonic thought ('I can kick my way out of this ruddy matrix when I like'). Intense emotions and verbal thought can stand in the way of the birth of thought through the caesura. Another magnificent description can be found on p. 279: 'I was keeping quiet, lying as close to your CNS as I could get and trying to make you have the sense to lie flat on the ground – drowned in adrenal stimulation'. And after passing the caesura, immediately language and logical thinking interfere and capture this foetal thought (p. 276: 'Words have no right to be rigid definitory caskets, preventing my birth'). The writing shows a nearly visceral aversion to definitory and closing language. On the contrary, Bion thought that great artists such as Leonardo da Vinci, Robert Browning, Homer, Virgil (p. 245) and Shakespeare (p. 524) are in touch with this basic, undifferentiated layer and are able to see the origin of Forms, and it is possible to distinguish art from kitsch for instance by using this criterion.

It is in this layer that one also finds the gist of language. When language loses contact with the basic layer and when the link with the constant conjunctions of the basic layer is gone, it becomes an oppressive prison. Being able to break up the rigidity of language creates figments of imagination, which are said often to be more powerful than many real things (p. 345). They are closer to the noumena, they are (p. 315): 'what did Berkeley call it? ghosts of departed quantities, Newton's nascent increments'.

Bion wants the patient and the reader to regain contact with their fundamental layer: 'All I purport to do is to give the individual the chance of observing his God-like assumption of God-like attributes' (p. 241). This compares to the essence, or, for Bion, the 'real self' of a person: P.A. states that 'we hope to introduce the person to his "real" self (p. 266) and that 'The difficulty is not only with the galactic centre. It is as difficult to see the centre of one's own personality. Distracted and fascinated by what is not one's self, the periphery is substituted for the centre' (p. 254).

Nevertheless, it can be dangerous to come too close to this centre, especially when one tries to know it or to possess it (–K): P.A. says: 'Intelligent people – Arjuna, Meister Eckhart, Jesus, Plato, Socrates, Aristotle, Saint Augustine and the rest – want to *know* God. They have been warned that, Icarus-like, they would single their waxen wings and . . . *fall*' (p. 359).

Meltzer (1994) interprets the dream meetings of the various characters in the second book as being under the influence of the basic assumptions: catastrophe, suspicion and dread of murder are present. Rosemary definitely becomes the central figure: her liveliness and spirit cut through the cynicism, pedantry, arrogance and especially the 'belief systems' of each of the characters. There is more tolerance of not-knowing, waiting and negative capability in the characters than in the first book. There is something frightening, however; Rosemary marries Man but 'Under the pressure of catastrophic change, it is uncertain whether the "foetal idea" is going to grow, kill itself, or be killed' (Meltzer 1994: 541).

Sandler (2005a) takes another approach and views the second book, *The Past Presented*, as a psychoanalytic session, in which the analyst can find several pieces of advice. He suggests that the book may even function as a kind of manual.

Third book: The Dawn of Oblivion

The third book, *The Dawn of Oblivion* (a reference to a verse by Milton), is written in a more coherent way. The characters in the third book no longer represent thoughts at different stages as in Book II, but are now stages of Bion himself. They are taken up again in his autobiography, *The Long Weekend*. Bion compares these stages to the layers of an onion. The basic layer where thoughts arise and which is described in book II nevertheless remains present, although Bion states that it takes a genius to regain contact with it.

In Bion's description of the coexisting layers of his own evolution, one can see his idea of a personality as functioning in different vertices that do not necessarily meet. He and his thoughts are both emmatures; that is, immature beings born in the formless infinite. They are thrown from the void of the womb into the infinite, *le Néant*. The psyche is born and dialogues with soma. Psyche and soma become separate, differentiated creatures with a life of their own.

PRE-MATURE	Get on with it – when were you born?
EM-MATURE	Don't hurry; I was coming to that.
EIGHT YEARS	You always are, but do not arrive.
EM	When I was only three somites old —
TWENTY-FOUR YEARS	That's not an age.

EM	Don't talk about matters you don't understand. If you have respect for your fore-bears —
EIGHT YEARS	You've spelled it wrong.
EM	When I spell it, it is right; when you spell it, it is wrong.
EIGHT YEARS	That is not how it seems to me, looking at it from my side of the barrier.
LEONARD	Shut up both of you and look at this drawing.
EIGHT YEARS	Not bad – what is it ?
EM	I see a great light
TWENTY-FOUR EARS	Open your eyes and you will see it is the darkness of the womb.
MILTON	The formless infinite – the void.
EM	The light is too intense.
TWELVE YEARS	'it is eye. Be not afraid. And 'e did 'it' is eye. And EM was afraid. Ha, ha, ha!
EM	What a dreadful oscillation of pressure!
THITY YEARS	Who is talking words you don't understand now?
LEONARD	Hair! Water! If you only looked you would 'see-what-I-mean', but
FORTY YEARS	No – only hair, water, words —
FORTY-TWO YEARS	No; if you listened you would only hear 'repetition compulsion' psycho-ese.
P.A.	Psycho-analysis?
EM	Stop! Stop! I can't bear it. I am blinded, deafened!

(Bion 1971: 430)

This is a nice example of the individual as a group and a barrier (caesura) between the unborn somapsyche, the hallucinatory layer, the emmatures and the born, especially the verbal ones, where Reason is dominating. As you can read, to Bion, psychic birth is there from the start (at three somites) but that cannot be understood by the verbal and reasonable ones. It takes a genius like Leonardo da Vinci (whirling water and hair drawings) and Milton (the infinite void) to get in contact with these undifferentiated layers of experience and psychic functioning in the womb. These experiences and this part of the personality are extremely sensitive; Bion describes the intense experience of the beginning of seeing and the pressure on the eyes, before a baby has words and thoughts to situate it. In this quote, the twelve years does it to the emmature. The point that Bion wants to make is that these zones of psychic functioning remain through life and psychoanalysis can make contact with it, if it does not retract in a closing deafening sterile conceptualization.

In this book, Bion describes how his childhood begins, with the presence of Bion's sister and mother. Adolescence and the Morals emerge ('sex, like sherry, often produces perfectly genuine feelings of love and affection' (p. 445)). Bion describes the 21-year-old soldier with passages about the humiliation of wearing a school cap, the bomb craters and the human soup at the Salient, and the battle of Amiens. These passages are written in a dialect that some of his comrades in the tank may have spoken, as yet another vertex. They are some of the most appealing passages about his psychic suffering as a soldier. He evokes the presence of scattered memories in his mind, wounded soldiers, one of his comrades dying near to him with his belly torn apart by a shell, mistaking walking soldiers for trees. All these things come together in a dissociated state of mind, while he is looking at a speck of mud. Bion evokes this extra-ordinary mental experience (in his war memoirs, it is the point where his war diary becomes psychic – see Chapter 12), and describes how his traumatic experience in the war takes a form arising from the undifferentiated hallucinatory layer. A memory of waiting at the front for a car to pick him up is mixed with memories from his childhood (arf-arfer: our father; king dumb: kingdom) and the dialect of his fellow soldiers and the traumatic experience of mistaking soldiers for trees. It shows how thoughts emerge from undifferentiated emotional experiences, voices, sensations. He describes in the same way what happened when they crossed the German lines in the attack of 8 August at Amiens of which Bion said that he died that day. On that day 30,000 German soldiers and 8,800 from the Allied Forces were killed.

Captain Bion

I stared at the speck of mud trembling on the straw. I stared through the front flap at the clods of earth spouting up all round us. I stared at the dirty, strained face of my driver Allen – my strained face as I sat by me; at the boomerang that Allen sent me from Australia. I got out and hovered about six feet above us. I knew 'they' would . . . and saw trees as woods walking. How they walked – walk! walk! They went like arfs arfing. Arf arf together, arfing's the stuff for me, if it's not a Rolls Royce, which I'd pick out for choice. Then a nice little Ford bright and gay, and when they came to that ford, styx I say, Valiant for S'truth passed over and all the strumpets sounded for him on the uvver side. Cooh! Wat'appened then? 'E talked a lot more about Jesus and dog and man and then 's sez, all sudden like, Throw away the uvver crutch! Coo! Wot'appened then? 'E fell on'is arse. And'is Arse wuz angry and said, Gett off my arse! You've done nothing but throw shit at me all yore life and now you expects England to be my booty! Boo-ootiful soup; in a shell-hole in Flanders Fields. Legs and guts . . . must'ave bin twenty men in there – Germ'um and frogslegs and all starts! We didn't 'alf arf I can tell you. Let bruvverly luv continue. No one asked'*im* to fall-in! No one arsed'im to come out either – come fourth, we said and E came 5th and'e didn't ½ stink. Full stop! 'e said. The parson'e did kum, 'e did qwat. 'E talked of Kingdom Come. King dumb come.

(Bion 1991: 53)

P.A.: Right – let's start. I remember how I felt when I was Twenty-one. We had just been ordered up the Line; I was terrified. I did not like the prospect at all. The orders were that we must not allow the enemy any rest, but carry on the pursuit now he had been beaten and a great gap torn in his lines by our victory on August 8th. Unfortunately I had been decorated for gallantry. Twenty-one knew I was terrified and hadn't the courage to get the doc. to invalid me out. I knew I had not the courage for 'heroic' deeds. Besides, I had 'flu; my runner was given a bottle of phyz. to dose me with. No one knew what I was suffering from so it was called p.u.o. – pyrexia of unknown origin. I hoped my death would be painless and sudden. The infantryman by my side had a hole in his belly. We looked at him coldly. 'He's a gonner – why waste time looking at him? Come on – zero hour'. I scrambled out of the trench and stared walking forward. I inhibited – as I learned to call it later – any whisper of fact to burst through my p.u.o. A grey-haired man with his legs worn round his neck like a scarf wanted me to 'help' him. It was annoying to be expected to disentangle his neck-wear. Besides, I was busy. 'No – stretcher bearers coming!' I knew they weren't; only regimental stretcher bearers help. Why did I tell him that? I had been taught – disciplined – so that in just such a crisis I would not have an unfamiliar, unthought-out problem to solve in inadequate conditions for its solution. As a doctor I now understand; as an influenza-sodden tank officer, 'S.B's coming!' I lied. 'Kamerad kaput!' yelled the little Boche as he ran towards me, his bottom wiggling furiously as he tried not to fall. I could tell the hideously disarticulated old Tommy to go to Hell – 'S.B'.s coming' – but I allowed the horrible little Boche to drag me to his cubby hole. No discipline – I knew he would murder me. I entered; in the dark another Boche with his legs wrapped round his neck for scarfwear. 'Kaput?' He dragged me to touch – 'Kaput?' I did. 'Yes, kaput'. He burst into tears. I told myself, 'Now – damn fool – get *out*'. Only then I snapped out – out of the hole, out into the air, out into the sense to carry my Smith and Wesson where I had been taught to carry it.

Priest You would not have felt any better if you had been a parson. I remember our pink-faced, jolly, card-playing padre and how scornful you were – you and that red-faced, non-conformist private – because he would not come up and bury the dead. Poor Smith! He was so rigorous mortis that we could not force his arms into our grave; we were in a hurry too.

(Bion 1991: 474–475)

Bion's anecdotes are illustrations of how the Mind works. He places the layers of the Mind side by side so that they can develop separately. Because of this, splits and conflicting vertices are preserved like conscious – unconscious, soma – psyche. Different characters represent different vertices.

What does it mean to mammals to have a mind, to experience the strange object which is growing there? Bion asks. One can read the text as a war going on between soma and psyche (Harris Williams 1983), a caesura between the purely experiencing pre-natals (the hallucinatory layer) and the post-natals that function on a higher level (thinking). What if they meet each other? Bion transcends the caesura by allowing them to coexist.

As De Bianchedi (2005) points out, the idea of a pre-natal and a post-natal level of functioning of the mind partly replaces Bion's former ideas of a psychotic and a non-psychotic functioning of the personality. Different transformations take place on the opposite sides of the caesura, and in the different vertices: 'if the somites could write, the book would be on the "interpretation of reality" and the theories would be what we call dreams' (1991: 470) (see Box 8.6). The other zone is making dreams about the reality that we meet. While this idea may sound strange, it is close to certain contemporary neuroscientific findings and hypotheses, like those of Friston (2013) who suggests that the function of dreams is to make interpretations and hypothesizes to prepare us for the unknown reality that we meet every day.[1]

The caesura of language between psyche and soma is now experienced as an opaque screen (1991: 467) rather than as a link as Bion had seen it in his ideas of the 1960s on verbal thought. Now Bion describes language as an exoskeleton, a chitinous carapace. Nevertheless, something can break through this caesura, like interpretations that have to be perspicacious and perspicuous (1991: 459). As we will discuss in Chapter 11, Bion finds that bigotry can play a role in breaking through this caesura. In bigotry the words may evoke an emotional reaction and are often embodied: 'bigotry and ignorance are two fundamental characteristics of psychoanalysis, we must stay alert for these' (1991: 524).

> Sometimes the 'acceptable convention' has to stretch, alter, to accommodate the thing that 'breaks through'; sometimes the 'conventionally acceptable' crushes the 'outbreaking impulse'. Usually it is a compromise between the two. Just now Alice allowed her ears and lips to be degraded by 'bloody cunt' and 'fucking bastard'; the rest of us have to allow ourselves to be limited by being polite and saying 'please'.
>
> (Bion 1991: 485)

Bion's mistrust of language extends to rational thinking. He considers dogmas and theories as futile and unreliable ('the words in which we dress ideas disguise already as they display the meaning to which we aspire', p. 478). Ideas are imprisoned within shells of words that act as preservatives and diminish their power. However, although psychoanalysis is dressed in tired language, the meaning is not tired and neither is illness; both retain their power and analysis remains a dangerous act (p. 533). Bion himself does not find it hard to let theories go (p. 447: he has no more difficulty than an insect has with 'the form it bursts out of'). His firm statement that psychoanalysis must break through the crust is repeated over and over: 'Robin: It took me years before I broke through the crust of training, by wich I learned to revere my superiors and their wisdom. I did achieve my freedom' (p. 547).

Without the shell of words and theories we are in touch with a pure intuition that arises from the somatic. Just as animals are aware of the imminence of an earthquake, humans can be aware of the imminence of an emotional upheaval. In our enormous ignorance, intuition can be an 'oeil en trop', as he prompts Green to say (p. 538): 'We can smell the danger'. Bion had lived with this sense of imminent catastrophe and found that it had often been a great help for him (p. 538). Thinking and Truth look megalomaniacal in this light: '"What is truth?" said jesting Pilate' (p. 449) and he ran away in order not to be killed. Truth is relative and a concept or ideal in itself; it is only in its relation with the infinite that it can be defined.

Bion seldom writes about sex. In *A Memoir of the Future* he talks about its potentially destructive power. His characters show different facets, vertices of it. He found sexual desire which is too easily satisfied mentally debilitating (p. 531) and suggests that undisciplined sexual love is reminiscent of a baby's love for food. Bion is not like Bataille, who explored the limits and unmentalized sides of sexuality and used these experiences to break through defences. Bion did not use experiences to try to go beyond beaten tracks and unfetter fixed mental attitudes, but tried to give a shock with words, with bigotry, in order to get real contact: for instance, when he began a lecture at the Menninger Clinic by saying 'bloody cunt' and then fell silent. It is unclear with what psychoanalytic object Bion wanted to share an emotional contact. For example, his concise two words might have been intended to point to the impact of the 'B.C.' whether in its bloody or non-bloody states, in function, capacity and meanings for human beings, male and female, young and old.

The power of sexuality and its potential to bring about catastrophic change is evident in the characters of well-educated Alice and Rosemary, who is the daughter of a prostitute but has an authentic sexuality. Bion describes how sexuality brings a catastrophic change and a role reversal in Alice.

The book with its different characters reflects the difficulty of integrating these facets, which are not good or bad but coexist as parts of a personality. Bion seems to find a possible integration in what he calls passionate love, which is different from passion and unrelated to an actual partner. It is more like a mental state and different from the soma. Bion does not seem to trust these bodily desires and talks about human beings always thumping with anger, fear, love. Or sex, like sherry, that entails tender feelings, which is something different than the capacity for passionate love (p. 445). The mental state of passionate love is of another order and even sexual maturity (p. 470) may disguise the absence of passionate love (p. 472).

As Sandler (2005a) states, there are still a lot of islands of (paranoid-schizoid) suffering in the third book, but the depressive position is more prominent. The inner objects are less fragmented. 'Priest' returns enriched, 'Woman' joins him. The Bion character only plays an 'insignificant' role. He no longer acts as the separate character Bion next to other personae, and identifies himself with the psychoanalyst. The book is like an interview with Bion at the end of his life. The style is no longer so wild and philosophical. In this book, Bion comes to the fore as a wise analyst who puts many classical questions in perspective. He prompts himself to say that at the age of 25, he hoped to be wise, not intelligent. At the age of 70 he admits that he cannot honestly say that he feels wise: 'In real life it gets off as fast as it grows' but he insists that 'knowledge must be augmented by wisdom, the chance of survival is decreased if the character cannot rely on being wise'. Wisdom is a becoming, not a possession. Only at the end of the book do Bion and P.A. once again become two separate characters, two differentiated vertices. Bion is the more questioning figure, who pricks defences. He states that he can hardly bear his own image of someone with a 'sane and balanced outlook and his fascinating sense of humour' (p. 522). He states that psychoanalysis is about becoming oneself, and this applies to the psychoanalyst as well as his patient.

In conclusion I could say that I struggled with *A Memoir of the Future* as many readers did. As Bion considered it as his major work, it is compelling to read it. It offers a lot of original insights and shows the large cultural background of Bion. It shows his 'negative capability' in looking at different vertices or parts of a personality communicating with each other, from different ages and points in the evolutions, and is in this sense a reflection of analytic work. We see Bion reflecting with his British ironical, often grotesque humour. There are many nice metaphors and quotes in the book. So it is really worth reading it, especially when being in a state of free-floating attention. It is like an exercise for psychoanalysts.

Bion wanted to get a liberated form and a liberated way of thinking, bringing readers in contact with the unknowable, with the emmature and life-giving side of our being. He did not really succeed in this effort; his work remains laborious, hard to read. It is does not go straight to the heart as some poems can do. You see Bion struggle with ideas on marriage, religion, sexuality and so on that are typical for the Zeitgeist in which he lived. But most of all, he does not seem to get freed from thinking, trying to convey something often at a philosophical level. Despite all his efforts, you still see the puppet master behind the work.

Note

1 See note 8 in Chapter 9.

11 LECTURES, SEMINARS AND SOME SHORT TEXTS AS PREPARATION FOR THE LECTURES (1973–1979)

Introduction

After the *Seven Servants*, Bion wrote no new theoretical works. He applied his insights but now began to write in a style more appropriate to his findings. *A Memoir of the Future* was an attempt to transmit his ideas in a lively way that would have the potential to provoke change. He also gave supervisions and lectures abroad. In his last years (between 76 and 82 years old) he was still in a process of becoming, perhaps now more than ever.

Bion's 'lectures' are actually associations in response to questions from the public. Bion never prepared them, although he would sometimes free associate about them on beforehand, and tape-recorded some of these musings, which are published in *Cogitations* (Bion 1992). His musings in preparation for the Italian lectures are published in *Taming Wild Thoughts* (Bion 1997).

Bion never knew beforehand what he would say. He saw his lectures as experiences and was often nervous before them, feeling unsure that he had anything to say to the audience (Culbert-Koehn 2011). He talked in a monotonous voice with long pauses. People often laughed at his strange associations. He made long detours which he compared with a helix. He never answered a question directly, which often made his interlocutors feel uncomfortable; some people found him infuriating while others attributed guru-like qualities to him.

As in *A Memoir of the Future*, Bion was looking for a new style that would allow him to resist what he considered to be the fixing effect of language. In his search for a living form he was often provocative. For example, at the lecture at the Menninger Clinic (see Chapter 7) he used bigotry 'as a well developed and ancient characteristic of the human being' that may 'show up in psychoanalysis with startling freshness' (Bion 1991: 524). According to Mason (2000), the audience were disturbed and people thought that he had 'lost his marbles'. There are few pictures of Bion in this period. We see a large, sturdy old man, usually in a white shirt, bow tie and jacket, with a neat moustache and a slightly surprised, uncomfortable look behind thick glasses. There is a film available on the internet of one of the Tavistock lectures (Bion 1977) where one can see Bion at work during the seminars.[1]

Like *A Memoir of the Future*, the lectures and seminars illustrate his peculiar approach during this period, showing reversal of perspective, binocular vision, awe for the unconscious and the unknown and an attitude of radical not-knowing. Bion strove to create works that were open enough to allow something new to happen in his audiences' encounters with them.

Segal (1981: 8) recalls that on a visit to California, she confronted Bion with a former statement of his: 'Psychoanalysis aims to produce that change in the mental apparatus which enables it to learn by experience'. He smiled and said: 'You know, it is rather like catching a tiger and saying "nice pussy cat"', meaning that in psychoanalysis there was much more urgency and danger than his earlier statement conveyed.

Although the catastrophic change that transformed Bion's later work was manifest in *A Memoir of the Future* and in the content of his communications, lectures and seminars, this manifest change seemed to be less present in his psychoanalyses (Grotstein 2002) and in his supervisions. In these contexts he was perceived as an orthodox Kleinian. Bion's clinical work and supervision did not reveal his inner state of mind, which he explored in his writing.

Box 11.1 Pilgrimages with Bion

Tustin (1981), Grotstein (2002) and Gooch (2002, 2011) have written about their analytic experiences with Bion, which sound basically Kleinian. Tustin and Grotstein both describe their analysis with Bion as pilgrimages.
Some excerpts from their impressions:

> I have often been asked whether Dr Bion talked in the somewhat inscrutable, oracular way in which he sometimes wrote. I can say very firmly that this was not so. He was always brief, to the point and extremely simple and clear . . . Looking back, I realise that for much of the time I was 'impenetrable' as Dr Bion once said I was. And yet, at the time, I thought I was one of the most co-operative patients he could have had. There is no wonder that in my professional work I have concentrated on 'autism' in its various manifestations, both normal and pathological. I might have been left in that twilight state, but for Dr Bion's incisive insight, his patience and persistence. On one occasion I remember his saying to me that I was feeling that it was 'better to be persecuted than half-dead'. For most of my life I had been 'half-dead', and I had a strong desire to stay that way. Life was easier . . . He provoked me to think for myself – to have a mind of my own. He did this by asking challenging questions and by making unexpected remarks rather than by imposing

(continued)

(continued)

a rigid interpretive scheme on what I said and did. . . . His generosity and integrity (and capacity to withstand boredom) were evidenced by the fact that in the fourteen years in which I was (on and off), a patient with him, he never altered the fees I paid . . . I always referred to him as 'a rock of Gibraltar'. The waves of my passions broke around him and he stood steady. And after I had finished seeing him in analysis, and I felt turned upside down and inside out by the changes I had fended off from making whilst I was with him, I knew that that rock was there and that I would find my focus and my fulcrum in the end. The 'slough of despond' was navigated and I emerged to continue the pilgrimage . . . It was Bion's respect for the organic process of analysis which he allowed to take its course, and which he never tried to manipulate that made me feel so safe.

(Tustin 1981: 175–176)

My Kleinian analysis with Bion revealed a radically different aspect of technique and of philosophy. I could easily discern that I was adequately performing my role as analysand merely by freely associating. I was not held responsible for conducting the analysis; that is, I was never 'accused' of being resistant. Bion understood that my unconscious derivatives, which were preconscious, not conscious, were all that I could or should produce. The rest was up to the analyst to fathom and to interpret. What the classical analyst would interpret as resistance, he (Bion) would point to as a focus of great anxiety and seek to unravel it.

Furthermore, the analytic undertaking was more of a dialogue than an audited monologue. It was basically analogous to a 'conversation' between infant and mother. We were partners, but he, the Kleinian analyst, worked much harder and demanded less than his classical counterpart. I didn't even have to 'associate' to dream elements. He assumed I already had done so unconsciously in my associations. The differences were profound. Classical analysts started on the surface and interpreted resistances, whereas the Kleinian analyst begins with the unconscious anxiety that causes the resistances. It was like the difference between snorkeling and scuba diving. Another phenomenological aspect of the Kleinian analysis was my experience of it transpiring just underneath my awareness or consciousness, as if I were in a trance.

(Grotstein 2002: 99)

I recall a particular session, probably within the first year of my analysis, in which he began an interpretation from something I had said, the link to which was clear at the time. The interpretation was in typical, Kleinian part-object language. I was utterly outraged by such a meaningless bunch of jargon, but before I could express outrage and dismay, Bion went on to say something like, 'I have no idea whether there is any truth in what I just said, nor what it would mean in more practical and concrete terms.

But you may; so I mention it to you in case you have some knowledge of it'. I was flabbergasted. The room seemed to literally brighten. I felt a rush of associations which were indeed emotionally alive, along with feelings of amazement, exhilaration, discovery, hope, and so on. I knew this was the way that, in time, one might carry on an ongoing self-analysis.

(Gooch 2002: 4)

When he made interpretations he always made it clear what the evidence was – he was meticulous about that. It was not a pronouncement, but a theory or an educated guess, and only I could know whether there was any truth in it or not. I increasingly could feel in the music, and the dance, the cadence . . . the timbre of his voice that he was speaking from his heart; that he had to be having an emotional experience himself to be speaking to me that way. So even though he would not tell me what his associations were, it was clear that he was in touch with something within himself that had been evoked by me. As a matter of fact, it was not an uncommon thing for him to say, 'Even though I tell you almost nothing about myself you're likely to know a good deal about me based on what I'm able to understand about you and I'm not able to understand in you.

(Gooch in Culbert-Koehn 2011: 79)

Grotstein describes Bion's style as somewhat outdated, military, English, disciplined and very gracious (Grotstein 2007: 34–35). The portrait of Bion as a sincere, surprising, wise and involved grandfatherly figure can be supplemented by the sometimes extreme self-deprecation in his autobiographical volumes, by his sharp humour and by the passionate letters he wrote to Francesca and to his children. While measured on the outside, he seems to have preserved maximal inner space for wild stray thoughts.

Bion's lectures began in August 1968 when he was invited to Buenos Aires for two weeks. The small but valuable companion *Introduction to the Work of Bion* by Leon Grinberg, Darío Sor and Elizabeth Tabak de Bianchedi (1971) was a result of these meetings. A new edition was published by the same authors in 1993. In 1969 Bion visited Amherst College in Massachusetts, for a Group Relations conference, where he was received as a guru, which 'did ultimately make me a bit angry and impatient' (Bion 1985: 159). In 1973 he was invited to São Paulo by Frank Philips, who had also left London in 1968. The conferences were a great success, with many participants. In the press Bion was described as 'the most famous psychoanalyst in the world' (Bion, F. 1995). In letters to Francesca, published in *All My Sins Remembered* (Bion 1985), he jokingly asked Francesca if she was not jealous of his success, but it seems to have made him feel a little insecure: 'My God, my God. Don't people *love* me! . . . Do you think that it is possible that Greta Garbo spoke the truth when she said she "wanted to be alone"?' (Bion 1985: 161) and

'Sometimes, I think my real trouble is having very easily a reputation which I don't and cannot possibly deserve, even in my wildest dreams. Do presidents of the US, prime ministers and such feel that?' (Bion 1985: 164).

However, this was not always the case. In the US he was received critically, even negatively. The 1974 lectures in Los Angeles where he had his practice were given in the Veteran Hospital to about five psychiatric residents, psychologists and social workers, not quite the big audience he had had in Brazil. The audience were psychotherapists who were somewhat familiar with his work. In a Socratic manner that verged on rudeness, he threw back their well-meant theoretical questions. In New York, he gave a lecture to the Institute of Psychoanalytic Training and Research, entering the lion's den, as the American Psychoanalytic Association did not approve of the Kleinian approach, and Kleinians were not allowed to do training analysis. Bion with his unorthodox views was regarded with even greater suspicion. Ralph Greenson, who, like Bion, worked in LA, was a key adversary. He was influential and well known as the analyst of Marilyn Monroe and other famous public figures and powerful as a professor at UCLA, generating large fundings for psychoanalysis. The questions from the audience were critical and at certain moments, the tension mounted (Bion 1978: 41, 53–62). Bion made no concessions and at all times remained master of the situation and the group dynamics, but he was less Socratic in his questions and provided more explanation. Nevertheless, he was criticized for interpreting rather than answering the questions.

In 1975, he stayed a month in the newly built capital Brasilia and was invited to give lectures in this unique city. He went three times in five years to São Paulo. His last visit took place in 1978 and according to Francesca Bion (2005), even at 80 years he 'held fifty clinical seminars, daily consultations, and ten evening meetings' during this visit. He took part in meetings in Topeka, Lyon, Paris, New York and Washington.

Bion returned to the UK on four occasions. His former colleagues didn't recognize the earlier, respectable analyst and former president of the British Psychoanalytical Association in him (Green 1980). The British psychoanalytic community tended to prefer Bion's earlier ideas, as they later appeared in *Second Thoughts*, and considered his later thinking mostly a deviation. His last lectures in Rome (1977) and at the Tavistock Clinic in London (1977, 1978, 1978) were more elaborated, while the earlier ones, like those given in London in 1976, tended to take the form of discussions, with brief answers, often in the form of questions. According to Grotstein (2005), every line of the lectures deserves to be quoted. Hinshelwood remarks that:

Each reader can make his own catalogue of the lectures, for instance in the Brazilian lectures one can find issues about time, the future and the present; the specific dimensions of psychoanalysis (the helix); the loneliness of the analyst with his inherently mysterious material; the importance of intuition and a state of openness; his remarks about memory and desire; problems of development posed in terms of 'being just like' or of 'becoming'; the problem of ignorance and of omnipotent interpretation; the substitution of knowledge and theories in the place of discovery and the unknown.

(Hinshelwood 1992: 124)

Bion worked like a jazz musician, improvising on basic themes. I have studied the lectures in chronological order rather than organizing them by location, in order to better see these repetitions and the major themes at certain periods. This approach allows us to read the texts as Bion proposes to listen to clinical material: looking at constant conjunctions and the emergence of patterns.

Chronology of published lectures

Lectures

São Paulo 1973	Brazilian Lectures (Bion 1990: 3–70)
Rio de Janeiro 1974	Brazilian Lectures (Bion 1990: 72–177)
São Paulo 1974	Brazilian Lectures (Bion 1990: 180–213)
Los Angeles, April 1976	Four discussions with W.R. Bion (Bion 1978)
London, June 1976	Tavistock Seminars (Bion 2005: 1–12)
New York, April 1977	Bion in New York and São Paulo (Bion 1980: 1–74)
Untitled, May 1977	Transcripts of recordings in preparation for the Italian Seminars
London, July 1977	Tavistock Seminars (Bion 2005a: 13–29)
Rome, July 1977	Italian Seminars (Bion 2005b)
São Paolo, April 1978	Bion in New York and São Paulo (Bion 1980: 75127)
London, July 1978	Tavistock Seminars (Bion 2005a: 39–72)
London, March 1979	Tavistock Seminars (Bion 2005: 79–94)

Small texts

Caesura Untitled I and Untitled II as preparation for the Italian Lectures

Clinical seminars

Los Angeles Seminars and supervisions 1967 – Aguayo and Malin (2013) Brasilia 1975 en São Paulo 1978 Clinical Seminars and Four Papers (Bion, F. 1994).

There are no published records available of the lectures in Massachusetts, Topeka, Lyon, Paris and Washington.

Lectures

I will try to highlight themes and patterns that run through the different lectures. The references in brackets indicate the lectures where the same theme was repeated. These repetitions convey a sense of the importance of certain themes in his thinking. However, the references are so extensive that they interrupt the flow of the text; it is better not to pay attention to them in reading the text as a whole.

Ignorance, mystery and truth

Bion cultivated ignorance as a fundamental characteristic (*Brazilian Lectures* 1990: 3), which he often called abysmal (*Brazilian Lectures* 1990: 32; Untitled 1997: 31). Again and again he quotes Maurice Blanchot's (1969: 15) phrase which he got from André Green: 'La réponse est le malheur de la question' (*Four Discussions with W.R. Bion* 1978: 21, 40; *Bion in New York and São Paulo* 1978: 116; *Tavistock Seminars* 2005: 8, *Tavistock Seminars* 2005: 30).

In the same way, Bion saw mystery as an important quality of psychoanalysis and defines it as follows:

> What I mean by the term is a capacity to have feelings of respect for the unknown; to have a capacity to respect something of which we are ignorant; not to be so frightened of what we do not understand that we want to say.
>
> (*Brazilian Lectures* 1974: 100)

> It is, therefore important that psycho-analysis both now and in the future should be capable of respecting the human mind, the human personality, and even respecting it if they do not know what it is or anything about it. This is a part of what I call remaining able to be mystified. We must be able to tolerate mystery and our own ignorance.
>
> (*Brazilian Lectures* 1990: 101)

In the same vein Bion saw the religious dimension as an innate sensitivity to the unknown. In his lectures, he no longer referred to the ultimate truth. On the contrary, he quoted Bacon from his essay on 'Truth': 'What is truth? said jesting Pilate; and would not stay for an answer' (*Tavistock Seminars* 2005: 69).

His definition of O became somewhat more pragmatic. When I use the letter, O, I mean it to indicate noumenon, the thing itself of which nobody can know anything.

(*Brazilian Lectures* 1990: 69)

That is what I have tried to signify by a letter O – to signify it, merely to indicate that this is 'some thing', but what it is I do not know. Kant might call it 'the thing-in-itself'. Some philosophers would disagree with that, but I think, nevertheless, that there is a great deal to be said for the idea that he did regard noumena and things which are noumenous as related to the thing-in-itself. If the discipline were what we might call 'religious', the thing-in-itself might be called 'godhead'.

(*Brazilian Lectures* 1990: 84)

Box 11.2   Ignorance

To Bion 'answers' are really space-stoppers, a way of putting an end to curiosity, especially if you believe the answer is THE answer. On another occasion he explained, 'when I feel a pressure – I'd better get prepared in case you ask me some questions – I say, "To hell with it. I'm not going to look up this stuff in Freud, or even in my past statement – I'll put up with it", but of course I am asking you to put up with it too'. And again, 'If you are looking for answers to questions you will not find them except through your own intuition and understanding'. Accordingly, his replies were aimed at clarifying the problem by approaching it by an indirect route; in due course it became clear that the apparently irrelevant answer had in fact illuminated the area of the question and beyond, like a circular tour bringing the traveller back to the point of departure but now seen with increased knowledge and experience gathered on the journey.

(Bion, F. 1995, www.melanie-klein-trust.org.uk)

The whole of psychoanalysis [might turn] out to be one vast elaboration of a paramnesia, something intended to fill the gap – the gap of our frightful ignorance.

(Bion 1987b: 244)

Twenty years ago I thought I knew something about psychoanalysis, now I'm not so sure, but I know that I know more than those who would try to usurp the void of my ignorance.

(Bion 1975: 17)

Observation

From this attitude of ignorance, what matters is observation of 'facts', of which Bion gives a peculiar definition (*Brazilian Lectures* 1990: 111; *Tavistock Seminars* 2005: 39): 'I believe there is a fundamental reality even if I don't know what it is: that is what I would call a "fact"' (*Four Discussions with W.R. Bion* 1978: 21).

Thoughts can help, acting as a kind of mental can-opener to allow us to see these facts (*Italian Seminars* 1977: 18). Bion draws an analogy with medicine, giving the example of how as a medical doctor he was once able to diagnose tuberculosis from the co-existence of a swollen knee and a cough. Bion regrets that there are no such clearly perceptible signs for psychic reality (*Four Discussions with W.R. Bion* 1978: 26). Feelings are probably the signs that are closest to the unknowable psychic reality. According to Bion, the origin of feelings is not sensuous and in trying to get to the essence of feelings (like anxiety), we are misled by our senses: 'we are prisoners of our senses' (*Four Discussions with W.R. Bion* 1978: 21). We must, as Freud had already said, blind ourselves to our senses: 'I often try to blind myself in order to examine these obscure places' (*Brazilian Lectures* 1990: 20). In the same vein, he states that 'the minimum condition for me to analyse that patient is to be allowed to remain silent' (*Italian Seminars* 2005: 20). He wants to be free from the senses and from looking for coherence in his effort to pierce through to this 'thing' behind (*Bion in New York and São Paulo* 1980: 60; *Four Discussions with W.R. Bion* 1978: 18). This attitude is well reflected in his quote of the blind Milton from *Paradise Lost*: 'that I may see and tell of things invisible to mortal sight' (*Italian Seminars* 2005: 62; *Tavistock Seminars*: 2005: 13–31).

Not-knowing and resistance to theory

Bion did not give his audiences what they wanted to hear (F. Bion, preface, *Italian Seminars* 2005). Since he believed that truth cannot be expressed directly, he gave indirect answers – circling around the subject and meandering to places far away from the question in order to return with a new point of view.

Common to all the lectures is his refusal to adopt an abstract theoretical point of view. In a Socratic manner, theoretical questions are bypassed, and he answered in an associative, elusive and often surprising way – breaking through defences and evoking vivid thoughts. For instance, when an analyst from the audience asked about the difference between mental and sensuous experiences, he answered:

Question: 'What is *that*, Daddy?' Answer: 'That is a cow'. Question: 'Why is it a cow, Daddy?'

Well, why is it a cow? Does any philosopher, biologist, psychoanalyst, medical man knows the answer to that question? Only two questions – what is that? Why is that a cow? – and you are right away in the unknown. The world of the unknown is before you: you are out in ultimate space. That is how feeble our knowledge is. It is just two questions deep – that is all – and then you are out in the mental stratosphere. However long one lives one still will not know the answer to 'What is that?', 'It's a psychoanalyst'. 'Why is it a psychoanalyst?' You *could* say the mental experience and the sensuous experience have been making love to each other – hence the psychoanalyst. These answers are rationalisations, that is, rational answers; but the question may not be answerable in rational terms; it may be outside the scope of rational answers, or rational knowledge.

(*Brazilian Lectures* 2005: 82)

When he was asked to give an example of the use of the time-space concept in psychoanalytic practice and about the Kantian a prioris which played an important role in his concepts about the mind, he replied:

I do not touch my patients. It is true that I speak to them and I see them, but I do not believe that that gives an adequate description of the meeting between the patient's mind and mine.

(*Brazilian Lectures* 1990: 92)

This answer is somewhat unexpected but goes right to the heart of the matter of his ideas about the a-sensuous reality. When someone – again with *Transformations* in mind – asked whether 'psychoanalysis must be made mathematical before it can be considered a science', he replied again unexpectedly:

I remember talking to an atomic physicist who seemed to feel that all this business of Greek and Latin and poetry and literature was a lot of nonsense, that Oxford University wasted a terrible lot of time. I would not quarrel with that, but that does not mean to say that I think, therefore, that one should encourage our monkey-like trick without also encouraging the growth of wisdom.

(*Brazilian Lectures* 1990: 99)

This answer reflects the difference in his attitude to scientific abstraction before and after the caesura. Again he insisted on the need to avoid wanting to conquer, to understand better and on the importance of receptivity

In answer to the question of whether the experience of time in psychoanalysis could be affected by successive experiences of omnipotence and impotence, he replied that:

One is certainly familiar with people who say, 'I can always wake up at the time of day I want by thinking about it overnight; if I want to wake up at five in the morning, I wake up at five in the morning'.

(*Brazilian Lectures* 1990: 102)

Several times, the audience questioned him about projective identification, a concept that plays an important role in his work and one that he elaborated in an interesting and original manner (see Box 4.2). As one would expect, he sometimes indicated that he did not see projective identification as a fantasy of the patient but as something that really happens and is transferred in the session (*Brazilian Lectures* 1990: 68; *Bion in New York and São Paulo* 1977: 21–31). But at other times he claimed that there is not much to add to Klein's definition and did not even mention his own contribution (*Four Discussions with W.R. Bion* 1976: 1). Or he said that it is just a theory, and noted that while for a biologist in theory a tiger and a kitten are both cats, for the ordinary man there is a huge distinction (*Brazilian Lectures* 1990: 54). 'A more sophisticated version is one which is related to concepts and theories such as projective identification but these theoretical terms are almost meaningless'; likewise, 'Transference, it doesn't mean a thing, one wants to know what the transference looks like in a particular instance' (*Brazilian Lectures* 1990: 56).

Bion always insisted that it is more important to 'read the patient' (*Brazilian Lectures* 1990: 64) than to waste time reading psychoanalytic books (*Italian Seminars* 1977: 93). 'Theory is at most good for a few sessions, as a kind of opening in a chess game' (*Bion in New York and São Paulo* 1980: 38; *Four Discussions with W.R. Bion* 1978: 14). Instead of using theory, Bion advocated the use of models 'which may be useful or not, and which can be discarded without all the upheaval involved in setting up a theory. Models are expendable, theories not' (*Bion in New York and São Paulo* 1980: 16). One of the meanings of many of his answers is that it was very important to Bion that a notion feels 'real', that one is able to feel a notion, as one can feel in New York what a capital is (*Bion in New York and São Paulo* 1980: 58).

Freud and Klein

Bion downplayed Klein's theory (*Bion in New York and São Paulo* 1980: 36–37) in the light of his experience of O and transformations in O. Freud's theory was also to a certain degree considered as a space-filler in order not to be afraid of upcoming thoughts (*Four Discussions with W.R. Bion* 1976: 39; *Bion in New York and São Paulo* 1977: 30; *Four Discussions with W.R. Bion* 1978: 2). He found the Freudian distinction conscious–unconscious outdated as a category (*Bion in New York and São Paulo*) and thought that after using it for a while 'it can become a bit of a pest' (*Tavistock Seminars* 2005: 31). Transference was seen as transitional and particular according to each case; Bion thought that there was no point in making a generalizing theory about it (*Brazilian Lectures* 1990: 57–86; *Bion in New York and São Paulo* 1980: 16; *Tavistock Seminars* 2005: 5; *Italian Seminars* 2005b: 27). He repeated that he was 'sick and tired of hearing psychoanalytic theories – if they don't remind me of real people they are of no use to me' (*Four Discussions with W.R. Bion* 1978: 44; *Tavistock Seminars* 2005a: 2).

Language

Bion saw language as unreliable (*Four Discussions with W.R. Bion* 1978: 14); therefore the psychoanalyst 'must draw up his own vocabulary . . . like a surgeon who has to sharpen his scalpels before and during the operation' (*Tavistock Seminars* 2005a: 14; *Italian Seminars* 2005b: 5). On the use of words, Bion's advice sounds Beckettian: 'cut them down to fewer and fewer, and then use them very sparingly, very exactly, only in order to say what you mean' (*Italian Seminars* 2005: 5). A solution can be found in a language of achievement (see Box 8.1).

The aim of psychoanalysis

However, the question remains of what the radical openness that Bion advocated – waiting for a pattern to emerge (*Four Discussions with W.R. Bion* 1978: 8; *Bion in New York and São Paulo* 1980: 11, 79, 121; *Tavistock Seminars* 2005: 19) and seeing constant conjunctions – can lead to in an analysis. As one questioner critically remarked: 'what happens then – black magic?' (*Four Discussions with W.R. Bion* 1978: 15). To this Bion's answer was that one must try to see what the patient can become without pinning him down with definitions and theories.

> I resist falling back on what I already know of the patient . . . we are presented with the debris . . . analogous to blowing up the embers of a fire so that some spark communicates itself to others, the fire is built up again, although it appeared nothing but dead ash. Can we look at all this debris and detect in it some little spark of life?
>
> (*Tavistock Seminars* 2005a: 44)

Again and again he stresses that the patient should be given back to himself (*Four Discussions with W.R. Bion* 1978: 5), introduced to himself (*Bion in New York and São Paulo* 1980: 12). He does not have to learn to behave like the others but to be himself (*Bion in New York and São Paulo* 1980: 12). It is the distinction between 'being just like a loving and affectionate person' and 'becoming one' (*Tavistock Seminars* 2005a: 9), acting like a surgeon or being one. Here he recounted the anecdote from *All My Sins Remembered* (37–38). The skin grafts of his master surgeon, Trotter, all took whereas his competent fellow surgeon's (Julian Taylor) failed (*Four Discussions with W.R. Bion* 1978: 20). Related to this is the distinction between being intelligent and being wise (*Four Discussions with W.R. Bion* 1978: 28; *Bion in New York and São Paulo* 1980: 121; *Italian Seminars* 2005b: 53). Intelligence is what he called the 'monkey trick business, a department far ahead of the rest' (*Brazilian Lectures* 1990: 32). In contrast, psychoanalysis is about the real thing (*Four Discussions with W.R. Bion* 1978: 31; *Italian Seminars* 2005b: 9), or becoming (*Brazilian Lectures* 1990: 90; *Four Discussions with W.R. Bion* 1978: 5, 32; *Tavistock Seminars* 2005b: 9).

The mind

A key idea from the first lectures is Bion's focus on the existence of a mind, personality and character (*Brazilian Lectures* 1990: 37; *Tavistock Seminars* 2005a: 3, 40; *Italian Seminars* 2005b: 3). In the course of the lectures, this became more and more prominent. The mind is the 'thing in the patient' (*Italian Seminars* 2005b: 30) which is, however, not knowable. It was striking that Bion here did not refer to the 'Thing-in-itself' with a capital T, but just used 'thing'. This thing is primordial (*Four Discussions with W.R. Bion* 1978: 40), in a certain sense primitive. Bion described it as a function to which we are not yet adapted: 'the disease is mind', 'the poor mammal grew a mind' (*Bion in New York and São Paulo* 1980: 81), an 'unwelcome development' (*Bion in New York and São Paulo* 1980: 91), 'mind is a nuisance' (*Tavistock Seminars*: 53). He supposed a caesura[2] (see Box 8.6), which we are best off keeping in working order to keep the 'thing' separated from psychic functioning. Later on, he will use the analogy of the Alpheus (Milton) that goes underground (*Tavistock Seminars* 2005a: 35, 72) (see Box 11.3). The essence of psychic functioning takes place there. Hence his question: 'Where did you go last night and what did you see?' (*Tavistock Seminars* 2005a: 21, 46). Are we as analysts prepared to go underground and to speak at the level of the thing? To reach this level it may be helpful to let 'speculative imagination' run its course (*Italian Seminars* 2005b: 59) (*Bion in New York and São Paulo* 1980: 25–28, 63; *Tavistock Seminars* 2005a: 6, 18; *Untitled* 1997: 40).

Box 11.3   The Alpheus

Bion used the image of the Alpheus to represent the subterranean flow of the ever-present and unknowable dream thought, which he later compared to a hallucinatory zone (Bion 2007) and to the world of the pre-natals, separated by a caesura from the world of the post-natals (Bion 2007). According to Bion, the analyst should intuitively experience this subterranean flow when it surfaces. It appears that not unlike Lacan, Bion's analytic experience is that at the core of our being are not the unconscious ideographs, Freud's thing representations, but an unknowable, infinite, undifferentiated stream of potentialities that have not yet been expressed.

According to Greek mythology, Alpheus is the God of the eponymous Peloponnesian river. On the banks of the Alpheus, the Olympics were organized. In the Alpheus myth, Alpheus fell in love with the nymph Arethusa, whom he secretly watched while she was bathing. When Arethusa became aware of this, she was overcome by shame and ran from him. Alpheus arose from the water and followed her. When she was trapped and had nowhere to run, the virgin desperately prayed to Artemis, who changed her into a spring and created an underground channel that carried her all the way to Sicily, where she emerged. Alpheus followed her down this channel and their waters mingled. To prove the relation of the source to the river, the myth relates how a cup thrown into the river in Olympia surfaced in the water of the source Arethusa. Moreover, every time cows were slaughtered on the edges of the Alpheus, the water of the source Arethusa turned red.

The Alpheus is present in Milton's *Paradise Lost* (Milton 1674) which Bion (1979: 257) quotes:

Return Alpheus, the dread voice is past,
That shrunk thy streams; Return Sicilian Muse . . .

(Milton, *Lycidas*)

and in the famous poem of Coleridge (1816), *Kubla Khan*:

In Xanadu did Kubla Khan
A stately pleasure-dome decree:
Where Alph, the sacred river, ran
Through caverns measureless to man
Down to a sunless sea

Conclusion

In sum, the Bion we encounter in the lectures and supervisions is a Socratic figure, as in the picture on the cover of his books where he is reading Plato. He questioned, opened up, did not know. This wise and balanced attitude to the outside, in which he felt in a sense imprisoned, has its counterpart in the turbulent inner world and thinking that we find in *A Memoir of the Future*, written in the same period. However, his indirect Socratic questioning with many detours challenges fixed and sterile ways of thinking and remains true to his insights about the difference between transformations in K and transformations in O. He focuses on experiences at an unknown basic level outside time, space and senses. The lectures together with *A Memoir of the Future* and Bion's autobiographical writings give us an opportunity to use binocular vision and perhaps thereby to glimpse the essence of Bion. At the core of his lectures and supervisions is an attitude of ignorance that allows this essence to reveal itself.

Clinical Seminars

In *Clinical Seminars and Four Papers* (Bion 1987) we see Bion at work during supervisions. The clinical supervisions presented in this book took place in the period when he was lecturing abroad between 1973 and the end of his life in 1979, when he was in his late 70s. They were recorded and published posthumously by Francesca Bion. This was not an easy task:

> During the seventies I undertook the task of editing his work for publication – in addition to typing, proof-reading and corresponding with publishers which I had already done for many years. It was obvious that he would never have the inclination to do the job nor the time available if he was to continue with the all-absorbing occupation of creative thinking and writing. By that time I felt that I knew him and his way of working and expressing himself as well as anyone was likely to, and being present at all his talks made it easier to recall not only what he said (if recordings were of poor quality) but also how he said it. A tape recording tells you only a limited amount about a speaker; it presents an editor with the problem of how best to transfer the spoken word to the printed page, preserving the individual style and spontaneity while at the same time producing smooth-flowing prose. The most difficult part of the whole job was persuading him to read the finished product; it would have been easier to get a child to take a dose of foul-tasting medicine. He expressed his feeling somewhat crudely but graphically: 'I don't like examining my own vomit'.
>
> (Bion, F. 2006)

The supervisions in Brazil took place in a warm and welcoming atmosphere. The complicated reasoning and philosophical thoughts that we are accustomed to struggling with in his theoretical writings are absent from this contact with colleagues. In these supervisions it is hard to find traces of the mystical inspiration with which one tends to identify the 'late' Bion. And yet the attitude described in *Attention and Interpretation* is present. He tried to look at the essence of the patient, but not from a knowing point of view. As described in *Attention and Interpretation*, the essence, seen from the O-vector as a becoming, moves towards the session where it can eventually be met. The analysis is just a small part of a large unknown with many possibilities. Bion radically accepted this not-knowing, and avoided attempting to pin down or understand. He was present, observed and questioned, remaining open to the unknown both at a conscious and an unconscious level.

Attitude during the supervisions

Bion was never didactic. His attitude was questioning, radically not-knowing, helping the analysand to ask questions. Bion's questions were often surprising, sometimes even hilarious in their concreteness, reminiscent of a Groucho Marx kind of humour, e.g., 'He prefers men to women, what of it? A great number of women prefer men to women' (*Clinical Seminars* 1987: 58). We see his characteristic attitude reflected in the supervisions: a dispassionate openness, with deep respect and reliability. He viewed the ability to be abstinent as a necessary condition for this kind of work.

Having himself suffered painful traumatic experiences allowed Bion to identify with his patients' deepest layers and to read and write from there about the essence of dealing with emotional reality. His attitude towards theory was somewhat milder than in some of the lectures:

That is what I say, by all means read all these books and everything else you want to, but don't let it get in the way of your forming your own opinion of the person with whom you are dealing.

(*Clinical Seminars* 1987: 59)

What matters is the patient in the here and now situation and being wide awake in the present situation of the session.

This story about her and her girlfriend will form the basis of an interpretation that you will give six sessions later, six months later, six years later. This is why it is so important to have your senses open to what is going on in your consulting room in front of your own eyes.

(*Clinical Seminars* 1987: 72)

These facts are important, but what is especially important is this which is taking place today. We often talk of past situations – it is quite useful – but the past is the past and there is nothing any of us can do about it. What we can do something about is the present. So what has happened that has made this patient talk like this today? She is no longer a baby.

(*Clinical Seminars* 1987: 80)

The goal of psychoanalysis

As in his lectures, Bion repeats that the goal of analysis is to set the psyche free, to let character be born; to help someone to become himself, whatever this may be; to deal with his or her own life. But this is of course never finished but a process of becoming:

What are we working in? What are we trying to make emerge? We hope that what will eventuate will be a human being capable of using his own life.

(Clinical Seminars 1987: 41)

Somewhere in the analytic situation buried in masses of neuroses, psychoses and so on, there is a person struggling to be born. It seems to me that the analyst's function is not to demonstrate all these neurotic and psychotic mechanisms, excepting as an incidental in the course of freeing the patient. It doesn't seem to be fanciful to say that just as Michelangelo, Leonardo, Picasso, Shakespeare and others have been able to liberate this mass of material, actual forms which remind us of real life, so the analyst is engaged in an analogous occupation – an attempt to help the child to find the grown-up who is latent there, and also to show that the grown person is still a child. These two might very well go together, not simply in order to make them indistinguishable, but in a creative or profitable manner. This patient is potentially a mother, but it is all covered up.

(Clinical Seminars 1987: 41)

The attempt to liberate the essence of a person, to see its evolution, is reminiscent of what was described earlier as the evolution of the psychoanalytic object along the O-vertex. Bion was not interpreting but looking at the evolution: 'the prostitute is the sexual person in herself that wants to be free' (*Clinical Seminars* 1987: 82). The analysis itself can provide such a real experience: 'it is quite likely that the analysis gives her the first chance she has ever had to feel rivalry, jealousy and envy without causing some kind of catastrophic reaction' (*Clinical Seminars* 1987: 47).

Any discussion of a case is full of questions, but Bion did not see this as a problem: 'You know nothing, but the patient knows nothing as well' (*Clinical Seminars* 1987: 30). He highlights the importance of keeping questions open, for example concerning a patient presented who suffers from passion: 'Is it passionate love, but what is this? An answer that nobody has yet found, so it is quite an adventure in which we are involved' (*Clinical Seminars* 1987: 91). Bion never took what the patient says for granted, or how he is diagnosed; he only believes his own observation (*Brazilian Lectures* 1973: 16).

Whenever we have to deal with a patient who says that he or she is happily married, I think we always need to see if we can bring out into the open this element of hatred for the partner in the sexual experience.

(Brazilian Lectures 1990: 16)

The psychoanalytic frame

In all his writings Bion stressed the need for a strict frame and an iron discipline:

In some respects I think it is fair to consider that an analysis is as serious as a surgical operation; the operating surgeon preserves a certain discipline.

I have only known one case in which a surgeon seemed to be allowing himself a freedom of action and behaviour with catastrophic results. Not that the surgeon was doing anything improper at all, but he seemed to be allowing a certain frivolity in the course of the operation – conversation, people joking. I think they were terribly misled by thinking that it was a very simple operation. So it was. But the patient, child, equally simply died.

(*Clinical Seminars* 1987: 74)

Like the work of a surgeon, an analysis is powerful but needs to be dispassionate:

If, for example, you were a surgeon and your son or daughter fell ill, I don't think you would like to operate on your blood relation; it would be sure to arouse very powerful feelings. That kind of emotional experience would interfere with the necessary clear thinking and destroy your dispassionate technical ability. Similar in analysis; if you begin to have feelings of love for a patient, that interferes with the analytic relationship and the capacity to think in a dispassionate manner.

(*Clinical Seminars* 1987: 184)

He never seemed to adapt the psychoanalytic frame, even when treating severe patients:

The analytic experience is a disciplined and unpleasant one – neither the analyst nor the analysand can do what they like. This helps to explain why analysts must have rests, must have some kind of life other than the analytic one. It is very unsatisfactory if they make their home life into a kind of psycho-analysis.

(*Clinical Seminars* 1987: 174)

This discipline is crucial to him; it floats and doesn't sink: 'fluctuat nec mergitur'[3] (*Clinical Seminars* 1987: 190).

Technique

The basic theoretical framework for supervision was Kleinian (e.g., *Brazilian Lectures* 1973: 49, *Brazilian Lectures* 1974: 82) and Bion's interventions were along the same lines, referring to inner objects and how they are repeated (*Brazilian Lectures* 1973: 35). Central topics included aggression, hostility, envy, rivalry, the parental couple and intercourse as imagos. When a patient can relive these dynamics in the analysis (*Brazilian Lectures* 1973: 47) this creates an opportunity. This sounds surprisingly classical, even more so when one considers the negative attitude towards Kleinian theory in the lectures. One may wonder to what extent Bion was less 'Bionian' than Bionians today. He remained true to classic psychoanalysis, and even if his thoughts took a large flight and he was not afraid of letting them turn in so-called stray dogs – it was always in a spirit of irony based on the awareness of the tragic, rigour, discipline.

Bion's main concern was to understand why and how the patient thinks. He conveyed a deep respect for the mental pain of the patient. He tried to be in contact with the mind, which was unknown to him, inflicted upon mammals who are not adapted to it (*Clinical Seminars* 1975: 161).

Many of Bion's interventions are quite direct. To give an example of his style:

you are feeling that, compared with you, I am a very unsatisfactory person. But you also seem to feel that if you are so superior to me, the right thing to do is to show your superiority by being rude and contemptuous.

(*Clinical Seminars* 1987: 31)

However, he found almost all interventions inadequate. The process is in the experience, in the learning itself. Transference was seen as a transient relationship (*Clinical Seminars* 1975: 151), a way of demonstrating patterns of behaviour and of relating to the patient. It is striking that Bion seldom mentioned countertransference, or containment, which are prominent in the contemporary neo-Kleinian approach that is influenced by his theories.

Conclusion

To become O in the session means being in contact with the 'zone', the hallucinatory layer, the level of undifferentiated psychic functioning. By contrast, thinking, getting a grip and judging usually result in getting out of this state of mind. Becoming O is a pure emotional experience in the here and now with the patient, made possible by the psychoanalytic setting (the analytic frame and the fundamental rule), which permits the analyst to try to maintain a radical free-floating attention, remaining as open as possible and analysing outside the temporo-spatial frame, as Bion called it. The analyst can identify maximally with the patient whilst being in contact with what happens in him/herself without feeling this distinction. To paraphrase Nishida (2001), he is like a musician playing in an orchestra, who is aware of his own notes while being part of the total experience. Being in a state of what Bion calls 'relaxed attention', a dispassionate state, facilitates this experience. The analyst should be at the threshold where infinite and finite meet, in a state just above sleep (see Box 11.2). The analyst must face the dark nothingness with faith and self-abandonment. He should jump into the unknown, so to speak. The analyst intuits what is emerging from the zone or hallucinatory layer. The emerging thoughts take form on many vectors going from infinite to finite. All the elements of the Grid can be seen as such vectors, which may or may not meet in mental space. Emotions are closer to the undifferentiated zone than images, thoughts and specific feelings as they are without form and are quickly and unconsciously shared.

Elements like feelings and images are transformations of the undifferentiated a–sensuous zone and can in turn be used as preconceptions; mental can-openers to facilitate further transformations. While the analyst may be at a vertex where infinity and finity can meet, where O meets K, the patient will be at another vertex. In order to keep the analytic function at a maximum level and to allow a transformation in O to happen, which will always be experienced as surprising, the analyst must strive to begin each session with an empty mind, a beginner's mind. Discipline and modesty are required in order to maintain this state of mind. Bion talks of blinding oneself so that as an analyst one may have dim apperceptions from the world behind the caesura (Taylor 2014). This creates the conditions that will allow constant conjunctions to light up as reflections of the psychoanalytic objects, the unknowable a–sensuous essences of a patient transforming and acquiring sensuous forms that are sensible. These essences are already present in the undifferentiated, a–sensuous zone as the irreducible part of the patient, which the analyst is expected to render in a living way to the patient. One may view these conjunctions in the a–sensuous zone that have not yet found expression in sensuous forms, as essences of a personality.

Bion also described a reverse movement; the 'dreamer who dreams the dream' looks at the facts of life, experiences and perceptions of the man-made world and transforms them; makes images, hypotheses and dreams about them. This way these experiences, perceptions and thoughts are accessible to the zone behind the caesura. The analyst may try to facilitate the movement between the two worlds, the two ways of functioning on each side of the caesura, by speaking a language that emerges from being at the vertex where O meets K, having an intuitive contact with O (see Box 8.1).

Box 11.4   Transformation in O, example

Bion discussed transformations in O in 1970, as a new emotional experience at an unrepresented level that happens maybe once or twice in an analysis, but that makes an analysis terminable. Such a transformation in O cannot be wanted; when it occurs it often surprises both patient and analyst. Transformations in O are psychic changes at an undifferentiated level of psychic functioning.

An example of T(O) is discussed in Vermote (2011) – the case of Trezebees.

Another example is the following: the patient came into analysis because she was stuck in a depressive-anxious attitude that blocked her to the point

(continued)

(continued)

that she had given up her job and was living an isolated life. She had begun to function better by the time of the episode I describe, a year into her analysis.

She dreamt that she had a tumour in her cheek. She wondered whether it was benign or malign. None of the six doctors that surrounded her could make her sleep; the last one said: now you will definitely sleep, but her bed rolled backwards and she escaped the high dose of anaesthesia. In the corridor some people that she knew saw her; also her boss passed by but did not see her, because he was flirting with a blonde woman.

Several interpretations sprang to my mind, some of them obvious: was I putting her to sleep or not paying attention to her? She had no associations, and I just said that the tumour looked as though something was pressing. I said no more in order to keep it unsaturated, so that the dream-work could go on.

In the next session, two days later, she associated about several things and said at some point that she connected being beautiful with being slim, which she is. Such a statement was new. She also made a slip of the tongue: 'het is naar de haantjes' instead of 'het is naar de vaantjes' (haantjes has a sexual meaning in Dutch). This was also rather new. Regarding the statement about beauty, the patient did not pay much attention to the way she looked and was always dressed in the same kind of clothes, jeans or sportswear. Although I am careful not to make interventions about behaviour or looks, I said that I had the impression that as in other parts of her life, she seemed to restrict the range of her experience of herself. She said that she would like to wear more feminine dresses. I wondered if nobody had admired her as a young girl, as fathers usually do. She did not react, but said later that she felt paralysed at this moment, wanted to cry, and then the session was over.

Three minutes later I received a text message from her. She had never sent me a message before: 'J is back'. J was a former boyfriend about whom she had barely spoken till then. I felt rightly criticized about my remark and understood that she had relived an experience with a criticizing man, an attitude that I had repeated without meaning to.

In the following session, four days later on Tuesday evening after the weekend break, I asked her what the former session had meant to her. She told me that she had cried and had been angry, she had sent me the message and had then switched her mobile phone off. Something strange happened. That weekend she ordered large mirrors to decorate her house. She rang a girlfriend with whom she had not had contact for a long time, and they talked about clothes and femininity and she went to a party, which was highly unusual. On Monday and Tuesday, she went to work feeling happy and got remarks about how friendly she was.

I said that I had colluded with a scenario that she had lived with her ex-boyfriend that I did not know of, and that her reaction to it seemed to have brought something new into the analysis. She was silent for the rest of the session.

In the last session of the week she told me a dream. Her mother served a meal with fish, which she likes a lot; however, her mother gave all the fish to her father; she was angry and destroyed the fish with her fork. It was new for her to dream of being angry about what she had missed. It was as though some venom had come out.

Later she told me that she wrote a letter to me when she came home after this session, and she gave it to me some weeks later (she had never given me a letter before). She wrote the letter because she never wanted to forget this week and wanted to be able to return to it when in difficulty.

In the letter, she wrote that she never had expected to experience consciously such a spectrum of emotions. After the session in which I made the remark about her clothes, she had the feeling of losing herself and after feeling intensely angry, she was overwhelmed with tears, feeling misunderstood; this then changed into a complete peace of mind and warmth. She felt it in her body around the cardiac region and had a lot of energy, which she equated with happiness. She went on to say that it felt as though we were bound with an indestructible bond and that there was an infinite trust that would never go away. It was as if she lived for a whole week absorbed in one never-ending thought, like someone who is drunk with passion.

It is striking that the words that she used in the letter were emotional, undifferentiated and infinite. She was feeling defenceless, raw and out of the armour of the obsessive-compulsive train of thoughts that she usually repeated endlessly.

This example of the analyst mentioning something about the patient's clothing style can be seen as a kind of seductive acting in – with a subsequent reaction of the patient. The point is, however, that the reaction of the patient to this session was an unexpected strong, sudden, generalized and lasting psychic change that altered her life. Such a deep-going phenomenon never happened again during the consequent years of analysis. I guess that having a similar changing reaction with a few words is what we are all looking for. The problem is that it happens without understanding it and without conscious control; it was at an unconscious level that something happened drastically.

The question now is whether it is correct to call this a T(O) and whether this makes sense clinically. Bion discussed transformations in O in 1970, as a new emotional experience at an unrepresented level that happens maybe once or twice in an analysis, but that makes an analysis terminable. This example shows the characteristics of a T(O) as described by Bion: it is an experience that happens unexpectedly and without wanting it at a level of experience and with a psychic change as a result. We may say that there was a contact with the patient at a non-verbal, non-differentiated and unconscious level. To phrase it otherwise: it is as if there was a contact in a kind of shared field which resulted in a unintentional kind of acting in by the analyst with the result that the patient felt seen. The happening was something that took us from behind, so to speak. In subsequent sessions this experience at this undifferentiated O level was found by her dreams; in other words the experience was taken up by her reverie or by her transformation in K. It is clear that the experience became possible because of the psychoanalytic device and the resulting field between analyst and analysand. Given the experience, the surprise and its transformational power, it is interesting to study it from Bion's concept of transformation in O.

Notes

1 www.melanie-klein-trust.org.uk/bion77d.html.
2 Several subjects were raised in the lectures that he worked into his later shorter texts such as the theory of black holes and turbulence (*Brazilian Lectures* 1990: 75; *Four Discussions with W.R. Bion* 1978: 5–23) and caesura (*Four Discussions with W.R. Bion* 1978: 22; *Bion in New York and São Paulo* 1990: 28).
3 Bion's motto was 'fluctuat nec mergitur' (be rocked and remain balanced, which is also the motto of the city of Paris).

12 AUTOBIOGRAPHY

Bion's four autobiographical writings about the Great War

Both World Wars played a major role in Bion's development as a person, as a psychoanalyst and as a thinker. Many of his theoretical concepts, like 'containment' (a military term), 'β-particles', 'nameless dread', 'the primary aim of a group is the survival of the group', 'the Unknown' and his account of the sense of urgency involved in thinking under pressure can only be fully understood against this background. Moreover, the war writings give an idea of Bion as a character.

However, Bion's four texts on the Great War are not easy reading. Readers can easily come to feel as though they are lost in a kind of fog, encountering a large number of names and diverging reports of the facts with very few clear indications of time and space. For this reason I have placed the content on a timeline. But in the first place the difficulty of reading is emotional, because of the traumatic nature of Bion's war experiences, which, over the years, is expressed in an increasingly painfully honest and sometimes brutal way.

The publication dates of the war writings do not correspond to the period when the texts were written. The two autobiographical texts, *The Long Weekend: Part of a Life 1897–1919* (1982) and *All My Sins Remembered: Another Part of a Life* (1985), were written last, at the time of *A Memoir of the Future*, but published respectively, three and six years after his death in 1979. Fifteen years later, Francesca Bion edited the account that Bion wrote when he was a 21-year-old student of history at Queen's College in Oxford: *War Memoirs 1917–1919* (1997). Having lost his diary, his aim was to give an impression of the 'life he led' (Bion 1997: 5) for his parents; he could not bear sending them letters during the war. The text is supplemented with drawings and photographs. As Parthenope Bion Talamo put it in her afterword: 'the diaries themselves are almost raw material, with hardly any emotional or intellectual elaboration'. *War Memoirs* contains two additional short texts in a more literary style. The first, entitled *Amiens*, was written when Bion was 61, when he passed the overgrown minefields of Amiens on a train journey through France. In this text he sketches critical psychological portraits of Captain Bion, his second lieutenant Asser and other soldiers and superiors in a rather self-consciously literary narrative voice, which was not entirely successful. In 1972 he wrote a ten-page-long *Commentary* (Bion: 1997, 199), after rereading his war diaries under 'Californian skies'. This takes the form of a critical dialogue staged between Bion as a young soldier and the 75-year-old analyst Bion.

Bion saw personality as constituted of layers like the skins of an onion. The four texts as a whole offer a unique insight into the different layers or the group of different characters that constitute Bion's self. Moreover, the 'palimpsest' or 'mosaic' of texts, as Parthenope Bion Talamo (1997) calls them, reveals the way in which the same experiences are in constant transformation in the course of his life as well as the undigested bits of experience that remain too traumatic ever to be fully worked through. Reading the war texts is difficult because of the emotional content and the scattered, unstructured data. However, this experience of reading without being able to get much grip on the narrative is an essential part of what Bion communicates about the war. Nevertheless, in this companion to his war texts we will describe Bion's war life chronologically as far as we have been able to reconstruct it from the four different texts. This may be of some help to the reader and may also reveal the psychic transformations that certain experiences underwent over the years.

Summer 1917: Belgium, the Salient

The account that Bion wrote when he was 21 offers a schoolboy's proud description of being a tank commander of the 5th Tank Battalion. Tanks were used for the first time in 1916, when four tanks cleared 10 kilometres of enemy trenches, taking the enemy completely by surprise, as they thought that the tanks were only transport vehicles. The other tanks got stuck in the mud and were easy targets, loaded with petrol. The casualty rate was almost 100%. After a short training, Bion joined the front with his tank on 31 July 1917 in the third battle of Ypres and Passchendaele in Belgium, the notorious Salient (a small curve of hills surrounding these cities) where 185,000 soldiers lost their lives only to win two to three kilometres. The front line was a quagmire of corpses, with a small track made of twigs bound together by wire. The 300 English, American, German and Canadian military graveyards that you can visit in the beautiful landscape are the sad testimony of it. There are two musea who make the nightmare visible.

Bion describes sitting with eight men in complete darkness in the tank, amidst the deafening roar of the engine and bullet hits, the air heavy with petrol fumes. When a bomb struck, the petrol-filled tanks caught fire and exploded.

Constant technical defects meant that the tanks were often sitting ducks. It is hard to believe nowadays that in the midst of shelling, the soldiers had to rely on pigeons to communicate with headquarters. Subsisting mostly on bully (canned beef) and biscuits, the crew hardly slept during battles and were sedated by the heat and fumes of the engine. As the commander, Bion was mostly outside the tank, wearing a white paper on his back in order to be seen from the tank, while he was being shot at and shelled. The soldiers plodded through the mud amid the nauseating stench of decaying corpses, chloride and lime, seeking shelter in shell holes left by previous attacks. The young Bion described the experience in a matter-of-fact way.

> One very big German shell that burst near us could be distinguished above the rest. It sounded like an express train coming through a tunnel – a gradually increasing roar as it came nearer. Then a deafening crash. As the nearer shells burst, the tank used to sway a little and shudder. This was very beastly, as one had previously felt that a tank was the sort of pinnacle of solidity. It seemed as if you were all alone in a huge passage with great doors slamming all around. I can think of no other way of describing it.
>
> (Bion 1997: 30)

Fifty-five years later Bion admitted that at the time he was unable to convey the intensity of the experience, and yet, even in the poor, clumsy descriptions of his diary, the truth of the overwhelming experience of fear does come through:

> Fear there certainly was; fear of fear was, I think, common to all – officers and men. The inability to admit to anyone, as there was no one to admit to without being guilty of spreading alarm and despondency, produced a curious sense of being entirely alone in a company with a crowd of mind-less robots – machines devoid of humanity. The loneliness was intense; I can still feel my skin drawn over the bones as if it were the mask of a cadaver. The occasional words exchanged echoed like a conversation from afar. 'Wipers' [= Ypres, a city in Belgium], 'Yes, the Salient', 'Guns sound a bit frisky'. 'Awful – but cheer up – you'll soon be dead'. 'You've said it'.
>
> (Bion 1997: 204)

At the age of 81, Bion gave a psychological account of these events, which he was unable to do at the time of his diary. 'I felt I was floating about four feet above my self . . . This dis-association, de-personalization was a way of achieving security – spontaneous, automatic, but potentially costly as it involved not-knowing of the imminence of death' (Bion 1982: 132).

Autumn 1917: France

In the autumn of 1917, Bion's battalion was transported from Ypres in Belgium to a small village near Metz in France, opposite the Hindenburg line.

Unlike Ypres, the countryside in this area was hardly touched. In the distance, they saw the enemy trenches outlined in low-bursting shrapnel: 'It looked like clouds of white with golden rain in bursts. It was very beautiful and very deadly' (Bion 1997: 47). Bion was later decorated for an act of heroism in this place. When their tank was being shot at, the crew left the tank and tried to hide in an enemy trench near the tank. 'Very excited', Bion took his Lewis gun and got on top of the tank behind the fascine that they carried, aiming at the snipers that were hiding in the woods and emptying his gun until it got blocked (Bion 1997: 50). Sixty years later, Bion emphasized the clumsiness and the lack of thought in this wild action (Bion 1982).

> Taking four drums of Lewis gun ammunition attached to my waste and a Lewis gun, I clambered clumsily onto the top of the tank and set up my gun under cover, as I thought, of the fascine . . . I was not aware of any danger and therefore experienced none of the fear which might have served as a substitute for my common sense which was wholly lacking. I commanded a good view of the little copse behind the wall, this I proceeded methodically to spray. I soon exhausted almost the whole of my four drums of ammunition.
>
> By this time my escapade had stirred up a veritable hornets' nest in the copse.
>
> (Bion 1982: 164)

In his diary the young Bion mentioned almost in passing that one of his old schoolmates, whom he met just before the attack, got shot through the head.

By November 1917, a few months later, the enemy had broken through the line at Gouzeaucourt. The tanks remained at a distance, waiting to take part in the action. The crew, sleeping underneath the tanks, became intoxicated by the exhaust fumes. Bion saved the life of his crew by pouring diluted doses of ammonia down their throats. From his position, he witnessed how the Guards took their position in closed formation accompanied by the music of bagpipes, refusing to back down. Fifty years later Bion repeated that it was 'a sight so perfect it might have been a parade-ground' (Bion 1997: 207). The sight of this disciplined determination provoked an impressive aesthetic experience in Bion, which he mentioned in several places in the war writings.

Winter 1917: hopelessness and decoration

Bion's account of the end of 1917 conveys his feelings of defeated hopelessness at this time. He was very critical of (all except one of) his superiors, who he described as weak-minded, underhand, incompetent and addicted to alcohol, and talking and behaving little better than animals. In *The Long Weekend* he described how when the soldiers were offered unlimited food and beer, some needed a week to get sober. The inefficient major and colonel were finally both removed from the company.

The period of relative calm that followed was marred by jealousy and envy about promotions and decorations. Bion was nominated for a Victoria Cross, the highest war distinction, for his action of shooting the sniper. However, in the evaluation procedure, he could not affirm whether he actually killed the sniper. Only at age 81 did he state that he shot the sniper from the trees, but he dismissed the heroic deed as a mixture of foolishness and mere luck. However, and obviously for psychological reasons, at the time he failed to confirm his deed, and therefore did not receive the Victoria Cross but was awarded a Distinguished Service Order (DSO) instead. In the *Commentary* he reflects on the psychological weight of the decoration and the ambivalent feelings it could provoke. 'Incidentally, I think the VC could have toppled *you* into a "breakdown". You were lucky not to get it' (Bion 1997: 204).

Bion always remained ambivalent and cynical about these distinctions: seeing himself as the 'public school boy dressed up as a soldier, complete with decoration' (Bion 1982: 200) but nevertheless feeling proud when he was awarded the medal at Buckingham Palace (Bion 1982: 187–189). He always mentioned his official military titles in his psychoanalytic books.

Mother and father

In his old age Bion regretted that his mother was not present for the award of his DSO (Bion 1997: 190–192) and that for psychological reasons he had failed to write home from the front.

A few striking images that occur in the early diary do hint at the importance and complexity of the mother figure:

> We walked slowly in front of the tanks and waited for shells. The strain had a very curious effect; I felt that all anxiety had become too much; I felt just like a child that has had a rather tearful day and wants to be put to bed by its mother; I felt curiously eased by lying down on the bank on the side of the road, just as if I was lying in someone's arms.
>
> (Bion 1997: 122)

The image of the bank in winter as a comforting mother seems chilling and can perhaps be linked to Bion's early separation from his parents, when he was sent from India to the UK. However, in his diary he only implicitly addressed his mother. Parthenope Talamo Bion interprets this as follows:

> It is his mother alone who is invoked every now and again as a reader, as though Bion felt that she was a fundamental participant in an internal dialogue. It is perhaps not too fanciful to suppose that the fact that he had not

'written letters' during the war had not only been part of a desire to spare his mother pain, but was also an unconscious attempt to preserve her in his own mind as a container as undamaged as possible by hideous news, and hence as a part of the personality capable of α-function.

(Bion 1997: 310)

Bion's father is not explicitly present in the war writings. When Bion was on leave from the front line, it was his mother who was in England to meet him. It is not clear why Bion did not send the letters and the diary home. He probably detailed the technical side of the tanks which were secret weapons with his engineer father in mind. Bion pictured his father as a mighty figure: a tiger hunter. He felt humiliated in front of him when he volunteered for the Great War and was rejected.

Spring 1918: back to Belgium

In France, the first months of 1918 were calm. Bion became a gunnery instructor, giving seminars, and was promoted to section commander. By April 1918, however, the Germans were breaking through in the North (Belgium) and pushed the front line back. The tank corps was called on in France to help Belgium, but now as infantry without their tanks, they were not trained for this and fought at the village of Bailleul amidst gardens, houses and fields of green. In his diary Bion described how digging small trenches was like gardening in the backyard.

When Bion discovered that the officer of the position next to him had left without handing over the position, leaving a serious gap in the British line, he left his own position (and crew) in order to fortify the part of the trench that was heavily bombarded. When he returned to his own section, he found that all of his men but one had been killed. From this incident on, the tone in the account written by the 21-year-old Bion became more attentive to psychic reality rather than just the facts of what happened. He was in a kind of dissociated state and 'stared for hours at a small piece of mud that hung from the roof by a grass and quivered to the explosion of the shells' (Bion 1997: 94) when he occupied what remained of three farms at Wuytschaete in May 1918. The same sentences return untransformed 60 years later (Bion 1982: 209). In the diary, the 20-year-old soldier describes how he made up his mind to come to terms with this trauma:

I was merely an insignificant scrap of humanity that was being intolerably persecuted by unknown powers, and I was going to score off those powers by dying. After all, a mouse must feel that it is one up on the playful cat when it dies without making any sport for its captor.

(Bion 1997: 95)

Sixty years later he wrote:

> It is peculiar that so many people feel that they will go mad – in another minute! – if the baby won't stop yelling, the dog won't stop barking, the telephone bell ringing – and now if the damn guns won't stop banging. No good telling them I would go mad if they didn't stop. I felt I couldn't stay there another minute!
>
> (Bion 1982: 209)

At the age of 81 he captured the essence of this 'murder of the spirit' (Bion 1997: 207–208) with a dream image:

> Night after night I found myself on my belly clinging by my toes and fingers to a glistening slope at the bottom of which was a raging torrent – the dirty trickle of the Steenbeck. Towards this I slithered. If I tried to arrest my progress by sticking in my toes or fingers it accelerated the descent; if I desisted, it again accelerated my descent. I did not make a sound. I just woke up bathed in sweat.
>
> (Bion 1982: 211)

During the subsequent battle around Mont Kemmel – a battle lost by the Allies, who were driven back into France – Bion's company was heavily shelled – 'literally, the whole earth seemed to be going into the sky'. Bion stepped out of the trench and walked to the top of the hill until he saw his men and addressed them from there:

> I may as well say now that from the point of view of sheer unadulterated lunacy what followed was the maddest and most dangerous thing I ever did. I must have been very nearly mad to do it. But I never *thought* more clearly in my life.
>
> (Bion 1997: 106)

In *The Long Weekend* he linked this action with his unspeakable guilt of having lost his men in Bailleul.

Fellow soldiers

In all his texts Bion shows a defiance of authority. Sometimes he was mercilessly scathing, for example in the short text 'Amiens', written when he was 61, where he described his colonel as fashion-driven in a fur coat at the front and the major as a port-drinking alcoholic. Twenty years later, he was milder: 'our senior officers were *not* inefficient, but we could not know that our world had reached its Niagara. We were bits that betrayed the accelerating speed of the flood' (Bion 1997: 205). Often he was cynical:

To be a jolly good officer, you need to be a jolly good liar, a scrimshanker, a man who keeps out of the way of any dirty job, the kind of man who unhesitatingly hits somebody below the belt, yes, and stamps on his face when he's got him down.

(Bion 1997: 233)

Bion (1982: 235) did not 'think much of these people who go in for religion and philosophy or that kind of thing' (Bion 1997: 294), although at the beginning of the war, he seems to have belonged to the religious Christian group in the army. At 75, he attacked his 'priggishness' and religiosity and was cynical about the 'pious brigade'. One of his religious fellow soldiers was Quainton, whose nervous breakdown made a deep impression on the young soldier. Quainton did not return from a period of leave, writing in a letter that he had had a car accident – which was interpreted as cowardice. The possibility of being suspected of being a fraud still overcame Bion at 61 with sensations of nausea and fear. Fourteen years later, after meeting Quainton in Oxford, Bion was milder when confronted with a man who had never recovered from the trauma of war and was but a shell of his former self: 'He was changed from a cheerful, frank fellow whom I had envied for his easy capacity for deep friendliness, into a timid, cautious and scared apology for a man' (Bion 1997: 204).

The friend who seems to have made the biggest impression on Bion was Asser. A year younger, Asser incarnated everything Bion felt he lacked: he was courageous, enthusiastic, capable of real loving and refused to surrender. It was a great loss when he died. In his diary Bion only mentioned that 12 August was the last night he spent in Asser's company (Bion 1996: 133). At age 75 he stated: 'His death killed me. At least, it made me feel I could never be a man with such intensity that I would knowingly embrace death' (Bion 1997: 210). And it is only in his last writings that he describes what happened: Asser, still holding his revolver, refused to put up his hands when he was captured. 'To the call to surrender he replied, "I'll be damned if I will"' (Bion 1982: 271).

I do not know if Asser was sustained by any religious belief. In the short time I knew him, he was always cheerful, modest, unassuming – how fast and trippingly the clichés come tumbling out. The currency is so debased that the very language of love, like the word 'love' itself, can hardly be used in the presence of the thing itself . . . 'And I, only, am left alone to tell thee'.

(Bion 1982: 272)

Summer 1918: The Battle of Amiens[1]

From May 1918 on, Bion was stationed in Berle au Bois in France, where it was initially relatively calm. He lectured at different military camps in the country and the young Bion describes pleasant dinners with his fellow officers. In August, however, his company was ordered to Amiens by General Douglas Haig as part of his offensive to clear the city. This offensive by the British, Canadian and Australian Corps was carefully planned and was meant to take the Hindenburg Forces around Amiens by surprise. Large troops were moved as much in secrecy as possible. In his diary, Bion provides photographs of the new German anti-tank guns and a tank crossing a trench (Bion 1997: 117–118). The aim was to take the enemy by surprise without any preliminary bombardments. For Bion, the battle began with a mission with Major Hotblack, a war hero with numerous distinctions, whom he greatly admired. Major Hotblack, who had been an intelligence officer in France, became a war hero with DSO and bar due to courageous actions in the Tank Corps. He was to Bion the ideal of the English imperturbable gentleman-officer and Bion was intimidated by him.

> Nevertheless Bion had felt extremely frightened. Whether he was more frightened of the enemy or of Major Hotblack would be difficult to say, but the upshot of it was that at one point he had become so extremely panicky that he had had to resort to taking a whole series of compass bearings of the position that he said he had to occupy with his tanks that evening.
>
> (Bion 1997: 224)

The coordinated attack of 8 August began at 4.30 am in a thick fog. In *The Long Weekend* Bion describes his fear of getting lost and the uncanny silence before the attack. When the tanks had to move blindly over a bridge, some took a wrong path and got stuck in a swamp. Initially, the Germans were taken by surprise, because the noise of the tanks was covered by aeroplanes. The attack of the Canadians and the Australians in the Centre and the South was a huge success; after a few hours they had taken more than 10 kilometres and made a gap of more than 20 kilometres in the Hindenburg line. The Germans were unaware of the concentration of Allied soldiers and were taken by surprise. Some of their staff were even taken while having their breakfast. For the British divisions north of the Somme, it was much more difficult. They had fewer tanks and the Germans had attacked there already on the sixth and expected a counter-attack. When the Germans fired back, the young Bion writes that 'their fire was so terrific that it seemed impossible to go on' (Bion 1997: 124). The soldiers had to take cover and Bion found himself lying in an old shell hole with a runner named Sweeting. The left side of the boy's body had been blown away, but he was not yet dead. He kept trying to cough and asked Bion to write to his mother. Bion pretended to bandage him and even sent a runner to take him to the dressing station, but to no avail. We can see the transformation of this traumatic incident through the different war writings. In his war diary the young Bion describes how badly this episode affected him:

This incident upset Hauser and me very badly, and we were very sick. I mention it in such detail, horrible as it is, because it had a great effect on me. The look in his eyes was the same as that in the eyes of a bird that has been shot – mingled fear and surprise. I didn't see then, and I don't see now, why that fellow and many like him should have been taken from their English homes (and their German homes) to die for a squabble they didn't understand and couldn't realize. It was simply the distrust, so frivolously sown by grown-up children who wanted to satisfy their childish ambitions, that led to Hell for us and misery for so many homes. The sooner people realize the criminal folly of their leaders the better.

(Bion 1997: 127)

Forty years later, Bion rewrote the episode in a dialogue form, which reveals the trauma when the boy died in his arms. 'Mother, Mother, Mother – never have I known a bombardment like this, he thought. I wish he would shut up. I wish he would die. Why can't he die?' (Bion 1997: 255–256). A few chapters later, he describes how stretcher-bearers came to get Sweeting. 'Well thank God he's gone, thought Bion, filled with a passionate hatred of himself for his hatred of the wounded man' (Bion 1997: 290). At age 81, Bion devoted an entire chapter to the event (Bion 1982: 247–250), describing his physical reactions to Sweeting's whimpering pleas, ranging from vomiting without having anything to vomit to utter exhaustion (Bion 1997: 249). The traumatic scene, which is vividly and painfully rendered in dialogue, ends thus: 'Sweeting. Gunner. Tank Corps. Died of Wounds. That for him, was the end' (Bion 1982: 250). The death of Sweeting haunted him throughout his life.

'Mother, Mother . . . You will write to my mother sir, won't you?' 'No, blast you, I shan't! Shut up! Can't you see I don't want to be disturbed?' These old ghosts, they never die. They don't even fade away; they preserve their youth wonderfully. Why, you can still even see the beads of sweat, still fresh, still distinct, against the pallor of their brows. How is it done? How is it done? Like the dewdrops on the petals of Rédoutés roses. Marvellous isn't it? So, so . . . death-like, isn't it? But of course it's just a trick – he's not *really* dead, you know. Please, *please* shut up. I will write, I really will. To Mother England – that old whore!

(Bion 1982: 264–265)

Bion felt that he himself had died on that traumatic day. 'They have a way of making people seems so life-like, but really we are dead. I? Oh yes, I died – on August 8th 1918' (Bion 1982: 265).

Bion's battalion had to walk through the gas-filled woods, so utterly exhausted that they had to prop themselves up against the tank. Passing the German front line with the tanks was easier than expected. Bion described his indifference when he encountered a crying German soldier. The battle was like an inferno: 'The whole place seems to rock and sway beneath us'

(Bion 1997: 145). The panicking infantry refused to get out of their trenches, to protect the tanks against the anti-tank guns. This had disastrous results. Bion described the cruel beauty of the destruction of the tanks, which they watched in a state of dissociation.

> We could only stand and watch, the Colonel almost demented, Hauser and I ghost-ridden. The tanks rolled up a gentle grassy slope. There was a soft muffled explosion. Robertson's tank opened as a flower in a nature film might unfold. Another thud; then two, almost simultaneous, followed. The whole four had flowered. Hard, bright flames, as if cut out of tinfoil, flickered and died, extinguished by the bright sun. One tank, crewless, went on to claw at the back of one in front, as if preparatory to love-making; then stopped as if exhausted. We stared, fascinated. Then we went to the Colonel, saluted and asked formally for permission to withdraw.
>
> (Bion 1982: 254)

Bion was miraculously saved and describes his state of mind, returning to the image of the cat and mouse that he had used before.

> Every course I had initiated had almost immediately seemed to be an irretrievable blunder. It was not a repetition, it was not a reminiscence, but again I had the sense of being a cornered rat which a giant was nonchalantly aiming to club to death. Even as a rat I was incompetent – like a mouse I had once seen sit up on its haunches in what looked like an attitude of prayer to Lord Cat Almighty who at that moment was luxuriously licking his paws and washing himself. I had escaped – apparently.
>
> (Bion 1982: 262)

Bion had lost his tanks, but no men. Everywhere men were lying with shell wounds, smashed legs or arms, crying for help and left to die alone. The battle went on for days. The young Bion tells in his diary how he had a bad flu and had to sip champagne to dull the fever, making it hard to read the maps.

> My impressions are mixed and are something like this: a tank route, which I wasn't to forget, whatever happened; terrific heat and a grey desolate landscape with white chalk diggings and old trenches shining in the sun; a few shells bursting near; a lot of dead horses and a few men, all very decayed and reeking; some shell-shattered woods; a burning tongue and a very sore heel; finally, lying in the long grass waiting for the tanks to come.
>
> (Bion 1997: 142–143)

The Battle of Amiens of 8 August was decisive for the outcome of the war. The morale of the German troops was damaged and several troops wanted to surrender. In a single day, the British Forces took 13,000 prisoners. The German losses were estimated at around 30,000, those of the Allied Forces at around 8,800. After the battle, Bion took a short period of leave in England and went to see a show in London. The comparison with the battlefield seems hyperbolic and absurd: 'That London show was a nightmare, and France was a nightmare – but the latter was positively healthy in comparison' (Bion 1997: 153). He went to Cheltenham to meet his mother, which was difficult.

> Relations with anyone I respected were intolerable, notably with my mother; I wanted nothing except to get back to the Front just to get away from England. I can only hope she had a similar wish to get rid of me. At last I had said good-bye and was leaning out of the train window. 'Mind the door', I warned her, 'it's filthy'. 'Everything', she said, near to tears, 'is dreadful . . . I mean nothing is really cleaned up nowadays'. And so we parted.
>
> (Bion 1982: 266)

Immediately after this passage, the 81-year-old Bion briefly described his mother's death, just before the Second World War. His emotions were expressed indirectly, by quoting her dying words: 'The heads of the flowers [in the vase] are drooping. I can hold them up no longer. Will you hold them up for me?'

After a very short leave, Bion was already back in France on 6 September 'in a very cheerful state of mind' (Bion 1997: 153).

Autumn 1918

By the end of September, Bion's battalion was preparing for the battle at Blangy. However, Bion had lost his nerve: 'Everything I did was difficult, in action I had to force myself to do my mere job. I had become more or less paralysed by the thought of action and my brain would *not* work' (Bion 1997: 156). While he was slowly sinking away in apathy and terror, he was awarded the Legion d'Honneur for 'gallantry in action on the 8th of August'. Bion was derisory of this decoration and all others that he was awarded.

> In actual point of fact it was practically arranged before that action that I should get something out of the lucky bag. The Brigadier had said that a DSO alone looked lonely and miserable – a touch of colour by its side would improve things to no end, he declared. The Colonel said that I needed an extra to make up for missing a V.C. One or two company officers said that I deserved it for having served under Aitches so long. The men were past being surprised at anything.
>
> (Bion 1997: 157)

The last action took place at Tara Hill, from where they had to go to the village of Sequehart in Picardie, North of France. In his diary, Bion adds numerous, rather moving photographs from the front. Just before the battle, he tried to capture the beauty of the sunset.

> As we walked forward, the sun came up behind Sequehart. It was magnificent sight and one I shall not forget. The miserable greys of dawn were suddenly shot with gold. The sun's beams were an angry blood-red, and its rising behind the village gave the whole scene an unrealistic appearance. The village, with its tall spired church in the centre, stood there clear-cut and black, like a cardboard model.
>
> (Bion 1997: 183)

Despite this idyllic image, the last fight was bitter. There was a strong counterattack and the small village was completely destroyed. They were shelled and gassed, taking ammonia as anti-poison. Bion was exhausted, hungry and lost all his lust to fight – in his diary he even mentioned that he felt bored. Bion finally decided to abandon the tanks and save the life of his crew, getting them out. Bion's decision was contradictory to his behaviour as a brave, dutiful officer and war hero. At age 81 he mentions that for years after the war, he was still plagued with feelings of guilt about it.

> I do not remember making any decision which I did not soon regret, but this was peculiar in that my feeling of guilt about my last battle grew steadily for many years after. I was able to compare the full account that I wrote at the time with the impression I had years later when the details had disappeared from my memory; the feelings seemed to have remained and even grown in intensity. Thus, looking back, I had an almost overwhelming sense of failure.
>
> (Bion 1982: 276)

By 1 pm they finally learned that the Hindenburg defences had fallen and that the war was over.

The end of the war

After 11 November the soldiers remained in France for a few more months, during which time they struggled to get used to the idea of no more war. One of the last images that Bion described in his diary is that of a young girl.

> Our attention was suddenly attracted by a young girl who came out of a house and crept across the street. We were both horrified; for although she was clearly about 16, terror seemed stamped on her face. I had never seen and never want to see again, such misery and horror disfigure any face. She walked half-way across the street, looked fearfully at us, and then dragged herself into a doorway opposite. We stared after her and then walked away quickly. We had both seen terrible things before, but there had always been

a relieving feature – fearful mutilations at least means escape from war, and death was no hardship. But from *her* misery there seemed to be no release. Some days after this, she gave birth to a German baby, but what happened to her I don't know. I can't see that the misery written on her face can't be accounted for by any system of ethics. I only hope she died because I can't imagine the possibility of her regaining life or happiness.

(Bion 1997: 191)

Quite strikingly, 50 years later, Bion rewrote the scene with the pregnant girl, introducing an element of sexuality that is not there in the diary. In *The Long Weekend*, he describes the image of the girl that haunts his dreams, as the utter shock of being confronted with femininity, pregnancy and attraction after the war.

'Scuse me asking, why the hell do you haunt my dreams you pasty faced little . . . little . . . school girl? Whore?
    So? I was shocked. After four years of war, and two years of combatant service, mostly fighting, I could say, 'Wot the bloody 'ell!', or, perhaps it was only 'What the bloody hell'. But sex, pregnancy even, that took some getting over . . . This little pregnant creature didn't look at all bad – really. She had gone past the civilised state, like the mobs chasing and taunting a mother with shaven head as she strode out angry and proud and defiant carrying her baby into shelter of a house in Rouen. There is a certain dignity about the wild animal to which this little child had come.

(Bion 1982: 281)

The return to England was an anticlimax. After an uncomfortable journey, the soldiers were disappointed by a lack of welcome. 'No one took any notice of us, no one seemed to know we had been fighting and were glad to be back' (Bion 1997: 194), except for an old lady who came out to greet the soldiers. Bion's war diary ends with the dissipation of the army and the men's return to civilian life: 'An hour or so later we steamed into London to separate and disappear again into that obscurity from which the world's most astonishing armies had emerged' (Bion 1997: 195). *The Long Weekend* ends on an even more despondent note, having lost faith – in the years of the atomic bomb and other weapons of mass destruction – not just in the British Empire, but in human nature and progress at large, except for the faint promise of art.

And as things have been they remain. Insignificance to Irrelevance in a few years. No one could explain that if the British Empire did not share the same fate it was because of a few poets. But what can poets do against nuclear fission or, even more potent, some germ being carefully tended and nurtured by biologists of marvellous skill and foresight – as is the way with that clever tool-making animal, man?

(Bion 1982: 287)

Ruddy heroes when you're wanted, so much muck when it's finished. It'll be the same next time as this . . . As things have been, they remain. Insignificance to irrelevance in a few years.

(Bion 1986: 287)

These sobering words of a survivor, years after the traumatic experience, reflect Bion's attitude as we have seen it evolve over the years in this book. Even if wars mark history, these feelings of insignificance in contrast with the intensity of the war that they were dropped in and the insignificance of their sacrifice after the war is over are the post-traumatic feelings of many survivors of whatever war who lived the misery and risked their lives.

This probably reinforced Bion's privileging of poetry and creativity over intelligence and reason. Having lived the irony of destiny, his attitude became a radical openness to the Unknown. He saw life as psychoanalysis as a 'game of snakes and ladders' (Bion 1977).

Note

1 A clear description of the background of the battle can be found at http://en.wikipedia.org/wiki/Battle_of_Amiens_ (1918).

13 THE FURTHER DEVELOPMENT OF BION'S IDEAS

The four periods in Bion's work and the contemporary elaboration of his ideas

Dividing Bion's work into four periods makes it easier to situate and understand his concepts and their elaboration by others. The periods can be seen as caesurae (Bion 1977) characterized by fundamental changes while invariants remain over the periods. The major caesura in Bion's work is between period 2 and 3, when a shift takes place from looking at mental phenomena from the perspective of transformations in knowledge, to an approach in terms of transformations in O. This book is structured according to this major caesura.

The pre-analytic or group period

Bion (1961) saw his groups as study groups and he deliberately refused to take the position of a leader. By this method regressive group phenomena became manifest. Bion realized that to a large extent humans are responding to the same dynamics as herd animals, a point of view that he shared with his admired teacher Trotter (Torres and Hinshelwood 2013). Individual needs are overruled by the reigning mentality that a group uses to survive. Bion (1961) described three group mentalities or basic assumptions: fight–flight, pairing and dependency. He suggested that one was always expressed in the foreground while the other two were unexpressed and undifferentiated in the background – a psychosomatic protomental matrix – from where they exerted a major influence on psychic functioning and change. Individual needs can only be expressed in the shifts that occur when a basic assumption moves from the background to the foreground; otherwise they are overruled by the reigning basic assumption in a group. Bion returned to the protomental matrix in his later works, in which he came to see it as an undifferentiated layer of psychic functioning which he called hallucinosis (Bion 1970). It is the alpha and the omega of his work.

Further developments of concepts from the group period

The Northfield experiment was the cradle of Bion's ideas on groups. Foulkes, Pines and Main continued in a more therapeutic way, so that Northfield became the origin of therapeutic communities all over the world. Bion's specific leaderless groups are still used in the Tavistock groups in London and the A.K. Rice Institute in Portland. In Italy there is a large culture of analytic group therapy based on Bion's ideas (Italian Institute for Group Psychoanalysis).

The major subsequent development of Bion's seminal ideas on groups seems to be the shift that Ferro (1999) initiated by linking Bion's ideas about the protomental matrix with the field theory of the Barangers; this underlined that analyst and patient alike are always working within a field, thereby acknowledging the great powers of this field. In a similar vein, Ogden (1994) linked these ideas with Winnicott's potential space, which led to his notion of the analytic third.

The epistemophilic period: transformations in knowledge

In trying to understand what goes wrong in psychosis, Bion (1962a,b) created a model of psychic functioning that combined Freud's (1911) 'Two Principles of Mental Functioning' with Klein's notion of unconscious phantasy and a British empiricist perspective on the mind (Vermote 2016b). His idea was that impressions on the mind are processed in an automatic way (Hume's reverie) which corresponds to Kleinian phantasy, a stream that underpins all psychic life (Segal 1991). Bion's model was the first to understand this as a process that has to be set in motion in communication with another, via the mother's containment of what is communicated to her by projective identification. Bion's (1962, 1963, 1965, 1970) four theoretical books constitute an elaboration of this basic idea of psychic functioning. He discerned many stages and uses of thoughts, located them as elements in a Grid and expressed the shifts between these elements in his formula: 'PS--D, $\venus\mars$, selected fact' (Bion 1963).

This process by means of which we passively become aware of constant conjunctions or patterns in the myriad of ever-changing phenomena that we deal with remains a theme throughout all of Bion's work and his guideline for practising psychoanalysis. These underlying patterns are psychoanalytic objects, which are unknowable and a-sensuous before they come to be expressed in sensuous phenomena. The reflection of the underlying psychoanalytic object in sensuous phenomena can occur without much change (rigid motion transformations), with deformations (projective transformations) or dispersed over a large space (hallucinatory transformations). The presence of a psychoanalytic object is never deduced by reason; we become aware of it through intuition.

The question is whether we can trace the origin (the psychoanalytic object) of what we see reflected and transformed in the phenomena of the sessions. Bion (1965) soon found that the origin (O) cannot be reached; the elements in the Grid that categorize all psychic phenomena are all at the level of representations. The origin itself is outside verbal thinking. It can only be intuited and is by definition non-dual, infinite, undifferentiated. We cannot know it. Bion concluded that real psychic change happens there (transformations in O) and not at the level of representations that he had studied so far.

Further development of the concepts of the epistemophilic period

Currently on Pep-Web alone, more than 12,000 papers refer to Bion. It is impossible to review them all; they are an indication of how many colleagues have constructed their own Bion (O'Shaughnessy, 2005). There are two major lines of development of Bion's ideas from this period. One starts from the influential so-called British post-Kleinian group and is characterized by an original elaboration of Bion's ideas, based on sophisticated clinical practice and an integration of them within the Kleinian body of theory. The other line of development starts from Bion's writings as a source independently of his Kleinian roots, and is more free this way. The writings of Californian authors (Grotstein, Ogden, Aguayo), Italian authors (Ferro, Civitarese, Lombardi, Beebe), French authors (Horowitz), Latin-American authors (Sandler, Fix) and North American authors (Levine, Eigen, Brown (2011)) are examples of this. Levine and Civitarese (2016) edited an international collection of recent original texts that offers an idea of the many lines of development.

The post-Kleinians are right that Bion remained very Kleinian as an analyst, although he changed many of Klein's ideas. Some of them, such as the paranoid-schizoid and depressive positions, and projective identification, acquired a less pathological connotation in his work. Some of the influences of his colleagues in the British Society of Psychoanalysis are manifest in his work; for example, Elliot Jacques (groups) and Roger Money-Kyrle (thinking). The influences of some of his non-Kleinian colleagues at the time are less manifest although there are similarities, for example with Marion Milner (creativity), Bowlby (attachment) and Winnicott (mirroring, incommunicado self). Bion's fellow Kleinian colleagues dealt with his ideas in a range of ways after his death. Segal (2006) saw Bion clearly in the line of Freud-Klein but makes an exception for his later ideas on O which she sees as too mystical. Betty Joseph (1989) integrated a lot of Bion's ideas in her influential ideas on psychoanalytic technique like the importance of experience in the here and now and transference-countertransference in the total situation of a session. Meltzer (1978), as an outsider, translated Bion's ideas and was an exception in the group in also actively paying attention to the ideas of the so-called late Bion, even editing a version of Bion's *Memoir of the Future*.

The contemporary post-Kleinians do original work with Bion's ideas from the T(K) period. For a long time there was a resistance towards Bion's later work that only recently seems to have diminished. For example, O'Shaughnessy (1994, 2005), who questions whether there is a continuity or a caesura between Bion's work from the T(K) and the T(O) period.

Britton (1989) introduced the notion of the Oedipal third and Britton and Steiner (1994) elaborated the notion of selected fact versus overvalued ideas in interpretation; Feldman (1993) wrote about projective identification; Taylor (2010) applies the notion of negative capability to interpretation and research; Bronstein (2011, 2014) relies on the protomental matrix in her study of psychosomatics. The influence of Bion's ideas is manifest in the writings of Bell (2016) on self-knowledge; Birksted-Breen (2003, 2012, 2016) on temporality and on the functioning of the mind; Abel-Hirsch (2010) on the life instinct and linking. Tuckett (2011) refers to Bion in his ideas of the essentials of psychoanalysis, to name some of them. Torres and Hinshelwood (2013) studied Bion's sources. Mawson made a major contribution with *Bion Today* (Mawson 2010) and the editing of the 16 volumes of the *Complete Works of W.R. Bion* (Bion 2014).

As it is impossible to deal with all these thoughts in detail, two seminal developments of Bion's thinking from the T(K) period will be highlighted.

The first was initiated by Bion's former analysand Frances Tustin (1986), who described a kind of sensory superficial feelings that defend against the non-thinkable separation which is experienced as a black hole; she described these as autistic barriers, which also exist in neurotic persons. This idea was taken up and further developed by Meltzer, Bick, Anzieu and Houzel who made it a psychic skin, and by Ogden (1989) who developed the idea of an autistic-contiguous sensory position which he distinguished from the paranoid-schizoid and depressive positions.

A second line of thinking is initiated by Ferro (2008), who did not only couple the Barangers' concept of the field to Bion's group idea (see above) but also further developed his theory of thinking, as a kind of transformational narrative process of and within this field. The task of the analyst then becomes to help the patient to transform with reverie what is not transformed. This is a radical new way of looking at psychoanalysis: seeing the analyst's task not as understanding – interpreting but as transforming together with the patient. Ogden (2004) took this up and developed a similar idea, seeing the analytic session as undreamt dreams that need to be dreamt in this field.

The transcendental period, transformations in O

The origin of transformations is infinite, ineffable and unknowable as it is not represented. Transformations in O are changes that happen outside verbal thinking but they can eventually be represented by transformations in K. The movement is always from O to K (Bion 1970). While a transformation in K is *representing* an experience that already happened, a transformation in O is a *new experience*. As O is outside verbal thought, it is by definition impossible to know and talk about O, just as one cannot sing potatoes (Bion 1965: 148). One can just become it – experience it. O is not an abstract thought, but the experience of O. In psychoanalysis, it is a concrete clinical experience often facilitated by a radical openness from the side of the analyst. Being outside verbal thought is being as close to the infinite, in the undifferentiated mode, as possible (Bion 1970). In Bion's idea the difference that matters for psychoanalysis is no longer between conscious and unconscious but between finite and infinite.

A transformation in O results in a change of a kind that makes a psychoanalysis terminable (Bion 1970) but this cannot be actively sought out; it happens automatically. This paradox is crucial.

Further developments of the concepts of the transcendental period

James Grotstein, who was analysed by Bion during his stay in Los Angeles, is best known for developing this aspect of Bion's work. In this regard he originated the concept of the transcendent position (a notion already used by Jung; see Dehing 1994). Grotstein saw it as a state of mind that was different from the paranoid-schizoid and the depressive positions. This state of mind reflects a deep contact at another, undifferentiated level:

> One intuits – internally 'senses' – the objectlessness of the object without ever contemplating it, yet experiences its presence. In the transcendent position, the individual must forsake the presence of the object in order to look inward into his or her own subjectivity.

It is not something 'higher'; Grotstein (2007) quotes Kant to say that it is bathos, the deep from where everything starts, the foundation of experience. O is the mute other that lies 'just beyond, within and around' where we are. One does not really experience O; one experiences experiencing O. The aim of psychoanalysis became for Grotstein the development of the infinite in the finite man. Grotstein's colleague Annie Reiner (2012) shares a similar perspective, using a more poetic approach.

In the same vein other psychoanalysts were developing an authentic linking of Bion's ideas with a thorough knowledge of mystical approaches, like M. Epstein with Zen (1995) and Michael Eigen (2012) with the Kabbalah. From a philosophical point of view the experience of O can be linked with the Kantian Sublime (Vermote 2011b, 2016c; Civitarese 2016c).

Actually experiencing O is a subject that has been written about extensively. In the many approaches, the watershed seems in Bionian terms, whether it is from K that one tries to get to O – which is doomed to fail; or whether the approach is from O – an intuitive experience – that gets expressed, found by K, and may be expressed in analogies or metaphors, images that emerge spontaneously – in short, a language of achievement (Bion 1970), a notion that Bion borrows from Keats.

The Socratic period

I have the impression that in this last period, Bion switches from pure emotional experience in the transcendental period to a more philosophical not-knowing, although this is fully in line with the transcendental period. O entails a fundamental not-knowing stance. In his *Memoir of the Future* Bion (1977) states that he has enough of understanding and being understood. He does not talk of O and a transcendental attitude anymore, but the Unknown is the invariant that he shares with the former period. He takes a deep uncompromising Socratic questioning approach. In his radical not-knowing, being truthful and non-defensive is the reference. His autobiographical work from this time reveals truths that he did not talk about before, like in his last war writings where he describes his self-image when he was young (Bion 1986). He is stripping, sandblasting all disguises. Psychoanalytic jargon is a particular target. A simple childlike question, such as 'What is a cow, Daddy?' can plunge us into the unknown (Bion 1994). When he was asked about projective identification in a seminar, a concept that was central to his way of working and his theory of the analytic process, he answered that it does not mean a thing (Bion 1990: 56). One could also argue that he made a rational progression in his thinking, leading him to use mystical metaphors in theory and practice in his transcendental period without really realizing them from within as mystics do. Ultimately he transformed them to a more philosophical Socratic stance of fundamental not-knowing in thinking about psychoanalysis in his lectures and supervisions of this last period.

CONCLUSION

In this book we have followed Bion's quest to discover the essence of psychoanalysis. The path is broken by caesurae, which introduce fundamental changes while still maintaining contact with the former vertices.

The main caesura is the leap from T(K) to T(O), which became a kind of dual track; both perspectives on psychic change coexist and touch at the caesura. Bion moved from a theory of thinking and verbal thought to lay emphasis on the importance of being, experiencing and intuition at a non-verbal level.

While looking at transformations, Bion focused more and more on beta-elements, the matrix, the emmatures, the hallucinatory layer, the Alpheus, O – which all point at the same formless, infinite, unknown, noumena. It is an undifferentiated matrix outside verbal thought, which is not represented and without separation and distinction. Bion used the metaphor of looking from the other side of Picasso's glass paintings. It is there at this pure experiential level that real changes take place (T(O)) that can be taken up at the level of representations (T(K)).

During his odyssey, we have seen changes in Bion's language and approach: from empiricist and positivistic when studying T(K) to the idealistic philosophers, and mystics who struggled with the same problem of expressing a truth beyond verbal thought and language when writing about T(O), and finally returning to a not-knowing, questioning Socratic attitude.

However, throughout all these changes, many things remained invariant, such as his dispassionate attitude, the oscillation between patience and security, his emphasis on poetry, and his move away from Reason.

Bion's unique theoretical background and life experiences allowed him to develop his tolerance of solitude, mental pain, growing, truth, integrity and remoteness in his isolation and further played an important role in his confrontation with personal misfortune and the Great War – he met unique individuals like Trotter, Beckett, Rickman, Paton and Klein who provided him with the building blocks for his original meta-theories that we can apply in many fields (psychoanalysis, art, philosophy, religion, community, etc.).

Immersing ourselves in his way of looking at things acts as a container that catalyses our own automatic-reverie capacity for psychic processing.

I would like to leave you with the following quotations, which I think together come close to what Bion discovered about the essence of psychoanalysis:

> After I had discovered in the course of my work with all members of my practice the obstructive quality of preconceptions, the patient's analysis became more lifelike. It did not matter whether the preconceptions had sprung from what I had consciously or unconsciously gathered from the contact with the patient, or whether it was something that I had heard in another context, or whether it was some psycho-analytic theory. The increase in lifelike quality was associated with an increased readiness to perceive non-verbal quality. As I became more practised at ignoring – or as Freud put it 'artificially blinding myself-to certain memories and desires, I found the patient's attempts to speak less able to demand my attention.
>
> (Bion 1989: 17)

> What is to be sought is an activity that is both the restoration of god (the Mother) and the evolution of god (the formless, infinite, ineffable, non-existent), which can be found only in the state in which there is NO memory, desire, understanding.
>
> (Bion 1970: 129)

ADDENDA

LISTENING TO AND READING BION

James S. Grotstein

Listening to Bion

Reading Bion is a unique experience in itself, but the combination of reading his works after listening to him, both in psychoanalysis and in lectures, was awesome and constituted an adventure in a different form of learning. I shall give an example of my listening experiences first. When I first entered analysis with him and for some time afterwards, I had not yet read his published works. I learned from my first day in analysis with him that he was different from my two previous analysts. He hardly ever *spoke* to me. He only (formally) *interpreted* my unconscious phantasies – and did so virtually from the first few moments after the analysis had begun. I still remember some of his interpretations, but I also recall, on the other hand, that I often did not recall many others of them even during the session and was frequently mystified when he spoke. Yet, after I left each of these session, I experienced feeling very alert and extraordinarily clear and did some of my best work with my own patients whom I saw afterwards. I only slowly began to believe that Bion's interpretations were addressed to my *pre*-conscious (unconscious) mind more than to my conscious one. The experience was not unlike hypnosis. I also recall an occasion when I attended a lecture he gave at a local psychoanalytic institute. I found that I was somewhat bored with his lecture and wasn't clear about what he was trying to get across. When I went home that evening, however, I found that I could not sleep. I got up from bed and felt compelled to write the skeletons of three psychoanalytic papers. In short, Bion was able to *telescope* his ideas in such a way that they had a mysterious delayed-action effect.

Once, he inadvertently revealed his 'secret' to me. After having presented me on one occasion with what I believed to have been a remarkable interpretation, I stated: 'That was a beautiful interpretation'. His reply was: 'Yes, "beautiful interpretation", you call it. The snag is that my "beautiful interpretation" was made possible by your beautiful associations. You were so keen on listening to me that you neglected listening to yourself listening to me'. In other words, the act of listening to how *I* feel about what he says became my revelation about Bion's analytic epistemology. He later made the statement that the analyst, while listening to the patient, should really listen to *himself* listening to the patient. This novel 'technique' can also be applied to reading his published work, and I have every reason to believe that that was how Bion desired for readers to approach his works: to listen to *their own* spontaneous thoughts while reading him, i.e., their own transformations of their own personal experiences upon reading him.

Reading Bion

Upon approaching reading Bion's published works, many readers become frustrated, perplexed, irritated and aversive. Some say that his style of writing closely resembles that of James Joyce's *Finnegans Wake*, particularly his three-volume novel, *A Memoir of the Future*. Thomas Ogden studied his style of writing and noted how it had changed from a formal to a more open and available style between his earlier and his later works. Virtually everyone agrees that his published works are dense, often recondite, abstruse and formidable. Some readers have come to grips with the often impenetrable nature of his style by reading him in groups. Others, including myself, have found that frequent readings, whether alone or with others, can be very rewarding and that he thereby becomes more understandable. It also must be remembered that Bion was an Edwardian and a graduate of a 'public school' as well as an Oxonian. His style of sentence structure seems to me to be clearly out of the Greek and especially the Latin classics. Sometimes, while reading Bion, I go into a trance and believe that I am rereading Virgil's *Aeneid*. Once when reading Bion, Borges' mystical story, 'The Book of Sand' came to mind. In this story the pages at the beginning and at the end proliferate to infinity as one approaches them. That's what happens to me when I read Bion.

Another impression I formed while reading Bion was that it seemed as if he were presenting his thoughts in a unique, private, idiosyncratic shorthand and that I, while reading his shorthand, was scanning it as one would do while speed-reading, i.e., using one's right cerebral hemispheric processing of the whole gestalt of the text while the left hemisphere processed the harvest of ideas and parts of ideas from the former. In other words, there was not a smooth, orderly sequential flow. The reader had to supply his or her own fill-ins. In this way I felt that I was reading Bion *actively*, i.e., that I was co-constructing the meaning of the text along with him while reading him. Put in other terms, I felt that I was liberated from being a passive acolyte searching for wisdom from a master and was, instead, joining an epistemological expedition or safari into the jungles of uncertainty.

I have often asked myself the question: (a) Was Bion's eccentric writing style due to an emotional problem of his about being forthright and direct (here I have in mind the tragedies of his life, including the trauma of World War I and the death of his first wife)? (b) Or was it due to an inborn gift, as it were, of presenting a mass of signifiers in a condensed way so as to present these seemingly disjointed signifiers in an economical manner? (c) Or was it a consciously and carefully contemplated technique to present his ideas in a manner that would avoid clichés and rhetoric and constitute indexical ideas that would spontaneously telescope and spread their variegated associations once encountered by the reader? Bion often used the phrase, 'I would like to draw your attention . . .'. I think his way of drawing our attention was to blind us to what he didn't want us to be distracted by. Francesca Bion, in her Preface to *Bion: New York and Sao Paulo*, states:

> It must be admitted that for those looking for cut-and-dried 'answers' Bion's method was inexplicable, frustrating and aggravating. Here was a man, thoroughly conversant with his subject, exceptionally articulate and therefore well able to supply questioners with what they wanted to hear – and he knew it. But he was steadfast in his respect for the truth and would not be persuaded against his better judgment to follow a course in which he could not respect himself. He believed that 'La reponse est le malheur de la question'; both in his professional and private life problems stimulated in him thought and discussion – never answers. His replies – more correctly, counter, contributions – were, in spite *of* their apparent irrelevance, an extension *of* the questions. His point of view is best illustrated in his own words: *'I don't know the answers to these questions – I wouldn't tell you if I did. I think it is important to find out for yourselves. I try to give you a chance to fill the gap left by me. I don't think that my explanation matters. What I would draw attention to is the nature of the problem. When I feel a pressure – I'd better get prepared in case you ask me some questions – I say, 'To hell with it, I'm not going to look up this stuff in Freud or anywhere else, or even in my past statement – I'll put up with it'. But of course I am asking you to put up with it too'.*
>
> (my italics)

In other words, Bion was interested – and wanted us to be interested – not in the answer to the question but to the virtual infinity of emerging questions which the transient 'answer' poses and is an indexical bridge to. Whereas Bion's earlier writings (up to *Transformations*, 1965) were written under Klein's – and Freud's – canopy, i.e., positivism, his later works reflected his move towards the Principle of Uncertainty, what he was to call 'O', the Absolute Truth about an ever unknowable, infinite, impersonal Ultimate Reality. Each new interpretation only points out the ever-growing disparity and asymmetry between what has just been learned while simultaneously realizing that one has just been introduced to how much more he does not know. The chasm of the difference mocks the knowledge one has acquired.

Bion's writings were thus moving from positivistic certainty (where the drives are first cause) to uncertainty and unfathomable mystery – from the answer to the question, rather than the other way around. I happened by chance once to be reading Plato's *Theaetetus* and serendipitously discovered what I believe to be the ultimate source of some of Bion's thinking and modes of explication. Bion was very Socratic. He became imbued with the importance of the ever-living question which mocks every attempt by answers to eliminate it. He also became imbued with Heraclitus's and Socrates' notion of 'flux', which he translated into 'evolution'. In *Theaetetus* we also see the origin of his later epistemological concept of 'become' (Socrates states that the perceiver must *become* the percept). He also discovered the Ideal Forms there and elsewhere in Plato's *Dialogues*, as well as the concept of the 'disciplined debate'. The Forms and flux were to characterize his later concept of O, and 'disciplined debate' was to characterize a defining theme in *A Memoir of the Future*.

Another way of characterizing Bion's style of presentation is to think of two images: one is a crossword puzzle and the other is an archipelago. In the former we see letters that are placed on a grid in such a way that the empty spaces between them are suggestive of other, unknown letters, which, when applied to the empty spaces, begin to constitute words. An archipelago is a group of islands in the ocean which, though seemingly disconnected on the visible surface, can be observed underneath surface of the ocean to be connected. Bion's writings are like both of those images. He presents a wide range of bursting ideas 'macilently' and compactly for us to absorb – without comment – and then to allow them to gestate in our unconscious – and see what happens.

A piece of Bion's writings

In *Transformations* Bion states:

> Part of the equipment of observation is *pre-conception* used as *preconception* – D4. It is in its D4 aspect that I wish to consider the Oedipal theory; that is, as part of the *observational* equipment of the analyst . . . The analyst's theoretical equipment may thus be narrowly described D4, E4 [conception-attention], F4 [concept–attention].
>
> (my brackets and italics: 50–51)

It took a great familiarity with Bion's writings for me finally to comprehend what Bion might have been suggesting here. He is discussing psychoanalytic technique. What I tentatively concluded about it was as follows: The analyst must on one hand listen to his patient without memory and desire (my background understanding of his concepts but not included in the citation) and also must observe his patient with a sound background in analytic theory, i.e., 'preconceptions'. One of the theories (preconceptions) is 'pre-conception', the knowledge of the Ideal Forms, i.e., inherent (*primary*) pre-conceptions, 'memoirs of the future', 'thoughts without a thinker', noumena, things-in-themselves. Moreover, each newly acquired *conception* not only progresses to the status of *concept*, it also recycles and reconstitutes a *secondary* pre-conception for the next iteration of transformation.

Let me explain my speculative imagining and reasoning in how I arrived at this hypothesis: I was at first puzzled by what I had read. Then, I believe, my preconscious α-function employed two of Bion's tools: concretism ↔ abstraction and P-S ↔ D. While my preconscious α-function was scanning the entirety of my knowledge about Bion's works, the knowledge that I had gained about preconceptions and pre-conceptions, which were 'filed', as it were, in knowledge assigned to the depressive position, now became regressively broken down, concretized and reassembled (abstracted) into a plausible new idea: The analyst must paradoxically *listen* to his patient without memory, desire, understanding or *preconception and* he must also *observe* the patient with preconceptions (theory, memory, experience), which include the inherent and acquired *pre-conceptions* that are on the alert to mate with their realizations in experience.

While working on this contribution I am simultaneously engaged in rereading Bion's *Transformations*, which I have read countless times before. This time I found myself reading it differently and ever more meaningfully. I felt that I finally comprehended what he is trying to get across in a deeper way. This time I was able to read him closely while remaining separate from him and his thoughts, i.e., I was not suffering from a 'transformation in hallucinosis' with him or his words (i.e., not hypnotized). I realized that this newfound ability required many years of immersion with his works. I came across a statement he made in *Transformations*: 'The growth of insight depends, at its inception, on undisturbed projective identification. If it is disturbed, mental development is hampered' (p. 36). Only at this latest reading did I realize the revolutionary epistemological importance of that statement. Projective identification serves the pleasure principle but in a way that also supports the reality principle. That is why Bion conflated Freud's primary *and* secondary processes in his concept of α-function.

I have come to see Bion in his earlier, more formal writings as a strained 'Prometheus bound', whereas in some of his later writings, especially in *Taming Wild Thoughts*, I see a 'Prometheus unbound', even playful. I cite the following from that work:

> If a thought without a thinker comes along, it may be what is a 'stray thought', or it could be a thought with the owner's name and address upon it, or it could be a 'wild thought'. The problem, should some thought come along, is what to do with it . . . [Y]ou could purloin it and hope either that the owner would forget it, or that he would not notice the theft and you could keep the idea all to yourself . . . What I am concerned with . . . is the wild thoughts that turn up and after which there is no possibility of being able to trace immediately any kind of ownership.
>
> (p. 27)

This is playful, imaginative Bion, now a Prometheus *Un*bound, having freed himself at last from the fetters of his former address, positivism and its sponsor, certainty.

When I first encountered Bion, I had authored (actually, co-authored) only one paper. After listening to and after reading – and digesting – Bion, I became prolific. In retrospect I think I owe this to his espousal and reverence for imaginative conjecture along with reasonable conjecture, i.e., his reverence and awe as to the products of imagination. In reading Bion one is best advised not to look to him for wisdom as a master. I advise the reader to allow him or herself to 'become' his or her own inner response to Bion. In the myth of Plato's cave, the subject observes shadows on the wall of the cave cast by a fire behind him, with the Forms situated between the fire and the back of his head. For too many eons we have been confusing the shadows with the Forms. Bion has at last come along and eliminated the 'middle man', the shadows, and now we can *experience the Forms* ('become' them) without needing to observe them.

In reading Bion the reader must abandon memory, desire (the desire to 'understand' him), preconceptions and (the myth of) understanding; he must cast 'a beam of intense darkness' into his mind so as to allows the text to affect him; he must allow for the effect of its spontaneous and mysterious incubation within him, and then he may ultimately – only ultimately – experience unpredictable results – but only transient results awaiting the next cycle of uncertainty's verdict.

MY INDEBTEDNESS TO BION

Antonino Ferro

My daily practice has been enriched by Bion's thought in several respects, not just in terms of the implicit basic theory, but especially in the realm of theory of technique. In other words, it has influenced the way I am in my consultancy room, during my routine work with patients.

I will try to briefly indicate some of these points.

The way of thinking about an interpretation as something insatiable: not everything has to be saturated with meaning; an interpretation must remain open to new scenarios, for what has not been thought yet. There is not one strong possessor of a knowledge, but two persons who are trying to approximate the bearable emotional truth (of both) on that particular day as closely as possible. In this work the patient is not merely the 'best colleague', but also the one who knows most about him/herself.

The way of thinking about theory not as something that guides and supports me, but as something that I discover and construct in a tentative and preliminary manner, without being afraid of this indefinite character and without shame when I later discover that it had been codified already. The preliminary nature of theories and thoughts in the consultancy room of the analyst implies that we are perpetually trying to escape from the light pollution and from the noise of everything that is already known. In his *Italian Seminars* Bion confirms that the only things that matter in the session are accessible to our senses. Only on this material – I would like to add – the truly metabolic, digestive and transformative operations can be performed. Only in this way can we enable durable introjection of the necessary instruments by the patients.

Abandon interest in the 'contents' of the story of the patient (which I nonetheless share with him/her – I will later say why) in favour of an interest in the instruments, the tools for thinking. What interests me are the modalities that enable the development of the α-function, the container, the attitude that is necessary to capture, to dream and to transform the proto-emotional and the proto-sensory states. In this respect, the most diverse contents can come into existence, without necessarily coming to the foreground.

In this view, 'the session is the dream'. From my perspective, what the patient tells me is a dream, what he or she replies to my interpretation is a dream (and often it is a dream about my interpretation), what s/he tells me already in the first encounter is a dream. What basically interests me is developing, both in the patient and in myself, a dream attitude towards our psyche. That is why I work on the development of the container (the threads of emotions that are interwoven and reinforced between me and the patient allow for increasingly intense contents to dance from one trapeze/psyche to the other, like acrobats in the circus, knowing that there is a safety net), on the development of the α-function, the apparatus that is capable of transforming the protosensations and proto-emotions in pictograms, audiograms, olfactograms (α-elements).

The development of the container is enabled by our capacity to be on the same wavelength with the patient, our capacity to be on the same emotional line. This allows the threads that I was talking about above to develop. It also demands the courage to – insofar as it useful – share the manifest meaning of the patient's story.

In my view, the α-function develops by means of the reverie of the analyst, by his attitude of continuous narrative deconstruction and by his capacity (which in turn becomes the capacity of the bipersonal field and finally that of the patient) to reconstruct the patient's communications as a dream.

The central position is occupied by what I absolutely consider to be Bion's most important conceptualization: his postulation of a dream activity in a waking condition (the α-function and her products) which continually alphabetizes sensory and unthinkable states. In an important remark in the *Tavistock Seminars* Bion emphasizes how little analysts are prepared to share this notion and, may I add, to believe in its theoretical-technical consequences of its implications. I believe that I have elaborated some of Bion's intuitions according to my personal point of view.

- The introduction of the concept 'narrative derivative' (Ferro 1999, 2002). Any manner in which a patient with a distanced attitude and with all kinds of deformation narrates what has happened between his psyche and the psyche of the analyst. And this without privileging one narrative genre (childhood, sexuality, anecdotes, stories in diary style, memories, etc.) at the expense of others (precisely because I am interested in the instruments that produce the stories and the transformations).
- The introduction of the concept 'character' that is so central in my thought (Ferro 1996). The character as a narrative nodal point bringing together different emotions that can be disentangled and joined together again in a different manner in order to form new characters. I noticed later that I owe this theme – apart from studies in narratology and semiotics – to the personifications that Bion made of psychoanalytic concepts in his *A Memoir for the Future*.

- The development of the concept 'field' not just in a horizontal, spatial realm that contains all divisions and intersections (the actual fractionated aspects of analyst and patient) but also in a vertical, historical realm that holds all temporal elements, including the transgenerational history of both. The concept of a group matrix of the psyche is definitely related to this point of view.
- A view of sexuality as a sexuality between psyches; that is, as the ongoing play between projective identifications and reverie that gives centre-stage to the psychical functioning/dysfunctioning of analyst and patient in the session. This way of looking at sexuality implies that we not only phenotypically take into account the sexes, but that we also consider the quality of mental pairing. In any type of couple male ♂♂ or female ♀♀ homosexual ways of functioning occur, as well as heterosexual ♀♂, as far as the interaction penetration/receptivity is concerned.
- An optimist vision of life and of the cure. Although I am convinced we are nothing but a 'joke of nature' (which could have ended worse), the rudimentary nature of the mental apparatus gives me hope that we will be more and more capable of developing the creative functions of the dream, of thinking and of emotions in the future. This is why I do not consider the death drive and destruction as a curse on our kind, but as a transgenerational accumulation of β-elements that we will probably be able to metabolize, to digest in order to transform them into creativity and the capacity to experience emotions.
- An essential identity between the analysis of adults, adolescents and children, due to the focus on mental apparatuses rather than on contents. The expressive language is different, not the essence of psychical functioning. In other words, I could say that the analytic session appears to me like a dream of psyches in which various stories, arising from different spaces and ages in the field, come together, are taken apart and reassembled. The shared experience is one in which the states of mind, affects, thoughts and characters are being circulated with the analyst (he too has a place in the field), who guarantees and maintains the framework and who facilitates the dream-like activity of the analytic couple.

To sum up, I could say that every session becomes a dream, shared, narrated together, acted together, which renounces real or historical truth in favour of an emotional-narrative truth, in which stories, transformations, insight and especially attitudes come to life – I mean the capacity to dream, to transform everything that imposes itself as sensoriality and proto-emotions into reverie, into an image.

Each session is a pearl, a bead on a rosary that through all its 'mysteries' leads not to contents, but to the capacity to make the journey, forwards and backwards, as in certain science fiction films, where it is possible to travel in time and space.

The motor of the analysis and of the story and myth-creating activity is the need to find a space/time for the unthinkable and the ineffable and a function that leads to the capacity to think and speak.

What it comes down to is to cooperate around the emotions present in the field, to weave them together and to reweave them again. This allows for the development of the container/contained ($\female\male$), throughout the reverie, through like-mindedness.

The result of all these transforming transitions, session after session, leads to the capacity to weave proto-emotions into images, into stories or memories that were previously sealed off, or even into memories of facts that never actually took place, but that were constructed in the field, and then put back into time, with continuously belated (*après coup*) movements.

The trajectory of the analysis becomes a function of the modality of the functioning of each analytic couple at work. The actual meaning of a natural process character is lost.

Each couple will have its own way of dealing with the analytic work. Likewise, the ups and downs of an analysis, the negative therapeutic reactions, psychotic or negative transferences (and counter transferences) will pertain to that couple.

Of course there is a limit to subjectivist derivation. This limit is grounded in the ethics of the analyst, in his personal analysis and preparation, and in his responsibility vis-à-vis the fact that only the narrated facts must be alphabetized by the analytic couple, and no other facts (such as the confirmation of the theories of the analyst, or the desire to avoid psychical pain).

It is clear that a field theory, in which the analyst is strongly implicated in the course of the analysis, demands a permanent vigilance on the part of the analyst as well as the maintenance of his main tool: his psychical functioning.

The session is played at the level of the mutual dream activity, either when the patient (when he is capable) 'dreams' the intervention of the analyst or his mental state, or when the analyst 'dreams' the answer that he will give to his patient. The more this answer is 'dreamed', the more it will be a factor that brings into being the alpha-function of the patient and that repairs its deficiencies if necessary.

The analyst in the session finds himself in the situation of a driver who must devote his attention to the entire set of instruments on board of a very complex car, or of an airplane, but only in the function of safe travel. Otherwise we would either run the risk of getting off course (or in serious trouble), or on the contrary, the risk that the analysis runs by itself without the journey progressing. We are after all dealing with a very paradoxical journey: its goal is to learn to travel in ever-expanding territories; in other words, to acquire a method.

The reverie as constant basic activity is the way in which the psyche of the analyst continually contains, metabolizes and transforms everything that is directed towards him by the patient, as verbal, para-verbal or non-verbal stimuli. The same activity of reverie is at work in the patient, in response to any stimulus (interpretative or not) coming from the analyst.

This fundamental activity of reverie is the basis of our mental life; health, disease, and the degree of psychical suffering depend on its functioning/dysfunctioning. The same can be said of the existence of a fundamental activity of projective identifications that are the necessary activators of any activity of reverie.

We cannot deny that the patient always knows the way in which we function psychically. This he tells us as well, by dreaming it in real time (Bion), but very often we don't want to know that dream. Instead, we take recourse to column 2 of the Grid: we tell ourselves lies, in order to protect us with them, even if we are dealing with an authentic feeling.

DISCOVERING BION
A Personal Memoir

H.B. Levine

Then felt I like some watcher of the skies
When a new planet swims into his ken;
Or like stout Cortez when with eagle eyes
He stared at the Pacific – and all his men
Looked at each other with a wild surmise
Silent, upon a peak in Darien.

(John Keats)

On first looking into Chapman's Homer

I first encountered Bion through the supervision of Harold Boris, when I was a neophyte psychiatric resident learning to lead an intensive, five-days-per-week therapy group on a 10-patient, psychoanalytically oriented in-patient service. Hal was a complex and charismatic figure. Not only was his psychoanalytic knowledge acquired outside an orthodox training institute – it was a time in the US when clinical training was not readily available to non-medical clinicians and would never be offered to a psychologist like Hal, who was without a doctorate – but he worked in the tradition of Klein and Bion at a time when their ideas were unknown and even derided in the ego-psychological world of the Boston Psychoanalytic Institute. Much of what he introduced me to ran counter to the conventional wisdom of my other teachers and, in retrospect, it was only through a kind of 'functional splitting' that compartmentalized my clinical self into 'group' and 'individual' personae that I was able to absorb some of what he taught and encouraged me to read. This solution worked for a while and I was even able to publish two papers based on our collaboration. Once I began my psychoanalytic training, however, the cognitive dissonance between ego psychology and Klein/Bion became so great that I could only survive by pulling away from the latter and what Hal had been trying to teach me. This early experience, however, did introduce me first-hand to emotional turbulence and cast a stone into the water that produced waves and reverberations that have proven to be of enormous importance to my formation and subsequent evolution as a psychoanalyst.

Soon thereafter, as a young graduate analyst, I became increasingly aware of two problems in my understanding of psychoanalysis. The first was that there seemed to be little correlation between successful analytic results and the initial assessment of analysability as it had been conveyed to me in my training. Even as a candidate, I had noticed that some patients with presumptively 'good' analytic prognoses and 'good enough' analysts did not necessarily do well in treatment, while other patients, with poor prognoses based on severity of diagnosis, could sometimes do quite well, if they had a favourable analytic match. The latter seemed more a matter of non-specific subjective factors, such as the analyst's 'emotional presence' or intuition, and the quality of the working relationship that was formed by each analytic dyad. This quality, which seemed to go beyond the ego-psychological sense of a 'therapeutic alliance', reached into something ineffable in the intersubjective encounter between analysand and analyst and appeared to be more powerfully determinative of analytic outcome than the presence or absence of objective patient-centred ego capacities. In retrospect, I had begun to learn that neither container nor contained could be considered in isolation from each other and that the interaction and fit between them was a vital consideration in understanding the unfolding of the analytic process.

A second problem that troubled me early in my career was the gap that existed between the reality of analytic practice and my assumption that if analysts were thorough enough in their analysis of resistances, then the necessary analytic data would appear in the associations of their patients. Much to my dismay, I found that especially with sicker patients – borderline and narcissistic personalities, perverse and action prone patients, psychosomatic disorders and adults with early or severe childhood trauma (e.g., adults who were sexually abused as children) – the relevant analytic material appeared, often dramatically, either in the subjectivity of the analyst or had to be imaginatively constructed de novo by the analytic pair.

This observation, strengthened by a growing American interest in the psychology of the analyst, led me to explore the literature on projective identification and the positive use of the countertransference and engaged my curiosity about the analyst's unconscious role and participation in the analytic process. Increasingly, these concerns led me to the work of the contemporary Kleinians and back to Bion, where I re-encountered his seminal formulations of the normative (communicative) role of projective identification in emotional development and the analytic process and its more general expression in his theory of container and contained.

As I now understand it, I would say that I had been straining against and beginning to escape from the strictures of a one-person psychology and the ego-psychological understanding of an 'archaeological' model, in which psychoanalysis was construed as an exploratory expedition that 'dug into' and uncovered the repressed areas of the patient's mind. This model, which was rooted in Freud's first topography and had great historical value, remained useful with neurotic patients or the neurotic portions of a patient's mind. As a general formulation for the treatment of the widening scope of analytic patients, the very cases that made up the bulk of my clinical practice, however, it was proving to be far too limited.

Assisted in part by my long-term collaborative interaction with colleagues in the Group for the Study of Psychoanalytic Process and the Klein/Bion Study Group of the Massachusetts Institute for Psychoanalysis, I began to achieve some resolution of the tensions that I felt, when I recognized the deeply intersubjective nature of the analytic process.

My convictions were strengthened and my understanding deepened by my subsequent encounters with the Bion-based writings of Antonino Ferro (2002, 2005), whose work also introduced me to the analytic field theory of the Barangers (1983). Slowly, in combination with my own clinical experience, I felt that I was now acquiring the essential elements with which to think about and describe the psychoanalytic process. These were rooted in Bion's revolutionary theory of thinking (1962) and in his conceptualizations of certain movements within the analytic process, such as the interplay of container and contained, the value of reverie, the central, constructive role of the analyst's intuition and the crucial differences between insight and experience, transformation and information, O and K and their relations to psychic change.

Subsequently, I found myself turning to Bion, especially his later works, not only for inspiration and stimulation in my attempts to understand mental functioning, transformation and psychic growth and for the elements of a truly psychoanalytic theory of intersubjective clinical relating broad enough to transcend the narrow, sectarian confines of rival analytic schools, but for the model of an analyst who had the encourage to entertain 'wild thoughts', take them seriously and to follow and learn from his experience, even when it went against the accepted wisdom of the establishment and the status quo.

While Bion did not elaborate a specific theory of psychoanalytic technique, his theory of mental functioning (Bion 1962) and perspective on the analyst's optimal listening stance ('without memory and desire') (Bion 1970) and role in the process of facilitating the transformation and development of the patient's psyche have had profound implications for my clinical work. Through study of his works, I have been helped to sharpen my awareness of and responsiveness to the patient's psychic reality, better tolerate uncertainty and allow myself to be more open to surprise.

In my reading of Bion, I believe that I have also discovered his conviction that in each analysis we must search for an irreducible starting point from which to examine our knowledge of the mind; a point of certainty, analogous to Descartes' cogito ergo sum, from which all else can follow. Taken in this way, Bion may be seen as preoccupied with two recurring fundamental questions about psychoanalysis and about existence: 'What do we know?' and 'How do we come to know it?' And his writings have addressed these questions in ways that have continued to open up the field for analytic investigation rather than constrict it. As Ferro (2002) has so clearly elucidated, Bion has given us a vision of the psyche that is always evolving and expanding; of an unconscious that is always in the process of being constructed; of a process of analytic exploration that enlarges, expands and creates the very subject that it seeks to explore.

Rather than forming a 'Bionian' school, Bion encouraged each of us to pursue the unique and personal developments that his ideas might stimulate. Thus, his work supports creativity in the analyst – 'mysticism' and 'genius' in Bion's (1970) terms – as he challenges the analyst to put his trust in intuition and inspiration. For Bion, consensually validatable experience, the 'usual' and accepted view of things, was a potential distraction from the true subject of psychoanalysis, the investigation of psychic reality. Elucidating the latter requires analysts to transcend the ordinary meaning of things and the commonplace assumptions about the relations that can seem to exist between the ordinary elements of life.

Bion thus posits a psychoanalysis that is not afraid of the idiosyncratic and the extraordinary and runs the risk of being perceived as dangerous to the Establishment and the status quo. He also invites a deeper rereading of certain Freudian texts (e.g., *Formulations on the Two Principles of Mental Functioning* (Freud 1911), which I think may be read as one of the key foundation texts for *Attention and Interpretation*) and for me has opened the way to the appreciation and study of leading French contributors, such as Green (2002, 2005), de M'Uzan (2003) and the Botellas (2005), whose work, especially in relation to unrepresented mental states and the development of mind, can be fruitfully approached through the fundamental lens and conceptual language that Bion has given us.

In an important sense, Bion's work stands in relationship to psychoanalysis, as it once did for me: as a source of emotional turbulence that may evoke disturbing, even threatening images of catastrophic change. But he has warned us that this is always the price to be paid for psychic development and has armed us with the conceptual means of making such threats thinkable. The disturbances his work produces are 'wild thoughts' in search of a thinker; the unbridled contained in search of a transforming container; not yet dared to be dreamed dream – thoughts in search of a suitable dream-work. Although it may be deeply appreciated, his legacy must perforce remain unfinished, even as it continues to inform and influence our work. As the evocative title of his autobiography indicates, his legacy is *A Memoir of the Future*. That is, a legacy not simply of contents uncovered, but of process and becoming. A legacy of searching for not only what once was, but for what has not yet dared to be.

REFERENCES

Abel-Hirsch, N. (2010) The life instinct, *Int. J. Psycho-Anal.*, 91: 1055–1071.

Abram, J. (1996) *The Language of Winnicott: A Dictionary of Winnicott's Use of Words*, London: Karnac.

Aguayo, J. and Malin, B. (Eds.) (2013) *Wilfred Bion: Los Angeles Seminars and supervision*, London: Karnac.

Ancona, L. (2000) Bion and Foulkes: A mythological encounter only, but it is already enough, *Funzione Gamma*, 34, www.funzionegamma.edu.

Angelus Silesus (1986/1737) *The Cherubinic Wanderer*, M. Shrady, J. Schmidt (Eds.) Mahwah, NJ: Paulist Press.

Anzieu, D. (1983) Un soi disjoint, une voix liante: l'écriture narrative de Samuel Beckett, *Nouvelle Revue Psychanalytique*, 28: 71–86.

Anzieu, D. (1984) *Le groupe et l'inconscient*, Paris: Dunod.

Anzieu, D. (1986) Beckett et Bion, *Revue de Psychotherapie Psychanalytique de Groupe*, 286: 5–6.

Anzieu, D. (1989a) *The Skin Ego*, New Haven, CT: Yale University Press.

Anzieu, D. (1989b) Beckett and Bion, *International Review of Psycho-Analysis*, 16: 163–169.

Anzieu, D. (1990) *Psychic Envelopes*, London: Karnac.

Anzieu, D. (1992) *Beckett et le psychanalyste*, Paris: Mentha, Archimbaud.

Anzieu, D., Monjauze, M., Bacon F. and Adda, E. (1993) *Francis Bacon, ou, le portrait de l'homme désespécé*, Lausanne: Aire, Archimbaud.

Appelbaum, D. (1995) *The Vision of Kant*, Shaftesbury: Element Books.

Badaracco, J.G. and Vermote, R. (2002) The nature of the problems of psychoanalysis with so-called 'difficult' patients, *International Journal of Psycho-Analysis*, 83: 689–694.

Bair, D. (1978) *Samuel Beckett: A Biography*, New York: Harcourt, Brace and Jovanovich.

Balint, M. (1968) *The Basic Fault: Therapeutic Aspects of Regression*, London: Tavistock.

Baranger de Bernardi, B.L. (2008) Introduction to the paper by Madeleine and Willy Baranger: the analytic situation as a dynamic field, *International Journal of Psycho-Analysis*, 89: 773–784.

Baranger, M. and Baranger, W. (2008) The analytic situation as a dynamic field, *International Journal of Psychoanalysis*, 89: 795–826.

Baranger, M. and Baranger, W. et al. (1983) Process and non-process in analytic work, *International Journal of Psychoanalysis*, 64: 1–15.

Barthes, R. (1981) *Camera Lucida*, New York: Hill and Wang.

Bate, W.J. (2009/1963) *John Keats*, Cambridge, MA: Harvard University Press.

Beckett, S. (1934) A Case in a Thousand, *The Bookman* 86, 241–242.

Beckett, S. (1938) *Murphy*, New York: Grove Press.

Beckett, S. (1958) The Unnameable, in *Three Novels* by Samuel Beckett, New York: Grove Press.

Beckett, S. (1984) *Disjecta*, R. Kohn, New York: Groove Press.

Bell, D. (2009) Is truth an illusion? Psychoanalysis and postmodernism. *International Journal of Psycho-Analysis*, 90: 331–345.

Bell, D. (2011) Bion: the phenomenologist of loss, In C. Mawson (Ed.) *Bion Today*, London: Routledge, 81–102.

Bell, D. and Leite, A. (2016) Experiential self-understanding. *International Journal of Psycho-Analysis*, 97: 305–332.

Bick, E. (1968) The experience of the skin in early object-relations, *International Journal of Psychoanalysis*, 49: 484–486.

Bion, F. (1981) Tribute to Dr. Wilfred R. Bion at the memorial meeting for Dr Wilfred Bion, *International Review of Psychoanalysis*, 8: 3–14.

Bion, F. (1991) La vie est pleine de surprises, in W.R. Bion, *Une théorie pour l'avenir*, Paris: Editions Métaillé.

Bion, F. (1995) The days of our years, *The Journal of the Melanie Klein and Object Relations Journal*, 13(1), online: www.melanie-klein-trust.org.uk and www.psychoanalysis.org.uk/days.htm.

Bion, F. (2000) Random reflections on Bion: past, present, and future (postscript January 1999), in P. Bion Talamo, W.R. Bion, F. Borgogno and S. Merciai, *W.R. Bion: Between Past and Future*, London: Karnac.

Bion, W.R. (1940) War of nerves, in E. Miller and H. Crichton-Miller (Eds.) *The Neuroses of War*, London: The Macmillan Company.

Bion, W.R. (1946) The Northfield experiment, *Bulletin of the Menninger Clinic*, 10: 71–76.

Bion, W.R. (1948) Psychiatry in a time of crisis, *British Journal of Medical Psychology*, XXI: 81–89.

Bion, W.R. (1950) The imaginary twin, paper presented to the British Psycho-Analytical Society, London (reprinted in *International Journal of Psychoanalysis*, 1955) also in W.R. Bion (1967) *Second Thoughts*, London: Heinemann.

Bion, W.R. (1957) Differentiation of the psychotic form the non-psychotic personalities, in W.R. Bion (1967/1984) *Second Thoughts*, New York: Jason Aronson.

Bion, W.R. (1959) Attacks on linking, in W.R. Bion (1967), *Second Thoughts*, London: Heinemann.

Bion, W.R. (1961) *Experiences in Groups*, London: Tavistock.

Bion, W.R. (1962) A theory of thinking, in W.R. Bion (1967/1984) *Second Thoughts*, New York: Jason Aronson.

Bion, W.R. (1962/1984) *Learning from Experience*, London: Karnac.

Bion, W.R. (1963/1984) *Elements of Psychoanalysis*, London: Karnac.

Bion, W.R. (1963/1997) *Taming Wild Thoughts*, Bion, F. (Ed.), London: Karnac.

Bion, W.R. (1963/1997) The Grid, in Bion F. (Ed.) *Taming Wild Thoughts*, London: Karnac.

Bion, W.R. (1965/1984) *Transformations*, London: Karnac.

Bion, W.R. (1966) Catastrophic change, *Bulletin of the British Psychoanalytical Society*, 5: 13–25.

Bion, W.R. (1967) Differentiation of psychotic from the non-psychotic personalities, in Bion, W.R. (1967/1984) *Second Thoughts: Selected Papers on Psychoanalysis*, London: Heinemann.

Bion, W.R. (1967/1984) *Second Thoughts: Selected Papers on Psychoanalysis*, New York: Jason Aronson.

Bion, W.R. (1967/1988) Notes on memory and desire, in E. Bott Spillius (Ed.), *Melanie Klein Today: Developments in Theory and Practice*, vol. II: *Mainly Practice*, London: Routledge.

Bion, W.R. (1970/1986) *Attention and Interpretation*, London: Karnac.

Bion, W.R. (1975) Brasilia clinical seminars, in Bion, W.R. and Bion, F. (Eds.) (1987) *Clinical Seminars and Four Papers*, Abingdon: Fleetwood Press.

Bion, W.R. (1976/1987) Making the best of a bad job in W.R. Bion and F. Bion (Eds.), *Clinical Seminars and Four Papers*, Reading: Radavian Press.

Bion, W.R. (1976/1987) On evidence in W.R. Bion and F. Bion (Eds.), *Clinical Seminars and Four Papers*, Reading: Radavian Press.

Bion, W.R. (1976) On a quotation from Freud, in F. Bion (Ed.), *Clinical Seminars and Four Papers*, Reading: Radavian Press.

Bion, W.R. (1976/1987) Emotional turbulence in Bion, in F. Bion (Ed.), *Clinical Seminars and Four Papers*, Reading: Radavian Press.

Bion, W.R. (1977/1989) Caesura, in W.R. Bion, *Two Papers: The Grid and the Caesura*, London: Karnac.

Bion, W.R. (1977/1989) *Two Papers: The Grid and the Caesura*, London: Karnac.

Bion, W.R. (1977/1991) *A Memoir of the Future*, London: Karnac.

Bion, W.R. (1977) Wilfred Bion speaking (Film, *Tavistock Lectures 1977: On Terminal Cancer*), online: www.melanie-klein-trust.org.uk/bion77d.html.

Bion, W.R. (1978) *Four Discussions with W. R. Bion*, Perthshire: Clunie Press.

Bion, W.R. (1980) *Bion in New York and Sao Paulo*, F. Bion (Ed.) Perthshire: Clunie Press.

Bion, W.R. (1980) *Entretiens Psychanalytiques*, Paris: Gallimard.

Bion, W.R. (1982/1992) *Cogitations*, London: Karnac.

Bion, W.R. (1985) *All My Sins Remembered: Another Part of a Life and The Other Side of Genius: Family Letters*, Bion, F. (Ed.), Abingdon: Fleetwood Press.

Bion, W.R. (1986) *The Long Weekend: 1897–1919 (Part of a Life)*, Bion, F. (Ed.), Abingdon: Fleetwood Press. (Original work published 1986).

Bion, W.R. (1987) *Clinical Seminars and Four Papers*, in F. Bion (Ed.), Abingdon: Fleetwood Press.

Bion, W.R. (1990) *Brazilian Lectures*, London: Karnac.

Bion, W.R. (1994) *Clinical Seminars and Other Works*, F. Bion (Ed.), London: Karnac.

Bion, W.R. (1997) *War Memoirs: 1917–1919*, F. Bion (Ed.), London: Karnac.

Bion, W.R. (2005a) *The Tavistock Seminars*, F. Bion (Ed.), London: Karnac.

Bion, W.R. (2005b) *The Italian Lectures*, F. Bion (Ed.), London: Karnac.

Bion, W.R. (2013) *Los Angeles Seminars and Supervision*, J. Aguayo and B. Malin (Eds.), London: Karnac.

Bion, W.R. (2014) *The Complete Works of W.R. Bion*, C. Mawson (Ed.) London: Karnac.

Bion Talamo, P. (1997) Bion: a Freudian innovator, *British Journal of Psychotherapy*, 14: 47–59.

Bion Talamo, P., Borgogno F. and Merciai, S.A. (Eds.) (1997) *Bion's Legacy to Groups*, London: Karnac.

Birksted-Breen, D. (2003) Time and the après-coup, *International Journal of Psycho-Analysis*, 84: 1501–1515.

Birksted-Breen, D. (2012) Taking time: the tempo of psychoanalysis, *International Journal of Psycho-Analysis*, 93: 819–835.

Birksted-Breen, D. (2016) Bi-ocularity, the functioning mind of the psychoanalyst. *International Journal of Psycho-Analysis*, 97: 25–40.

Birksted-Breen, D., Flanders, S. and Gibeault, A. (Eds.) (2010) *Reading French Psychoanalysis*, London: Routledge.

Blanchot, M. (1969) *L'entretien infini*, Paris: Gallimard.

Bléandonu, G. (1994) *Wilfred Bion: His Life and Works, 1897–1979*, New York: Guilford Press.

Bollas, C. (1979) The transformational object, *International Journal of Psychoanalysis*, 60: 97–107.

Bollas, C. (1987) *The Shadow of the Object*, New York: Columbia University Press.

Bollas, C. (2013) *China on the Mind*, Abingdon: Routledge.

Borges, J.L. (1985a) 'The Sea' in N.T. Di Giovanni (Ed.) *Jorge Luis Borges: Selected Poems 1923–1967*, London: Penguin Books.

Borges, J.L. (1985b) 'A Rose and Milton' in N.T. Di Giovanni (Ed.) *Jorge Luis Borges: Selected Poems 1923–1967*. London: Penguin Books.

Borges, J. L. (1985c) 'The Yellow Rose' in N.T. Di Giovanni (Ed.) *Jorge Luis Borges: Selected Poems 1923–1967*. London: Penguin Books.

Borgogno, F. and Merciai, S.A. (2000) Searching for Bion: cogitations, a new 'clinical diary'?, in P. Bion Talamo, W.R. Bion, F. Borgogno and S. Merciai (Eds.), *W.R. Bion: Between Past and Future*, London: Karnac.

Botella, C. and Botella, S. (2001) Figurabilité et régrédience, *Revue Française de Psychanalyse*, 4: 1150–1239.

Bridger, H. (1985) Northfield revisited, in M. Pines (Ed.), *Bion and Group Psychotherapy*, London: Routledge.

Bridger, H. (2005) The discovery of the therapeutic community, in G. Amadoo and L. Vansina (Eds.), *The Transitional Approach in Action*, London: Karnac Books.

Britton, R. (1989) The missing link: parental sexuality in the Oedipus complex, in J. Steiner (Ed.), *The Oedipus Complex Today*, London: Karnac.

Britton, R. (2011) The pleasure principle, the reality principle and the uncertainty principle, in C. Mawson (Ed.), *Bion Today*, London: Routledge, 64–81.

Britton, R., Feldman, M., O'Shaughnessy, E. and Steiner, J. (Eds.) (1989) *The Oedipus Complex Today: Clinical Implications*, London: Karnac.

Britton, R. and Steiner, J. (1994) Interpretation: selected fact or overvalued idea? *International Journal of Psycho-Analysis*, 75: 1069–1078.

Bronstein, C. (2011) On psychosomatics: the search for meaning, *International Journal of Psycho-Analysis*, 92: 173–195.

Bronstein, C. (2015) Finding unconscious phantasy in the session: recognising form, *International Journal of Psycho-Analysis*, 96: 925–944.

Bronstein, C. and O'Shaughnessy, E. (2017) *Attacks on Linking Revisited: A New Look at Bion's Classic Work*, London: Karnac Books.

Brown, D.G. (1985) Bion and Foulkes: basic assumptions and beyond, in M. Pines (Ed.), *Bion and Group Psychotherapy*, London: Routledge.

Brown, D.G. (2003) Pairing Bion and Foulkes: towards a metapsychology?, in Lipgar R.M and Pines M., *Building on Bion: Branches, Contemporary Developments and Applications of Bion's Contributions to Theory and Practice*, London, New York: Jessica Kingsley Publishers.

Brown, L.J. (2011) *Intersubjective Processes and the Unconscious: An Integration of Freudian, Kleinian and Bionian Perspectives*, London: Routledge.

Cambien, J. (1998) Bion: geneeskunde versus filosofie. In J. Dehing (Ed.), *Een Bundel Intense Duisternis (A beam of Intense Darkness)*, Leuven, Apeldoorn: Garant Carhart-Harris, R.L. and Friston, K.J. (2010) The default-mode, ego-functions and free-energy: a neurobiological account of Freudian ideas, *Brain*, 133: 1265–1283.

Civitarese, G. (2016a) *Truth and the Unconscious in Psychoanalysis*, London: Routledge.

Civitarese, G. (2016b) Sense, senseible, sense-able: the bodily but immaterial dimension of psychoanalytic elements, in H. Levine and G. Civitarese (Eds.), *The W.R. Bion Tradition*, London: Karnac.

Civitarese, G (2016c) On sublimation, *International Journal of Psycho-Analysis*, 97: 1369–1392.

Coleridge, S.T. (1816/2004) *Christabel, Kubla Khan, and the Pains of Sleep*, 2nd edition, W. Bulmer, London, 1816. Reproduced in *The Complete Poems*, W. Keach (Ed.), London: Penguin Books.

Conci, M. (2011) Bion and his first analyst, John Rickman (1891–1951): a revisitation of their relationship in the light of Rickman's personality and scientific production and of Bion's letters to him (1939–1951), *Int. Forum Psychoanalysis*, 20: 68–86.

Connors, S. (1998) *Beckett and Bion*, paper presented at the Beckett and London Conference, Goldsmiths College, London 1998.

Correale, A., Fadda, P. and Neri, C. (Eds.) (2006) P. and D. Faugeras (translation Letture Bioniane, Borla editions, Rome), *Lire Bion*, Paris: Eres.

Cryan, J.F. and O'Mahony, S.M. (2011) The microbiome-gut-brain axis: from bowel to behaviour, *Neurogastroenterol Motil.*, 23(3): 187–192.

Culbert-Koehn, J. (1997) The intersection between Bionian and Jungian vertices: a personal experience, paper presented at the Bion Centennial, Turin.

Culbert-Koehn, J. (2011) An analysis with Bion: an interview with James Gooch, *Journal of Analytical Psychology*, 56: 76–91.

Damasio, A (2000) *The Feeling of What Happens*, London: William Heinemann.

de Bianchedi, E.T. (1995) Theory and technique: what is psychoanalysis?, *Journal of Clinical Psychoanalysis*, 4: 471–482.

de Bianchedi, E.T. (2005) Whose Bion? Who is Bion? *International Journal of Psycho-Analysis*, 86: 1529–1534.

De M'Uzan, M. (1989) Pendant la séance, *Nouvelle Revue de Psychanalyse*, 40: 147–163.

De Maré, P.B. (1985) Major Bion, in M. Pines (Ed.), *Bion and Group Psychotherapy*, London: Routledge.

Dehing, J. (1994) Containment – an archetype?: Meaning of madness in Jung and Bion, *J. Anal. Psychology*, 39: 419–461.

Dehing, J. (Ed.) (1998) *Een Bundel Intense Duisternis (A beam of Intense Darkness)*, Leuven, Apeldoorn: Garant.

Donnet, J.L. and Green, A. (1973) *L'Enfant de ça. La psychose blanche*, Paris: Édition de Minuit.

Eaton, J.L. (2005) The obstructive object, *Psychoanalytic Review*, 92: 355–372.

Eckhart (1293/1981) *Meister Eckhart: The Essential Sermons, Commentaries, Treatises and Defences*, E. Colledge, B. Mc Ginn (translation), New York: Paulist Press.

Edelman, G.M. (1992) *Bright Air, Brilliant Fire*, New York: Basic Books.

Eigen, M. (1981) The area of faith in Winnicott, Lacan and Bion, *International Journal of Psycho-Analysis*, 62: 413–433.

Eigen, M. (1992) The fire that never goes out, *Psychoanal. Review*, 79: 271–287.

Eigen, M. (1998) *The Psychoanalytic Mystic*, London: Free Association Books.

Eigen, M. (2001) Mysticism and psychoanalysis, *Psychoanalytic Review*, 88: 455–481.

Eigen, M. (2012) *Psychoanalysis and the Kabbalah*, London: Karnac Books.

Epstein, M. (1995) *Thoughts without a Thinker*, New York: Basic Books.

Feldman, M. (1993) Aspects of reality, and the focus of interpretation, *Psychoanal Inquiry*, 13: 274–295.

Ferenczi, S. (1949) Confusion of the tongues between the adults and the child (the language of tenderness and of passion), *International Journal of Psycho-Analysis*, 30: 225–230.

Ferris, P. (1977) *Dylan Thomas*, London: Hodder.

Ferro, A. (1996/2002) *In the Analyst's Consulting Room*, London: Brunner-Routledge.

Ferro, A. (1999) *The Bipersonal Field: Experiences in Child Psychoanalysis*, The New Library of Psychoanalysis, D. Birksted-Breen (Ed.), London: Routledge.

Ferro, A. (2005a) Bion: theoretical and clinical observations, *International Journal of Psycho-Analysis*, 86: 1535–1542.

Ferro, A. (2005b) *Seeds of Illness, Seeds of Recovery*, The New Library of Psychoanalysis, D. Birksted-Breen (Ed.), London: Routledge.

Ferro, A. (2006c) *Psychoanalysis as a Therapy of Storytelling*, The New Library of Psychoanalysis. D. Birksted-Breen (Ed.), London: Routledge.

Ferro, A. (2006d) Clinical implications of Bion's thought, *International Journal of Psycho-Analysis*, 87: 9891003.

Ferro, A. (2008) *Mind Works: Technique and Creativity in Psychoanalysis*, The New Library of Psychoanalysis, D. Birksted-Breen (Ed.), London: Routledge.

Ferro, A. (2017) Attacks on linking or uncontainability of beta-elements? In Bronstein, C. and O'Shaughnessy, E. (Eds.), *Attacks on Linking Revisited: A New Look at Bion's Classic Work*, London: Karnac Books.

Fonagy, P. and Allison, E. (2016) Psychic reality and the nature of consciousness, *International Journal of Psychoanalysis*, 97(1): 5–24.

Fonagy, P., Gergeley, G., Jurist, E.L. and Target, M. (2002) *Affect Regulation, Mentalization, and the Development of the Self*, New York: Other Press.

Freud, S. (1911) Formulations on the two principles of mental functioning, *The Standard Edition of the Complete Psychological Works of Sigmund Freud, Volume XII*, pp. 213–226.

Freud, S. (1915) The Unconscious, *The Standard Edition of the Complete Psychological Works of Sigmund Freud, Volume XIV*, pp. 159–215.

Freud, S. (1923) The ego and the id, *The Standard Edition of the Complete Psychological Works of Sigmund Freud, Volume XVIIII*, pp. 1–64.

Freud, S. (1933) New introductory lectures on Psycho-Analysis, *The Standard Edition of the Complete Psychological Works of Sigmund Freud, Volume XXII*, pp. 1–182.

Freud, S. (1940) Splitting of the ego in the process of defense. *The Standard Edition of the Complete Psychological Works of Sigmund Freud, Volume XXIII*, pp. 271–278.

Friston, K. (2013) Life as we know it, *J R Soc Interface*, 10: 2013.0475. http://dx.doi.org/10.1098/rsif.2013.0475.

Gallese, V., Eagle, M.E. and Migone P. (2007) Intentional attunement: mirror neurons and the neural underpinnings of interpersonal relations, *Journal of the American Psychoanalytic Association*, 55: 131–176.

Glouberman, S. (2005) Building on Bion: roots, origins and context of Bion's contributions to theory and practice, and Building on Bion: branches, contemporary developments and applications of Bion's contributions to theory and practice, R.M. Lipgar and M. Pines (Eds.), London, New York: Jessica Kingsley Publishers, International Library of Group Analysis (vols. 20, 21), 2003, 272, 320; *Canadian Journal of Psychoanalysis*, 13: 131–134.

Godfrind, J. (1993) *Les deux courants du transfer*, Paris: Presses Universitaires de France.

Gooch, J. (2001) Bion's perspective on psychoanalytic technique, shortened version of paper given at The International Psychoanalytical Association, Nice, July 2001.

Gooch, J. (2002) *Bion's perspectives on psychoanalytic technique*, www.psychoanalysis.org.uk/gooch2002.htm.

Green, A. (1980) Au delà? En deça? de la théorie, in W.R. Bion, *Entretiens Psychoanalytiques*, Paris: Gallimard.

Green, A. (1998) The primordial mind and the work of the negative, *International Journal of Psycho-Analysis*, 79: 649–665.

Green, A. (1999) *The Work of the Negative*, London: Free Association Books.

Green, A. (2000) The central phobic position: a new formulation of the free association method, *International Journal of Psycho-Analysis*, 81: 429–451.

Grinberg, L. (1962) On a specific aspect of countertransference due to the patient's projective identification, *International Journal of Psycho-Analysis*, 43: 436–440.

Grinberg, L., Sor, D. and Tabak de Bianchedi, E. (1975) *Introduction to the Work of Bion*, Perthshire: Clunie, Roland Harris Educational Trust.

Grinberg, L., Sor, D. and Tabak de Bianchedi, E. (1993) *New Introduction to the Work of W.R. Bion*, New York: Jason Aronson.

Grotstein, J.S. (Ed.) (1983) *Do I Dare Disturb the Universe? A Memorial to W. R. Bion*, New York, London: Karnac.

Grotstein, J.S. (1999) Bion's transformations in O and the concept of the transcendent position, in Bion Talamo, P., Borgogno F. and Merciai, S.A. (Eds.), *W.R. Bion: Between Past and Future*, London: Karnac.

Grotstein, J.S. (2001) *Who is the Dreamer who Dreams the Dream: A Study of Psychic Presences*, Hillsdale, NJ: Analytic Press.

Grotstein, J.S. (2002) One pilgrim's progress toward the psychoanalytic citadel, *Psychoanalytic Inquiry*, 22: 90–105.

Grotstein, J.S. (2005a) 'Projective transidentification': an extension of projective Identification, *International Journal of Psycho-Analysis*, 86: 1051–1069.

Grotstein, J.S. (2005b) *Memoirs of the Future*. International Dictionary of Psychoanalysis, www.encyclopedia.com.

Grotstein, J.S. (2007) *A Beam of Intense Darkness*, London: Karnac.

Guignard, F. and Bokanowski, T. (Ed.) (2007) *Actualités de la pensée de Bion*, Paris: Editions in Press.

Harris, B and Redway-Harris, L. (2013) Braitwaite and the philosophy of science. In N. Torres and R.D. Hinshelwood (Eds.), *Bion's Sources*, London: Karnac.

Harrison, T. (2000) *Bion, Rickman, Foulkes and the Northfield experiments: advancing on a different front*, London, Philadelphia: Jessica Kingsley Publishers.

Hebbrecht, M. (2010) *De droom: verkenning van een grensgebied*, Utrecht: de Tijdstroom.

Hill, J. (1992) A brief personal memoir of Wilfred Bion, *British Journal of Psychotherapy*, 9: 70–73.

Hinshelwood, R.D. (1989) Communication flow in the Matrix, *Group Analysis*, 22: 261–269.

Hinshelwood, R.D. (2016) Containing primitive-emotional states: approaching Bion's later perspectives on groups, in H. Levine and G. Civitarese (Eds.), *The W.R. Bion tradition*, London: Karnac.

Hume, D. (1739/1985) *A Treatise of Human Nature*, London: Penguin Classics.

Ijsseling, S. (2015) *Denken en danken, geven en zijn*. Nijmegen: Uitgeverij Vantilt en Samuel Ijsseling.

Isaacs, S. (1948) The nature and function of phantasy. *Int. J. Psycho-Anal.*, 29:73–97.

Joseph, B. (1985) Transference: the total situation. *Int. J. Psycho-Anal.*, 66: 447–454.

Joseph, B. (1989) *Psychic Equilibrium and Psychic Change: Selected Papers of Betty Joseph*, London, New York: Tavistock/Routledge.

Joseph, B. (1999) Appreciation: Parthenope Bion Talamo, *British Journal of Psychotherapy*, 15: 368–369.

Kandel, E.R. (1999) Biology and the future of psychoanalysis: a new intellectual framework for psychiatry revised, *American Journal of Psychiatry*, 156: 505–524.

Kant, I. (1781/1929) *Kritik der reinem Vernunft* (Critique of Pure Reason, tr. Kemp Smith), London: Macmillan.

Karnac, H (2008) *Bion's Legacy: Bibliography of Primary and Secondary Sources of the Life. Work and Ideas of Wilfred Ruprecht Bion*, London: Karnac.

Katz, D. (1999) *Saying I No More: Subjectivity and Consciousness in the Prose of Samuel Beckett*, Evanston, IL: Northwestern University Press.

Keats, J. (1817/1931) Letter to George and Thomas Keats, in M.B. Forman (Ed.), *The Letters of John Keats*, London: Oxford University Press.

Kernberg, O and Ahumada, L. (2000) Bion: a binocular view: groups and individuals, *International Journal of Psycho-Analysis*, 81: 991–994.

Kinet, M. and Vermote, R. (2005) *Mentalisatie*, Leuven, Apeldoorn: Garant.

Kiplin, R. (1996/1936) *Just So Stories*, New York: Harper Collins Publishers.

Kirk, U., Downar, J. and Montague, P.R. (2011) Interoception drives increased rational decision-making in meditators playing the ultimatum game, *Frontiers Neuroscience*, 18; 5: 49.

Klein, M. (1929) Infantile anxiety situations reflected in a work of art and in the creative impulse, in M. Klein, *The Writings of Melanie Klein Volume I: Love, Guilt and Reparation*, London: Hogarth Press.

Klein, M. (1935) A contribution to the psychogenesis of manic-depressive states, in M. Klein, *The Writings of Melanie Klein. Volume I: Love, Guilt and Reparation*, London: Hogarth Press, 262–289.

Klein, M. (1946) Notes on some schizoid mechanisms, *International Journal of Psycho-Analysis*, 27: 99–110.

Klein, M. (1961) Narrative of a child analysis, in M. Klein, *The Writings of Melanie Klein Volume IV*, London: Hogarth Press.

Kline, M. (1967) *Mathematics for the Nonmathematician*, New York: Dover Publications.

Knowlson, J. (1997) *Damned to Fame: The Life of Samuel Beckett*, London: Bloomsbury.

Kohut, H. (1971) *The Analysis of the Self*, New York: International University Press.

Lacan, J. (1947/2000) La psychiatrie anglaise et la guerre, *L'Evolution Psychiatrique*, 3, 293–312, in *Autres Ecrits*, Paris: Seuil, 2001; P. Dravers and V. Voruz (translators) British Psychiatry and the War, *Psychoanalytical Notebooks of the London Circle 4, Psychiatry and psychoanalysis*, Spring 2000.

Lacan, J. (1964/1973) *Les quatre concepts fondamentaux de la psychanalyse*, Le séminaire, Livre XI, Paris: Seuil.

Lacan, J. (1960/1995) Position of the unconscious, in R. Feldstein, B. Fink and M. Jaanus (Eds.), *Reading Seminar XI: Lacan's Four Fundamental Concepts of Psychoanalysis*, New York: State University of New York Press.

Letley, E. (2014) *Marion Milner: The Life*, London: Routledge.

Levine, H. (2016) Is the concept of O necessary for psychoanalysis?, in H. Levine and G. Civitarese (Eds.), *The W.R. Bion Tradition*, London: Karnac.

Levine, H. and Civitarese, G. (Eds.) (2016) *The W.R. Bion Tradition*, London: Karnac.

Lewin, K. (1935) *A Dynamic Theory of Personality. Selected Papers*, New York: McGraw Hill Book Company Inc.

Lichtenberg-Ettinger, B. (1997) The Feminine/Prenatal Weaving in Matrixial Subjectivity-as-Encounter, *Psychoanalytic Dialogues*, 7: 367–405.

Lipgar, R.M. and Pines, M. (Eds.) (2003) *Building on Bion: Branches, Contemporary Developments and Applications of Bion's Contributions to Theory and Practice*, New York: Jessica Kingsley Publishers.

Locke, J. (1689/1975) *An Essay Concerning Human Understanding*, Oxford: Oxford University Press.

López-Corvo, R. (2003) *The Dictionary of the Work of W. R. Bion*, London: Karnac.

Lowe, E.J. (1995) *Locke: On Human Understanding*, London: Routledge.

Lucas, R. (1993) The psychotic wavelength, *Psychoanalytic Psychotherapy*, 1: 15–24.

Luquet, P. (2002) *Les Niveaux de Pensée*, Paris: Presses Universitaires de France.

Lyotard, J.F. (1991) *Lessons on the Analytic of the Sublime*, Stanford, CA: Stanford University Press.

Lyotard, J.F. (2000) *The Confession of Augustine*, Stanford, CA: Stanford University Press.

Lyth, I.M. (1980) *Bion's Contribution to Thinking about Groups* (read at Memorial Service for Bion).

Lyth, O. (1980) Obituary: Wilfred Ruprecht Bion (1897–1979), *International Journal of Psycho-Analysis*, 61: 269–274.

Mahon, E. (1999) Yesterday's silence: an irreverent invocation of Beckett's analysis with Bion, *Journal of the American Psychoanalytic Association*, 47: 1381–1390.

Mason, A. (1989) Le voyage Californien de Bion, *Revue Française de Psychanalyse*, 5: 1383–1395.

Mason, A. (2000) Bion and binocular vision, *International Journal of Psycho-Analysis*, 81: 983–988.

Matte-Blanco, I. (1988) *Thinking, Feeling and Being: Clinical Reflections on the Fundamental Antinomy of Human Beings*, London: Routledge.

Mawson, C. (Ed.) (2010) *Bion Today*. D. Birksted-Breen (Series editor), London: Routledge.

Meissner, W.W. (1996) *The Therapeutic Alliance*, New Haven, CT: Yale University Press.

Meltzer, D. (1975) *Explorations in Autism*, London: Karnac.

Meltzer, D. (1975) Adhesive identification. *Contemporary Psychoanalysis*, 11: 289–310.

Meltzer, D. (1978) *The Kleinian Development, Part III: The Clinical Significance of the Work of Bion*, Perthshire: Clunie Press.

Meltzer, D. (1997) The evolution of object relations, *British Journal of Psychotherapy*, 14: 60–66.

Meltzer, D. and Williams, M.H. (1985) Three lectures on W.R. Bion's: *A Memoir of the Future*, in Hahn, A. (Ed.), *Sincerity and Other Works. Collected Papers of D. Meltzer*, London: Karnac.

Meltzer, D. and Harris Williams, M. (1988/1990) *The Apprehension of Beauty: The Role of Aesthetic Conflict in Development, Art and Violence*, Perthshire: Clunie Press [Buenos Aires: Spatia, 1990].

Miller, I. and Souter, K. (2013) *Beckett and Bion: The (Im)patient Voice in Psychotherapy and Literature*, London: Karnac Books

Milner, M. (1957) *On Not Being Able to Paint*, New York: International Universities Press.

Milton, J. (1674/1968) *Paradise Lost: Paradise Regained*, London: Penguin Books.

Mitrani, J.L. (2001) 'Taking the transference': some technical implications in three papers by Bion, *Int. J. Psycho-Analysis*, 82: 1085–1104.

Morgan, G. (2005) Dylan Thomas's *In the Direction of the Beginning*: towards or beyond meaning ? *Cycnos*, 20: 2, http://revel.unice.fr/cycnos/index.html?id=84.

Najeeb, S. (2014) Bion the mystic, *Back Issues. Issue 11* www.psychoanalysisdownunder. com.au.

Nakagawa, H. (1988) *Jusqu'ou suis-je moi? Lacan et la chose Japonaise*, Paris: Editions Navarin.

Nishida, K. (2001) *Uber das Gute. Eine Philosophie der Reinen Erfahrung*, Frankfurt am Main: Insel Verlag.

Norton, D.F. (1993) *The Cambridge Companion to Hume*, Cambridge: Cambridge University Press.

O'Shaughnessy, E. (1994) What is a clinical fact? *International Journal of Psycho-Analysis*, 75: 939–947.

O'Shaughnessy, E. (2005) Whose Bion? *International Journal of Psycho-Analysis*, 86: 1523–1528.

Ogden, T.H. (1989) *The Primitive Edge of Experience*, Northvale, NY: Jason Aronson.

Ogden, T.H. (1994) The analytic third – working with inter subjective clinical facts. *Int J Psycho-Analysis*, 75: 3–20.

Ogden, T.H. (1997) Reverie and metaphor: some thoughts on how I work as a psychoanalyst. *International Journal of Psycho-Analysis*, 78: 719–732.

Ogden, T.H. (2004a) An introduction to the reading of Bion, *International Journal of Psycho-Analysis*, 85: 285–300.

Ogden T.H. (2004b) This art of psychoanalysis: dreaming undreamt dreams and interrupted cries, *International Journal of Psycho-Analysis*, 85: 857–877.

Ogden, T.H. (2004c) On holding and containing, being and dreaming. *International Journal of Psycho-Analysis*, 85: 1349–1364.

Ogden, T.H. (2007) On talking-as-dreaming, *International Journal of Psycho-Analysis*, 88: 575–589.

Oppenheim, L. (2001) A preoccupation with object-representation: the Beckett–Bion case revisited, *International Journal of Psycho-Analysis*, 82: 767–784.

Pao, P.N. (1979) *Schizophrenic Disorders: Theory and Treatment from a Psychodynamic Point of View*, New York: International Universities Press.

Pfeiffer, E. (1963) *Sigmund Freud and Lou Andreas-Salomé Letters. The International Psycho-Analytical Library*, 89: 1–242. London: The Hogarth Press and the Institute of Psycho-Analysis.

Pick, I.B. (1985) Working through in the countertransference. *International Journal of Psycho-Anal.*, 66: 157–166.

Pines, M. (Ed.) (1985) *Bion and Group Psychotherapy*, London: Routledge.

Pines, M. (1987) Bion: a group-analytic appreciation, *Group Analysis*, 20: 251–262.

Pontes Miranda de Ferreira, R.B. (1997) The fundamental role of the Grid in Bion's Work, in P. Bion Talamo, F. Borgogno and S. Merciai (Eds.), *W.R. Bion: Between Past and Future*, London: Karnac.

Powell, A. (1989) The nature of the group matrix, *Group Analysis*, 22: 271–281.

Quinodoz, J.M. (2005) *Reading Freud: A Chronological Exploration of Freud's Writings*, London: Routledge.

Quinodoz, J.M. (2007) L'identification projective: développements Bioniens et post-Bioniens, in Guignard, F. and Bokanowski, T. (Eds.), *Actualité de la pensée de Bion*, Paris: Editions in Press.

Ramachandran, V.S. and Blakeslee, S. (1998) *Phantoms in the Brain: Probing the Mysteries of the Human Mind*, New York: William Morrow.

Reiner, A. (2012) *Bion and Being: Passion and the Creative Mind*, London: Karnac.

Rey, J.H. (1994) *Universals of Psychoanalysis in the Treatment of Psychotic and Borderline States*, London: Free Association Books.

Rilke, R.M. (1912/2001) *Duino Elegies*. D. Young (Transl.), New York: Vintage Books.

Rosenfeld, H. (1987) *Impasse and Interpretation*, London: Karnac.

Saint Augustine (400/1998) *Confessions: A New Translation by H. Chadwick*, New York: Oxford University Press.

Sandler, P.C. (2005a) *The Language of Bion: A Dictionary of Concepts*, London: Karnac.

Sandler, P.C. (2005b) *Bion's Work Presented: A Memoir of the Future: Some Thoughts on its Oblivion and Dawn*, Funzione Gamma, 20, www.funzionegamma.edu.

Sandler, P.C. (2006) The origins of Bion's work, *International Journal of Psycho-Analysis*, 87: 179–201.

Schermer, V.L. (2003) Building on 'O': Bion and epistemology, in R. Lipgar and M. Pines (Eds.), *Building on Bion: Roots*, London: Jessica Kingsley Publishers.

Segal, H. (1957) Notes on symbol formation, *International Journal of Psycho-Analysis*, 38: 339–343.

Segal, H. (1991) *Dream, Phantasy and Art*, New York: Routledge, Chapman and Hall.

Segal, H. (2006) Reflections on truth, tradition, and the psychoanalytic tradition of truth, *Amer Imago*, 63: 283–292.

Simon, B. (1986) *I Cannot Promise Communication of Pure Non-Sense Without the Contamination by Sensea Case of Beckett and Bion* (unpublished manuscript).

Simon, B. (1988) The imaginary twins: the case of Beckett and Bion, *International Review of Psycho-Analysis*, 15: 331–352.

Spillius, E.B. (1992) Clinical experiences of projective identification. *New Library of Psychoanalysis*, 14: 59–73.

Stein, G. (1922) Sacred Emily. In G. Stein (1999), *Geography and Plays*, New York: Dover Publications.

Steiner, J. (1985) Turning a blind eye: the cover-up for Oedipus, *International Review of Psycho-Analysis*, 12: 161–172.

Steiner, J. (1993) *Psychic Retreats*, London: Routledge.

Stevens, V. (2005) Nothingness, nothing, and nothing in the work of Wilfred Bion and in Samuel Beckett's Murphy, *Psychoanalytic Review*, 92: 607–635.

Sulloway, F. (1979) *Freud, Biologist of the Mind: Beyond the Psychoanalytic Legend*, New York: Basic Books.

Sutherland, J.D. (1985) Bion revisited: group dynamics and group psychotherapy, in M. Pines (Ed.), *Bion and Group Psychotherapy*, London: Routledge and Kegan Paul.

Symington, J. and Symington, N. (1996) *The Clinical Thinking of Wilfred Bion*, London: Routledge.

Symington, N. (1993) *Narcissism: A New Theory*, London: Karnac Books.

Taylor, D. (1983) Some observations on hallucination: clinical application of some developments of Melanie Klein's work, *International Journal of Psycho-Analysis*, 64: 299308.

Taylor, D. (2010) Psychoanalytic approaches and outcome research: negative capability or irritable reaching after fact and reason? *Psychoanal Psychotherapy*, 24: 398–416.

Thomas, D. (1985/1934) Letter to Glyn Jones, dated 14th March, 1934, *Collected Letters*, London: Dent.

Thomas, D. (2000) *Collected Poems 1934–1953*. D. Walford and R. Maud (Eds.), London: Phoenix.

Thys, M. (2005) *Fascinatie. Een fenomenologische en psychoanalytische verkenning van het onmenselijke*. Amsterdam: Boom.

Thys, M. and Vermote, R. (1995) *Trauma en Taboe: Psychoanalytische Beschouwingen over Incest*, Leuven-Apeldoorn: Garant.

Torres, N. (2003) Gregariousness and the mind: Wilfred Trotter and Wilfred Bion, in R.M. Lipgar and M. Pines (Eds.), *Building on Bion: Branches, Contemporary Developments and Applications of Bion's Contributions to Theory and Practice*, New York: Jessica Kingsley Publishers.

Torres, N. and Hinshelwood, R.D. (Eds.) (2013) *Bion's Sources: The Shaping of his Paradigms*. Abingdon: Routledge.

Trist, E. (1985) Working with Bion in the 1940s: the group decade, in M. Pines (Ed.), *Bion and Group Psychotherapy*, London: Routledge and Kegan Paul.

Trist, E. (1987) Some additional reflections on working with Bion in the 'Forties', *Group Analysis*, 20: 263–279.

Trotter, W. (1916) *Instincts of the Herd in Peace and War*, London: Unwin.

Tuckett, D. (2011) Inside and outside the window: some fundamental elements in the theory of psychoanalytic technique, *Int. J. Psycho-Analysis*, 92: 1367–1390.

Tustin, F. (1981) A modern pilgrim's progress: reminiscences of personal analysis with Dr Bion, *Journal of Child Psychotherapy*, 7: 175–192.

Tustin, F. (1986) *Autistic Barriers in Neurotic Patients*, New Haven, CT/London: Yale University Press.

Tustin, F. (1990) *The Protective Shell in Children and Adults*, London: Karnac.

Van Lysebeth-Ledent, M. (2016) Le travail onirique du Moi inconscient, *Bulletin de la Société Psychanalytique de Paris*, 111–189.

Verhaeghe, P. (2011) Lacan on the body, in J. Borossa (Ed.), *The new Klein Lacan Dialogues*, London: Karnac.

Vermote, R (1994) Le mythe d'Oedipe à la lumière du mythe du Sphinx, *Revue Belge de Psychanalyse*, 24: 29–43.

Vermote, R. (1995) Réalités psychiques et formes, *Revue Belge de Psychanalyse*, 27: 39–55.

Vermote, R. (1998a) Entretien avec Parthenope Bion, *Revue Belge de Psychanalyse*, 32: 43–49.

Vermote, R. (1998b) Les transformations psychiques et la 'Grille' de Bion, *Revue Belge de Psychanalyse*, 32: 49–65.

Vermote, R. (1999) Projective identification and PI. Response to J.S. Grotstein, Conference with J.S. Grotstein, organisatie: Jungiaanse School voor Psychoanalyse, Kortenberg, October 1999.

Vermote, R. (2000a) Les transformations psychiques et la 'Grille' de Bion, in J. Dehing (Ed.), *Autour de W.R. Bion. Essais Psychanalytiques*, Paris: L'Harmattan.

Vermote, R. (2000b) Psychose et souffrance, in M. De Hert, J. Peuskens, E. Thys and G. Vidon (Eds.), *Raisonner la déraison*, Bruxelles: Epo, Frison-Roche.

Vermote, R. (2003) Two sessions with Catherine, *Int. J. Psycho-Analysis*, 84: 1415–1422.

Vermote, R. (2005) A dictionary of the work of Bion by Lopez-Corvo, *Tijdschrift voor Psychiatrie*, 46: 862–864.

Vermote, R. (2008) Quelques notes sur l'inconscient selon Bion, *Revue Belge de Psychanalyse*, 53: 89–99.

Vermote, R. (2009a) Experiencing the shadow of the future, *Int. Forum Psychoanal.*, 18: 100–103.

Vermote, R. (2009b) The basic layer of the interpersonal field, in A. Ferro and R. Basile (Eds.), *The Analytic Field: A Clinical Concept*, London: Karnac Books.

Vermote, R. (2010) Bion's critical approach of psychoanalysis, in C. Mawson (Ed.), *Bion Today*, D. Birksted-Breen (series editor), The New Library of Psychoanalysis, London: Routledge.

Vermote, R. (2011a) Getting to know the 'early' Bion, *Int. Forum Psychoanalysis*, 20: 116–118.

Vermote, R. (2011b) On the value of 'late Bion' to analytic theory and practice, *Int. J. Psycho-Analysis*, 92: 1089–1098.

Vermote, R. (2011c) Rudi Vermote's response to David Taylor, *International Journal of Psycho-Analysis*, 92: 1113–1116.

Vermote, R. (2013) The undifferentiated zone of psychic functioning: an integrative approach and clinical implications, *Bulletin of the European Federation of Psychoanalysis*, 13: 16–27.

Vermote, R (2014a) Free association, meeting the patient halfway, keynote lecture at the UCL Psychoanalysis Conference, London, 11–15 December 2014.

Vermote, R. (2014b) Transformations et transmissions du fonctionnement psychique: approche integrative et implications cliniques. *Revue française de psychanalyse*, LXXVIII, 2, 389–405.

Vermote, R (2014c) *Das "incommunicado self" bei Winnicott und Bion*. Schweizerische Gesellschaft für Psychoanalyse. Wochenende der Mitglieder und Kandidaten. Bern, 26 January 2014.

Vermote, R. (2016a) Le corps a des raisons que la raison ne connaît pas, in J. Press and I Nigolian (Eds.), *Corps parlant, corps parlé, corps muet*, Paris: Editions in Press.

Vermote, R. (2016b) On Bion's text 'Emotional Turbulence': a focus on experience and the unknown, in H. Levine and G. Civitarese (Eds.), *The W.R. Bion Tradition*, London: Karnac.

Vermote, R. (2016c) Reaching the transcendent position by a borderline patient in reading Beckett, in A. Reiner (Ed.), *Of Things Invisible to Mortal Sight: Celebrating the Work of James S. Grotstein*, London: Karnac.

Vermote R. (2017). "Attacks on linking" revisited from Bion's later work. In: Bronstein C., O'Shaughnessy E. (Eds.), *Attacks on linking revisited*, Chapt. 4, (pp. 75–87). USA: Routledge.

Visser, G. (2008) *Gelatenheid. Gemoed en hart bij Meester Eckhart*, Boom: Sun.

White, R.S. (2011) Bion and mysticism: the western tradition, *American Imago*, 31: 147–158.

White, R. (n.d.) Gelassenheit, from three points of view, www.robertwhitemd.com.

Williams, M.H. (1985) The tiger and O: a reading of Bion's memoir and autobiography, *Free Associations*, 1: 33–56.

Wieland, C. (2013) Freud's influence on Bion's thought: links and transformation. In Torres, N. and Hinshelwood, R.D. (Eds.), *Bion's Sources*, London: Karnac, 104–124.

Williams, M.H. (1983) Underlying pattern in Bion's *Memoir of the Future*, *International Review of Psycho-Analysis*, 10: 75–86.

Winnicott, D.W. (1963) Communicating and not-communicating leading to a study of certain opposites, in *The Maturational Process and the Facilitating Environment: Studies in the Theory of Emotional Development*, New York: International UP Inc., 179–193.

Winnicott, D.W. (1965) *The Maturational Processes and the Facilitating Environment: Studies in the Theory of Emotional Development*, The International Psycho-Analytical Library, 64: 1–276. London: The Hogarth Press and the Institute of Psycho-Analysis.

Winnicott, D. (1969) The use of an object and relating through identifications, in D. Winnicott (1970) *Playing and Reality*, New York: Basic Books, 101–111.

Winnicott, D. (1970) *Playing and Reality*, New York: Basic Books.

Winnicott, D. and Rodman, F. (1987) *The Spontaneous Gesture: Selected Letters of D.W. Winnicott*, London: Karnac Books.

Wisdom, J.O. (1978) Bion's place in the Troika, *International Review of Psycho-Analysis*, 14: 541–551.

Wright, H. (1987) Is Bion beyond me? How can I understand if I do not dream? *Group Analysis*, 20: 271–273.

INDEX

Abel-Hirsch, N. 141, 231
abstractions, description of 89–90
abstract systems 90
acting and thinking 161
action 103
act of Faith 152, 153; *see also* faith
Actualité de la pensée de Bion 4
Aguayo, J. 5
Ahumada, L. 54
algebraic geometry 114, 115
All My Sins Remembered (Bion) 2, 11, 138, 193, 201–202, 213
alphabetization 112
alpha-elements 28, 76, 78, 82, 84–85, 99, 103, 106, 112, 113
alpha-function 76, 78, 82, 83–85, 86–87
Alpheus 83, 84, 202–203
always present phantasying 75
'Amiens' (Bion) 213–214, 219
Amiens, Battle of 6, 7, 185–186, 220–224
analytic couple 87
analytic third 87–88, 229
Anzieu, D. 4, 66, 67, 68–69, 103, 231
archetypes 25
Aristocracy 61
Army 61
a-sensuous zone 17, 209
Asser 214, 220
asymmetrical psychic functioning 30n3
'Attacks on Linking' (Bion) 67, 73
attention 102–103
Attention and Interpretation (Bion) 13, 54, 81, 110, 115, 129n2, 132, 135, 137–138, 140–167, 205
Augustine 127, 150, 157
authority, defiance of 219–220
autistic-contiguous continuum 64, 231

autobiography 212–227
automatic mental associations 28
awe 152, 155, 157

Bacon, F. 197
Bail 135
Bair, D. 67, 68
Balint, M. 62
Barangers, M. and W. 4, 64, 112, 229, 231
Barthes, R. 94n8
basic assumptions 54–56, 60–61, 62
basic emotional links 88
'Basic Fault' 62
basic group level 58
Bataille, G. 188
bathos 149, 232
Beam of Intense Darkness, A (Grotstein) 3, 167
Beatrix, R. 96
Beckett, S. 12, 24, 66–69, 179
Beckett and Bion (Miller and Souter) 5
Beckett et le psychoanalyste (Anzieu) 4, 68–69
Being and Time (Heidegger) 175
Belgium 214–215, 218–219
Bell, D. 231
Bergson, H. 27, 30, 57, 93
beta-elements 28, 82, 84, 85–86, 97, 99, 103, 106, 111, 126, 143
beta-screen 85
Bick, E. 68, 231
bigotry 187, 188, 190
binocular vision 51, 53–54, 58, 60, 62, 145, 181
biographical information 6–11, 135–139
Bion, F. 2, 6, 9, 11, 13, 64–65, 96, 97, 136, 137, 138, 139, 171, 177, 193, 204, 213
Bion and Being (Reiner) 5

Bion's Legacy to Groups 2
'Bion's Sources' (Torres and Hinshelwood) 5
Bion Talamo, P. 2, 4, 5, 6, 7, 12, 48, 103, 155, 213, 214, 217–218
Bion Today (Mawson) 5, 231
bipersonal field 64
Birksted-Breen, D. 231
bizarre objects 70, 86
Blake, W. 172
Blanchot, M. 196
Blatt 21
Bléandonu, G. 3, 81, 97
blindness, artificial 161, 198
Borges, J.L. 124–125
Borgogno, F. 138
Botella, C. and S. 4, 64
Bowlby, J. 230
Braithwaite, R.B. 27
Brandschaft 135
British empiricists 27, 28–29
British Psychoanalytical Society 20–21, 49
Britton, R. 72, 231
Bronstein, C. 73, 231
Brown, L. 3

caesura: concept of 132–133; continuity before and after 134; in *Dawn of Oblivion* 187; description of 12–14, 234; meaning of 1
Caesura (Bion) 133, 134
calculus 101
Carroll, L. 115
causality 119–120
causation 125–126
cave allegory 119
C-elements 99, 112–113
'chronic murder' 117
chronology of lectures 195
Church 61
Civitarese, G. 5, 230
clinical material, notation and presentation of 169–171
Clinical Seminars and Four Papers (Bion) 204
Cogitations (Bion) 2, 82–83, 96, 137, 138, 151, 190
Coleridge, S.T. 164, 202
commensal lie 159
commensal relationship 158
'Commentary' to *Second Thoughts* (Bion) 64, 67, 169–176, 214, 217
common emotional view 76–77

Complete Works of Bion (Mawson) 5, 231
concept 101
conception 101
Conci, M. 49, 50
Confessions (Augustine) 157
Connors, S. 67
constant conjunctions 28, 71, 96, 102, 114, 116–117, 119, 121, 132–133, 150, 159, 162, 163, 229
contact-barrier 84–86
container and contained 92, 105, 158, 159, 163, 229
containing object 73–74
containment 71, 72, 76, 77, 155, 158
Controversial Discussions 48
counteridentification 72
countertransference 157
creativity 18, 227
Critique of Aesthetic Judgement (Kant) 31n5
Critique of Pure Reason (Kant) 29
Culbert-Koehn, J. 25

da Vinci, L. 182, 184
Dawn of Oblivion, The (Bion) 138, 180, 183–189
daydreaming 82
deadening attacks 19
death drive 16, 19, 70
de Bianchedi, E.T. 180, 186
De Cusa, N. 150
De Docta Ignorantia (De Cusa) 150
definitory hypothesis 102
Dehing, J. 25
delusions 85–86
de Masi 78
denial 102
dependency 55, 56, 59, 61, 228
depersonalization 62
depressive position *see* paranoid-schizoid and depressive positions (PS-D)
Descartes, R. 114
description of 151
desire 147–149, 154, 155, 161, 163, 174, 175
'Development of Schizophrenic Thought, The' (Bion) 69–70
Dictionary of the Work of WR Bion (López-Corvo) 4–5
'Differentiation of the Psychotic from the Non-Psychotic Personalities' (Bion) 22–23, 70

Dilke 164
diseases 55–56
disinterestedness 165
Distinguished Service Order (DSO) 217
Dodgson, C. 115
Do I Dare Disturb the Universe? (Grotstein) 3, 167
Donne, J. 103
Dream, The (Bion) 138, 180–181
dreams 70, 82–84, 107, 147–148, 187
dream thought 16, 18, 29, 75, 77, 82, 99, 202
dream-work alpha 29, 82–84
drives 82

'East Coker' (Eliot) 175–176
Eaton, J.L. 74
Ecclesiasticus 135
Eckhart, M. 124, 149, 150, 159, 160, 173, 175, 176
Eco, U. 113
Eigen, M. 3, 24, 155, 167, 232
elements: description of 95; geometrical theory of 90; psychoanalytic object and 106–107; theory of 98; transition between 104–106
Elements of Psycho-Analysis (Bion) 81, 95–113, 115, 119, 120, 138, 145, 153, 159, 162
Eliot, T.S. 175–176
embryonic infinite layer 8
emotional experiences, processing of 88–89, 99, 101
empathic identification 165
'empty thoughts' 75
envy 19, 85, 165
epistemophilic instinct 19
epistemophilic period 229–231
Epstein, M. 3, 167, 232
Euclid 95, 114, 162
Experiences in Groups (Bion) 10, 18, 48, 53–54, 143

faith 149, 150, 151–152, 153, 155
fantasy 15–16, 82
father, Bion's 218
feelings, Grid and 109
Feldman, M. 231
Ferenczi, S. 48
Ferris, P. 141
Ferro, A. 4, 64, 112–113, 229, 231, 244–248

field of poppies metaphor 115–116
field theory 49, 56
fight-flight 55, 56, 59, 61, 228
figments of imagination 182
'*fluctuat nec mergitur*' 8
Form 28
formulas 80, 91
'*Formulations on the two principles of psychic functioning*' (Freud) 14–15
Foulkes, S. H. 51, 57–58, 229
fragmentation 110, 164, 165
France 215–216, 220–221
Freud, A. 111
Freud, S.: comparison with 14–18; ego and 102; lectures touching upon 200–201; Matte-Blanco on 63; negative and 110–111; on origins of thinking 75; on perception 147; psychosis and 77; Rickman and 48; theory of thinking and 81–82, 87; Trotter and 52; unconscious and 83
Freudian ego 61
Friston, K. 187
frustration tolerance 15, 75–76, 78, 108, 120, 146, 163–164, 182
functions: application of 85; concept of 80, 81–82, 92–93

Galileo 80
Gelassenheit 175, 176
genius, psychoanalytic 165
genius function 10, 158
Gooch, J. 163, 191, 192–193
good–bad categorizing 20
good internal breast 18–19
Green, A. 4, 78, 110–111, 196
Greenson, R. R. 137, 194
Grid 95–104, *100*, 107, 108–109, 112, 120–121, 123, 126, 145, 154
Grinberg, L. 72, 78, 97, 193
Grotstein, J.: analytic experiences of 191, 192; on Bion's move to California 136; on Bion's style 193; on diverging perspectives 54; on Grid 97; invitation from 135; on lectures 194; on listening to and reading Bion 238–243; in Los Angeles group 3; on *Memoir of the Future* 178–179; on noumenon 128; on O 143, 149, 166–167; on openness to unknown 14; organizing of seminars by 137; on projective identification 72; on psychic functioning 63; psychosis and 78;

on Seven Servants 81; transcendent position and 232
group mentality 51, 53
group period 228–229
group(s): Bion's attitude in conducting 50–51; experience of 58–60; Klein and 18
Guntrip 135
gusto 165

Hadfield, J.A. 66
Haig, D. 221
hallucinatory infinite zone 141
hallucinatory layer 8, 142–143, 180, 182, 208
hallucinatory transformations 229
hallucinatory zone 202
halluncinatory matrix 64
Harris, M. 178
Harris, R. 180
Harrison, T. 49
Harris Williams, M. 178, 179, 180
Hate link 16, 19, 88, 157
Hazlitt, W. 165
Heidegger, M. 175
Heilungsversuch 83
herd instinct 52, 60
Hinshelwood, R.D. 5, 52, 194, 231
holding function 22
Homer 182
Hopkins, G.M. 182
horizontal axis of Grid 102–103
Horowitz, M. 4
Hotblack, Major 221
Houzel 231
Hume, D. 28–29, 54, 87, 93, 119
humour 24

Idea 15, 28
idealist philosophers 29–30
ignorance 5, 152, 196–197
imaginary order 70
'Imaginary Twin, The' (Bion) 65–66, 67, 169–170
imagination 28, 182
Impressions 28
Incarnation 160
incommunicado true self 23
infinity 64, 172–173
inquiry 103
Instincts of the Herd in Peace and War (Trotter) 12

intelligence 202, 227
internal Mafia gang 19
internal obstructive object 120
internal parents 128
'In the beginning' (Thomas) 141
intrapsychic zone 64
Introduction to the Work of Bion (Grinberg, Sor, and Tabak de Bianchedi) 193
intuition 30
invariants 116–117, 119
Isaacs, S. 137
isometries 114

Jacques, E. 92, 230
Jardine, B. 11, 50
Johnson, Doctor 142
Jones, E. 52
Jones, G. 141
Joseph, B. 72, 135, 230
jouissance 27
Joyce, J. 179
Jung, C. 24–25, 67
'just above sleep' state 151

Kant, I. 25, 28–30, 54, 115–116, 119, 124, 128, 149, 157, 167, 168n7, 197, 232
Karnac, H. 5
Keats, J. 110, 164–165, 175, 233, 249
Kernberg, O. 54
Kierkegaard, S. 168n6
Kipling, R. 81
Klein, M.: Bion in analysis with 60; fantasy and 82; groups and 61; influence of 18–20, 21–22; lectures touching upon 200–201; negative and 111; paranoid-schizoid and depressive positions and 90, 93, 105, 163–164; phantasy and 229; projective identification and 72, 87; +psychosis and 77; on regression 8; Rickman and 48, 49; *see also* phantasy
K-link 12, 16, 19, 88–89, 93, 103, 157
knowledge (K): frustration tolerance and 120; relation to 107; transformations in 14–17, 18–20, 21–24, 26, 27, 28–29, 119–120, 126, 144–145
Kubla Khan (Coleridge) 202

Lacan, J. 4, 13, 25–27, 68, 78
lamelle 26
Langton, B. 142
language 69, 76, 140–141, 166, 179, 181, 182, 187, 190, 201

language of achievement 127, 141, 150, 166, 175, 179
Language of Bion, The (Sandler) 3
Laplanche 26
layer of hallucinosis 143, 153, 156, 228
Leaderless Group Project 52
leaderless groups 10
leadership 10
learned ignorance 150
Learning from Experience (Bion) 14–15, 80–94, 96, 98, 101, 105–106, 115, 119, 120, 125–126, 153–154, 162–163
Leclaire 26
lectures: chronology of 195; conclusion regarding 203–204; overview of 190–195; themes and patterns in 196–203
Legion d'Honneur 224
Levine, H.B. 3, 5, 230, 249–252
Lewin, K. 49, 56
Lichtenberg-Ettinger, B. 64
lies 159
Lipgar 4
Lire Bion 4
Locke, J. 28, 54
Loewenberg, P. 137
logical thinking 90
Long Weekend, The (Bion) 2, 6, 138, 177, 179, 183, 213, 216–217, 219, 221, 226
López-Corvo, R. E. 4–5, 97
Los Angeles Psychoanalytic Society and Institute 136, 137
love 11–12
Love link 16, 19, 88, 157
Lyotard, J.F. 123

Main, T. 51, 57, 229
Malin, B. 5
Man of Achievement 141, 164
Mason, A. 5, 13, 54, 135, 136–137, 158, 190
matrix 57–58, 62–63
Matte-Blanco, I. 30n3, 62–63
Matter and Memory (Bergson) 27, 30
Mawson, C. 5, 231
Meltzer, D. 6, 13, 115, 128, 135–136, 138–139, 178, 180, 183, 230
Melville, H. 152, 171
Memoir of the Future, A (Bion): aim of 11, 190; catastrophic change and 191; Grid version of 96, 97; inner world in 19, 203; Jung and 25; main discussion of

177–189; Meltzer and 230; multiple points of view and 54; O in 154; opacity of memory in 129n7; publication of 138, 213; style of 13; unborn self in 67; Unknown and 233
memory 83, 129n7, 147–149, 151, 154, 155, 161, 163, 174, 175
Menninger lecture 137, 188, 190
mental pain 108
mental space 144–145
Merciai, S. 4, 138
Middle Group 48
Miller, I. 5
Milner, M. 230
Milton, J. 124, 135, 179, 180, 183, 184, 198, 202
mind, in lectures 202
minus state 106
mirror motor neurons 72
Mitrani, J.L. 74
model, description of 89
model–abstractions approach 89–90
models 170–171, 200
Money-Kyrle, R. 136, 230
Monroe, M. 137, 194
moralizing judgement 125–126
Moran 141
mother: Klein and 19; Lacan and 26; projective identification and 72; in war writings 217–218, 224; Winnicott and 21, 22; *see also* containment
M'Uzan 64
mystery 152, 155, 157, 196–197
mystical metaphors 138
mysticism 127, 150, 159–160
myths 25, 107–109

Najeeb, S. 175
nameless dread 67
naming 59, 60
narcissism 19
narcotization 113
narrative derivatives 113
narrative links 111
narratology 113
negative 110–111
Negative Capability 110, 164–165, 175, 231
negative growth 110
New Introduction to the Works of Bion 3
Nietzsche, F. 158
Nishida, K. 208

non-sensuous reality 174
Northfield experiments 9, 50, 57, 229
notation 102
'Notes on Some Schizoid Mechanisms'
    (Klein) 72
Notes on the Theory of Schizophrenia
    (Bion) 69
not-knowing 198–200
noumena 29, 112, 124, 128, 182

O: attitude of analyst and 148–149; contact
    with 147–148; containment and 158;
    different notions of 154; direct contact
    with 122–123; experience of 149–150;
    faith and 151–152; former concepts and
    126–127; infinite and finite modes of
    transformations in 122; introduction to
    118–119; language and 140–141; notion
    of 12; openness to 125–126; pleasure
    principle and 154; preverbal matrix and
    143; psychic truth and 142; quotations
    on 143–144; shift towards 115, 123–124;
    summary of 230; transformations in
    17–18, 20, 25, 26–27, 29–30, 123, 125,
    209–211, 231–232; unconscious and 153
observation 198
obstructive object 19, 73–74
Oedipal third 231
Oedipus myth 50–51, 71, 89, 104, 107,
    108, 109, 121
Ogden, T.H. 64, 87–88, 229, 231
'On Arrogance' (Bion) 64, 71, 174
'On Hallucination' (Bion) 70, 117
opacity of memory 129n7, 151
operative thinking 4
Oppenheim, L. 67
O'Shaughnessy, E. 73, 139, 231
Other Side of Genius, The (Bion) 2, 138
O-vertex 146, 153, 156, 158, 159, 161

pain 108–109, 154, 156
pairing 50, 54–55, 56, 59, 61, 228
Palinurus, death of 109
Paradise Lost (Milton) 180, 198, 202
paranoid-schizoid and depressive positions
    (PS-D) 18, 61, 67, 69, 78, 90, 93, 105,
    111, 148, 163–164, 180, 229
parasitic lie 159
parasitic relationship 158
Pascal, B. 68, 114, 118, 144
Past Presented, The (Bion) 138, 180,
    181–183

patience 146, 163–164, 175
Paton, H.J. 27
phantasy 15, 16, 18, 19, 21, 72, 75, 82,
    93, 229
Philips, F. 135, 193
philosophical background 27–30
Picasso, P. 133
pilgrimages 191–192
Pines, M. 4, 51, 57–58, 136, 229
Plato 28, 29, 115, 119, 124, 157, 160
Platonic Forms 115, 124, 160, 179, 182
pleasure principle 15, 82, 87, 154, 156
poetic anthology 171–172
poetry 127, 140, 164, 171–172, 227
Poincaré, H. 27, 90, 105, 114
points of view, multiple coexisting 54
positive growth 110
post-Kleinians 230–231
potential space 229
pre-analytic period 228–229
pre-conceptions 75, 101, 102–103, 117
preverbal matrix 143
Profumo affair 59
projective geometry 114
projective identification: bad objects
    and 75–76; beta-elements and 99;
    communication through 19, 87, 92, 93,
    229; containment and 73; failure of 71;
    group and 56, 61; obstructive object
    and 74; overview of 72; psychoanalytic
    object and 163; psychosis and 77, 117;
    questions on 200, 233; reversed 70
projective transformations 117–118,
    119, 229
projective transidentification 72
protomental matrix 56–57, 62, 228, 231
protomental system 55–56
proto-organizations 92
proto-thoughts 86–87, 92
psyche 186–187
psychic functioning: infinite and finite
    modes of 122; models of 63–64,
    229; switching from content to 66;
    undifferentiated layer in 62
psychic processing 72
psychic skin 231
psychic truth 142
psychoanalysis, aim/goal of 201–202,
    205–206
psychoanalytic frame 206–207
psychoanalytic object: apprehending
    145–146; awareness of 229–230;

continuity in 134; elements and 106–107; evolution of concept of 162–163; experience of O and 149–150; in formula 91, 93; noumena and 112; O and 161; transformations and 119; transformations in O and 126; unknown 20

psychopathology 126–127
psychose blanche, La (Green) 4, 78
psychosis: contact-barrier and 85–86; infinity and 172–173; mental space and 144; O-vertex and 156; papers on 64–79; as thought disorder 77; T(K) and 142
psychosomatic illnesses 4

Quainton 220
Quakers 50
Quinodoz, J.M. 72

Real (Lacan) 26, 27
reality principle 82, 87
Reality scale 97, 126
Reason 15
reductive analysis 66
regression 8, 24, 57, 110
Reiner, A. 5, 172, 232
religion 12, 220
religious mysticism 124
resistance 154, 198–200
resonance 85
reverie 29, 76, 87–88, 90, 93, 119, 147, 179
reversed/reversible perspective 108, 181
'Re-View' (Bion) 60
Rice, K. 8, 58, 59
Rickman, J. 12, 25, 48–50, 66
Riemann, G. 114
rigid motion transformations 117, 119, 229
Riviere, J. 21
rose 124–125
Rosenfeld, H. 19, 135
Royal Anthropological Society 49
Royal Cemetery at Ur 109
rudimentary zone 64

Salient 214–215
Salome, L.A. 17
Sandler, P.C. 3, 4, 5, 27, 54, 143, 180, 183, 188
schizophrenia 64–65, 69–70
scientific deductive system 101

secondary process 15
Second Thoughts (Bion) 54, 64, 69, 169–176, 194
security 146, 164, 175
Segal, H. 18, 70, 82, 135, 136, 191, 230
selected fact 90–91, 93, 105, 111, 146, 163, 171, 229, 231
Self (Jung) 25
seminars: list of 196; overview of 190–195; themes and patterns in 204–208
sense-impressions 81–82, 85
Sermons (Eckhart) 175
sessions, state of mind during 151
Seven Servants 81, 190
sexuality 10–12, 188
Shakespeare, W. 125, 164, 165, 182
singing 6–7
Skin Ego, The (Anzieu) 4
Socratic period 233
solitude 6, 7, 8
soma 186–187
sophisticated group level 58
Sor, D. 193
Souter, K. 5
speculative imagination 181, 202
Spender, S. 141
sphinx 50–51, 71, 107, 109
splitting 16–19, 61–62, 69–70, 78, 85
state of mind during sessions 151
Stein, G. 125
Steiner, J. 231
Stevens, V. 67
St John of the Cross 159
Strachey, J. 21
Sublime 157, 232
Sweeting 221–222
symbiotic lie 159
symbiotic relationship 158
Symbols and Transformations (Jung) 25
Symington, J. 4
Symington, N. 4, 97
symmetrical psychic functioning 30n3

Tabak de Bianchedi, E. 193
Taming Wild Thoughts (Bion) 190
tanks 214, 216, 223
Tara Hill 224–225
Tavistock Clinic 10, 49, 50, 58–59
Tavistock lectures 191
Taylor, J. 202, 231
technique 160–161, 207–208
theory, description of 89

'Theory of Thinking, A' (Bion) 64, 75–77, 81–82, 161
therapeutic groups 60
thing-in-itself ('Ding an sich') 115, 116, 119, 160, 168n7, 197, 202
Things-in-themselves 29, 30
thinking: logical 90; theory of 75–77, 78, 81, 87, 104–106, 154, 161, 173
thinking emotional experience 98
Thomas, D. 141, 153
Thorner 135
thought, level of 102–104
thoughts: classification of 75; genesis of 98
three-dimensional mental world 144–145
Thus Spoke Zarathustra (Nietzsche) 158
Torres, N. 5, 27, 52, 56–57, 231
Tower of Babel 107, 109
training analysis 146
transcendental period 231–232
transference 157, 200–201, 208
transformation, theory of 112
transformational process 112–113
transformation in hallucinosis 118, 119
transformation in infinity 118
transformations: focus on 116–117; geometrical concepts applied to 117–118; geometrical theory of 114, 115; origins of 118–119; visual metaphors for 115–116
Transformations (Bion) 13, 54, 81, 114–128, 132, 154, 162
transformations in knowledge: British empiricists and 27, 28–29; finite space for 144–145; Freud and 14–17; Klein and 18–20; Lacan and 26; O and 126; Winnicott and 21–24
transformations in O: causation and 125; effect of 123; example of 209–211; Freud and 17–18; idealist philosophers and 29–30; Jung and 25; Klein and 20; Lacan and 26–27; philosophical background for 175–176; precluding 156–157; summary of 231–232; Winnicott and 24
Tree of Knowledge 107, 109
Trist, E. 56, 59
tropisms 121–122
Trotter, W. 12, 52, 56, 201–202, 228
true self 23, 24
truth 125–126, 141, 142, 143, 188, 196–197
Tuckett, D. 231
Tustin, F. 13–14, 191–192, 231

'Two Principles of Mental Functioning' (Freud) 15, 81–82, 102, 154, 157, 161, 229

Ultimate Reality 127
unborn self 67
unconscious, O and 153
unknown, attitude of analyst and 157
unknown psychoanalytic object 20
Untitled (Bion) 154
'Use of an Object and Relating through Identification, The' (Winnicott) 13, 23, 24

valency 58, 60
veil of illusions 157
verbal thought 69, 73, 77–78
Verhaeghe, P. 26
Vermote, R. 97, 209
vertical axis of Grid 99, 101
vertices 145
Victoria Cross 217
Virgil 182
visual metaphors 115–116

waking dream thought 18, 29, 75, 82–84, 88, 112
War Memoirs (Bion) 2
War Memoirs 1917–1919 (Bion) 213
war writings 213–227
White, R. 175
Whitehead 57, 93
Who is the Dreamer Who Dreams the Dream? (Grotstein) 167
Wieland, C. 17
Wild Thoughts Searching for a Thinker (López-Corvo) 5
Wilfred Bion: His Life and Works 1897–1979 (Bléandonu) 3
Williams, M.H. 6
Wilson 8
Winnicott, D. W. 8, 13, 20–24, 57, 87, 94n6, 111, 135, 229, 230
wisdom 189, 202
Wisdom, J.O. 177–178
Wordsworth, W. 164
work group 58, 60, 62
Work of the Negative, The (Green) 4, 110
World War I 6–7, 213–227
WR Bion Between Past and Future 2
W.R. Bion Tradition (Levine and Civitarese) 5
Wu-Wei 175

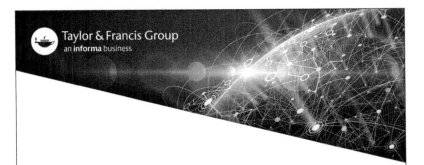

Capri '86

Ta Da!

Wanderlust

Wanderlust

Interiors that Bring the World Home

MICHELLE NUSSBAUMER

Foreword by Hutton Wilkinson

RIZZOLI
NEW YORK

New York Paris London Milan

To my one love—for always encouraging me in my endeavors, for letting me be my true self, and for showing me that there is poetry in every sunset and music in every dawn. Just the sound of your name alone calms my soul. Thank you for accompanying me on this grand adventure. I love you, Bernard.

To my four spirited, intrepid children: Nile, Jean-Axel, Anaïs, and Andreas. Your passion for life is an inspiration to me; your joy is my joy. Thank you for teaching me what is truly important in this life. I love you all to the moon and back.

To Jean Nussbaumer, who started the journey long ago and lit the way for us all—may your torch always burn bright.

Foreword *8*

Introduction *11*

Living Out Loud *20*

Nomads at Rest *70*

Dreaming in Color *114*

Culture Tripping *144*

Sailing to Byzantium *226*

Finding Shangri-la *262*

Resources *298*

Acknowledgments *302*

FOREWORD *by Hutton Wilkinson*

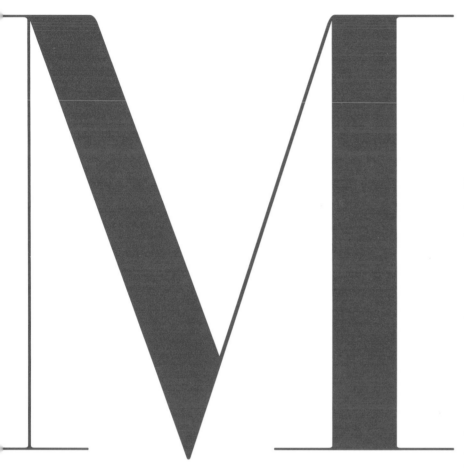

Michelle Nussbaumer. How shall I describe the indescribable? A living, breathing voluptuary, Michelle Nussbaumer creates works of intense originality that have the power to astonish, heal, and even protect. These amazements spring forth from her unlimited imagination, materializing as designs for living that alter our workaday world in the form of pure enchantment.

Her clients, realizing they've discovered an alchemist with the ability to weave straw into gold, must sit back in wonder as Michelle, with what seems a mere gesture, makes dreams

come true. You see, Michelle is a dream catcher, a three-dimensional storyteller, a seductive sorceress whose enchanted vision must be obeyed. In her magnificent interiors, there is no sleight of hand and no room for negative thinking. The objects are real and precious. And by bravely taking chances with her unorthodox choices, she makes the perils to herself and to others visceral, courageously pairing high with low, Oriental with Occidental, the modern with the ancient. To achieve her goals, she juxtaposes not only colors but also textures, diverse cultures, and her own unique vision with those of her clients. To the uninitiated or the faint of heart the results can at first appear alarming, unconventional, or even bizarre. But I can assure you they are always transcendent, as the beauty she creates is always greater than the sum of its parts. This is Michelle Nussbaumer's genius. This is what sets her work apart from the run-of-the-mill, mindless decors of the last century and places her at the forefront of the new maximalist movement going forward.

A modern-day Marco Polo, Michelle Nussbaumer revels at being a twenty-first-century explorer. Intrepidly, she scours the earth for treasure and carries it home, optimistically spreading it before us while knowing full well that many won't understand its worth. It's only after she enhances what she finds—polishes and cuts, sets diverse pieces together, places them ceremonially in their desired space—that many of us will finally see and understand at last her artist's vision. Michelle's extraordinary work requires a leap of faith, a trust that cannot be questioned, and a serious commitment from her clients to see her vision through to the end. Those are the three necessary ingredients for creating magic. There are not many individualists like Michelle who are working in the decorative arts today or who can achieve results that not only feed their own souls but also inspire individuality and creativity in their clients and in those fortunate enough to experience the finished product. In this respect she is one of the chosen few in the pantheon of the world's great designers, including the likes of Elsie de Wolfe, Tony Duquette, and Renzo Mongiardino.

The cognoscenti who know Michelle's work understand its value, for it embodies the very definition of luxury as "something custom, something one of a kind, something only one person can have." This rarified brand of luxury does not come without a price. And that price cannot be calculated in mere gold, but in something far more marketable, a passion for all-consuming work. Michelle Nussbaumer tirelessly searches the world for her inspirations. Her wanderlust turns to wonder-lust through the environments she creates. These rooms are not preconceived but spontaneous, organic, living, breathing works of art. Hers are not stagnant stage sets but rooms at once alive, environments constantly in flux not just because families are living in them but also because Michelle has arranged them for change, growth, and livability.

So I ask myself again, "How shall I describe the indescribable?" And the answer comes back, "With great difficulty," because the work of Michelle Nussbaumer is purely subjective, something that one must see, feel, and experience firsthand, and because like all great art it is innately sensual, uplifting, and joyous. Look inside these pages and be amazed, for here is an introduction to a world that I hope one day you may have the joy of experiencing in person—as I have.

INTRODUCTION

I have always had wanderlust. Even as a child I dreamed of travel, of bringing home what I found from worlds far from home. Those dreams have come true for me. I was born a Texan, but have become a citizen of the world having lived and worked abroad, with homes in Italy, Switzerland, and Mexico. My far-flung experiences have given me a unique perspective on the world of design and the art of decoration. Taking diverse elements from a multitude of cultures and making them my own is what inspires me. My style absorbs everything and transmogrifies it so that the rooms I create are greater than the sum of their parts. I think of this as my own unique American design tradition!

My passion is searching out treasures from the world's most fabled markets—the Medina in Fez, the Grand Bazaar in Istanbul, the Marché aux Puces in Paris, the neighborhood markets in India, the night markets in Beijing, and the European Fine Art Fair in Maastricht. I love to pull together objects and elements of decoration that I have discovered on and off the beaten track and mix them with important antiques and modern art to create an atmosphere deep with personality, exotically perfumed, and enlivened with a touch of the eccentric. This is what I do for the houses of my clients, my own houses, and my gallery of design in Dallas. Ceylon et Cie is where I present furniture with provenance, because I believe every home should have objects with stories to pass on to future generations.

Because my family has always loved beauty, my eye was trained from a young age. My mother is a well-known painter, and was forever dragging me along to museums and galleries. One summer, she took me all the way to Spain, as she was a huge fan of the work of Joaquín Sorolla y Batista and decided she had to study his work in his own home, which is now a museum. Our house was full of art, antiques, and her fellow artists. My aunt Betty was an antiquarian and lover of all things French. I also had a traditional grandmother and a rather glam grandmother. My more conventional grandmother, who played bridge and wore pearls, had a very ladylike, country-club sort of house. She was the keeper of the family treasures, and I have the most wonderful memories of helping her polish the antique silver and setting the table with heirloom china and crystal for family occasions. My more theatrical grandmother was just the opposite, an Auntie Mame personality with purple velvet sofas, leopard-print carpets, and an imperial-yellow convertible sports car. She and my grandfather, who lived on a magical estate in West Texas, also had a place in New Mexico with an authentic big bunkhouse. Their homestead there was like a stage set for the movie *Giant*. She and my grandfather had filled their rooms with crazy treasures, bearskin rugs, snowshoes, Asian antiques, her paintings, modern furniture, and wonderful pieces that we found at the Apache reservation nearby, where my love of the tribal was born. The plurality of taste among these extraordinary women informed my own taste. Their styles shaped mine. You can see all these influences play out in the work on these pages. This has been true since I was that little girl always redecorating my room and, to my mother's chagrin, painting my furniture a myriad of different colors.

As a theater major in college—I intended to be an actor—I had to take practicums in every aspect of stagecraft from lighting design to makeup. Set design sparked something in me that I couldn't ignore, so I switched gears. That is what ultimately led me to interior design. After all, what is a house if not a stage for living? Soon after university, I met my husband, who is Swiss, and we moved almost immediately to Rome. With one small child and another on the way, I started shopping for our houses—in Rome, a villa on the ancient via Appia Antica,

and in Umbria, a sixteenth-century tower. Before I knew it, our storage spaces were overflowing so I began selling the overflow of beautiful objects to friends. And when family and friends would come to visit us from the States, I would take them shopping to all my special haunts and secret places around Italy.

Our house in Rome, Il Fortino, was a classical, tinted-plaster villa in a gated compound on the Appia Antica—and completely fabulous. That area of the city is full of the ruins of Imperial Rome, and today part of it lies within the city's archeological park. Sandwiching us were Valentino's house on one side and the house of Franco Zefferelli, the acclaimed film and opera director, on the other. Paths ran through the compound, and we could catch glimpses of their houses through the hedges. In the grass of his garden, Zefferelli had columns, capitals, and arches strewn around like just-uncovered archeological fragments. Peeking through the hedges on the other side of the walkway, I could see Valentino's English-meets-Italian gardenscape. Even digging in the garden of our villa to plant a rosebush was an adventure: with my shovel and spade, I would turn up remnants of Roman pottery and sculpture, like the beautiful arm of a marble goddess from the classical era that we've had in our living rooms ever since. Life there was a complete fantasy for me—utterly beautiful and wildly magical in its reality—a Fellini film as only Rome can be.

The way the Italians live—and the way I learned to live while we were there—is very laissez-faire. Americans love rules, and we tend to think our decor has to be correct and proper, a certain way, one specific style. Europeans don't. No matter where you go in Europe, rooms contain a mix of collected family pieces alongside throwaway things. That exuberance about life—honoring history and family, but with humor and a great feel for the now—is what I have always tried to bring to my work. The English are masters at this, as their great English country houses show. Just think of Chatsworth, where Lucian Freud's spectacular painting of the Duchess of Devonshire hangs amid those fabulous seventeenth-century family portraits. Each successive generation that took over the house added its own possessions and experiences of life. When that happens, a house stays alive. That aesthetic, that

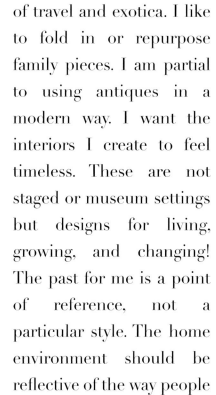

way of being, is not just about the visual—it engages all the senses. Those eventful years living in Italy were crucial to my aesthetic. It is as if I spent my formative years as a designer there. We later moved to Los Angeles, where I began selling antiques with a few girlfriends as part of a little shop. Ceylon et Cie was born from that experience. And that is where designing as a professional started for me.

I have discovered through my travels and the time I have spent living abroad that there are no definite rules for design. There are principles, however, and mine inform every choice I make in each project that I do. My interiors are about passion—and about bringing passion into my clients' lives. I want the rooms I create to show that individuals are present and at home. I try to translate my understanding of who my clients are into the rooms I design for them. I will almost always include elements of travel and exotica. I like to fold in or repurpose family pieces. I am partial to using antiques in a modern way. I want the interiors I create to feel timeless. These are not staged or museum settings but designs for living, growing, and changing! The past for me is a point of reference, not a particular style. The home environment should be reflective of the way people live, of the style of the house and what it dictates, of the place where the house is. My goal is always to create personal spaces with a little bit of whimsy and fantasy. I am not going to take a Georgian house and do a Mediterranean interior. If someone has a midcentury house, I would certainly include at least one midcentury element. But I would still mix in something of tribal origin or from a faraway place or an antique.

I have been to Africa, Asia, India, and all over Europe hunting for pieces that will make my projects and my shop unique and special. But I set off just as often for love of travel and without a specific purpose in mind. Three of my favorite places are Mexico, India, and Morocco. Strangely, they are similar to one another in many ways. Each is a desert environment where color blooms. Desert peoples very often love bright, saturated colors, because the sere landscape that they inhabit is just so many shades of brown. Diana Vreeland called pink—hot pink—the navy blue of India. That pink in India? It's a red in Mexico and Morocco. That color literally comes from the earth. Perhaps that is why I have never seen a color I didn't love.

Every place has its own character and culture, and wonderful adventures come with the process of discovering their similarities and differences. The world's tribal and indigenous peoples all use the same materials, each in their own way. I like exploring that in my work. Almost every culture from Bali to Bangladesh, including the Native Americans, has an ikat, whether woven or printed. Ikat has been prevalent for centuries, and is now in vogue again. I take delight in the research, in searching out the craftspeople and artisans who make the material culture of their community—tiles, baskets, textiles, you name it. Meeting and working with craftspeople and translating their traditional techniques into something new is one of the greatest design journeys of them all. Very often the indigenous

people have stuck to their traditional patterns, forms, and colors for hundreds of years, making textiles, rugs, pottery, and furnishings exactly as their ancestors did. Collaborating on new patterns, forms, and colors with a master craftsman using age-old techniques handed down from generation to generation is incredibly rewarding for me creatively, and a way to bring them more income. Wherever I go—Africa, Mexico, India, Morocco, and elsewhere—if I meet someone who's very talented, I try to take advantage of the opportunity. In Senegal not long ago, I met someone who makes hand-blocked textiles. We worked together on a collection of block prints that I sell in my shop. All these arts are dying all over the world. If we can revitalize interest in them, perhaps they can survive.

Much of what I do is based on old-world design. Very often something specific, like a pattern motif seen in a Turkish sultana's gown from the fourteenth-century, provides the starting point. Changing the scale of a pattern or ornamental theme—and recoloring it—can make it modern and new.

Just from traveling, the eye changes. Witnessing a Bedouin tribe using the very dishes that you have hung on a wall in a grand house, watching how exactly they use them, seeing the color of the clay they were made from, the clothes the women are wearing, and the tattoos on their faces—all of that affects

every design decision in one way or another. The mind goes through its creative gyrations and one day, somehow, the idea of that tattoo gets incorporated into an edge treatment along a wall. Being with people in Africa while they weave baskets, as they have done for centuries, and taking in the gorgeous color of their hands with the lovely hues of the rushes—that beautiful combination stays deep in the subconscious, there for when it is needed and appropriate.

Wherever I am, I search out textiles, antique and modern. I might use one for a pillow, another as a tablecloth for a dinner party, still another for a wall treatment. Sometimes I will frame a textile and show it off as the work of art it happens to be. Or I might patchwork pieces of cloth together to create another fabric for a specific purpose. Antique textiles bring layers of warmth and beauty to a room, and sometimes even a pop of modernity. That they show their wear, that the colors have the ombrage of age, only adds to their appeal. I may apply them sparingly because they are fragile, but those small fragments and pieces of antique cloth often have an outsize effect.

Since I started my travels, I have seen the world change profoundly. Of course, I have changed, too. Depending on where our four children have lived in the world, I have pursued and taken on projects in those places, primarily Mexico, Switzerland, America, France, and England. I have been lucky in that, and I have great clients. Now I am starting to work with my clients' children. That is wonderful because I have seen them grow up, and I still have the notes they sent to me when they were eight years old to say, "Thank you for being my decorator."

I want people to live in and enjoy their environment, to have their own personal world at home, one that excites, soothes, and pleases all the senses. I want every part of the house to be used and lived in—and to be elegant and beautiful, too—so that people feel their home is fun and open to all. That is the kind of environment I try to create for each of my clients. Nothing should be so precious that people can't use it, and nothing should be there only to be looked at and admired.

One of my daughters has a blind friend who is a Rhodes Scholar, an amazing, learned young man and an inspiration to anyone who knows him. He paid me the biggest compliment I have ever received as a designer. When he walked into our house in Dallas, he exclaimed, "It smells like God lives here." It is important that the house smells delightful. That it is full of fresh flowers. And pets. And music. And people, most of all. As much as I love the poetry of design and the beauty of objects and art—and I do—they are inanimate. But when we discover, select, and bring them home as reminders of our experiences, they are not only treasures, but also treasuries of meaning and memory. That is why I see what I do as less about a house than about a life. A house should never be finished. It is alive, and because it is alive it needs to be breathing, evolving, and changing.

LIVING
OUT LOUD

hen my husband asked my father for my hand in marriage, my father said yes, but with a caveat: "As long as you don't ever take my daughter away." We knew even then, in our twenties, that we wanted a home like those we grew up in—a place where you live your life through the years, raise your children, make and keep memories. We also knew that we were not those people who buy one house after another, always in a state of flux. As soon as we got married, we bought a beautiful house in Dallas, built in the 1940s by Wilson McClure, an iconic Dallas architect, with a Hollywood Regency vibe that we just loved. Many people told us it was too much house for a young married couple—eight bedrooms, a library, and so on—but we didn't listen. We knew that we wanted a large family and a house that we could grow into. Almost immediately, though, we moved to Rome. So my father didn't necessarily get his wish.

For all those years we lived elsewhere—in our remarkable villa on the Appian Way and then in Los Angeles—we kept this house because we loved it and felt that we might return to Texas someday. When we finally did, we came home to this house, which had been waiting patiently for us all those years. We raised four children here and myriad animals—a complete menagerie, from dogs, cats, and gerbils to a duck, Claire, which my daughter had hidden in her bathtub. The house was always full of family, friends, cooking—of life. My children would do their homework in the living room. There was never any place in the house that was off-limits to anybody, of any age.

I always tell my clients that if you really love a piece, it will work in any space. This house is living proof of that ideology. I am not the kind of designer who finds it necessary to redo each house from scratch, especially not my own. I've always bought what I loved and loved what I bought, just as I advise my clients to do. The rooms have not changed much in all these years, although I will occasionally paint walls a different color and reupholster key pieces.

All the furnishings in our Dallas house have been collected over many years. Some of the objects and antique furnishings are inherited, but most I purchased. That process took me a while—and a lot of traveling—because I have always tried to buy the best that I could. I try to help my clients do the same so that they end up with heirlooms instead of just used furniture.

My beloved Venetian bombé commode, eighteenth-century English and Italian sofas and chairs, eighteenth-century blue-and-white Chinese porcelains, Syrian tables, antique textiles, and yes, even the ancient marble arm that I dug up one afternoon in Rome while planting a rose bush—these are the same pieces we lived with in Rome and Los Angeles. They have been back and forth across the ocean three times. All are timeworn. Each holds memories. Some of these special pieces have now moved to our house in Mexico. My children have taken others as well. So while these pieces have all had lots of different incarnations, they always make our house feel like home.

My passion is finding exquisite treasures as I travel the world. I love to pull together the objects that I have discovered and mix them with important antiques to create an atmosphere that captivates with personality and a hint of the eccentric.

PAGE 26: My collection of Indian paintings on fabric and silk hangs over the Tree of Life pattern that my mother painted on the stairwell wall when my husband and I purchased the house. When we finally moved into it twenty years later, I had another artist continue the pattern up the stairs. PAGE 27: One of my favorite possessions is this portrait of an Indian maharajah, painted on canvas. PREVIOUS SPREAD, LEFT: A nineteenth-century Beaux-Arts plaster replica of Cheops tops an eighteenth-century Italian console on the upstairs landing; flanking it is a pair of chairs deacquisitioned from the Maharajah of Jaipur's palace. PREVIOUS SPREAD, RIGHT: I love tulips, and I find them especially beautiful when their petals are just about to fall. LEFT: A detail of the painting of the maharajah. OPPOSITE: A view into our library, where the Venetian blackamoor from my husband's family stands watch over a Venetian grotto chair that I found when we lived in Rome. Egyptian fragments and Imari porcelain sit atop a Syrian table inlaid with ivory.

PREVIOUS SPREAD: The colors and sensibility of the rooms at Chatsworth inspired my own living room, which contains so many beloved pieces that I have collected over the years. Atop the table are marble urns, bronze censers in the shape of elephants, and a Beaux-Arts plaster cast of an arm. An Aubusson tapestry covers the Louis XVI chair.
LEFT: Bronze-doré boar candlesticks rest atop a nineteenth-century gueridon.
OPPOSITE: A Regency console with a Greek key detail and shell-and-garland ornament makes a perfect home for a French girandole and blue-and-white Chinese porcelain.

RIGHT: The sofas in my great room are by Syrie Maugham, and I slipcovered them in raspberry linen. FOLLOWING SPREAD: A damask-covered table topped by favorite things sits at the center of my library. Surrounding it are chairs covered in Suleyman, one of my fabrics. I have layered the floor with nineteenth-century rugs that I've found on my travels. Stacks of textiles from my latest trip are piled high on a gilded Venetian grotto chair.

LEFT: My posse of ceramic pugs sits atop the desk in the library. OPPOSITE: I've placed favorite family photographs into the frame of a portrait of a distinguished Russian count that hangs over the desk. On the library walls hang some of the Orientalist paintings that I collect. FOLLOWING SPREAD: The Chinese wedding bed once belonged to Tony Duquette. It is a perfect spot for an afternoon catnap, and does double duty when the house overflows with guests. Of course, my dogs love it too.

THE WORLD IN VOGUE PEOPLE. PARTIES. PLACES

A GRAND ITALIAN EPIC
VALENTINO GARAVANI

CONTESTED VISIONS
IN THE SPANISH COLONIAL WORLD

FASHION DRAWING IN VOGUE

VENETIAN VILLAS

If children grow up surrounded by beautiful things, they tend to appreciate them even more as they grow older.

PREVIOUS SPREAD, LEFT: Dappled light in the library animates a clutch of ikat- and suzani-covered pillows on my Chinese wedding bed. PREVIOUS SPREAD, RIGHT: Pieter Estersohn, who took this photograph of me, collects nineteenth-century portraits of odalisques. Dressed in an antique sari, I am stretched out on an Italian sofa that I've upholstered in an eighteenth-century Kirman rug. LEFT: In this early incarnation of our dining room, my son Andreas sits on a settee that I found in Venice. The column capital was rescued from a Venetian palazzo.

LEFT: A Waterford chandelier festooned with drops and bobeches adds drama and sparkle to our dining room. OPPOSITE: A sleek, elegant, William "Billy" Haines–designed black lacquer dining table from the Jack Warner estate that I purchased when we were living in Los Angeles sits center stage. One of my ikats adds pattern to the back of the black patent-leather-covered dining chairs. I recently wallpapered the ceiling with a detail, blown up to giant size, of a photograph by my friend Richard Bettinger. FOLLOWING SPREAD: I love to set the table with an interesting mix of antique and vintage pieces. Here, I've combined German and Chinese porcelain with Bohemian glass and Mexican and Venetian goblets.

I think every home should have a certain level of intimacy. As houses have become larger in recent years, everyone craves a spot for cocooning. For me, it's my bedroom.

PREVIOUS SPREAD, LEFT: To pump up the volume in our master suite, I recently decided to paint the ceiling in a heavenly shade of pumpkin.
PREVIOUS SPREAD, RIGHT: Here I am in bed with three of my four-legged best friends! To balance the bold Sumatran textiles, Chinese porcelains, and Venetian mirror, I used a simple American ticking on the walls. RIGHT: I am a great believer that design is in the details. In my bedroom, I've combined Murano dishes, lacquerwork, bohemian Turkish vases, Chinese blue-and-white porcelains, and obviously much more.

LEFT AND OPPOSITE: Children always find the smallest, coziest room in the house. Ours is the TV room, where a ceremonial mask from Africa rests in one corner. FOLLOWING SPREAD: The room was wrapped in a bronze wallcovering from the 1950s that I love. Balancing the mask on the other side of the window is a painting from the 1940s. My grandmother's tables flank the sofa.

LEFT AND OPPOSITE: In my older son's room, a tapestry hangs above the bed. I painted the lampshades with a Joan Miró–inspired pattern and a quotation to match. He's had the faux-painted cabinets since he was small. On the floor is a Moroccan rug; the bedskirt is a ticking fabric and the coverlet is a suzani. Though he is now grown up and living on his own, his room still feels like a comfortable room for a young man.

FOLLOWING SPREAD: My younger son, who is still in college, clearly loves strong color, a bold mix of patterns, and texture as much as I do.

PAGES 68–69: In my daughter Nile's bedroom, my Scheherazade headboard is covered in my Chevron linen printed in a delicious lemon gold. She inherited the collecting gene and has filled her room with art and treasures found on her own travels.

64

NOMADS AT REST

eep in our genes, we carry the traces of our nomadic past—that time when we were hunter-gatherers seasonally on the move, finding ways to create stable, safe places; to protect our families; and to rest our heads. That is why the ideas of home and hearth resonate so deeply with each of us—and why we work so hard to create beautiful, comfortable rooms full of meaning and memories.

Because of my own wanderlust, I make much of the drama and discovery that comes with travel. In just about every interior I design, I introduce visible evidence of that nomadic spirit—and some of the artifacts of actual nomads that have taught me so much about pattern, color, and the culture of design. Antique textiles and tribal fabrics speak to me. They have always drawn me in, both in my life and in my work. When designing ikats for my clients, I rely heavily on my collections of gorgeous ethnic and antique fabrics, carpets, embroideries, and weavings for inspiration. For the palettes and patterns in my designs, I often look to Moghul miniatures from India, with their remarkable colorations and combinations of hues.

I may treat the walls of a room to suggest a faraway place. Antique Chinese wallpaper, scenic panels, or a parade of hand-painted pagoda silhouettes above a dado do more than create a theatrical entrance: they create an environment in which the imagination can take flight. A Chinese wedding bed in a gentleman's study offers a piquant element of both the foreign and the homey; dressed with piles of ikat and suzani pillows, it offers a cozy place for people to sit and chat or, alternatively, to have a private moment or, better yet, to nap. A daybed has the same effect of imbuing a room with the potential for fantasy. I think you can do that in just about any environment. When there are piles of silk pillows on the floor, for example, people can sit around and drink coffee at a low table. It is always possible to make a space just that much more fun and adventurous, especially for a party.

Sometimes I will use the lighting to create pattern, for nothing says glamour—or sets the mind wandering—more evocatively than active shadows all around, especially in a dining room. I may select furniture for the same purpose, because the carving on the legs, back, and arms or the silhouette itself can establish pattern or contribute to the language of pattern that is already in place. I will very often take an element of what I have seen on my travels and incorporate it into what I am designing, whether it be fabric or furniture or glassware or stemware or pottery.

The first time I went to the Egyptian Museum in Cairo, in 1981, it was possible to touch everything there: mummies, fabric, monuments, murals, you name it. There were no cases, no glass vitrines, none of today's reverence for the objects as precious repositories of cultural memory. When I saw the pyramids on that trip, I was able to walk right up to them—no tourists anywhere in sight. Times change. So do we. And so do the places we wish to visit. But our memories are always with us, wherever we rest, whenever we bring them home.

There is nothing more compelling than the grandly scaled spaces of converted industrial lofts and classic salons and great rooms. The challenge lies in creating intimacy within the openness.

LEFT: A rock crystal–encrusted bust from J. Antony Redmile stands guard in our Dallas foyer.
OPPOSITE: The enormous raw concrete columns remind me of an ancient Egyptian temple like Karnak or the Temple of Isis at Philae, and yet feel right at home surrounded by my client's beautiful eighteenth-century French furnishings. FOLLOWING SPREAD: In the loft's living room, we've assembled a quiet mélange of pieces from around the world that reflects a wanderer's eye for beauty. Here, a French daybed, Chinese leather trunks, a French bombé chest, nineteenth-century French caned chairs, a Persian rug, a Venetian mirror, Moroccan urns, and bowls filled with crystal fragments all live happily together.

One thing that I
learned, and still
value, from my days
in the theater is
the importance of
setting a scene.

PREVIOUS SPREAD, LEFT: With its Chinese porcelains,
eighteenth-century French furnishings, and
remarkable antique mirror, this dining area looks
as if it might inhabit a mini château rather than a
converted American warehouse. PREVIOUS SPREAD,
RIGHT: For intimate dining tables, I usually have
several different cloths made to fit so that, with a
simple shift, the hostess can change the mood of the
table; on the table here is a watery blue linen and
silk velvet. RIGHT: This very diverse collection of
ceramics embraces everything from English
transferware to Korean and Chinese pieces. What
could be a discordant display of disparate elements
finds harmony through the beauty of the color blue.

82

Context matters a great deal when it comes to the design choices we make for our homes. But I believe that if you do what you love, are passionate about it, and avoid trends, you'll end up with interesting rooms that reflect you.

PREVIOUS SPREAD, LEFT: The Italian wrought-iron console, originally intended for outdoor use, lends a bit of heft to the French antiques. PREVIOUS SPREAD, RIGHT: In the master bedroom area, the bed, a lit à la polonaise, is undressed and open to the ductwork. Really fine bed linens like these from D. Porthault are never, ever a mistake. OPPOSITE, TOP RIGHT: The guest room occupies one end of the loft, with the kitchen behind a curtain, which creates an interior wall and maintains formality. OPPOSITE, BELOW LEFT: Sometimes, a spontaneous decision—like resting a sterling silver chandelier atop magazines in a bronze Indian baby bed—makes for a really happy decorative moment.

There is nothing more exciting to me than searching out artisans around the world and creating beautiful objects with them, like this chandelier modeled on a classic Turkish lantern. The team that produced it and I collaborated closely to create a fixture that stays recognizably true to its tradition but that suits the scale of the room, and with the proportions, pattern, and ornament of our contemporary lifestyles. At the flick of a switch, light and shadow spill across the ceiling and over the walls in a fantastic filigree that transports you to the era of Scheherazade.

The lantern crowns the upstairs vestibule, which leads into the master suite. A tranquil palette of mouse-ear gray and cream emboldened with strong accents of black feels both serene and sophisticated. In another shadowing effect, the silhouettes of pagodas painted on the walls mimic the ivory pagodas atop the console. Though Turkish accents are overhead and underfoot with an Oushak carpet, Chinese references abound, from the blanc de chine porcelains to the armchairs with the Chinese bamboo motif.

OPPOSITE: I love bold color, but I am also passionate about the subtleties and sophistication of neutrals when the occasion suits. In this second-floor vestibule that leads to the master suite, a palette of mouse-ear gray, cream, and black makes perfect, quiet sense.

LEFT: In a sitting room off a master suite, I created a pair of Chinese daybeds to give the couple a private place to be together. FOLLOWING SPREAD, LEFT: An overscale Arabic-patterned wallpaper covers the walls of this intimate, dark space with vaulted ceilings. FOLLOWING SPREAD, RIGHT: Establishing a strong focal point, an Indian mirror hangs over an antique marble fireplace. The Orientalist theme carries through to Paul Montgomery scenic wallpaper and the custom-made sconces.

91

I often use symmetry to balance asymmetry. When properly placed, corresponding pairs of like or similar furnishings and objects can establish clarity and order within unusual spaces.

PREVIOUS SPREAD: Twenty years ago, I covered the walls and sofas of my Dallas sunroom in leopard print. With four children and a house full of dogs, of course I've recovered the sofas since then—but always with the same leopard-print fabric. I still love the way it looks, especially since I've added the emerald-green pillows and Moroccan pottery. On the coffee table are some of my truly most favorite things, including a fourteenth-century bronze arm from Thailand. LEFT: For me, green is a neutral hue, but then so is leopard print. Both come directly from nature. OPPOSITE: Manipulating scale with oversize elements brings high drama to any environment. The pair of dolphins was once owned by Tony Duquette.

In a grand salon made asymmetrical with three pairs of French doors opening to a terrace, a careful arrangement of pairs endows the space with a strong, central core. Embellishing the elements of upholstery with tape and trims creates a European yet modern look. The sophisticated black-and-white marble floor adds even more bold pattern underfoot.

LEFT: For many of us, objects have meaning and evoke memories. My client found the hand-chased silver parrot candlestick in Brazil. I have perched it proudly next to an English tortoiseshell box and an enchanting little English tea caddy in a shell-covered tray from Vietnam, which rests on a French table. OPPOSITE: For an art-collecting family with a bohemian spirit, I developed this living room around a French sofa in a rose-petal shade of velvet and tribal textiles.

KEEFFE & ALFRED STIEGLITZ

TWO LIVES

A CONVERSATION IN PAINTINGS AND PHOTOGRAPHS

ASSOULINE

LEFT: Another of my favorite bone-inlaid Syrian chests sits in the bedroom of my art-loving, bohemian-spirited client. The top of the chest provides a perfect place for her personal mementoes, including a Persian shoe that she found in Paris. FOLLOWING SPREAD: At left, tile shards and other mosaic materials form fantastic patterns in a *pique assiette* urn that stands tall on a side table in this sunroom; I find these ceramics in France, and I love their fragmented look. Across the room, a large Moroccan urn filled with lilacs provides a counterpoint atop a table from Rome draped in Turkish velvet. A wall-sized painting by John Alexander dominates the room. PAGES 112–13: Three works of art by Andy Warhol hang over a sofa made even more enticing with Moroccan textiles.

109

DREAMING
IN COLOR

I really do dream in color. And I have never met a color I didn't like. But if I had to choose just one shade out of the entire spectrum, it would be vermilion red—Eugène Delacroix's red, pomegranate red, the red in Mexican colonial houses, the red of a Cartier box and of Burmese rubies—because it is passion incarnate.

Azure always reminds me of the things I love: Delft porcelain, the blue of Greece, ancient tribal textiles, Fez pottery, my children's eyes. I also find it to be incredibly practical from a design perspective. When I want to combine European elements with exotic ones, azure is very often the great harmonizer. As for azure and white together—or any shade of blue and white—that, to me, is happiness.

Every room needs moments to rest the eye so that the palette and the pattern don't become too confusing or overwhelming. I love using black for that purpose. For me, black brings stillness to a room. I use it to frame vignettes, to establish a focal point, and to add some weight to the rest of the palette, especially when the palette is particularly colorful. Very often I will paint doors black.

I love Mother Nature's vast and seasonal tones, too—all those wondrous hues from the earth, the ocean, the mountains, and the sky, from the plant world and the animal kingdom. Sometimes the exuberance of color can be daunting. That is when, to chill things down, I might mix wintry elements, such as rock crystal, with a color scheme as pale and as various as ice itself. No matter what I add, I make sure that each element heats up the visual temperature by another degree of cool.

When the architecture is limited and there is no way to change it, I am catalyzed to really dream in color and pattern. You cannot put high heels on a low ceiling, so if the space is small and the ceiling constrained, I find that it is best to accept it and love it. Why not paint that kind of room a dark color and think of it as a jewel box? That is what I often do. Many of my clients with large houses end up spending a disproportionate amount of time in that one cozy jewel box of a room because people love to cocoon.

I get so much joy from mixing unconventional patterns that might not seem to go together but that in the end create an overall harmony that is rich and many layered. The way to do that is by keeping the colors similar—whether with my beloved blues or with the exuberant colors that bring me so much joy or even with the paler shades that speak of subtlety and nuance. First, I establish a visual theme. Once the theme is clear—blue-and-white pottery from different countries, for example—those repeating threads of color reinforce the pattern and pull together the mixture. Everything works together, because the colors are in harmony.

People sometimes are frightened of strong color, and they often want to hold back. But I find it is important to look, leap, and carry the power of the palette to its maximum strength. Color is emotion, memory, and mystery. There is nothing more potent than creating a personal space with some whimsy and fantasy.

LEFT: When my daughter Anaïs was small, she loved to cool off by dipping her toes into the pond in our Dallas garden, under the watchful eye of two zinc statues purchased from the Jack Warner estate in Los Angeles. OPPOSITE: An antique sideboard that I discovered on a trip to England when I was very young anchors our Dallas breakfast room. Its Gothic-esque details influenced the chairs, which I designed when we moved into the house and are still in my line. Because our children were quite young then, I based the chairs on a nineteenth-century church model with a hidden storage space for place mats or coloring books. Even with all the antique references, the room feels quite contemporary because of the wallpapered ceiling and the floor.

Large-scale patterns with giant repeats have a unique form of fabulous charm. There are so many wonderful options now that it feels as though bold pattern is having a true revival moment.

PREVIOUS SPREAD: For a couple of newlyweds who wanted a sophisticated, modern living space, I assembled a collection of midcentury furnishings and traditional pieces. With the addition of strong colors and bold patterns, the blend creates a context that feels very "of the moment." RIGHT: Saturated shades of emerald, black, and sunny yellow recur in pattern themes and design variations throughout the couple's home.

OPPOSITE: A Regency mirror hanging proudly above a double fireplace and a burled wood desk faced with a pair of custom chairs create a serene, feminine atmosphere in this lady's office. RIGHT: For Dwell with Dignity, a wonderful organization that supports homeless families, I created this room with donated furnishings that include a vintage sofa covered in my chevron ikat in a shade of dusky dark charcoal that I call Caviar. Appliquéd to the wall for ornament are banana leaves that I cut from a roll of shelf liner with an X-Acto knife. FOLLOWING SPREAD: In this family room, a wall of paintings hung gallery style above the sofa inserts additional saturated hues into a quiet palette sparked with brilliant yellows. I love the way the zigzag of the bargello-patterned fabric on the lounge chairs echoes in diminishing scale through the leaf pattern on the pillows and the sea urchin shell atop the coffee table.

129

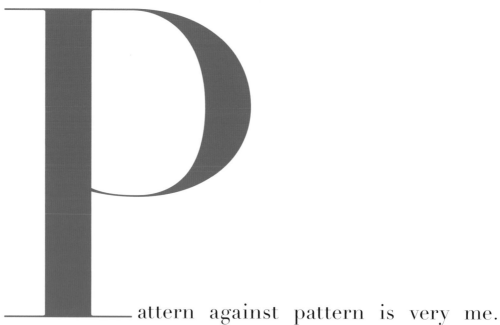

Pattern against pattern is very me. When items share a cultural lineage, related visual motifs, and complementary palettes—such as an eighteenth-century blue-and-white Chinese gourd vase standing proudly in front of eighteenth-century Chinese painted wallpaper—an arranged marriage feels like a match made in heaven.

In my design lexicon, the combination of blue and white is a neutral—but then so is leopard print—and a piece of blue-and-white porcelain enhances every room. If the item happens to be large and antique, I like to set it on a contemporary plinth or a minimal pedestal to create drama and pull the object—and whatever it may be paired with—into the twenty-first century.

I am always on the hunt for antique textiles and antique wallpapers, plus vintage fragments and pieces of fabric that are large enough to frame. A room done entirely in eighteenth-century painted wallpaper panels may be completely dreamy. But there is something about framing one large panel and hanging it as a work of art that makes it feel much more contemporary—and somehow much more fun.

OPPOSITE: Whether on a grand scale or a miniature one, the play of pattern on pattern enhances rooms—and lives—in an endless variety of ways. FOLLOWING SPREAD, LEFT: Seagrass furniture painted lavender and dhurrie rugs bring so much freshness to this wonderful outdoor sala. FOLLOWING SPREAD, RIGHT: The Spanish Colonial–inspired architecture sets the tone for this villa's breakfast room, where Venetian chairs assemble around a table dressed with a cloth made from a Carleton Varney ikat. Tracing through the air above is a delicate French eighteenth-century chandelier.

RIGHT: Early nineteenth-century pieces of Wedgwood's Duke of Wellington pattern adorn our breakfast room wall.
FOLLOWING SPREAD: For her Goop pop-up shop in Dallas, I collaborated with Gwyneth Paltrow and the Goop team to create a space that showed off her distinctive, stylish brand to perfection. The mix of pieces included some of my beloved blue-and-white Chinese porcelains and French furnishings from the 1940s.

ne morning a few years ago, my assistant walked into my office to tell me that Gwyneth Paltrow was on the phone. I didn't believe her. But she wasn't kidding. When I got over my surprise, Gwyneth told me that she was planning a series of pop-up shops to promote her Goop brand around the country. She said she had heard that if she was going to do one in Dallas, I was the person to help her. I was immensely flattered. Given Gwyneth's fabulous sense of style, who wouldn't be?

I designed the space, which Gwyneth filled with Goop product. The furnishings and decorative elements of the room were all custom-made. I created them with her in mind—a mesh of her style and mine. I had a Gracie panel with an Indian motif done in a dark charcoal gray that Gwyneth loves. I did one of my pagoda beds in a paler shade of gray, also very much her vibe. Most of the decorative items came from my shop. The Goop pop-up was a great success—and a memorable collaboration.

OPPOSITE: Among the elements I included in the Goop environment was my Dia polka-dot fabric, which I recolored just for the occasion, as well as one of the Peruvian gods on a stand that I offer in my own shop, Ceylon et Cie. I purchased the French 1940s desk in Paris. The sculptural metalwork table lamps are by Curtis Jeré.
FOLLOWING SPREAD: In the Goop space, my plaster bull's head hangs on a wallpaper by Andrew Martin that I offer at my shop. Goop's linens dress the table alongside my eighteenth-century Chinese plates. My Milagro glasses, which I designed to aid a charity in Mexico and are handblown there, add finishing touches to the setting.

CULTURE
TRIPPING

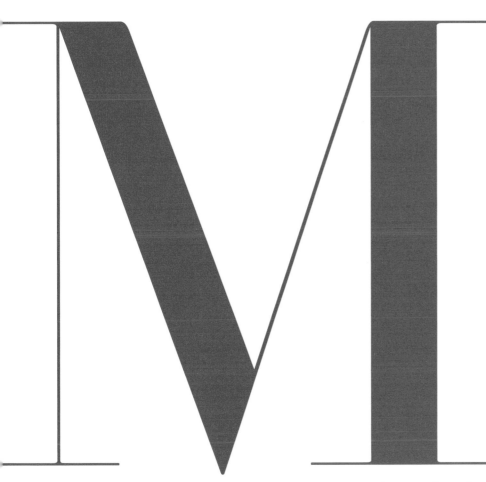

y mother says that I was born under a wandering star. During any given year, I may go to Africa, Asia, India, Mexico, England, France, and the rest of Europe shopping for projects and for my shop—and, yes, I confess, just for love of travel. When I am on the road, I do not generally have a specific purpose in mind, and I am rarely in search of anything in particular. But I am always looking for that special something—that unique and different object, textile, piece of furniture, or work of art—to incorporate into the homes I happen to be working on then, and even those that are meant to be complete.

Wherever I go, I love meeting local craftspeople and working with them to translate their traditional techniques into something new and modern. We Americans tend to be rather casual, plainspoken, and direct, unlike so many other cultures. Elsewhere in the world, courtesy calls for a certain formality of greeting and a little conversation before business begins, so I usually try to learn a few key phrases in the language of the country I am visiting. (I speak Spanish and Italian fluently, French badly, enough Turkish to get by, and a tiny bit of Urdu.) People appreciate the effort, even when they know English.

I love hunting for exquisite treasures and bringing them home to create unusual spaces. Mixing decorative-arts gems and glorious examples of indigenous crafts with other remarkable elements is, in my eyes, the best way to impart high drama to the living environment. Sculptural artifacts fit beautifully into any design scheme, whether it is minimalist and modern or luxe and antique filled. Nothing speaks to me more forcefully of exotic elegance and glamour than a worldly room of eighteenth- and nineteenth-century French and English pieces, enhanced with unusual, unique, and tribal items discovered on a globe-trotting trek.

My goal is to create eye-filling, eccentric, beautiful assemblages—a merging of the precious and the playful, pulled together with a century's best bits and pieces and curiosities, enlivened with important antiques and art. I like visual drama. And I enjoy thinking outside the box. A Spanish Colonial house with a mix of period colonial and contemporary furnishings and noteworthy art makes complete sense to me. So does a Chinese pagoda daybed, inspired by one found at Chatsworth, in a bohemian Dallas loft.

I try to envision the culture of each house I design—that is, the way my clients inhabit and use it. Sometimes I will switch the functions of various rooms and spaces because of the needs of the family. For clients who are voracious readers living in a house without a library, I might dedicate the foyer to that purpose, and fit it out with a center table and shelves. Every space in the house needs attention, and there is really no area that can't be made into something useful and beautiful.

Other cultures provide such inspiration, wonder, and richness. In learning about others, we learn about ourselves. It is part of the American heritage to take diverse elements and make them one's own. What is great about American design is that it has no limitations, and it ultimately absorbs all influences.

People now are much more receptive to integrating exotic and tribal styles into their living spaces. I can be attracted to something extremely valuable as easily as I can be to something that's fun, whimsical, and not very expensive at all.

LEFT: A detail of Moroccan tassels shows the skill used in their intricate crafting. OPPOSITE: For a theme-and-variations play on vermilion, a Coromandel vase filled with poppies stands tall amid Venetian glass paperweights, a fabulous piece of faux coral, and a contemporary Chinese lamp with a red lacquered shade. FOLLOWING SPREAD, LEFT: A trellis from the garden center spray-painted black adds both pattern and texture to the walls of a bohemian bungalow. FOLLOWING SPREAD, RIGHT: This library reflects the passions of my clients, who travel frequently to Africa and are also avid collectors.

Wherever I happen to be, I search out textiles, antique and modern. I might use one for a pillow, another to dress the table for a dinner party, still another for a wall treatment.

Pillows made from fragments of a vintage Panamanian flag add brilliant color to a settee upholstered in a bold faux-zebra pattern. An Indian side table with bone inlay sits nearby for convenience and added visual delight.

155

LEFT: Vintage suzani textiles and brilliant emerald-green lacquer bring fresh life to a mix of inherited pieces. A painting by Angelbert Metoyer hanging over the fireplace adds another cross-cultural reference. OPPOSITE: For high-impact drama, this collage wall contains modern and family works hung salon style. Panel draperies made from Sumatran textiles that I had sewn together add to the effect of floor-to-ceiling, wall-to-wall pattern.

156

THE WAY WE LIVE

MESTIC ART   ASSOULINE

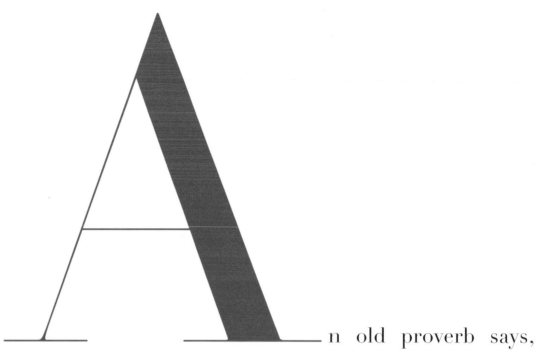

An old proverb says, "We are all wanderers on this earth. Our hearts are full of wonder, and our souls are deep with dreams." I know this is true for so many of my clients, all of whom appreciate beauty. They do not want just throwaway things, so we will often continue work on their houses over the years until that special piece—the one they've dreamed of—appears.

Many contemporary objects and furnishings that look beautiful in the moment are often too trendy to last. The stage after trendy is déclassé—what is fabulous one year may easily turn into the opposite the next. Many of us learn this lesson the hard way. Even so, it is important to take chances. A brilliant green stain can completely refresh a classic French desk with ormolu accents and gold details. An overscale, zebra-inspired pattern on the floor will add to the play of periods and cultures, while a rock-crystal-and-stone-studded brass box reminds us of the force of nature.

Start with the best, and use it as long as possible—that is what I believe.

OPPOSITE: A modern rug from The Rug Company sets off a vintage desk in a mesmerizing shade of green topped by one of my brass boxes set with stones and crystals. FOLLOWING SPREAD: Primary colors always make a bold statement. The blanc de chine cranes and a red vase set off a vintage Chinese cabinet lacquered a fetching shade of blue. Midcentury modern sculptural lamps by Curtis Jeré flank a photograph of Napoléon III's dining room taken by my husband.

RIGHT: A piece of modern art by Cameron McClain captivatingly reflects in a French-polished dining table that is surrounded by matte-white plaster chairs with arabesque backs. FOLLOWING SPREAD: In another fantasia of color and pattern, a Parsons chair covered in my own Dazzle fabric pairs with a vintage, green-lacquered desk. Atop the desk is a leather tray in Hermès orange full of wondrous things. Oversize botanicals hang nearby in the stairwell.

When young people ask me to help them, I am always flattered, especially when I have worked for their parents. We often include modern pieces in their projects because they are very educated about what is up-to-date in design and they want to reflect that in their houses.

PREVIOUS SPREAD: A mix of saturated color brings a happy hue to this young family's den. Furnishings are a mélange of contemporary and vintage pieces. A custom handmade ceramic lamp sits on a chinoiserie desk. RIGHT: A point-counterpoint of contemporary details and accents illustrates the more modern vibe of these rooms done for several of my younger clients.

LEFT: A faux-bamboo bar cart houses crystal Baccarat tumblers and an array of antique blue-and-white Chinese porcelains, all made sunny with brilliant yellow lemons and mums.

OPPOSITE: The bar cart flanked by beaded African chairs anchors one wall of an office made casually elegant with Danish modern furniture atop a Moroccan rug. I love to hang art on colored walls, because very often they show off the art better than the more expected plain, bright white.

The entry to every house is its opening act, so I always advise my clients to "go bold" there. Even when I am striving to create a dramatic effect, I want to distill what each client loves down to the perfect expression. When a client shares my love of red and my delight in blue and white in its many forms and combinations, I know just what to do—and how to do it.

A smallish foyer painted a gorgeous shade of vermilion always creates a memorable entry. The front door of this house opens onto a small, Chinese red–painted hallway with a fantastic red nineteenth-century Chinese cabinet—the first focal point. My client here, though young, has a passion for blue-and-white porcelain that almost rivals my own. Since I knew her before she got married, I suggested she add blue-and-white pieces to her wedding registry. She did. And now she has begun a wonderful collection. Some of these pieces she uses. They and others sit in the cabinet in her entry hall. To my eye—and to hers—they fill it up perfectly.

OPPOSITE: Finding ways to help young clients establish and build their collections is always fulfilling. That's why I suggested that this young woman, whom I knew before she got married, add the blue-and-white porcelain she longed for to her wedding registry. FOLLOWING SPREAD, LEFT: One of my rules is always to have fresh flowers. They make every space they're in feel alive. FOLLOWING SPREAD, RIGHT: To bring interest to an unlikely corner of a dining room, I hung an eighteenth-century Chinese ancestor portrait above a vintage Chinese porcelain palace urn. Chinese floral wallpaper plays to the Chinese and floral themes.

RIGHT: A large Herez sets the tone for this young woman's exuberant living room space, which opens to an equally exuberant dining room with walls covered in a Chinese floral paper from F. Schumacher. A contemporary acrylic coffee table sits in front of a blue velvet-covered sofa festooned with pretty pillows. Yellow silk covers a pair of midcentury bucket chairs.

FOLLOWING SPREAD, LEFT: The pairing of a French desk lacquered in black with a midcentury bronze chair creates a ladylike corner.

FOLLOWING SPREAD, RIGHT: A period Georgian table feels and looks ultra modern in this breakfast nook where my Dazzler fabric mixes with textiles from other collections. The portrait of John Lennon makes the assemblage feel groovy.

KELLY WEARSTLER ...

MILES REDD ...

KEN KIFF

YOUSSEF NABIL

VOGUE & THE METROPOLITAN MUSEUM OF ART COSTUME INSTITUTE
PARTIES. EXHIBITIONS. PEOPLE

Gaston Migeon &
Henri Saladin ART OF ISLAM

Chinese Art

My style has been described as having old-world elegance with a touch of the exotic. My goal as a designer is the eye-filling, eccentric, beautiful assemblage—a merger of the precious and the playful, pulled together with a century's best bits and pieces and curiosities, enlivened with important antiques and art.

In my rooms, elements from the eighteenth-century feel right at home with interesting, unexpected pieces from many other periods and distant countries of origin.

For a young client's guest room, we wanted to develop a decorative scheme that was neither too masculine nor too feminine. For that reason, we went with a neutral palette. I custom colored the kaleidoscope prism wallpaper with my friends at the Newlon Collection. The headboard shape is one we use often. I named it Darby after a favorite client.

LEFT: A raffia bull's head hangs above a Chinese plate and an ivory lacquered Chinese Chippendale chair from my line, in a detail of the room pictured opposite. OPPOSITE: For me, blue proves a perfect background for hanging art of all kinds. On the top of a mother-of-pearl Syrian chest happily packed to the point of overflow with blue-and-white porcelains, an African basket and a ship's knot make a cultural counterbalance and add interesting rustic notes to the refined surfaces.

186

Serge Roche and Dorothy Draper used plaster inventively in the 1940s. I like to incorporate elements inspired by them into my rooms for unexpected drama.

LEFT: A vintage sectional sofa gets updated with sumptuous linen velvet in Hermès orange. The vintage carpet dates to the 1960s. A plaster side table adds a glamorous touch. Large-scale citrine geodes from my shop bring a natural sparkle to the room. FOLLOWING SPREAD, LEFT: In a niche beside the fireplace, plaster brackets from Axel Vervoordt support mirror-black Chinese vases. I had the flower wall ornaments carved and gilded in Mexico. FOLLOWING SPREAD, RIGHT: In front of the quartet of drawings by Salvador Dalí sits a plaster lamp from the 1960s.

LEFT: In this breakfast room, midcentury brass stools covered in bright orange cowhide pull up to the breakfast bar. A vintage Mark Shaw photograph of a model in front of Harry's Bar in Paris brings a splash of brilliant color to the Andrew Martin wallpaper. OPPOSITE: With its reflective discs, a contemporary brass chandelier refers to the shape that dominates the wallpaper pattern. A contemporary British rug provides foundation for the Hollywood Regency dining chairs.

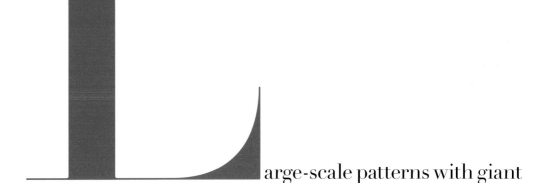

Large-scale patterns with giant repeats have a unique form of fabulous charm in my view. There are so many wonderful choices now that it feels as though bold pattern has made a comeback and is having a true revival moment. I love to use these eye-catching designs for curtains. It is a case of scale meeting scale. The window panels and draperies are large enough to ensure that the entire pattern is visible, but contained enough so that it doesn't overwhelm. If I choose, I can also manipulate the pattern into some other form by pleating, folding, piecing, or draping the fabric. To my eye, the scaled-up motifs also add a movement to the room as the light changes throughout the day.

It may seem contradictory, but I have a similar philosophy about incorporating strong color into a home. When a client responds to saturated hues but doesn't want to make an overwhelming statement, I will suggest trying a limited dose: paint a smaller space top to bottom, including the doors, entirely in one dynamic, startling shade—like Schiaparelli pink.

OPPOSITE: Curtains made with my Palais Jamais fabric filter the daylight beautifully as it kisses the blue-and-white Chinese gourd vase. The honey-toned burled wood of the Biedermeier chair creates a quiet moment amid all the bright colors and layers of pattern that surround it. FOLLOWING SPREAD: In this dining room, the accent color in the curtain fabric picks up the precise shade of underwater aqua that washes over the walls and ceiling. A beaded palm-frond chandelier glams up the interior. On the floor is an antique Peking Chinese rug. PAGE 198: On the dining table, roses in a deep shade of pink echo the warm tones used in the glazes on the teapots and coffee pots. PAGE 199: I find it interesting to use and display objects in unexpected ways, like hanging the occasional piece of porcelain with its backside facing front.

LEFT: I lacquered this laughing Buddha just the right, happy shade of red. RIGHT: My pagoda daybed reigns imperially over this room papered in a red chinoiserie pattern from de Gournay. The plaster plinth and urn atop the pedestal offer a perfect setting for the orchids. The shagreen-framed mirror over the mantel reflects the opposite side of the room.

If I had to choose just one hue from the entire spectrum, it would be vermilion red— Eugène Delacroix's red, pomegranate red, Chinese red, the red in Mexican colonial houses, the red of a Cartier box and of Burmese rubies—because it is passion incarnate.

RIGHT: Details of this Chinese-inspired fantasia reveal my eye for pairing hot hues with cool. Two of my favorite clients sit on an antique French chair, which I purposely left in a state of dilapidated grandeur.

PREVIOUS SPREAD, LEFT: In the hallway of the home of a world-traveling photographer and filmmaker, a 1940s French iron console takes center stage. An antique French chair dressed in my Dancing Deity fabric flanks it. PREVIOUS SPREAD, RIGHT: In the contemporary dining room on the other side of the hall, an antique crystal chandelier sparkles in front of a mirrored wall. Dominating the tabletop is a fruit-filled African sculpture. LEFT: A large work of art by Masatake Kouzaki hangs above an iron console strewn with small flowers made of hand-painted Coca-Cola cans from Africa. The vase is Sicilian.

207

Between a pair of custom sofas sits my Anaïs lacquered coffee table. Contemporary art brings a contained burst of strong color to an otherwise pale palette. A pair of my plaster lamps frames the fireplace.

LEFT: Hats and fezzes collected by a globe-trotting client crown the fireplace mantel. A contemporary Indian painting by M.F. Husain hangs above the mix.
OPPOSITE: Two Moroccan lanterns and a pair of gilded mirrors make this foyer come alive with color and reflected light. The spirit of the mix expresses the background and joie de vivre of my international client.

RIGHT: A pair of gilt wood fauteuils upholstered in one of my ikat fabrics flanks an art deco console topped by one of George Sellers's plaster rhinoceros heads and a beaded African walking stick.
FOLLOWING SPREAD: I used African textiles that my client has collected on her travels over the years to cover the chairs in this breakfast room. The geometric pattern on the ceiling reflects that of the rug below. The electric blue silk curtain panels pull the whole mélange together. In the background hangs an ethereal photograph by the client.

212

LEFT: In this quiet corner of a worldly client's home, an important French desk from the 1940s is topped off by a Picasso terra-cotta vase.
OPPOSITE: In her guest room, I used an antique sari from her mother's collection to cover the Scheherazade headboard. A brilliant paisley from Cole and Son spreads its arabesques across the walls.
FOLLOWING SPREAD, LEFT: In a second-floor reading room, the client's collection of minerals, both earthly and celestial, finds a home in a cabinet of curiosities that I had finished in black lacquer.
FOLLOWING SPREAD, RIGHT: In the same room, the malachite bar is stocked for all occasions.

216

LEFT: On a desk ornamented with chased bronze-doré, a woman figurehead fitted over the curve of a leg gazes down on a contemporary British rug from The Rug Company. OPPOSITE: Handed down from one generation to the next, the desk dominates the home office of my client, a sports agent who is delighted to safeguard such a treasured family heirloom. We've surrounded him with a cool, contemporary mix of art, photography, and other unusual vintage pieces and antiques that play off the decoration of the desk.

In a young client's master suite, the frame of the bed is lacquered in a cameo hue to match the velvet upholstery. The gold-leafed grasscloth from Phillip Jeffries sets a Hollywood tone, which stems from the client's photograph of Faye Dunaway taken by Terry O'Neill the day after she won her Oscar for *Network* in 1977 (partially seen over the bed). The Maison Baguès rock crystal sconces add even more sparkle. The leopard pattern reinforces the movie magic.

222

Old Hollywood is still
so inspiring to me.
I love reinterpreting
that special glamour
in modern terms.

For this client—a chic, young sophisticate—the
Hollywood references make such perfect sense. I
encouraged her to start collecting, and now we've
begun to assemble significant pieces, including a
gritty Western image of a cowhand by Laura Wilson,
a former assistant of Richard Avedon.

SAILING TO BYZANTIUM

e sail through life in stages, marked by the passage of time. Our homes provide us with safe harbor, but they also reflect the experiences we've had on our crazy odysseys—and sometimes those we still hope to have. When we're in those young decades of growing a family, home usually means a welcoming nest, one that functions easily for all ages and for every activity from casual to formal. When the children leave that nest, it may be time to consider another kind of habitat because, almost overnight, the house that's been so full of life, laughter, and bustle grows quiet. How do we keep the house happy and ourselves, too? Do we redecorate while holding on to all our beloved furnishings and objects? Or do we just save those things that are precious because they mean the most to us and place them, beautifully, with new treasures, in a new setting?

When we change our homes—location, decoration, or both—there's anticipation and wonder. That's true whether we're doing something on a small scale, like repainting a room or re-covering a sofa, or something much more major, like relocating from the suburbs to the city, from a traditional, grand dream house to another more eccentric dream, like a loft in a converted factory downtown. Our journeys don't have to be far-flung, though that's my passion.

Coming a long way but a short distance can be just as satisfying. Suddenly the everyday is redesigned, full of surprise, pleasure, and excitement.

True collectors aim to find—and live with—objects and furnishings that express their pilgrimages; I do this almost without thinking. When a client has the same urge, there's nothing more fascinating or fun. The design process becomes an embarking point for a trip through the maze of interests, passions, and history—and beautiful furnishings, antiques, textiles, objects, and art.

Rooms have to function. Seating arrangements are very important to how a space flows and how people use it. Each room needs to include enough seating—and several different areas of seating—so that people can sit down and feel comfortable, not just perch. Every bedroom should have a desk and some bookshelves. And every bedroom—especially a child's bedroom—should express the individual's personality and serve his or her particular needs. Guest bedrooms are extremely important, too. The right mirror, lamps for reading on each side of the bed, soft enough lamplight so one person can read and the other can sleep—it's necessary to take into account all these details of living.

The quality of natural light—its saturation, hue, and intensity—changes from place to place and continent to continent. The clear, bright light of North Africa, which inspired John Singer Sargent to such a degree, calls for one type of color. The gray northern light of Sweden, Denmark, and Norway suggests a paler, softer palette. So, where we are dictates the colors that we live with. I study the way colors alter as the light changes through the day and into the night. For me, blues are the best beta testers—the most important colors to watch at different hours. Yet, as intensely as I love full displays of color, I also love monochromatic palettes, which are a great way to incorporate color—and lots of individuality and personality—into a room without making a crazy commitment.

Our journeys don't
have to be far-flung,
though that's my
passion. The joy of
coming a long way but
a short distance can be
just as satisfying.

LEFT: A carved wooden Buddha, holding offerings of
amber and roses, sits atop an antique Oceanic chair.
OPPOSITE: For cultured clients with a literary bent and a
passion for collecting, chocolate-colored walls create
a sophisticated background for furnishings, art, and
objects. With four children in the family, we decided
to slipcover the upholstery in linen. Next to the sofa,
Spanish Colonial statues stand atop a nineteenth-century
Chinese table inlaid with mother-of-pearl. FOLLOWING
SPREAD: An antique Tabriz adds subtle pattern to the living
room floor; old-master drawings add such quiet beauty.

PREVIOUS SPREAD, LEFT: These clients are in the magazine publishing industry, and are major book lovers. Because they live in a house that lacks a library, I transformed their very large entryway to serve the purpose. A quartet of nineteenth-century Spanish leather chairs surrounds the central table. Overhead is a contemporary brass lamp. PREVIOUS SPREAD, RIGHT: In the entrance to another client's house, midcentury lamps flank a camel-bone mirror. A photograph of Barbra Streisand provides a touch of old-school glamour. LEFT: In one corner of the living room, an eighteenth-century portrait of St. Jude hangs above a midcentury chair found in Paris. Atop the desk is a nineteenth-century American Indian basket filled with Queen Anne's lace from the garden. OPPOSITE: A bowl of yellow mimosa brings happiness to a tabletop with an eclectic mix of favorite things.

238

orocco, Mexico, Turkey, and India—each of these ancient cultures continues to have a very strong handicraft culture, which I find makes their different styles easy to meld. Mexican and Rajasthani carvings—such as this door and pair of columns, respectively—often resemble one another so closely in handwork and ornament that it can sometimes be difficult to tell the two apart. Fold in a Turkish Oushak carpet, also made by hand, also with a tribal motif, and voilà: instant tribal harmony.

A home's entry is a place of first impressions. It should be dramatic, and it should set the stage for what's to come. This client is of Mexican heritage and Catholic, parts of her story that we represented through the altar sticks that flank the door and the censer-style chandelier from a church that hangs on high. The French tapestry hails from Paris. Because she has young children, we decided to keep things casual and drape it nonchalantly over the bannister. It's an irreverent moment, but a quiet one.

OPPOSITE: When my clients purchased this house, the Rajasthani columns were already in place. The antique carved doors from Mexico and other decorative pieces give the villa a colorful flavor. The altar sticks that flank the door and a censer-style chandelier that once hung in a church are perfect finishing touches.

RIGHT: In this light-filled living room, modern and antique elements create an up-to-date mix. An ancient stone pedestal table made originally for a garden sits conveniently beside a modern sofa. A Syrian folding chair nestles next to an eighteenth-century Spanish table that provides a perfect home for blue-and-white porcelains. The pair of seventeenth-century French chairs that flanks the fireplace are dressed in one of my ikats. FOLLOWING SPREAD: In the master bedroom, a posy of lavender chrysanthemums adds a voluptuous note. Custom lamps of petrified palmwood from my collection and Chokwe African masks adorn the bedside table, a custom design finished in raffia. The comforter fabric is a Peter Dunham design.

Whenever an opportunity presents itself to create a glamorous, private, personal retreat for the lady of the house, my creativity goes into overdrive. Here is one instance of what I consider a perfect lady's space. Symmetry works its quiet magic. The palette is serene and natural, and it glows divinely in the flood of natural light. An ample bath beckons in the center of the room. Art provides focal points, and silk balloon shades unfurl in an added layer of voluptuousness.

246

I'm a great believer that guest bedrooms should have all the comforts of home, from a delicious, inviting bed to adequate storage space, a comfortable chair, and sufficient lighting. This guest bedroom has all that. Pretty midcentury Lucite lamps sit atop a matched pair of eglomise bedside tables. The draperies lend a sunny glow, and the Pratesi linens couldn't be more luxurious. The Capa headboard is from my line.

249

Pale colors always need some kind of a counterbalance to give them gravity. Robin's-egg blue with a hint of green—a shade that I absolutely love—feels very ethereal because it reflects light so well, especially when it is adjacent to any kind of gilded or metallic surface. To bring things back to earth, I often use black as a kind of trim, almost like eyeliner.

I love working with reflections and colors. And light absolutely amazes me. We are all so reactive to it. It is itself endlessly variable, and it transposes and transforms everything it touches. When I am working on a house, I always visit several times to see what sort of chameleon the particular color I've selected is and how it responds to the different qualities of light at various times of the day and at night. My beloved robin's-egg blue has a million different moods and shades depending on the hour and the season. And at night, well, it has an entirely dissimilar repertoire.

OPPOSITE: This client is in fashion—and is a glamour girl! The quality of light in this room of her house is so ethereal and beautiful, especially as it filters through the silk curtains. From day to night, the color of the room changes profoundly. A gilded Venetian blackamoor bracket supporting a Chinese porcelain vase adds so much sophistication. FOLLOWING SPREAD: In the entranceway, French furniture in the same pretty shade of robin's-egg blue sets the scene for what's to come. Fresh flowers always provide a feeling of welcome—and of life.

LEFT AND OPPOSITE: In a monochromatic living room enhanced with delicate bursts of blue, a pair of nineteenth-century fauteuils upholstered in a classic, modern David Hicks textile perch on a pale Oushak. Flanking the chairs is a pair of nineteenth-century bronze-doré gueridons purchased in Paris. At the center of the seating arrangement is a French table from the 1940s.

FOLLOWING SPREAD: In the dining room, contemporary fauteuils covered in silk surround a French rosewood table and bar from the 1940s. Presiding over all is a Murano chandelier. A voluptuous flower arrangement in a nineteenth-century Japanese tea caddy creates a lovely centerpiece for a table setting that sparkles with crystal Venetian tumblers and the sheen of polished porcelain glazes.

ANOTHER MAN MEN'S STYLE STORIES
Compiled by Alister Mackie

Comfort means different things to different people. For some, using a consistent color palette in every room of a house creates a sense of cohesion and inevitability that delights the eye and relaxes the mind.

PREVIOUS SPREAD: In the master bedroom of a woman in the fashion world, an ink-on-paper work by Jack Cornell rests atop a custom mirrored bedside table that I created to reflect light around the room. My Rock Candy box sits with a grouping of celadon porcelains and my rock crystal Luna lamp, which is mounted on acrylic.
RIGHT: When the color palette remains constant from one room to the next, I'll create interest by playing with it in different textures, finishes, and materials.

FINDING SHANGRI-LA

staad is a winter wonderland, Shangri-la, Nirvana, and Santa's North Pole all rolled up in one—a wondrous fantasia of a place. Our family has been going to this mountain paradise forever—and my husband, who is Swiss, all his life. All of his family have chalets there. For our children, it has been their other home as they all went to Institut Le Rosey, the boarding school in Rolle that my father-in-law acquired in the 1970s. During our early visits there, though, we found ourselves staying in chalets that really didn't work for the family. I kept hunting for our perfect place. And one day—finally—I found it. When I took my husband to see it, he was flabbergasted. He had grown up coming to that house, because his best friend had lived there. We felt it was meant to be—and not just for that reason. When we lived in Rome, our address was 37. Our hacienda in Mexico has a 37 address. Every time we find our favorite, most wonderful, magical places, they each seem to have a 37 address. I don't know why. But this chalet—our chalet—was a 37, too, so it had to happen.

Built in 1739, our chalet began its life as a working farm. And if its walls could talk, I'm sure it could tell fantastic stories. Here's one that I do know: The house once belonged to Paul Sacher, the founder and conductor of the Basel Chamber Orchestra. During his tenure there, Sacher commissioned several pieces from Béla Bartók, the Hungarian composer. Each time he did, he offered the chalet to

263

Bartók as a quiet retreat to write. In the summer of 1939, not long before he left Europe altogether, Bartók composed his *Divertimento for String Orchestra* there.

One of the qualities that I loved about our chalet from first sight was that so much of its history was intact: the low ceilings, because rooms used to be so expensive to heat; all the original woodwork, paneling, and floors; even one of the dining room's big, beautiful stoves, which would have kept dishes warm through the meal. By Swiss standards the chalet itself is large, but the rooms are very small, which is typical of that vernacular style.

In Switzerland, there's snow for half the year, and it's so quiet you can hear a pin drop. I decided to have a maximalist explosion of color inside the house because it becomes very lonely, in a way, when you're there by yourself. It's beautiful in its loneliness, but with bursting color inside, it feels more exuberant and alive. Yet there's serenity, also, because of the antiques.

The rooms are a mix of the things we all love. Swiss furniture. Moroccan bowls. Chinese porcelains. French paintings. English pieces. Spanish plates. A French 1940s armchair upholstered in Mongolian fur. English chairs covered in one of my fabrics, whose pattern I named for the wife of a Turkish sultan. Some of the pieces were inherited. Some I bought. Some were in the chalet when we got it, and had probably been there for hundreds of years. Some I sent over by container from America, including all the bed treatments. The house is always full of flowers inside and outside—freshly cut from the garden in season and, in the winter, floral prints in wild colors.

Each family member has their own space, and I did each room to reflect the inhabitant's personality—trying to incorporate those things that I know they love. We hope that our children will use the chalet for many years, and that someday their families will, too.

PAGE 268: Cindy the cow heads to the kitchen bringing morning milk. I wove her crown with fresh flowers. PAGE 269: In our breakfast room, nineteenth-century Swiss farm chairs face a period Swedish sofa. Vintage French curtains bring it all together. To add to the fantasia of pattern, I lined the bookshelves with a modern, English wallpaper. PREVIOUS SPREAD: Our mudroom, which is part of the kitchen, opens to the breakfast room. I found the antlers at a local flea market. The fabric is all from my collection. RIGHT: Our living room is always filled with family and laughter; it peeks into the dining room, where a suzani-covered table seats eighteen. I love to keep the large French majolica cachepot on top of the draped coffee table full to the brim with flowers. An eighteenth-century painted Swiss chest dominates one wall.

272

PREVIOUS SPREAD, LEFT: The French majolica cachepot provides a perfect home for a garden bouquet of roses and lilacs in my favorite reds and oranges. PREVIOUS SPREAD, RIGHT: I think pillows are a perfect way to layer in pattern, color, and texture. On the living room sofa, I've placed a suzani textile from Istanbul next to a silk damask and an Italian paper–inspired fabric made by the artist Kelly O'Neal, a dear friend. RIGHT: Playing with scale is one of my favorite aspects of design. In this corner of our low-ceilinged living room, a wall covered in a mural of an old-master painting blown up to twenty times its actual size seems to open up an entirely new world. Through the doorway is our library, which I swathed in my Sultana fabric in shades of raspberry and azure.

276

PREVIOUS SPREAD, LEFT: It seems as if we're always having a dinner or lunch party, and to me that means flowers and greenery as well as food. In winter, I decorate the chandelier with holly and fir. An eighteenth-century mirror reflects the dining room. PREVIOUS SPREAD, RIGHT: Beautiful table settings are a passion of mine. This one layers eighteenth-century Spanish plates with a beloved tablecloth with a Tree of Life pattern. RIGHT: Our library makes me happy. One of the seventeenth-century portraits in my collection hangs over the settee. The antique Bukhara rug echoes the color palette of my Sultana fabric. FOLLOWING SPREAD, LEFT: In Switzerland, everything grows brilliantly. These flowers are from our garden. FOLLOWING SPREAD, RIGHT: An Indian tapestry hangs above the bed in the bedroom of one of my daughters.

All of these rooms
house a mix of the
things my entire
family loves. Old
and new, serious
and silly, found here
and there, gathered
in our travels—
when these things
surround us,
we know that we
are home.

So often people have redone—and overdone—the interiors of these chalets. In ours, all the pine woodwork is original, and hundreds of years old. That is one reason why, when I found this house, I knew it had to be ours.

RIGHT: The upstairs has twin guest bedrooms. FOLLOWING SPREAD: A view into one of the guest bedrooms. In one corner, a pillow covered in the Swiss silhouette fabric that I designed just for this house rests on a wicker chair that sits next to a Moroccan pouf. I found the photograph of a Rajasthani prince in Jaipur. The coverlet fabric sports a vintage English rose pattern. PAGES 294–95: No matter the season, every room in the house has flowers. On my bedside table, tulips grace a bronze-doré chalice placed next to the Spanish dish where I put some of my jewelry. Covering our bed is a museum-quality eighteenth-century suzani. PAGE 296: I love overscale monograms. PAGE 297: Cindy and I are headed back to the barn.

RESOURCES

USA

ABELL AUCTION COMPANY
2613 Yates Avenue
Los Angeles, California 90040
323 724-8102
abell.com
auction house

BONHAMS
Showrooms worldwide
bonhams.com
auction house

CARLETON V LTD.
To-the-trade showrooms worldwide
carletonvltd.com
fine fabrics and wallcovering

CEYLON ET CIE
1319 Dragon Street
Dallas, Texas 75207
214 742-7632
ceylonetcie.com
*antiques, designer fabrics, antique
textiles, art, and custom furniture*

DRAGONETTE LIMITED
711 North La Cienega Boulevard
Los Angeles, California 90069
310 855-9091
dragonetteltd.com
antiques, modern art, and photography

EXQUISITE SURFACES
To-the-trade showrooms nationwide
xsurfaces.com
antique flooring

F. SCHUMACHER
To-the-trade showrooms worldwide
fschumacher.com
designer fabrics

FORTUNY
To-the-trade showrooms worldwide
fortuny.com
designer fabrics

HOLLYWOOD AT HOME
703 North La Cienega Boulevard
Los Angeles, California 90069
310 273-6200
hollywoodathome.com
Peter Dunham designer fabrics

HOLTON ARTS
1177 Clare Avenue #6
West Palm Beach, Florida 33401
877 846-5866
holtonarts.com
decorative finishes and murals

JED ANTIQUES
27 Washington Street
Sag Harbor, New York 11963
631 725-6411
antiques and curiosities

JF CHEN
1000 Highland Avenue
Los Angeles, California 90038
323 463-4603
jfchen.com
*antiques and midcentury furniture
and arts*

KELLY O'NEAL
Design Legacy by Kelly O'Neal
2200 Big Town Boulevard #140
Mesquite, Texas 75149
214 748-5118
koneal.com
works of art

LEONTINE LINENS
3806 Magazine Street
New Orleans, Louisiana 70115
504 899-7833
leontinelinens.com
monogrammed linens

THE NEWLON COLLECTION
903 217-6911
newloncollection.com
*wall coverings by photographic artist
Richard Bettinger*

PHILLIP JEFFRIES
To-the-trade showrooms worldwide
phillipjeffries.com
wall coverings

QUADRILLE FABRICS
To-the-trade showrooms worldwide
quadrillefabrics.com
designer fabrics

REMAINS LIGHTING
Showrooms worldwide
remains.com
Tony Duquette lighting

ROBERTA ROLLER RABBIT
336 West 37th Street, Suite 700
New York, New York 10018
877 695-7655
robertarollerrabbit.com
printed bed linens

THE RUG COMPANY
Showrooms worldwide
therugcompany.com
contemporary rugs

SHERLE WAGNER
To-the-trade showrooms worldwide
sherlewagner.com
designer hardware

MEXICO

AMORA TALAVERA
Avenida del Salvador #5
Col. Santa Teresa
Dolores Hidalgo, GTO 37800
+52 418 185 9002
amoratalavera.com
tiles

LA BUHARDILLA
La Aurora SN, Aurora
37715 San Miguel de Allende
+52 415 154 9911
*works of art from Frida Kahlo
and Diego Rivera and
important colonial furniture*

SOLLANO 16
10 Sollano No. 16
San Miguel de Allende
Colonia Centro 37700
Guanajuato
+52 415 154 8872
cintia.sollano16@gmail.com
*contemporary Mexican furniture
and textiles*

ENGLAND

ANDREW MARTIN
To-the-trade showrooms worldwide
andrewmartin.co.uk
wallpaper, furniture, and fabric

WILLIAM YEOWARD CRYSTAL
270 King's Road
London SW3 5AW
+44 (0) 20 7349 7828
williamyeoward.com
crystal

FRANCE

GALERIE YVES GASTOU
12 rue Bonaparte
75006 Paris
+ 33 1 53 73 00 10
galerieyvesgastou.com
the best of French 1940s furniture

LEYLA LEBEURRIER-AHI
Marché Dauphine
140 rue des Rosiers
93400 Saint-Ouen
+33 6 13 40 31 10
leylaahi@hotmail.com
antique textiles

MARCHÉ DAUPHINE
134 rue des Rosiers
93400 Saint-Ouen
+33 6 64 03 94 15
nineteenth-century Orientalist art

S.D.C. ANTIQUITÉS
Marché Serpette
110 rue des Rosiers, Allée 3, Stand 1
93400 Saint-Ouen
+33 6 98 83 64 04
antiques

TAJAN
Ventes aux Enchères
37 rue des Mathurins
75008 Paris
+33 (0)1 53 30 30 30
tajan.com
auction house

THIERRY DE MAIGRET
Commissaire Priseur
5 rue de Montholon
75009 Paris
+33 1 44 83 95 20
auction house

XXL ANTIQUE MIRRORS
Showroom: 121 rue des Rosiers
93400 Saint-Ouen
Main shop: 97 rue des Rosiers
93400 Saint-Ouen
cadresanciens.com
xxl-antique-mirrors.com
antique mirrors

ZUBER
To-the-trade showrooms worldwide
zuber.fr
scenic handblocked wallpaper and paint

SWITZERLAND

GALERIE CAROLINE FREYMOND
Menus Plaisirs: Objets d'Exception
Promenade 6
3780 Gstaad
+41 33 744 9242
antiques and contemporary art

LA VERAND'ANNE
Rialtostrasse 5
3780 Gstaad
+41 33 744 20 02
laverandanne@bluewin.ch
suzanis and tabletop

TURKEY

GALLERY MEVLANA
Misir Carsisi No. 41
Eminomu, Istanbul
+90 212 511 9378
suzanis

GRAND BAZAAR
Istanbul

INDIA

DILLI HAAT
New Delhi
*traditional Indian market
with handicrafts*

PARAS UDAIPUR
Near Paras Mahal
Hiran Magri Sector 11
Udaipur 313001
Rajasthan
blog.parasudaipur.com
parasudaipur.com
handmade inlaid furniture

MOROCCO

AUX MILLE ET UNE CHOSES, CHEZ
KIKI
24 Souk des Teinturiers
Marrakech
+212 024 39 13 49
GSM: 066 30 72 02
copper and brass lanterns and lighting

BAZAR MIFTAH ELKHAI
9 Bis Kissariat Miftah Alkhair rue
Lekssour
Marrakech
+212 06 46 83 83 93
antique carpets

EL MOUMAN ABDELKRIM ET SON
FILS
Souk el Hanna, No. 77-83
Souk el Kabir près des Souk des
Babouches
Marrakech
+212 06 61 54 17 11 / 06 10 52 27 96
blue-and-white Fez pottery

FRÈRES HAMZA & MOHAMMED
45-72 Souk Semmarine
Marrakech
+212 06 68 94 45 29
hamzadt@hotmail.com
traditional Moroccan leather poufs

KENYA

ANNA TRZEBINSKI
Stores in Nairobi and Aspen,
Colorado
annatrzebinski.com
*custom furniture, textiles,
and home decor*

ACKNOWLEDGMENTS

Most of all, I thank my wonderful clients for inviting me into their homes and into their lives. There would be nothing here without all of their support and trust: Christine and Wick Allison, Deborah Cass, Steve Dunbar and Vatana Watters, Ted Fields, Laura Ginsburg-Pierson and Lloyd Pierson, Karla and Mark McKinley, Capa Mooty, K.J. Murphy, Gwyneth Paltrow and the Goop team, Beau and Bonnie Purvis, Julia Sands, Lekha Singh, Carrie and Kent Smith, Medley and Worth Turner, Robin and Warren Wilkes, and Susanna York and Sorna Dnyaneshwar.

I so appreciate the many editors and the magazines who have supported me over the years: Christine Allison, Orli Ben-Dor, Michael Boodro, Rob Brinkley, Dara Caponigro, Carolyn Englefield, David Feld, Allison Hall, Pamela Jaccarino, Karen Marx, Holly Moore, Lisa Newsom, Margaret Russell, Mary Jane Ryburn, Rebecca Sherman, Clint Smith, Maxine Trowbridge, Newell Turner, Christopher Wynn, *Architectural Digest*, *D Home*, *Elle Decor*, *House Beautiful*, *Luxe Interiors + Design*, *Modern Luxury*, *PaperCity Magazine*, *T Magazine*, *Traditional Home*, and *Veranda*. There are no words for my gratitude.

I cannot forget the many talented photographers who came on this journey with me and shot the beautiful photographs on these pages: Melanie Acevedo, Mali Azima and Mark Roach, Grey Crawford, Pieter Estersohn, Miguel Flores-Vianna, Terri Glanger, Stephen Karlisch, Bernard Lucien Nussbaumer, Dan Piassick, Carter Rose, James Schroder, Agi Simoes, Troy Steakley, Ann Stratton, Arturo Rodriguez Torres, Peter Vitale, and Ka Yeung. I thank them all for their endless talent and energy—they are the essence of this book.

I am forever indebted to Jill Cohen, who gave me encouragement and excellent advice through the arduous process and had faith in the book from the start; to Doug Turshen, for making everything he touches magical—the work he did on these pages speaks for itself and I am eternally grateful; to my publisher at Rizzoli, Charles Miers, for believing in me; to Philip Reeser, my editor and kindred spirit in our love of the English country house, for his invaluable advice; to Judith Nasatir, for being my voice with such sensitivity and understanding; to the two Lizzies for not giving up on me and keeping me on track; and to everyone who worked tirelessly with such passion.

I thank my friends and fellow interior designers for the many years of support and friendship. To Mary McDonald, the sister I chose in this life, for intrepidly accompanying me on many, many adventures, from India to Capri, and for getting in that car with me in the deserts of North Africa, even though she knew better, just because she was afraid I might die if I went alone. I thank my other soul sister, Robin Wilkes, for her endless friendship. To Hutton Wilkinson, whose talent and style make the world a more beautiful place, I thank him for his presence in my life—and for writing the foreword to this book. To Anne Barbier-Mueller, Natalie Bond-Bloomingdale, Janis Brous, Patty Dedman-Nail, Sally Donn, Beverly Field, Nicole Gill-Ottinger, Nandu Hines, Kim Isaacsohn, Heidi Kier, Kelly O'Neal, Myrna Schlegel, Ka-haiya Sophia, and Caroline Whitman. I thank Jack Deamer and Arnaud Fioramonti, my brothers from other mothers; Jimmy Hensley; Richard Holton; David Nelson; Gavin Smith; and Jim Williamson.

I especially thank all the Ceylon et Cie team for their endless work and passion. JR Hernandez, Troy Steakley, Ashley Hightower-Cole, Rachel Richardson, Julia Arena, Katherine Auffenberg-Hill, Ali Brasher, Nathalie Garza, Paul Fiorella, Will Kolb, John McCarley, Maggie Corrigan, Jeff Woodrum, Alexis Stool, Gavin Cross, Lazaro Valencia, Lourdes Calix, Kirk Roark, and my beautiful daughter Nile Nussbaumer for putting up with me as a boss and a mom. Abe Studer, who always brightened my day, I miss him and know that God's home must be looking pretty swanky now.

Last but not least, I thank my family for always supporting me and letting me be myself. To my mother, who put that first paintbrush in my hand. And to John B, who taught me that the world was my oyster. To Krystal, I smile because she is my sister and I laugh because there is nothing she can do about it. I love you all. And if there's anyone I've inadvertently neglected to mention, please forgive me.

First published in the United States of America
in 2016 by

Rizzoli International Publications, Inc.
300 Park Avenue South
New York, NY 10010
www.rizzoliusa.com

Philip Reeser, *Editor*
Alyn Evans, *Production Manager*
Elizabeth Smith, *Copy Editor*
Doug Turshen with David Huang, *Design*

ISBN: 978-0-8478-4891-1
Library of Congress Control Number: 2016935204

Distributed to the U.S. trade by
Random House, New York
Printed and bound in China
2016 2017 2018 2019 / 10 9 8 7 6 5 4 3 2 1

PHOTOGRAPHY CREDITS

© Melanie Acevedo: Pages 1, 6, 13, 23, 26–29, 36, 38, 41, 44 (upper center, middle center, and middle right), 45 (upper left and lower right), 50–52, 54, 55, 62, 67–69, 96, 121, 265, 266 (middle right), 267 (middle center), 268–82, 284–86, 288 (bottom), and 289–95

© Mali Azima and Mark Roach: Pages 31, 48, and 120

© Grey Crawford: Pages 102 (upper right, middle left, and lower right) and 103 (middle left and lower right)

© Pieter Estersohn: Pages 2, 3, and 47

© Miguel Flores-Vianna/The Interior Archive: Pages 73, 89, 90, 92, and 93

© Terri Glanger: Pages 147, 158, and 159

© Stephen Karlisch: Pages 5, 10, 16, 34, 35, 40, 44 (upper left and right, middle left, and lower images), 45 (upper center and right, middle images, and lower left and center), 46, 60, 61, 64–66, 76–78, 80, 81, 82–87, 94 (right), 95 (right), 104–8, 110–12, 124, 126, 127, 129, 133, 138, 139, 141–43, 161–68, 170–73, 175–85, 194, 196–206, 208–17, 229, 233, 234, 236–39, and 300 (left)

© Bernard Lucien Nussbaumer: Endpapers; pages 24, 25, 74, 75, 102 (upper left, middle right, and lower left), 103 (upper images, middle right, and lower left), 118, 119, 148–50, 230, 231, 266 (upper images, middle left, and lower center), and 267 (upper left and center, middle right, and lower imges)

© Dan Piassick: Pages 30, 117, 244, and 245

© Carter Rose: Page 303

© James Schroder Photography: Pages 18, 19, 56–59, 94 (left), 95 (left), 122, 123, 186–90, 192, 193, 218–25, 232, 251–61, 266 (lower left and right), 267 (upper right and middle left), 300 (right), and 301

© Agi Simoes: Page 288 (top)

©Troy Steakley: Pages 98 and 100

© Ann Stratton Photography: Page 136

© Arturo Rodriguez Torres: Pages 152–54, 156, and 157

© Peter Vitale: Pages 128, 134, 135, 241–43, and 246–48

© Ka Yeung: Pages 15, 32, 42, 130, and 151